VEECK—*As in Wreck*

ABOUT THE AUTHORS

Bill Veeck was treasurer and assistant manager of the Chicago Cubs from 1933 to 1941; he was president and owner of the minor league Milwaukee Brewers (1941–45), the Cleveland Indians (1947–49), the St. Louis Browns (1951–53), and the Chicago White Sox from 1959 to 1961 and again from 1976 to 1980. From 1957 to 1958 Veeck was a sports announcer for NBC-TV, and in 1993 he was elected to the Baseball Hall of Fame. His books include *The Hustler's Handbook* (written with Ed Linn) and *Thirty Tons a Day*.

Ed Linn is best known for his writing on the New York Yankees and the Boston Red Sox. His many books include three collaborations with Bill Veeck as well as *Inside the New York Yankees: The World Championship Year*, *Steinbrenner's Yankees*, *Hitter: The Life and Turmoils of Ted Williams*, *The Great Rivalry: The Yankees and the Red Sox 1901–1990*, and *The 100,000,000 Dollar Game* (with Mel Durslag). Linn's articles appeared in *Sports Magazine*, *The New York Times*, and *The Saturday Evening Post*.

VEECK—As in Wreck

THE AUTOBIOGRAPHY
OF BILL VEECK *with Ed Linn*

The University of Chicago Press

The University of Chicago Press, Chicago 60637
The University of Chicago Press, Ltd., London
Copyright © 1962 by Mary Frances Veeck and Edward Linn
Afterword copyright © 1976, 1986 by Edward Linn
Foreword copyright © 2001 by Bob Verdi
All rights reserved. Originally published 1962
University of Chicago Press edition 2001
Printed in the United States of America
05 04   6 5 4 3

Library of Congress Cataloging-in-Publication Data

Veeck, Bill.
   Veeck as in wreck : the autobiography of Bill Veeck / with Ed Linn. — University of Chicago Press ed.
      p.   cm.
   Originally published : New York, Putnam, 1962. With new foreword.
   ISBN 0-226-85218-0 (pbk. : alk. paper)
   1. Veeck, Bill. 2. Baseball team owners—United States—Biography. 3. Baseball promoters—United States—Biography. I. Linn, Edward. II. Title.

GV865.V4 A3   2001
659.2'9796357'092—dc21
[B]   00-053249

To MARY FRANCES—Not because I think
I should but *because I want to*

CONTENTS

FOREWORD

It's not as much fun anymore. We hear that often these days, about real life and sports, too. People live longer and are stronger than ever, our economy is robust, and if the internet doesn't occupy your time, there are something like 500 television channels available.

But we don't laugh as we once did, and by all means, that applies to the industry of games, where athletes reap salaries we once would have thought unbelievable. In fact, they seem unbelievable as we speak. Yet, the business of pleasure has also become exponentially more serious, and that is one reason why I miss Bill Veeck more than ever. I suspected on the very day he died—January 2, 1986—that he would leave a void. But the grim faces around sports—particularly his passion, baseball—serve as a reminder that Bill literally was in a league by himself.

Physically, of course, Veeck was not all there. His body was a mosaic of broken parts on borrowed time, founded in no uncertain terms by the prosthesis, the result of a war injury and his most visible calling card, besides that impish smile. Bill never paid much attention to such minor annoyances and ailments. He built a makeshift ashtray in the stump, and when guests started to fade during his late-night vigils, he would remark, "I have an advantage over you . . . people say I can drink beer as though I've got a wooden leg."

Bill Veeck never wasted a minute when it came to savoring this precious gift of life. He beat the sun up each morning, then tucked it to bed each evening. He was indefatigable, and expected nothing less of those around him. Sleep was optional, a necessary evil, and Veeck surrendered to bed and pillow only under duress, and then only briefly.

One of my first experiences with Bill occurred at spring training in Sarasota, Florida, in 1976. He had just regained control of the Chicago White Sox, and naturally, there were never enough hours in the day for him. I was young then, and so was Roland Hemond, the White Sox general manager who was on the peripatetic side. But Veeck represented another dimension altogether. Hemond on occasion would dine with someone other than Bill, a wise choice because I don't recall ever seeing him eat, either. Anyway, Hemond would then return to the Sox's hotel headquarters in dire need of some shuteye. He would tiptoe around bushes and sidewalks, unlock the door to his room ever so furtively, brush his teeth in the dark, then collapse in a heap. Sleep at last!!

Not so fast. Hemond's phone would ring. It would be Bill, inviting him over to his room for a cold one and more baseball talk. Roland says he worked five years for Veeck, but it seemed like ten, because he never closed his eyes. Or his mind. Veeck did that to you. He could discuss anything, because everything interested him. Call him a voracious reader and you would be correct. Call him a voracious thinker and you would truly define him. I don't ever recall being bored in his company, and most of those hours were spent listening because I did feel vastly inferior to his intellect, not that he would impose on you with his knowledge. Bill would invariably ask your opinion on a subject. Just as surely, his ideas were better than yours.

Veeck was suspicious of pretense and formality, and if you wore a necktie, especially on a hot afternoon, you were automatically overdressed. This posture did not especially endear him to fellow owners and executives from baseball's grim and officious pinstriped gang. And that was then, when a goodly number of the sport's power brokers at least were brought up in or around the game. Now, baseball is overrun by accountants, and I daresay this flock of bean-counters would put even Bill's sense of humor to a test. Not that he didn't see the day coming when inflationary spirals would threaten baseball's very essence.

"It's not the high price of stardom that bothers me . . . it's the high price of mediocrity." That's what every baseball mogul is saying now, and Bill said it a quarter of a century ago. He was both a visionary and a man who lived for the present. He was blessed with a fertile imagination and basic values gleaned from his father, who was Bill's idol. That combination made it easy for Bill to handle everything from the constant pain of his sore limbs to the aggravation of one run losses. When he got angry or frustrated, rubbing that hearing aid of his, the mood would surely pass. Veeck would figure out today just in time to afford tomorrow a proper and fitting welcome.

I never heard him swear, but I did see him clomp out of the Comiskey Park on a searing summer Sunday afternoon to dive into a fight among fans. That kind of rough stuff didn't belong in the ballpark. It was dangerous and uncouth and besides, it violated Bill's law— the game is about joy. When Bill said that the sweetest sound on earth was that of bat hitting ball, he wasn't selling tickets. He was merely unbuttoning his shirt so his heart could fall out.

By necessity, Bill departed baseball upon the advent of free agency — an era characterized by unprecedented dollar-slinging. Bill simply couldn't cope with the new math; sports has become increasingly corporate. All bankbooks being equal, however, I suspect Bill could have dealt with the new attitudes. For all his old-fashioned virtues, Veeck was modern, contemporary, hip. Could Vince Lombardi coach today's independently wealthy football players? I think so. The great ones always find a way, and besides, Veeck had something you can't buy. He loved baseball. *Veeck as in Wreck* is all about that love. It takes you back to when baseball was still a game and somebody like Bill Veeck could make it fun even when his team was losing.

Had Bill still operated a franchise into the turbulent '80s and '90s, however, I imagine he would have implored baseball players and officials to enjoy their privileged existence. It's a job, baseball is, for those who depend on it for a paycheck, but a job needn't feel like work. Then again, maybe it's just as well he left us when he did. Bill Veeck could not have tolerated the disgrace of 1994, when the World Series was canceled because labor and management argued over money.

Bill Veeck had the business of pleasure in perspective. I remember him, answering his own phone in an office where the door was never closed. I can't recall if it even had a door. And I also remember him, hobbling around the ballpark, oblivious to all those aches, and I often wondered: who *is* really handicapped, him or us?

Bob Verdi
September 2000

A Can of Beer, a Slice of Cake— and Thou, Eddie Gaedel | 1.

IN 1951, in a moment of madness, I became owner and operator of a collection of old rags and tags known to baseball historians as the St. Louis Browns.

The Browns, according to reputable anthropologists, rank in the annals of baseball a step or two ahead of Cro-Magnon man. One thing should be made clear. A typical *Brownie* was more than four feet tall. Except, of course, for Eddie Gaedel, who was 3'7" and weighed 65 lbs. Eddie gave the Browns their only distinction. He was, by golly, the best darn midget who ever played big-league ball. He was also the only one.

Eddie came to us in a moment of desperation. Not his desperation, ours. After a month or so in St. Louis, we were looking around desperately for a way to draw a few people into the ball park, it being perfectly clear by that time that the ball club wasn't going to do it unaided. The best bet seemed to be to call upon the resources of our radio sponsors, Falstaff Brewery. For although Falstaff only broadcast our games locally, they had distributors and dealers all over the state.

It happened that 1951 was the Fiftieth Anniversary of the American League, an event the league was exploiting with its usual burst of inspiration by sewing special emblems on the uniforms of all the players. It seemed to me that a birthday party was clearly called for. It seemed to me, further, that if I could throw a party to celebrate the birthdays of both the American League and Falstaff Brewery, the sponsors would be getting a nice little tie-in and we would have their distributors and dealers hustling tickets for us all over the state. Nobody at Falstaff's seemed to know exactly when their birthday was, but that was no great problem. If we couldn't prove it fell on the day we chose, neither could anyone prove that it didn't. The day we chose was a Sunday doubleheader against the last-place Detroit Tigers, a struggle which did not threaten to set the pulses of the city beating madly.

Rudie Schaffer, the Browns' business manager, and I met with the Falstaff people—Mr. Griesedieck Sr., the head of the company, Bud and Joe Griesedieck and their various department heads—to romance our project. "In addition to the regular party, the acts and so on," I told Bud, "I'll do something for you that I have never done before. Something so original and spectacular that it will get you national publicity."

Naturally, they pressed me for details. Naturally, I had to tell them that much as I hated to hold out on them, my idea was so explosive I could not afford to take the slightest chance of a leak.

The Falstaff people, romantics all, went for it. They were so anxious to find out what I was going to do that they could hardly bear to wait out the two weeks. I was rather anxious to find out what I was going to do, too. The real reason I had not been willing to let them in on my top-secret plan was that I didn't have any plan.

What can I do, I asked myself, that is so spectacular that *no one* will be able to say he had seen it before? The answer was perfectly obvious. I would send a midget up to bat.

Actually, the idea of using a midget had been kicking around in my head all my life. I have frequently been accused of stealing the idea from a James Thurber short story, "You Could Look It Up." Sheer libel. I didn't steal the idea from Thurber, I stole it from John J. McGraw.

McGraw had been a great friend of my father's in the days when McGraw was managing the New York Giants and my daddy was president of the Chicago Cubs. Once or twice every season he would come to the house, and one of my greatest thrills would be to sit quietly at the table after dinner and listen to them tell their lies. McGraw had a little hunchback he kept around the club as a sort of good-luck charm. His name, if I remember, was Eddie Morrow. Morrow wasn't a midget, you understand, he was a sort of gnome. By the time McGraw got to the stub of his last cigar, he would always swear to my father that one day before he retired he was going to send his gnome up to bat.

All kids are tickled by the incongruous. The picture of McGraw's gnome coming to bat had made such a vivid impression on me that it was there, ready for the plucking, when I needed it.

I put in a call to Marty Caine, the booking agent from whom I had hired all my acts when I was operating in Cleveland, and asked him to find me a midget who was somewhat athletic and game for anything. "And Marty," I said, "I want this to be a secret."

I never told Marty what I wanted him for. Only five other people knew. Mary Frances, my wife; Rudie Schaffer; Bob Fishel, our publicity man; Bill Durney, our traveling secretary; and, of course, Zack Taylor, our manager.

Marty Caine found Eddie Gaedel in Chicago and sent him down to be looked over. He was a nice little guy, in his mid-twenties. Like all midgets, he had sad little eyes, and like all midgets, he had a squeaky little voice that sounded as if it were on the wrong speed of a record player.

"Eddie," I said, "how would you like to be a big-league ballplayer?"

When he first heard what I wanted him to do, he was a little dubious. I had to give him a sales pitch. I said, "Eddie, you'll be the only midget in the history of the game. You'll be appearing before thousands of people. Your name will go into the record books for all time. You'll be famous, Eddie," I said. "Eddie," I said, "you'll be immortal."

Well, Eddie Gaedel had more than a little ham in him. The more I talked, the braver he became. By the time I was finished, little Eddie was ready to charge through a machine-gun nest to get to the plate.

I asked him how much he knew about baseball. "Well," he said, "I know you're supposed to hit the white ball with the bat. And then you run somewhere."

Obviously, he was well schooled in the fundamentals. "I'll show you what I want you to do," I told him.

I picked up a little toy bat and crouched over as far as I could, my front elbow resting on my front knee. The rules of the game say that the strike zone is between the batter's armpits and the top of his knees "when he assumes his natural stance." Since Gaedel would bat only once in his life, whatever stance he took was, by definition, his natural one.

When Eddie went into that crouch, his strike zone was just about visible to the naked eye. I picked up a ruler and measured it for posterity. It was 1½ inches. Marvelous.

Eddie practiced that crouch for awhile, up and down, up and down, while I cheered him on lustily from the sidelines. After a while, he began to test the heft of the bat and glare out toward an imaginary pitcher. He sprang out of his crouch and took an awkward, lunging swing.

"No, no," I said. "You just stay in that crouch. All you have to do is stand there and take four balls. Then you'll trot down to first base and we'll send someone in to run for you."

His face collapsed. You could see his visions of glory leaking out of him. All at once, I remembered that the twist in the James Thurber story was that the midget got ambitious, swung at the 3-0 pitch and got thrown out at first base because it took him an hour and a half to run down the baseline.

"Eddie," I said gently, "I'm going to be up on the roof with a high-powered rifle watching every move you make. If you so much as look as if you're going to swing, I'm going to shoot you dead."

Eddie went back to Chicago with instructions to return on Saturday, August 18, the day before the game. In the meantime, there were details to be attended to. First of all, there was the question of a uniform. No problem. Bill DeWitt Jr., the seven-year-old son of our vice-president, had a little Browns' uniform hanging in the locker room. Rudie stole it and sent it out to get the number 1/8 sewed on the back. Scorecards are traditionally printed up on the morning of the game, so listing him would be no problem at all.

Just for the heck of it, I took out a $1,000,000 insurance policy to protect us in case of sudden death, sudden growth or any other pernicious act of nature. Somehow no opportunity to tell anybody about that policy ever came up, no great loss since the whole thing cost me about a buck and a half.

We were hiring Eddie for one day at $100, the minimum AGVA scale for a midget act. Still, if he was going to play in an official game he had to be signed to a standard player's contract, with a salary set on an annual basis and a guaranteed 30-day payment upon termination. That was no real problem, either. We computed the salary on the basis of $100 a game and typed in an additional clause in which Eddie agreed to waive the 30-day notice.

I must admit that by the time Eddie came back to St. Louis we were playing the cloak-and-dagger stuff a bit strong. Eddie went directly to a hotel suite we had hired for him about ten blocks from the park. Instead of bringing the contract to his room, Bob Fishel set up a meeting on a street corner a block or two from the hotel. Bob drove up in his old Packard and Eddie slid into the front seat, scribbled his signature on two contracts and jumped back out. One of the contracts was mailed to league headquarters on Saturday night, which meant that it would not be delivered until Monday morning. The other contract was given to Zack Taylor, in case our promising rookie was challenged by the umpires. The morning of the game, I wired headquarters that we were putting player Edward Gaedel on our active list.

On Sunday morning, we smuggled Eddie up to the office for further instruction on the fine art of crouching. That was a little dangerous. I have always taken the doors off my office and encouraged people to walk right in to see me. We posted a lookout and from time to time either Mary Frances or Bob or Rudie would have to hustle Eddie out to the farm-system offices in the back. Always they'd come back with the same story. As soon as Eddie got out of my sight he'd turn tiger

14

and start swinging his little bat. "He's going to foul it up," they all told me. "If you saw him back there you'd know he's going to swing."

"Don't worry," I'd tell them, worrying furiously. "I've got the situation well in hand."

Don't worry. . . . Just as I was leaving the office to circulate among the customers as they arrived at the park, Eddie asked me, "Bill . . . ? How tall was Wee Willie Keeler?"

Oh, boy. . . .

"Eddie," I said, "I've got your life insured for a million dollars. I've got a gun stashed up on the roof. But don't you let any of that bother you. You just crouch over like you've been doing and take four pitches, huh?"

As I was going out the door, I turned back one final time. "Wee Willie Keeler," I told him, "was six-feet-five."

Falstaff came through nobly. We had a paid attendance of better than 18,000, the biggest crowd to see the Browns at home in four years. Since our customers were also our guests for the Falstaff Birthday Party, we presented everybody with a can of beer, a slice of birthday cake and a box of ice cream as they entered the park. I also gave out one of Falstaff's own promotional gimmicks, salt-and-pepper shakers in the shape of a Falstaff bottle. The tie-in there was that we were giving the fans *midget* beer bottles as souvenirs of the day, a subtlety which managed to elude everybody completely.

The most surprising thing to me, as I moved through the crowd during the first game, was that nobody seemed to have paid the slightest attention to the rather unique scorecard listing:

1/8   Gaedel

Harry Mitauer of the *Globe-Democrat* did ask Bob Fishel about it up in the press box, but Roberto was able to shunt the question aside. (The next day, we had a hundred or so requests from collectors, so I suppose there are quite a few of the Gaedel scorecards still in existence around the country.)

Every baseball crowd, like every theatre audience, has its own distinctive attitude and atmosphere. You can usually tell as they are coming into the park whether it is going to be a happy, responsive crowd or a dead and sullen one. With the Birthday Party and the gifts and the busfuls of people from the outlying towns, the crowd arrived in a gay and festive mood. Not even the loss of the first game could dampen their spirit.

We went all out in our between-games Birthday Celebration. We

15

had a parade of old-fashioned cars circling the field. We had two men and two women, dressed in Gay Ninety costumes, pedaling around the park on a bicycle-built-for-four. Troubadours roamed through the stands to entertain the customers. Our own band, featuring Satchel Paige on the drums, performed at home plate. Satch, who is good enough to be a professional, stopped the show cold.

In our own version of a 3-ring circus, we had something going on at every base—a hand-balancing act at first base, a trampoline act on second and a team of jugglers at third. Max Patkin, our rubber-boned clown, pulled a woman out of the grandstand and did a wild jitterbug dance with her on the pitcher's mound.

Eddie Gaedel had remained up in the office during the game, under the care of big Bill Durney. Between games, Durney was to bring him down under the stands, in full uniform, and put him into a huge 7-foot birthday cake we had stashed away under the ramp. There was a hollowed-out section in the middle of the cake, complete with a board slab for Eddie to sit on. For we had a walk-on role written in for Eddie during the celebration; we were really getting our $100 worth out of him. As a matter of fact, the cake cost us a darn sight more than Eddie did.

As I hustled down the ramp, I could hear the crowd roaring at Patkin. Eddie could hear it too. And apparently the tremendous roar, magnified underground, frightened him. "Gee," I could hear him saying, "I don't feel so good." And then, after a second or two, "I don't think I'm going to do it."

Now, Bill Durney is 6′4″ and in those days he weighed 250 lbs. "Listen, Eddie," he said. "There are eighteen thousand people in this park and there's one I know I can lick. You. Dead or alive, you're going in there."

I arrived on the scene just as Bill was lifting him up to stuff him inside. Eddie was holding his bat in one hand and, at that stage of the proceedings, he was wearing little slippers turned up at the end like elf's shoes. Well, it is difficult enough, I suppose, for anybody to look calm and confident while he is being hung out like laundry. Nor do I imagine that anybody has ever managed to look like a raging tiger in elf's shoes. Taking all that into consideration, you could still see that Eddie was scared. He wanted out. "Bill," he said piteously, as he dangled there, "these shoes hurt my feet. I don't think I'll be able to go on."

We weren't about to let him duck out this late in the game. Durney dropped him in the cake, sat him down and covered the top over with tissue paper.

16

Up on the roof behind home plate we had a special box with a connecting bar and restaurant for the care and feeding of visiting dignitaries. By the time I got up there to join Bud Griesedieck and the rest of the Falstaff executive force, the cake had already been rolled out onto the infield grass. Along with the cake came Sir John Falstaff or, at any rate, a hefty actor dressed in Elizabethan clothes. *There* was a touch to warm the cockles and hops of the Falstaff crowd.

"Watch this," I chuckled.

Our announcer, Bernie Ebert, boomed: "Ladies and gentlemen, as a special birthday present to manager Zack Taylor, the management is presenting him with a brand-new Brownie."

Sir John tapped the cake with his gleaming cutlass and, right on cue, out through the paper popped Eddie Gaedel.

There was a smattering of applause from the stands and a light ripple of laughter.

In the Falstaff box, there was nothing but stunned silence.

"Holy smokes," Bud said, "this is what your big thing is? A little midget jumps out of a cake and he's wearing a baseball uniform and he's a bat boy or something?"

"Don't you understand?" I said. "He's a real live Brownie."

"You put funny shoes on a midget and he's a real live Brownie and that's going to get us national coverage?"

Karl Vollmer, their advertising manager, was plainly disgusted. "Aw, this is lousy, Bill," he said. "Even the cake gimmick, you've used that before in Milwaukee and Cleveland. You haven't given us anything new at all."

I begged them not to be too unhappy. "Maybe it isn't the best gag in the world," I said, "but the rest of the show was good and everybody seems happy. It will be all right."

They were determined to be unhappy, though. The gloom in that box was so thick that our Falstaff could have come up and carved it into loaves with his cutlass. (That didn't seem like a very good idea at the moment, however, because Vollmer looked as if he was just about ready to grab the cutlass and cut my throat.) "This is the explosive thing you couldn't tell us about," Vollmer muttered. "A midget jumps out of a cake and, what do you know, he's a real live Brownie."

I did my best to look ashamed of myself.

In the second game, we started Frank Saucier in place of our regular center fielder, Jim Delsing. This is the only part of the gag I've ever felt bad about. Saucier was a great kid whom I had personally talked back into the game when I bought the Browns. Everything

17

went wrong for Frank, and all he has to show for his great promise is that he was the only guy a midget ever batted for.

For as we came up for our half of the first inning, Eddie Gaedel emerged from the dugout waving three little bats. "For the Browns," said Bernie Ebert over the loudspeaker system, "number one-eighth, Eddie Gaedel, batting for Saucier."

Suddenly, the whole park came alive. Suddenly, my honored guests sat upright in their seats. Suddenly, the sun was shining. Eddie Hurley, the umpire behind the plate, took one look at Gaedel and started toward our bench. "Hey," he shouted out to Taylor, "what's going on here?"

Zack came out with a sheaf of papers. He showed Hurley Gaedel's contract. He showed him the telegram to headquarters, duly promulgated with a time stamp. He even showed him a copy of our active list to prove that we did have room to add another player.

Hurley returned to home plate, shooed away the photographers who had rushed out to take Eddie's picture and motioned the midget into the batter's box. The place went wild. Bobby Cain, the Detroit pitcher, and Bob Swift, their catcher, had been standing by peacefully for about 15 minutes, thinking unsolemn thoughts about that jerk Veeck and his gags. I will never forget the look of utter disbelief that came over Cain's face as he finally realized that this was for real.

Bob Swift rose to the occasion like a real trouper. If I had set out to use the opposing catcher to help build up the tension, I could not have improved one whit upon his performance. Bob, bless his heart, did just what I was hoping he would do. He went out to the mound to discuss the intricacies of pitching to a midget with Cain. And when he came back, he did something I had never even dreamed of. To complete the sheer incongruity of the scene—and make the newspaper pictures of the event more memorable—he got down on both knees to offer his pitcher a target.

By now, the whole park was rocking, and nowhere were there seven more delirious people than my guests in the rooftop box. Veeck the jerk had become Willie the wizard. The only unhappy person in that box was me, good old Willie the wizard. Gaedel, little ham that he was, had not gone into the crouch I had spent so many hours teaching him. He was standing straight up, his little bat held high, his feet spraddled wide in a fair approximation of Joe DiMaggio's classic style. While the Falstaff people were whacking me on the back and letting their joy flow unrestrained, I was thinking: *I should have brought that gun up here. I'll kill him if he swings. I'll kill him, I'll kill him.*

Fortunately, Cain started out by really trying to pitch to him. The first two deliveries came whizzing past Eddie's head before he had time to swing. By the third pitch, Cain was laughing so hard that he could barely throw. Ball three and ball four came floating up about three feet over Eddie's head.

Eddie trotted down to first base to the happy tune of snapping cameras. He waited for the runner, one foot holding to the bag like a pro, and he patted Delsing on the butt in good professional exhortation before he surrendered the base. He shook hands with our first-base coach and he waved to the cheering throng.

The St. Louis dugout was behind third base, which meant that Eddie had to cut completely across the infield. If it had been difficult to get him into the cake earlier, I was worried for awhile that I would have to send Bill Durney out there again to carry him off the field. Eddie, after all, was a performer. In his small, unspectacular way he was a part of show business. He had dreamed all his life of his moment in the spotlight and now that it had come to him, he was not about to bow his head and leave quietly. He crossed that field one step at a time, stopping in between to wave his hat or bow from the waist or just to raise an acknowledging hand to the plaudits of the crowd. When he disappeared, at last, into the dugout he was the happiest little man you have ever seen.

If the thing had been done right, Delsing, running for Gaedel, would have scored and we would have won the game, 1–0. I was willing to settle for less than that. I was willing to win by one run, regardless of the final score, as long as that one run represented Eddie Gaedel. As it was, there being a limit to the amount of help you can expect from either the St. Louis Browns or fortune, Delsing got as far as third base with only one out and was then left stranded. We lost the game, 6–2.

Nothing remained but to wait for the expected blasts from league headquarters and, more particularly, from the deacons of the press, those old-timers who look upon baseball not as a game or a business but as a solemn ritual, almost a holy calling.

The press, for the most part, took the sane attitude that Gaedel had provided a bright moment in what could easily have been a deadly dull doubleheader between a 7th and an 8th place ball club. Vincent X. Flaherty of Los Angeles pretty much summed up the general reaction when he wrote, "I do not advocate baseball burlesque. Such practices do not redound to the better interests of the game—but I claim it was the funniest thing that has happened to baseball in years."

It's fine to be appreciated for a day; I recommend it highly for the soul. It's better for the box office, though, to be attacked for a full week. I was counting on the deacons to turn Gaedel into a full week's

19

story by attacking me for spitting in their Cathedral. They didn't let me down, although I did feel the words "cheap and tawdry" and "travesty" and "mockery" were badly overworked. The spirit was willing, but I'm afraid the rhetoric was weak.

Dan Daniel, a well-known high priest from New York, wondered what "Ban Johnson and John J. McGraw are saying about it up there in Baseball's Valhalla," a good example of Dan's lean and graceful style. Non-baseball fans should understand that baseball men do not go to heaven or hell when they die; they go to Valhalla where they sit around a hot stove and talk over the good old days with Odin, Thor and the rest of that crowd. (I am assuming that the baseball people haven't driven the old Norse gods out to the suburbs. You know what guys like Johnson and McGraw do to real-estate values.)

To Joe Williams, Daniel's colleague on the New York *World-Telegram,* I was "that fellow Veeck out in St. Louis."

"It didn't matter that this made a mockery of the sport or that it exploited a freak of biology in a shameful, disgraceful way," Williams wrote. ". . . What he calls showmanship can more often be accurately identified as vulgarity."

I have never objected to being called vulgar. The word, as I never tire of pointing out to my tireless critics, comes from the Latin *vulgaris,* which means—students?—"the common people." (If you don't believe it, Joe, you could look it up.) I am so darn vulgar that I will probably never get into Valhalla, which is a shame because I would love to be able to let McGraw know how he helped that little boy who used to listen to him, enraptured, over the dinner table. From what I can remember of McGraw, he would roar with delight.

What that fellow Williams in New York didn't seem to realize—or did he?—was that it was he who was gratuitously and publicly calling Eddie Gaedel a freak. Eddie was a professional midget. He made his living by displaying himself, the only way we permit a midget to earn a living in our enlightened society. In more barbaric times, they were able to achieve a certain stature as court jesters. My use of him—*vulgaris* that I am—was the biggest thing that ever happened to him. In the week that followed, I got him bookings that earned him something between $5,000 and $10,000. I kept getting him bookings here and there for the rest of his life. Eddie hungered for another chance at the spotlight. Whenever he came to a town where I was operating he would phone and say, "OK, Boss, I'm ready."

I did use him for a couple of my gags. One of the last times was at Comiskey Park in Chicago, about a year before his death. Eddie and three other midgets, all dressed in regimental Martian clothing (gold helmets and shoes, coveralls, oxygen tanks), somehow dropped out of the heavens in a helicopter and landed directly behind second base. Quickly capturing our tiny second-base combination, Nellie Fox and Luis Aparicio, they made them honorary Martians and informed them —over the remarkably handy public-address system—that they had come down to aid them in their battle against the giant earthlings.

It was during this historic meeting that Eddie Gaedel uttered those immortal words, "I don't want to be taken to your leader. I've already met him."

The battle with league headquarters had begun before Eddie stepped into the batter's box. Will Harridge, the league president—for reasons best known to himself—had gone to his office that Sunday and had seen the report come over the Western Union teletype that I was trying to send a midget up to bat. While Hurley was still looking over the papers, our switchboard operator, Ada Ireland, sent word to me that Harridge was on the phone threatening to blow a fuse unless someone in authority came out to talk to him. I sent back word that we had all disappeared from the face of the earth.

A few minutes later, I was told that Will was trying to get me on the office teletype, which is in direct communication with headquarters. I told them to turn off the machine.

The next day, Harridge issued an executive order barring Gaedel from baseball. A new rule was promptly passed making it mandatory that all player contracts be filed with and *approved* by the president.

Naturally, I was bewildered and alarmed and shocked. I was a few other things too: "I'm puzzled, baffled and grieved by Mr. Harridge's ruling," I announced. "Why, we're paying a lot of guys on the Browns' roster good money to get on base and even though they don't do it, nobody sympathizes with us. But when this little guy goes up to the plate and draws a walk on his only time at bat, they call it 'conduct detrimental to baseball.'"

If baseball wanted to discriminate against the little people, I said, why didn't we have the courage to be honest about it, write a minimum height into the rules and submit ourselves to the terrible wrath of all right-thinking Americans. "I think," I said, "that further clarification is called for. Should the height of a player be 3 feet 6 inches, 4 feet 6 inches, 6 feet 6 inches, or 9 feet 6 inches?" Now that midgets had been so arbitrarily barred, I asked, were we to assume that giants were also barred? I made dark references to the stature of Phil Rizzuto, who is not much over five feet tall, and I implied very strongly that I was going to demand an official ruling on whether he was a short ballplayer or a tall midget.

I hammered away at the phrase "little people," which had a solid political currency in those days. I had given Eddie Gaedel a speech on that theme too. "Everybody talks about protecting the little man these days," he was supposed to say, "and now that someone has finally taken a direct step to help the plight of the little man in baseball, Harridge has stepped in and ruined my career."

Political connotations, unfortunately, were lost on Eddie. When the time came for him to deliver his statement, he blew it. "Now that someone has finally taken a direct step to help us short guys," he said, "Harridge is ruining my baseball career." Ah well, you can't win them all.

In the end I had to agree, reluctantly, to bow to superior authority. "As much as it grieves me," I said, "I will have to go along with this odd ruling." I thought that was rather big of me, especially since I had only hired Gaedel for one day.

Something else happened, though, that I was not disposed to be so amiable about. The good deacons of the press had been wailing that unless Harridge acted immediately, the name of Eddie Gaedel would desecrate the record books for all time. Harridge dutifully decreed that Gaedel's appearance be stricken from all official records. This I wouldn't stand for. I had promised Eddie that he would live forever in the record books, which are cast in bronze, carved in marble and encased in cement. Immortality I had promised him, and immortality he would have. I reminded Harridge that Gaedel had a legal contract and had been permitted to bat in an official game presided over by the league's own umpires. If Gaedel hadn't batted, I pointed out, it would also mean that Bobby Cain hadn't thrown the pitches and that Swift hadn't caught them. It would mean that Delsing had come in to run for no one, and that Saucier had been deprived of a time at bat. It would mean, in short, that the continuity of baseball was no longer intact, and the integrity of its records had been compromised. If Desecration was the game they wanted to play, then I held a pretty strong hand myself.

Eddie crept back into the record books and remains there today. When he died, he got a front-page obituary in *The New York Times,* a recognition normally accorded only to statesmen, generals and Nobel Prize winners.

I did not recognize at the time that Gaedel's moment was my moment too. I knew it was a good gag. I knew it would delight the fans and outrage the stuffed shirts. I knew, in other words, that it would be a lot of fun. It never entered my mind, however, that it would be the single act with which I would become permanently identified. Even

22

today, I cannot talk to anybody from St. Louis without being told that they were there the day the midget came to bat. If everybody was there who says he was there, we would have had a tidy gathering of 280,000.

I have done a few other things in baseball, you know. I've won pennants and finished dead last; I've set attendance records and been close to bankruptcy. At the age of fifteen, I was taking care of Ladies' Day passes at Wrigley Field. I owned my first ball club when I was twenty-eight. I have operated five clubs—three in the major leagues and two in the minors—and in three of the towns I won pennants and broke attendance records. Two of the three teams to beat the Yankees since I came to the American League in 1946 were my teams, the 1948 Cleveland Indians and the 1959 Chicago White Sox. The only other team, the 1954 Indians, was made up for the most part of my old players.

But no one has to tell me that if I returned to baseball tomorrow, won ten straight pennants and left all the old attendance records moldering in the dust, I would still be remembered, in the end, as the man who sent a midget up to bat. It is not the identification I would have chosen for myself when I came into baseball. My ambitions were grander than that. And yet I cannot deny that it is an accurate one. I have always found humor in the incongruous, I have always tried to entertain. And I have always found a stuffed-shirt the most irresistible of all targets.

I'm Bill Veeck, the guy who sent a midget up to bat?

Fair enough.

A Man of Dignity | **2.**

MY daddy, William Veeck Sr., became president of the Chicago Cubs in 1917 when I was three years old. There is a story that he was hired by William Wrigley after he had written a series of articles in the Chicago *American* blasting the way the Cubs were being run. The story is not really inaccurate, it is simply overstated. He did not blast the Cubs, he wrote a sane and thoughtful series telling, in a sane and thoughtful way, what changes he would make if he were running the club. I can remember seeing that series a long time ago, and it was what you so often hear about and so seldom see: constructive criticism without any attempt to be either colorful or clever. My father was not one of the great sportswriters of his time, he had little facility with words. But he was a good, solid reporter.

If you asked anybody who knew my daddy to describe him in a word, that word would undoubtedly be "dignified." And then they would be constrained to add, "dignified without being stuffy." He had a good sense of humor and he was always scrupulously fair. I can say, without any fear that I might be a little prejudiced, that he was the most popular fellow in baseball.

I can remember one time—I was no more than eleven—when he took me to the ball park with him. The ticket sellers had just brought the day's receipts in to the club secretary, Margaret Donahue, and her desk was covered with money. "You know, Bill," he said, "it's a very interesting thing. You look at that money and it all looks exactly the same, doesn't it? You can't tell who put it into your box office. It's all exactly the same color, the same size and the same shape. You remember that."

Although it was years before I came to understand his point, I've always remembered it.

One of the great differences between my father and me is that he was always "Mr. Veeck" to everyone who knew him and I am always "Bill." Not even the members of the Cubs' operating staff, all of whom remained with him throughout his entire 16-year tenure, would have dreamed of calling him by his first name.

For my part, I have wandered around a bit in baseball. Wherever I land, I make it clear to the girls at the switchboard and the guys who run the elevators that I am "Bill." I believe very strongly that we are all working together for the best interests of the ball club. I cannot see why the fact that I own some stock and they don't should have any bearing on our personal relationship. I do not have my father's inborn sense of dignity, and false dignity annoys me.

My father was a completely self-educated man. He was born in Boonville, Indiana, in 1877, the son of a wagon builder, and he went to work himself after only four years of schooling. My mother, Grace DeForest, was his childhood sweetheart. He first became a working newspaperman with the Louisville *Courier-Journal*. At the age of twenty-five, he came to Chicago to work for the Chicago *Inter Ocean*, a newspaper that folded a year later. With its collapse, he moved to Hearst's Chicago *American* as a reporter and rewrite man. Eventually, an opening developed on the sports desk and my father, a good baseball man and a close friend of the paper's great sportswriter, Ring

Lardner, took over the newspaper's stock sports byline, Bill Bailey.

I went to school with the Lardner boys. In Chicago, our families lived in the same apartment house, and when we moved to Hinsdale, a suburb, the Lardners moved to nearby Western Springs.

It was as Bill Bailey that my daddy wrote the series that brought him to the attention of William Wrigley, who had only recently bought control of the club. Mr. Wrigley invited him to his home for dinner and in the course of the subsequent discussion and dissection, told him, "All right, if you're so smart why don't you come and do it?" And so he did.

Mr. Wrigley contented himself with being a fan and left the running of the club entirely to his new president. The only argument they ever had arose over the hiring of Rogers Hornsby as manager. Wrigley had become so convinced that Hornsby was the answer to all the Cubs' problems that he bought him from Boston, over my father's head, for $120,000 and five players, a fantastic outlay in those days. My father immediately resigned. Mr. Wrigley got him to return only on the promise that he would never interfere again.

Unlike me, my father was far too dignified a man to pull any promotional stunts. He was a man of imagination, though, and easily the greatest innovator of his time. It was my father who first brought Ladies' Day to the big leagues. He was also the first to broadcast his ball games, and he did it in the face of furious protests from every other team in the league. In 1922, he formally proposed a round robin of inter-league games at the halfway point of the season, an idea so progressive that when I next suggested it, in 1949, it was still considered visionary by the forward-looking fossils who run the game.

In an era when managers came exclusively from the ranks of the great players, he hired a minor-league manager who had never played a game in the majors in his life, Joe McCarthy. With McCarthy, the Cubs won their first pennant in 21 years.

And, finally, it was William Veeck who fought the attempts to retain the weak three-man governing Commission, after the Black Sox scandal of 1919, and not only insisted upon a single Commissioner with absolute powers but nominated Judge Kenesaw Mountain Landis, a close personal friend, as the logical choice.

His system certainly worked for him, with or without promotion. His Cubs were the first team to ever draw more than a million people during a season, and he set a Chicago attendance record that lasted until we broke it with the White Sox in 1960.

From the time I was ten, my daddy began to take me to the park with him. When I was fifteen, I was put to work mailing out Ladies'

Day tickets. Ladies' Day, which was held every Friday, had become such a smashing success that it had become impossible to handle all the ticket seekers at the park. The women would write in—there being only a ten-cent tax in those happy days—and I would stuff the envelopes and mail them out.

It doesn't really seem fair, then, that it was a Ladies' Day crowd that gave my father his darkest hour. As somebody or other has said, the revolution always eats its own children.

My daddy's own little Black Friday came with McGraw's Giants in town. The Cubs were challenging the Giants for the first time within my memory, and the women—with and without tickets—descended upon the park *en masse*.

The men descended, too, money in hand, but, out of the native shrewdness of our sex, they knew better than to mix with the babes who crushed, like bargain-crazed Christmas shoppers, around every turnstile and ticket window. When the box office is under that kind of a blockade a call goes out to the head man.

Down came the Veecks, father and son. My daddy, like all men of good will, had a childish faith in the powers of pure reason. They were, he told the ladies, more than welcome to come into the park as the guests of the club. He was, he said, heartened by the interest they were displaying in the fortunes of the Chicago Cubs and it was his fervent hope that the team would never let them down. At the same time, he went on—getting to the heart of the matter—he was sure they realized that, under the regrettable conditions that obtained, the paying customers had to be given priority.

In front of the mob was a huge blockbuster of a woman named Emmie. Later, I got to know Emmie very well. She was the wife of a milkman and a fan, I would say—if I had any guts—of the first water. Emmie was a regular. Her emotional tie to the Cubs was more than partisan, it was maternal. If we'd had a good day, she would stand at the bottom of the clubhouse stairs and pat the players on the head as they passed. If they had behaved badly out there on the field, she would stand there anyway and pat them on the head to show them that, for all their sins, she loved them still.

The opposition was something else again. The opposition was the enemy, and she abused them in a voice that carried to the shores of Lake Michigan. Her knowledge of the public and private lives of the opposing players was almost unlimited, and she shared this knowledge unselfishly with even those poor souls in the farthest reaches of the bleachers.

Emmie had a sense of the fitness of things. She would go through her husband's pockets for money to pay her way into the park, and only when she came up empty would she come to me for a ticket. "Well, Willie," she would say, "the bookies got the money this week." I would then take her through the turnstiles and escort her to her favorite seat, just behind the boxes. It was always a good idea to escort her because, although her seat was unreserved, she looked upon it, quite rightly, as her private property. If someone happened to be sitting there already, she would ask him—once—to move. If he offered any objection, she would pick him up bodily—and I mean bodily —carry him to the exit and heave him out. Down would come Willie to brush him off and present him with a season ticket to show the Cubs' good will—and to forestall any possible damage suit.

Every now and then, of course, the police would beat me to the scene and I would have to assure them that the provocation must have been great indeed to have moved so gentle and loving a soul as Emmie to an act of naked violence.

We became dear friends, Emmie and I. But that was later. My father was not familiar with Emmie as he addressed the Ladies' Day crowd milling around the park that day, and for that matter neither was I. The first time I ever heard her voice, which might be compared —allowing for the inadequacies of the language—to the tender murmurings of a lady buffalo, she was answering his request to stand back and let the paying customers through. "Open up all the gates," she roared, "and then we can all get in!"

My father patiently explained that to throw open the gates would be to let everybody in free, the men as well as the women, a rather inefficient way to run a profit-making organization.

"Well," said Emmie, "you have your troubles and I have mine. I'm coming in!"

She took one step backwards, broke into a ladylike trot, somewhat similar to an Ohio State fullback cutting between guard and tackle, and plowed right through the gate and into the secondary. Behind her came 15,000 women.

Even as a young boy, I came equipped with a hard head, reasonably broad shoulders and a healthy instinct for self-preservation. I dove for cover. As I hit the ground, my father was still speaking in that clear and courteous voice with which he would address a group of ladies in his own living room. The next I saw of him, he was being trampled in a stampede of spike heels.

When the dust cleared—and it took some time for the dust to clear —he picked himself up slowly, brushed himself off carefully and tucked his shirt cuffs under his jacket. Without a word or a glance, he walked past me and went up the stairs to his office, full of elbow marks, small punctures and long thoughts.

On the drive home that night not a word was said. He never mentioned Veeck's famous last stand to me or, as far as I know, to anybody else in the world. His dignity had been affronted and he could not bear to speak of it.

As long as he lived, my father never again left his office on Ladies' Day, and for five years, I always made it a point to handle the gate on Fridays.

I saw him forget his dignity only once. He was entitled to this one fall, for it came at the end of the greatest ball game I have ever seen. In Hinsdale, my buddy was Marsh Samuel. We started together as delivery boys for the local florist and, in subsequent years, he became our publicity director at Cleveland. Marsh and I had the same last-period class on the first floor of Hinsdale High, a class presided over by a marvelously named Latin teacher, Annie Euripides Goodchild. The Cubs were in another hot race with the Giants that season—it was the year we finally won our first pennant—and since Marsh and I didn't want to miss the start of any of those crucial late-season games we would arrange for a friend to make a racket outside our classroom shortly after the roll was taken. While Annie was out in the hall restoring law and order, Marsh and I would leap out the window and head for the park. After a few innings, when our presence wouldn't be too suspicious, we would work our way down to the president's box.

Late in the season, we were playing the Giants to break a tie for first place, a game of such importance that we found Judge Landis sitting with my father. The Giants seemed to have the game sewed up right into the ninth inning when the Cubs scored four runs to tie it up. The Giants bounced right back with four runs in their half of the tenth.

In our half, the first two batters went out. Mark Koenig kept us alive with a home run. The next three batters got on to load the bases. Up came Kiki Cuyler, representing the winning run. And Cuyler belted one. The ball was still climbing over the fence when William Veeck Sr. let out a rebel yell and vaulted over the railing. Marsh and I had leaped out toward the railing too, but we were somewhat delayed because we had to untangle ourselves from the *harrumphing* Commissioner. By the time we got onto the field, my father was in the very center of a mob scene, grabbing for Cuyler's hand.

I am not going to say that I had a "close relationship" with my father but only, understand, because that phrase has taken on a rather ridiculous connotation these past few years. He was thirty-seven years old when I was born. He was my father and I was his son and there was never any nonsense that we were pals or wanted to be pals or could be pals. I had something more than a play-acted palship with him. I admired my father and I liked him.

Early in my life, after I had done something deserving of punishment, he told me, "I'm not going to spank you, and I'm not going to go through any tiresome routine of taking things away from you or depriving you of any privileges. I'm going to do something much worse. When you do something stupid, I'm going to embarrass you. Then it will be up to you whether you want to keep on being stupid or change. The only thing is that I hate to think of a son of mine being stupid."

He did embarrass me. The first time he caught me swearing, he said, "When people can't think of anything else to say, they fall back on the old tried cusswords. I don't care what words you use. If you want to show people that you're stupid, that's up to you."

There's no doubt that he got to me, for I have not used profanity since I was a boy. Not that I'm prudish about it. I couldn't care less what kind of language my friends use. With me, it long ago became a matter of pride to find the word that best expresses what I want to say.

With a father who ran a ball club, my boyhood was the kind most kids dream about. For, hanging around the ball park, I got to know all the players. During my early years, our great star was Grover Cleveland Alexander. Alex was always extraordinarily kind to me. In one of the golden moments of my boyhood Alex took me to Riverview, an amusement park in Chicago, and was challenged at the baseball-throwing concession. In those days you didn't just throw baseballs at a pyramid of pins in a boardwalk booth. They'd have a cage, with a guy sitting on a collapsible platform. The customer would throw the baseball at a round, metal disc, and if he hit the disc, the platform would spin up and dump the guy into a tank of water. To make it even more delightful, if you dumped him you didn't have to pay.

The guy on the platform was also the shill. It was his job to insult the people as they walked by and keep them so riled up that they'd keep throwing just for the pleasure of dunking him in the water. As Alex and I were strolling past, the guy on the platform yelled, "Hey, you bum. You don't look as if you could hit the side of a barn. You don't frighten me, you bum. Come on, step up and let me see what you can do."

Well, here I am with the man who could control a baseball better than anybody else in the world—even if he did look like a bum. "Come on, Alex," I said. "Let's show them something."

Alex could have hit that disc all night. He almost drowned three different guys. They'd slide off the platform, hit the tank, climb out, and before they were halfway back onto the platform—splash!—back into the water again.

Alex, as everybody connected with baseball knew, was an alcoholic. Not just a heavy drinker, an alcoholic. Still, I can't ever remember seeing him drunk. The first drunken ballplayer I was really aware of was Rabbit Maranville. Maranville was always loaded.

For, as much out of character as it may seem at first glance, my daddy built his pennant winners with the most rollicking, raucous, rowdy and roistering crew in big-league history. Drinkers didn't bother him at all. It may have been because he had seen, with Alex, that a man could be an alcoholic and still be a marvelously disciplined craftsman on the field. It may have been merely the coincidence that his tenure as president of the Cubs (1917–1933) spanned the Prohibition era in Al Capone's Chicago. The real reason, I think, was that, being such a fair-minded and tolerant man, he could not bring himself to hold a man's personal habits against him professionally. He'd sometimes talk to me about it on the way to the park. "If a player is ready to play when he puts on his uniform and if he doesn't bring any adverse publicity to the club, it's none of our business what he does away from the park."

It works. It worked for my father and it worked for me. This may bring no particular comfort to health-food addicts, temperance workers and moralists, but both Alexander and Maranville played in the big leagues until well into their forties and played so well that they were both elected to the Hall of Fame.

I'll show you how little it bothered my father. He was able to get Maranville and Charlie Grimm, two blithe souls, from Pittsburgh for a couple of used Confederate soldiers, because they had been driving the excitable Pirates' owner, Barney Dreyfus, nuts. Maranville and Grimm teamed together very well, for the Rabbit had peered into the bottom of many an empty bottle and Charlie, though a non-drinker, had studied the top of many a rising sun.

Each of them was made manager of the Cubs at a time when my father felt the players needed to relax. Maranville got the job during his first year with us and he took it so seriously that he never drew a sober breath. But Grimm took over a good ball team, following Hornsby's reign of terror, and relaxed them right into a pennant.

I first laid eyes on Maranville and Grimm on the golf course, the day they reported to spring training at Catalina, Mr. Wrigley's private island. Because of their reputation for high jinks and low humor, a photographer was posing them with Charlie lying flat on his back, a golf tee clenched between his teeth, and Rabbit holding a driver as if he were about to swing.

The photographer said, "OK. Good. Hold it." Whereupon, Rabbit took a vicious swing and knocked the ball cleanly out of Charlie's teeth and over the photographer's head. Charlie arose, white as a sheet because, in case I have neglected to mention it, Rabbit had only played a few rounds of golf in his life.

That was Rabbit Maranville. A little rascal to his dying day. A few days after he reported, he disappeared onto the mainland overnight—meditating or something—and returned to the island on the excursion boat. Upon debarking, he snatched up a coal scuttle full of ashes, for he had learned that it was Ash Wednesday. Stationing himself at the entrance of the huge dining room of the St. Catherine Hotel, he dabbed ashes onto the foreheads of all the incoming guests. Regrettably, he was so loaded that he couldn't tell their foreheads from their elbows and he was flinging the ashes all over the place. The management had to serve more than 100 meals over again.

The year after Maranville and Grimm arrived to enliven the Cubs' roster, my father picked up Hack Wilson in the minor-league draft. Hack, one of the idols of my youth, was an oddly built, stocky little barrel of a man, with clothes hangers in his shoulders and a watermelon in his gut. Below the waist he was so small that when I was twelve years old his shoes were too small for me. Hack was a warm and cheerful and full-blooded human being, well flavored by the malt and well seasoned by life. The fans in Chicago loved him whether he was hitting his home runs or misjudging fly balls. He had what is always defined as that indefinable something, that personal glow that warmed people to him from a distance of 500 feet—me included—and made him the most important person on the ball field.

For years I found it impossible to look at any round outfielder who could hit a long ball without deciding that I had found myself another Hack Wilson. It took a long time before I got it through my thick head that you can no more manufacture colorful players like Hack Wilson than you can manufacture a colorful fan like Emmie. They have to be authentic. There is nothing quite so phony as a phony phony.

I very rarely went into the clubhouse or onto the field. My father had impressed upon me from the first that it wasn't my place to intrude upon the players. I had to go down one morning, though, to carry a message to our trainer, Andy Lotshaw, himself a rich and pungent character. Andy had Hack in one of those big, high old tubs, sobering him up. In the tub with Hack was a 50-pound cake of ice. Well, what would you do if a 50-pound cake of ice jumped into your bathtub with you? You'd try to jump out, right? That was precisely what Hack was trying to do. Enthusiastically but not successfully. Every time Hack's head would bob up, Andy would shove it back down under the water and the cake of ice would come bobbing up. It was a fascinating sight, watching them bob in perfect rhythm, first Hack's head, then the ice, then Hack's head, then the ice.

The date would be easy enough for any scholar to find. That afternoon Hack hit three home runs for the first and only time in his life. It was the same year that he hit fifty-six home runs, a National League record that still stands.

Hack's only trouble was that he was overgenerous. He gave everything away he had. Always. His money, the shirt off his back—little things like that. Chicago was the toddling town in those days. Hack's drinking buddies, a rollicking crew of about two dozen Chicagoans, would wait for him after the game and they'd toddle over to the joints on the North Side and the West Side. Hack picked up every check. When he longed for the companionship of his teammates there were always a dozen or so heading out on the town. The players' favorite joint was the Hole in the Wall over in Cicero, a speakeasy which could easily be defined as the fallout shelter of the Prohibition era; it was the gangster hangout and that made it the safest place in town. At the core of the rollickers, in addition to Hack, was Pat Malone—a name to inspire any old Cub fan to hoist a mug of beer himself. Pat Malone was another of the perennial minor-leaguers. My father bought him cheap and he pitched us to the pennant. And, ah yes, there was—as I remember—a nonplaying member of this roistering crew of blessed memory, young Bill Veeck. By the time I was fifteen, I was getting around pretty good.

I even developed the habit of stopping at Hinsdale's friendly neighborhood speakeasy on my way home to dinner. My father and mother would drop into the same speakeasy when they were going out—and inevitably they found out about my patronage.

One evening, when I arrived home, my father was waiting for me with two cocktails.

Oh, oh, I thought.

I needn't have worried, of course. "Look," he said. "You always have a cocktail before dinner. I don't recommend it at your age but if you're going to do it anyway you might as well not be sneaky about

32

it. I think it's a kind of sorry state of affairs when you do something away from home that you can't do here."

My work around the park, I should make clear, was nothing more than a way for me to make a few dollars during the summer. There was never any plan for me to make a career in baseball. My father was always a newspaperman at heart, and like most old newspapermen, his dream was to own a small-town paper. Our plan was to start a paper in Lincoln or Sterling or some other little Illinois town, after I graduated from college, and run it together.

As a self-educated man, my father always stood in awe of the printed word. Reading had always been a great part of his life, and so it became a part of the life of the family. As long as I can remember, he read to us after dinner: Robert Louis Stevenson, James Fenimore Cooper's *Leatherstocking Tales,* Dumas. Every Christmas he would give me the complete works of two or three authors, sometimes as many as fifty books altogether. I'd have them all read in three months, and he'd keep feeding me more. By the time I was fourteen, I had read virtually all the accepted classics.

Throughout my life, I have read an average of five books a week. I read everything, my tastes being both catholic and indiscriminate. I have the literary digestion of a garbage-disposal unit. I can go from Gibbon to the best-seller list to a trade journal and find something to interest me in all of them.

The kind of life I have led has been conducive to reading. For one thing, I've had to do a lot of traveling on trains and planes. And from the day I injured my leg on Bougainville, I have spent an awful lot of time in hospitals. Since my right leg was amputated in 1946 I have had to bathe the stump an hour or two every day. So I lie in a hot tub, soaking and reading.

It was important to my father that his children have the very best formal education. Thus after grammar school, I was sent to Phillips Academy in Andover, Massachusetts. I became terribly homesick after the first semester and came back to Hinsdale for my first two years of high school. After that, I went to the Los Alamos Ranch School in New Mexico, on the site where the atomic bomb was later developed. The Ranch School was right up there with the most expensive private schools in the country; tuition was $5,000 a year. The students had to wear short pants, just so we'd know we were better than the long-trousered masses. It was a fine school, though, with only two or three students to a class. It guaranteed to get its graduates into any college in the country, and it could. My classmates were the sons of the heads of some of the biggest corporations in the country.

33

I didn't get along at all. Even at Hinsdale, there had been a certain kind of kid who roiled my insides. Not because they were wealthy but because they felt that out of some divine ordering of the universe they had been created from a finer clay. A remarkable number of them seem to end up inheriting baseball clubs.

To give you an idea, I was known as "that public school rowdy," a description that put me just one rung above the loinclothed savage. I got into a lot of fights. Someone would make a wisecrack and I'd pop him.

To make me feel really ill at ease, I began to sprout like a stalk of summer corn. Until I was sixteen, I was a skinny little kid, 105 lbs. and 5'3" or 5'4". In my first year at the Ranch School, I grew 8 inches and put on about 50 lbs. I didn't just grow out of my clothes, I grew through them. The most humiliating two days of my life came when I had to travel back to Chicago by train for the Christmas vacation wearing clothes so short that my jacket sleeves barely came halfway down my forearms.

In my senior year, I departed the Ranch School for the Easter vacation with the understanding that I would not be coming back, a genteel way of being kicked out.

I still haven't graduated from high school, even though I did attend Kenyon College. I had been a good enough blocking-back at Hinsdale High, despite my lack of size and speed, to have attracted the interest of a couple of small colleges. Kenyon, to keep the record straight, was not yet the excellent small college it has since become. Because I had no diploma, I had to pass the College Boards, including an exam in ancient history, a subject I had never taken. By virtually memorizing the textbook I managed to pass.

Boy, Kenyon was one long party for me. There was, in fact, a party going full blast in the dormitory the day I arrived. It developed into a permanent floating party, moving from one floor of the dorm to the other and rolling on, unbroken, for a full month.

It tells something about the school to say that I was elected president of the freshman class, quite possibly on capacities having little to do with my capacity for study. But then, I was a pro among amateurs. I had studied this course with big-leaguers.

The year came to a fitting conclusion for me the day of the freshman dance. I was standing out on the ledge of the recreation room window, 4½ floors aboveground, surveying the incoming females, one hand clutched firmly to a bottle of beer, the other holding onto the inside wall.

A buddy waved to me from across campus. I waved back. Being

34

in a somewhat befuddled state, I used the wrong hand, waved myself right off the ledge and toppled like a sack of wheat to the ground. A sober man would probably have been killed. I got away with two broken legs.

The scene of the party was promptly shifted from the campus to the hospital.

My memory of the next two days comes to me darkly, as through a red haze. The cast on my left leg had been put on much too tight, cutting off most of the blood flow to my brain. What blood did get through was well diluted because all my visitors were thoughtful enough to bring along their flasks.

There is a philosophy of life that goes: Things are never so bad that they couldn't be worse. Right. The Betas, the fraternity to which I had been pledged, were holding their induction ceremonies that same night. Quite obviously, they were not going to take any chance of losing a prospective member as talented as I in such diverse arts as drinking, blocking and falling. A committee arrived at the hospital to claim me. The good Sisters who ran the hospital intercepted them, and a tug-of-war took place over my precious body. If I had not been practically unconscious, I might have found it quite flattering. In the end, the hospital surrendered, probably to keep me from being torn in half. It is possible that the nurses also felt that, with luck, nobody would bother to bring me back.

The next day, when my father and mother arrived, I was so far gone that I didn't know who they were. Fortunately for me, my daddy insisted upon getting me to his own doctor at once. He carried me to his car, the cast still on my leg, and drove me back to Chicago. The cast was cut off, the leg was reset and I promptly returned to the world of the living.

The next September, I was back at Kenyon to start the football season. But, sadly, not for long. A few weeks after school started, I was told that my father had been stricken with leukemia, an almost unknown disease in those days. I jumped into my car and rushed home.

The doctors told me there was no hope. They also told me that the last thing a dying man can hold in his stomach is wine. I had done little enough for my father, I knew, and I was determined that he would go out in some comfort and some style.

Prohibition had just ended. The bootleg supply was drying up; the legitimate wineries were not yet in full production. But there was one man in Chicago, I knew, who would know where the best champagne was to be had. Al Capone. I knew him slightly from the ball park and

I knew some of his boys even better. Ralph Capone, Al's brother, was a great Cub fan. We had a ticket man, named Red Thompson, whom the mob guys always dealt with. Whenever I got a $100 bill in Red's bank in later years, I knew that Ralph Capone and his boys were at the game.

I hurried to Al Capone's headquarters at the Hotel Metropole and told him what I wanted and why. "Kid," he said, "I'll send a case of champagne right over." The case was there when I got back. Every morning during these last few days of my father's life, a case of imported champagne was delivered to the door.

The last nourishment that passed between my daddy's lips on this earth was Al Capone's champagne.

The Battle of Wrigley Field | 3.

FROM a purely financial standpoint my father's death, coming as it did in the midst of the Depression, could not have occurred at a worse time. We had lived well. Now his investments, like everybody else's, had gone sour. I returned to Kenyon to finish out the football season, then went to the Cubs' office and asked for a job. William Wrigley had died two years earlier. Phil Wrigley, his son, hired me as office boy at $18 a week.

That was all right. In the eight years I remained with the Cubs I received a sound and solid education in every phase of a baseball club's table of organization. The same week I went to work for the Cubs, I began to work the switchboard for the Chicago Bears who, of course, played their football games at Wrigley Field. During the winter, I worked on the ground crew. The next winter, Mr. Wrigley got me a job at the Cubs' advertising agency and he soon had me putting out a magazine—and a pretty good one—to be sent to Cub fans.

I ran the commissary and I worked with the ushers. I worked the ticket windows and the ticket office. I ran the tryout school for high school players. I was in charge of park maintenance at the time Wrigley Field was being rebuilt and, at the end, I was the club treasurer and assistant secretary. Turn my wallet upside down and union cards will come tumbling out.

To everything, there is a craft. Take tickets. George Doyle, the head of our ticket department, not only taught me the tricks of the trade, he got me jobs in arenas and theatres all over town. I like to think that I can still count tickets fast enough to get a job anywhere in the country. A professional, working under pressure, picks up a whole block of tickets and riffles them alongside his ear, like a gambler counting a deck of cards. After a great deal of experience, you know through a combination of the sound and the feel exactly where to stop. And you have to be accurate; close doesn't count. When Doyle requested that the front office send me down to check the ticket windows during the 1935 World Series, I felt highly honored; each ticket, representing three home games, was worth $39.60.

Concessions are a whole little world in themselves, a world that has continued to fascinate me. You would be amazed how much sheer psychology is involved in selling a hot dog and beer. In designing the new concession stands at Wrigley Field, I wanted to install fluorescent lighting. I was told that fluorescent lighting could not be used outdoors because, as everyone knew, the lights wouldn't work in the cold. Well, baseball isn't exactly a winter sport. I told them to put in the fluorescents anyway and we'd see what happened. What happened was that the lights worked fine (they also worked fine during the football season and would presumably work splendidly in any well-appointed igloo).

What also happened was that our business immediately fell off drastically. I had made the mistake—in the luck of the draw—of choosing a hard blue-white fluorescent, a lighting particularly cruel to women. Women seem to be born with some tribal instinct about these things; they would not come to the stands no matter how hungry they were. We changed to a soft rose-white, which is flattering to women, and quickly picked up all the old business and more besides.

At the same time I learned something so elementary that it is generally ignored in baseball. Female customers are not the same as male ones.

By working in the concession stands myself, I had come to understand the importance of space. In a baseball park, people run up to the concessions between innings or stop off briefly on their way out. I found that when I was able to get from the red hots to the beer and coffee without having to move. I would sell both the red hot and a drink. If I had to take but one step, the beverage sales would begin to drop. I was even able to reduce it to a precise formula. *One extra step costs you 10 percent of your gross.* I therefore designed the concession stands myself and have been designing my own ever since.

An architect will draw you a beautiful stand. So beautiful and spacious that you'll go broke.

I was in a position to be designing stands and supervising construction only because of Boots Weber, the man who had replaced my father. My father left me a far more valuable and lasting legacy than money. He left me a good name. All my life I have run across old friends of his eager to show their affection for him by helping his son. Boots had been running Wrigley's Los Angeles franchise, a post to which my father had reappointed him, and as a way of showing his affection and admiration, Boots more or less adopted me.

It was Boots who sent me to night school to study the subjects that would be most valuable around a ball park. I went to Northwestern to study accounting and business law—which have been invaluable—and to Lewis Institute for designing and blueprint reading.

With a couple of hours to kill every night before going to school, I'd stay around the office with Boots and try to be helpful. Before long, I was his assistant and we were running the club together.

Difficult as it may be to say how much one man can owe another, I owe more to Boots Weber than to anyone else. Years later in Cleveland, I found a bright, clean-cut young boy named Stanley McIlvaine working behind the press-room bar. I sent him to night school to take accounting and business law, and moved him into the office to work with us during the day. When he finished night school, I sent him to Zanesville, Ohio, to run our Class-D club. Stanley is still in baseball. Last year, he was general manager at Dallas. It was my way of thanking Boots, in the way I thought he'd like to be thanked.

I stayed on with the Cubs, after the first few years, only because of Boots. Life with Phil Wrigley was always a battle between the baseball men and the gum men. Boots and I had to stand back-to-back to protect each other from sudden attack.

It is hard to understand how a father and son can be as completely different as William and Phil Wrigley. The father, who practically invented chewing gum, was the last of the super salesmen, a man who made his name synonymous with his product. He was a well-upholstered, jovial man who liked people and knew what made them tick.

The son is one of those men who is difficult to describe in a quick few words. I always called him Mr. Wrigley when I worked for him, I still call him Mr. Wrigley when I see him, and half the time I even think of him as Mr. Wrigley.

As a young man he was quiet and introspective and always perfectly happy to be overshadowed by a dynamic father whom he wor-

38

shiped. His father left the club to him personally rather than to the estate, the only direct bequest in his will, and so Phil Wrigley assumed the burden out of his sense of loyalty and duty. If he has any particular feeling for baseball, any real liking for it, he has disguised it magnificently.

The one point on which we clashed, perennially, was promotion. I wanted it. He didn't. He was the boss. He won every argument. Mr. Wrigley, as a shy man, isn't interested in the press. It's more than that, though; he's a little afraid of writers. He sometimes leaves the impression he is afraid that if he opens himself up to them they'll compare him unfavorably with his father.

He isn't really a lesser man, he's just different. Let's have no misconceptions on this point, Mr. Phil Wrigley is a brilliant man. He has taken his father's company and built it into an international colossus, and don't give me any of that nonsense about it being easy for a son to step into an established enterprise. I have seen too many rich men's sons run their father's businesses into the ground. Mr. Wrigley would have been successful at anything he put his hand to. And that, in fact, is where he is happiest, putting his hands to things. He is a mechanical genius. His greatest relaxation is to strip an old automobile apart and put it back together.

He has invented several tools. One of his inventions, for example, is a screwdriver which slips into small openings and then is locked, by means of a lever, into the screw. But once he has built a prototype to prove to himself that it works, he loses all interest in it. The rights are given over to his mechanic.

A more honest and selfless man would be hard to find. While I was with the Cubs, he had an unbelievably altruistic working arrangement with Milwaukee. Wrigley did not believe in farm systems. It was his belief—and he was right—that baseball could only remain healthy if the minor-league clubs were free to develop their own players and sell them to the highest bidder. He put his money where his mouth was. He subsidized Milwaukee, through a direct cash grant, and renounced all rights to their players. As a result, Whitlow Wyatt, the best pitcher in the minor leagues, was sold not to the Cubs but to the Dodgers. Two years later, Wyatt pitched the Dodgers to a pennant.

With all these virtues, Phil Wrigley has one overriding flaw. He knows more about things and less about people than any man I have ever met. In the eight years I worked for him, he almost never had a visit from a personal friend. He has few personal friends. Business associates, yes; friends, I don't know.

Because he is such a shy man, the associates he feels most comfortable with are not the ball-club employees—who are a gregarious, outspoken lot—but the gum company people. And so while he kept all my father's employees—the old group remained intact for 40 full years until death began to thin them out a couple of years ago—he also surrounded himself with a kitchen cabinet of gum executives who were always undercutting Boots and me.

Wrigley is one of those men who insists he despises yes-men. What he really means is that he wants you to talk a little before you agree with him. If you can reach *his* conclusion for your own reasons, so much the better. The gum men never gave him an argument about baseball. They couldn't. Eddie Gaedel knew more about baseball than most of them.

In the general area of promotion, Wrigley and I agreed on only one thing: keeping the park clean. My father had always had a phobia about a clean park. Phil Wrigley carried it even further; he made the park itself his best promotion.

While he was doing it, he taught me perhaps the greatest single lesson of running a ball club. Wrigley compared the Cubs' won-and-lost records with corresponding daily-attendance charts and showed me that the two followed a practically identical pattern. His conclusion was inescapable. A team that isn't winning a pennant has to sell something in addition to its won-and-lost record to fill in those low points on the attendance chart. His solution was to sell "Beautiful Wrigley Field"; that is, to make the park itself so great an attraction that it would be thought of as a place to take the whole family for a delightful day. It was no accident that the title of the magazine I edited for him was *Fan and Family*.

Wrigley kept the park freshly painted. He threw out all the sidewalk vendors, newspaper boys and panhandlers. He stationed ushers out front to guide people to their sections. He insisted that the ticket sellers be polite and courteous.

We sold "Beautiful Wrigley Field." We advertised "Beautiful Wrigley Field." The announcers were instructed to use the phrase "Beautiful Wrigley Field" as often as possible. We sold it so well that when I came back to Chicago in 1959 as president of the White Sox, across town, I found "Beautiful Wrigley Field" my greatest single obstacle. Because "Beautiful Wrigley Field" tacitly implied "that run-down, crummy joint on the South Side."

By 1959, Wrigley was no longer keeping the park freshly painted. The neighborhood had deteriorated badly. None of that mattered. People came into Wrigley Field *knowing* they were comfortable. Just

40

as people who had not been to Comiskey Park in years *knew* it was a crumbling ruin.

"Beautiful Wrigley Field" was a marvelous promotion based on a completely valid premise. The trouble was that I could never get its creator to take the next logical step: to give the customers what they really set out for the ball park hoping to find—entertainment and excitement.

There was only one promotional gimmick I ever got away with. Mr. Wrigley permitted me to install lights on top of the flagpole to let homeward-bound Elevated passengers know whether we had won or lost that day. The flagpole was on top of the new scoreboard, and at its summit I put a crossbar with a green light on one side and a red light on the other. The green light told the El passengers we had won, the red that we had lost.

All right, it wasn't much, but it was all I had and I was proud of it. Not long after it was up, I glanced out the window of my office in the Wrigley Building and saw, to my horror, that a furious wind was whipping down the street. In my mind, I could see my flagpole toppling over. I ran out into the street, grabbed a taxi and headed for the park. (One of the many things Boots and I could never get Mr. Wrigley to do was to move the office to the park so we wouldn't have to spend half our lives traveling back and forth.)

Trees were toppling over all along the route. Windows were being blown out of store fronts. Still, it never occurred to me that I was in the middle of Chicago's worst hurricane in a decade. I had my own problems. I had computed the strains and stresses for the flagpole myself and I was checking over my figures to find out how much of a wind I had allowed for. Arriving at the park, I dashed to the scoreboard and climbed out through the trap door onto the narrow roof.

As soon as I got out there, needless to say, the wind practically blew me back downtown. I grabbed the flagpole and hung on for dear life as it swayed back and forth. The El trains were moving slowly on the tracks behind, and I could just imagine one homeward-bound fan turning to the guy beside him and saying, "Yeah, I *know* green means we win and red means we lose, but what means a pale-faced young man waving back and forth?"

Eventually, I got Cliff Westcott, who did the real engineering work for us, to check my specifications. He found I had built in 50 percent more stress than would have been needed for the worst hurricane in Chicago history. That wasn't very bright of me. I had wasted Mr. Wrigley's money and I had let down the Lewis Institute. Still, as I thought of myself swaying back and forth on that pole, I cannot say I was too unhappy.

When it came to beautifying Wrigley Field, Mr. Wrigley was open to all suggestions. If he wanted something, money was no object. Time was something else again. Time *was* an object. What Phil Wrigley wants he wants right now.

In planning the construction of the new bleachers, he decided that an outdoor, woodsy motif was definitely called for. Since I had always admired the ivy-covered bleacher walls at Perry Stadium in Indianapolis I suggested that we appropriate the idea for ourselves. Almost absently, I added, "And we can put trees or something in the back."

What I had in mind was a circle of small trees outside the park. Mr. Wrigley didn't want the trees *outside* the park and he didn't want to wait any ten years while they grew up over the bleachers. He wanted them *in* the bleachers, on the steps leading up to the scoreboard, and he wanted them planted full-grown.

What he got were the most expensive tree plantings in the history of the world. Just for openers, we had to build tree boxes into every step, which meant new concrete footings and new steel supports to carry the weight.

That's a routine construction job, though. From there on in, the routine stopped. Chicago, you see, is situated on Lake Michigan. A strong wind comes off the lake. Someday, a poet is going to give Chicago some kind of appropriate nickname, like, say, The Windy City. We planted all of Mr. Wrigley's giant trees, and a week after we were finished the bleachers looked like the Russian steppes during a hard cold winter. Nothing but cement and bark. The leaves had all blown away.

Mr. Wrigley put that down as bad luck. We pulled out all those barren trees and planted a whole new set of leaf-bearing trees. Along came the wind to blow all those leaves away too. We kept putting in trees, and we kept having bad luck. We could have turned the Grand Canyon into a forest with all the trees we planted, since it took about ten sets of trees before Mr. Wrigley began to spot a trend. The trees were quite inexpensive; the footings cost about $200,000.

That left me with the ivy. I had planned on planting it at the end of the season, after the bleachers had been completely rebuilt. By the time the new season came around, the ivy would have caught and Mr. Wrigley would have his outdoor atmosphere.

The Cubs were ending the season with a long road trip, returning home only in the final week for one last series. The day before the team was to return, Mr. Wrigley called me in to tell me he had invited some people to the park to watch the game and gaze upon his ivy.

"Holy smokes," I said, "I haven't even ordered it yet, let alone planted it. But I'll see what I can do."

John Seys, the vice-president, called a friend who owned a nursery. He informed us that ivy couldn't be put in overnight.

"Well," I said, "what can I put in that will take the place of ivy?"

"Bittersweet," he said.

Bob Dorr, the grounds keeper, and I strung light bulbs all along the fence to enable us to work through the night. When the morning sun broke over the grandstand roof, it shone upon a bleacher wall entirely covered with bittersweet. We had planted the ivy in between and, in time, the ivy took over.

I spent a sleepless night getting the scoreboard up, too, although I can hardly blame Mr. Wrigley for that one. While I was fooling around with the blueprints, an inventor walked into my office with a working model based upon an entirely new concept. Instead of having lights switching on and off, like all other scoreboards, his model featured brightly painted eyelids which were pulled up and down magnetically.

The inventor was a shy, hesitant, somewhat apologetic man, proof enough for me—out of my long experience scouting inventors—that he was the real thing. In addition, the model worked to perfection. Predictably, Mr. Wrigley was fascinated by it. "This is what we want," he said. "Something different. Just so long as he can have it ready before the end of the season."

I asked my genius if he could have it ready.

You bet your sweet life he could.

The day before the delivery date stipulated on the contract, I phoned his factory to find out what kind of help he was going to need from our ground crew. Nobody answered. I sped immediately to the factory address and found a small second-floor loft. It was deserted.

My genius, as I later learned, had invented a great deal in his life but he had never actually built anything this big. Thus, he had assembled all the necessary material in his loft, had completed a good part of the work, and then, with the moment of truth staring him in the face, he had panicked and run out.

I summoned the ground crew from the park. The wiring, I could see, was similar to switchboard wiring, so I called a friend at Kellogg Switchboard Co. and borrowed a couple of dozen of his electricians. We all rolled up our sleeves and went to work. I drilled the frames.

The ground crew put the frames together and the Kellogg electricians wired them. We built the whole scoreboard in that loft during the night, carting it to the park unit by unit, where the park electricians assembled it.

It worked perfectly. It is the scoreboard still being used at Wrigley Field.

Not to leave the story hanging, I paid the inventor every cent the contract called for, without even deducting the amount we had paid the extra help. There was no denying it, his scoreboard did work. Thus heartened and encouraged, he went into the scoreboard business. Every now and then he would write me a chatty letter letting me know how he was getting on. I'd write back telling him about the ball club. Neither of us ever wrote one word about the way he had ducked out on us.

Two years ago, while I was looking around Chicago, without success, for someone to build me an exploding scoreboard for Comiskey Park, my friend phoned to let me know he wanted to bid on it. By that time, understand, he had a thriving business. "Nothing doing," I said, growing a little indignant twenty years after the fact. "I don't want to have to go out and put this one up myself, too."

There was one thing I was unable to persuade Mr. Wrigley to do, even for the park. In 1934, the year before Larry MacPhail installed the first lights in a major-league stadium, I tried to get Mr. Wrigley to put lights in Wrigley Field. "Just a fad," he said. "A passing fancy."

Every year, I'd bring it up again. Every year he would come up with a new reason for not doing it.

"Those light towers look terrible sticking up there," he'd say. "They'll spoil all this beauty we've worked so hard to create."

I got together with Cliff Westcott and a hydraulic engineering firm to work out a system for placing the "baskets"—the platforms on which the lights are mounted—on telescoping towers. During the day, the baskets would be tucked completely out of sight. At night, when they were needed, they would rise out, fully lighted.

That was all well and good, said Wrigley, except that the lights themselves were so garish that they would spoil the whole effect he had been trying to create for his beautiful field.

OK. I got Westinghouse to run tests on lighting a field with fluorescents. They found it could be done. Mr. Wrigley, of course, had a reason for not wanting it done that way either. No matter what I came up with, he had a reason for not doing it.

Old men, playing dominoes across the hearth, like to say that Phil Wrigley is the last of the true baseball men because he is the only

44

owner who still holds, in the simple faith of his ancestors, that baseball was meant to be played under God's own sunlight.   ,

I know better. Having blown the chance to be first with lights, Mr. Wrigley just wasn't going to do it at all.

I could at least talk to him about things like lights. When it came to promotion ideas, he wouldn't even listen. He could tell from some manic gleam in my eye what was coming, and as soon as I opened my mouth, he would say, "No, no, no."

And yet, everybody fools you. Just when you're sure you have somebody figured out down to the soles of his feet, he'll do something to confound you.

One afternoon, I was called to Mr. Wrigley's office. It's a big office with a big desk in front of a big window. Seated in one of the easy chairs alongside the desk was a ferret-faced, wizened little guy in a checkered suit. He was puffing on a cigar in that self-pleased, self-important way that only a cigar can bring out.

You could see that Mr. Wrigley was pleased with himself, too. "He's going to help us," he told me. "He's going to give us a psychological advantage."

From the look of this little bum, I'm thinking that the only psychological advantage he could give us would be to sneak into the visitors' locker room before every game and steal the spikes off their shoes—an assignment for which he seemed eminently suited.

Almost as if he had read my mind, he jumped out of the chair, fixed me with an awesome and terrible glare and began to circle around me, making cobralike passes at me with one hand like Bela Lugosi.

While I was watching this dance, fascinated beyond belief, Mr. Wrigley was comparing his discovery to a wrestling manager who was supposed to be able to put a whammy on his boy's opponents, a wonderful publicity gag that was getting a big play in the Chicago papers.

Holy smokes, I thought, suddenly getting it. Old Phil has come up with a real good one. Who'd have thought the old boy had it in him? I had finally got to him, I figured. Things were going to get interesting around Wrigley Field.

Two days later, during a meeting in Wrigley's office, I began to talk up our whammy man, because I thought it was pretty funny. "What are we holding back for?" I said. "Let me give it to the papers today."

A chill came over the room. "There's nothing funny about this," Mr. Wrigley said evenly. "This man may help us. And don't go talking to your newspaper friends about it. Or anybody else, either."

What can you say to a multimillionaire? I could think of a lot of things. Like, "When I was a boy, my daddy told me that if a little man ever came up to me in a checkered suit, took the cigar out of his mouth and told me he was going to win a pennant for me by putting a whammy on my opponents, I should, despite my sweet and trusting nature, take the elementary precaution of checking him out with the Better Business Bureau for past performance."

He had contracted to pay this guy—may Ford Frick be elected to another term as Commissioner if this is not the truth—a flat $5,000 fee plus an additional $25,000 if we won the pennant.

For the rest of the year we carried our Evil Eye around the league with us. At home, he sat directly behind the plate, gesturing furiously at opposing pitchers, none of whom seemed disposed to enter into the spirit of the thing at all. (He was, I must admit, able to cast his strange spell over the customers sitting nearby, most of whom could be seen edging cagily away from him—which proves that Beautiful Wrigley Field did attract a most discriminating clientele.)

Our man operated under a severe handicap for such a chancy profession. He could not stand cold weather. (Which led me to believe that he was a fraud—not an Evil Eye at all but a voodoo chief who had served his apprenticeship in equatorial Africa.) On cold days, he would go up to the office, stand over the Western Union ticker and put the whammy on the tape as the play-by-play came in.

Let me make it clear that I don't want this to be taken as a blanket indictment of all Evil Eyes. Most Evil Eyes, I'm sure, are honest, tax-paying, respectable citizens. It's only that rotten 3 percent who don't give you an honest day's work for an honest day's pay who give the whole profession a bad name.

In 1940, Boots Weber retired. Jim Gallagher, who became a close friend too, replaced Boots and although I stayed around to help him break in, I was already looking for my own club. Early in 1941, there were rumors that the Milwaukee team, no longer under a Wrigley subsidy, was in trouble. Soon afterwards Harry Bendinger, the owner, came to Chicago to try to sell the club to us. I recommended to Mr. Wrigley that he buy it. Mr. Wrigley, who still didn't believe in farm clubs, wasn't interested.

The next day, I called George Trautman, the president of the American Association, at his office in Columbus. I was told he was right in Chicago, at the Morrison Hotel, on his way to Milwaukee to see what he could do about the situation. I called Trautman at the hotel and announced that I was his buyer.

"Have you any money?" he asked, a logical enough question.

"No," I said, an honest enough answer.

"How are you going to buy it then?"

"I don't know," I said. "But I'll get the money somehow."

"Come on over," Trautman said. "We'll talk about it."

As soon as he saw how serious I was, Trautman promised to help me. "I just want you to understand one thing," he said. "I think you're crazy."

Just to keep everything clean and aboveboard, I went back to Wrigley to find out whether he'd had any second thoughts about buying the Brewers. When he repeated that he wasn't interested, I told him I was going to buy the club myself.

Knowing Wrigley, I was pretty sure how he'd react. "All right," he said, "I'll help you. How much money do you need?"

"No," I told him. "I have to do this myself. I've got a lot of ideas I want to try, and I know you don't agree with them. I don't want to feel responsible to anybody or be attached to anybody."

The one man I did want was Charlie Grimm. Charles and I had always been very good friends. He had gone from managing the Cubs to broadcasting their games and I had been helpful in bringing him back to the Cubs that year as a coach. "Charles," I said, "I think we can make a good deal out of this. You'll manage and you'll have twenty-five percent ownership and we'll have a lot of fun."

As a prospective co-owner, Charlie had one slight liability. He was just as broke as I was.

Trautman, however, had already spoken to Herbert Uihlein, the owner of Schlitz Beer, about backing me in return for the broadcasting rights plus the exclusive right to sell beer in the park. George and I arrived at Uihlein's home in Milwaukee at ten in the morning, and the deal was worked out. At eleven, Uihlein's wife came into the room, picked up our balance sheet and began to glance through it. Mrs. Uihlein is quite a woman. She ran through the figures at a gallop, then threw the papers back on the table and shook her head. "All you've got here," she said, "is a paper company."

Between the time Mrs. Uihlein picked up the balance sheet and the time she threw it down, we blew the deal.

By this time, Bendinger was willing to hand the club over to me just to keep it from being thrown into bankruptcy. He owed the City National Bank of Milwaukee $83,000 and had another $25,000 or so in pressing debts. The bank, terrified over the prospect of waking up with a baseball club on its hands, was willing to go along with any kind of a deal that was made.

As we left the Uihleins' I told Trautman that one way or another

I'd come up with enough money to operate the club. "Nobody else will," he said. "I'm almost tempted to sell it to you without any money. Can't you just come up with $25,000 to cover the immediate, pressing bills?"

It isn't easy, I discovered, to raise money for a bankrupt minor-league baseball team.

I finally raised it because Clarence Rowland, vice-president of the Cubs, volunteered to sound out his son, Clarence Jr., who worked at a brokerage. Clarence Jr. wasn't eager to recommend the loan to his house but he did introduce me to a colleague at the brokerage, Arthur Vyse. Vyse was in the fortunate position, from his point of view, of having a wealthy father-in-law. He was in the even more fortunate position, from my point of view, of having a small chunk of his father-in-law's money to invest.

Vyse and I had dinner, and he somehow got the impression—I can't imagine how—that we had several other investors who had already agreed to put up $25,000. Under the terms of my proposal, Vyse could have got 100-percent return on his money for every complete calendar year we kept it. In other words, we would owe him $50,000 at the end of the first year, $75,000 at the end of the second, et cetera, et cetera, et cetera.

This was the kind of high finance that gave Ponzi a bad name. It also got me my ball club.

For a week I had been traveling back and forth between Chicago and Milwaukee on the Elevated, instead of by railroad, to save a few dollars. When it came to taking over our ball club, Grimm and I felt it incumbent upon us to arrive by train, as befitted the owners of a Triple-A team—even a bankrupt one. We arrived at the Milwaukee station on a cold, drizzling Saturday afternoon with a grand total of $11 between us. Immediately, we crossed the street to a tavern and drank $10 worth of toasts to the glorious future that lay ahead. The other dollar I framed. Some businessmen, I have heard, have the quaint custom of framing the first dollar they earn. I framed the last dollar I had before I opened up shop.

I was twenty-eight years old. I had a wife and two children. I was dead broke. But I had my ball club and a bountiful belief that I was going to make the baseball world sit up and take notice.

Call it supreme egotism or call it the ignorance of youth. I don't really think it was either. I'm not as smart as most people I've run across in my travels. I knew that then, I know it even better now. I decided very early in life that while I couldn't outsmart anybody,

48

there was one thing I could do: I could work harder and longer than anybody else was apparently willing to work.

I came to Milwaukee ready to work 24 hours a day. My head was exploding with the ideas I had been gathering in Chicago. I had a good friend at my side and a city I was sure would respond to my kind of promotion.

What more could any man ask?

The First Fine Careless
Rapture of Milwaukee

4.

FROM the tavern, Charlie and I went directly to Borchert Field to introduce ourselves to our customers. We found 22 loyalists in the stands. Theoretically, it was supposed to be Boy Scout Day, but all except three of the Boy Scouts had apparently decided to stay home and tie knots, an undeniable proof that the future of the nation lay in good hands. The three Scouts present and accounted for turned out to be the Honor Guard. They, poor kids, hadn't been permitted to beg off.

The record of the Brewers as we took control was 19-43. We were already 5½ games out of seventh place and a light year or two out of first. By the end of the day we were even farther behind. My Brewers were absolutely the worst Triple-A team I had ever seen.

Borchert Field was a ramshackle, rundown wooden park which had not seen a fresh coat of paint in 17 years. Between the time Bendinger signed the team over to me and the time Charlie and I arrived, I had returned to the City Bank and asked for a $50,000 loan to clean the joint up.

"You've gone this far with me," I told Irwin Weinhold, the bank president. "Why not go all the way?" Mr. Weinhold handed the money over without a whimper. I thought at the time he was so happy the club hadn't been dumped into his lap that he was willing to go for anything. I was probably wrong. In my wanderings, I have found that bankers get such a kick out of having a backer's interest in a baseball team that their normal prudence about stuffy things like, say, collateral is forgotten.

I had already hired 100 cleaning women. After the game, we put the lights on and began to scrub the park down with soap and water.

49

Seats, walls, floors, fences, everything. Charlie and I were right in there, through the night, scrubbing along with them.

The townspeople, attracted by the lights in the early morning hours, came in to see what was going on, giving the cleaning women a far greater audience than the ballplayers had drawn all year. The papers sent photographers, and gave us a lot of ink during the next two days. Rain washed out the Sunday game, and Monday was an open date. That gave us all the time we needed to get things into shape. We brought in a crew of painters to cover everything with a light, bright gray. A construction crew started putting in a completely new ladies' room. All this activity whipped up a lot of interest; it created the feeling that things were beginning to happen, that better days lay ahead. There was even a vicious rumor that Charley and I had invested $100,000 of our own money; I can't imagine how talk like that gets started.

We could only hope that the interest would be translatable at the box office. Having rid myself of the $50,000 in two days, I was once again without operating funds. I now owed the bank $133,000. When Tuesday night came around, we had to have some money passing through those freshly painted ticket windows.

We drew 4,800 fans, the largest crowd in years.

In Chicago, I had always wandered around the park talking to the fans, because I have always felt that the only way to know what the people want is to ask them. Besides, I enjoy talking baseball with people. I especially enjoy talking to people while I'm watching a ball game.

I stood at the main gate to greet the fans as they entered, and I stood at the exit gate to talk to them as they left. I continued to do this every night I was in Milwaukee, win, lose or humiliated.

During the game, I moved around from section to section, sitting with one group of fans for the first half of an inning and another group the second. Fans always have good suggestions; some of my best ideas through the years have come from them.

One of their complaints was about the field itself. Borchert Field, an architectural monstrosity, was so constructed that the fans on the first-base side of the grandstand couldn't see the right fielder, which seemed perfectly fair in that the fans on the third-base side couldn't see the left fielder. "Listen," I told them. "This way you'll have to come back twice to see the whole team."

After the game (which, incidentally, we won) I was joined on the receiving line outside our only exit by Charlie Grimm and by Sam Levy of the *Journal*. I had been warned about Sam Levy before

I came to town. He had the reputation of being a knocker, a killer, a headache to any operator. Instead, I found Sam to be one of the most helpful and honorable writers I have ever come across.

After the last hand had been shaken, Charlie, Sam and I retired to a nearby pub to discuss the problems that confronted us. I could always talk to Sam with complete honesty and he would always protect me by printing only what he knew wouldn't hurt me. In one way he was unique. Sam was one of the best newspapermen I've ever known and yet he was one of the poorest writers. His mind was like a vacuum cleaner in the sense that it had swept up all kinds of odd bits, pieces and wisps of information through the years. I'd say "John Smith," wait for the wheels to turn and the gears to reverse, and out would come everything he had ever heard about John Smith down to the tiniest detail.

The most important thing that happened to me in Milwaukee, though, was that I bumped into Rudie Schaffer. Wherever I have gone, I have had the great good fortune of bumping into exactly the fellow I needed. In Chicago, of course, it had been Boots Weber. In Milwaukee it was Rudie.

Rudie was a public accountant who had been working for the Brewers for six full years out of a boundless love for baseball. He had been the entire office staff, with duties ranging from keeping the books to opening up the park. His salary was almost negligible, which was just as well because he seldom had been paid.

The morning after that triumphant opener, Rudie grabbed me as I came into the office. "Hey," he said, "where were you? You didn't come down to see how much money we took in."

"Why should I worry about that?" I asked. "You're the one who handles that department."

"You mean you don't care?"

"Of course I care," I told him. "I'd be a fool if I didn't. But what's the sense of both of us worrying about it? You're the secretary-treasurer of the company."

"Since when?"

"Since I met you," I told him.

Rudie has been with me ever since, in every club I've ever operated, as business manager. He has freed me completely from worry over details, business or otherwise. If I decided I wanted some entertainment for the next afternoon, I'd say, "Rudie, get me a jazz band." The band would be there. If I wanted to give somebody an award, I'd say, "Rudie, I think we ought to have the biggest cup we can get."

Rudie might just grunt, leaving a casual visitor to wonder whether he had heard me. When the time came, the cup would be there.

Rudie dug up a big, four-foot cup, a gorgeous thing, to present to Charlie Grimm while we were honoring him for something or other shortly after we took over. Charlie was quite pleased with it until we needed a cup to honor Mickey Heath, our radio announcer, and later, our vice-president. Rudie had a new plate attached, with suitable inscription, and we gave the cup to Mickey. He didn't keep it long either. Every time we felt the need to honor a player, Rudie would change the inscription plate. If the fans wanted to believe we were doing a heavy traffic in cups rather than inscription plates, that was their business.

One of the first things we did to entertain the customers was to form our own band, featuring Charlie Grimm, who is usually billed as "baseball's only left-handed banjo player." Rudie manned a home-made bull fiddle, Mickey Heath played the washboard drums and the ever-popular Bill Veeck was on the jazzbo (a sliding tin whistle). The other member of the band was an excellent violin player and a terrible pitcher. A *terrible* pitcher. We kept him on the roster all season just to play the violin, but we rarely let him get near the mound.

The band wandered through the stands serenading the customers. When things got a little dull for Charlie on the coaching line during the game—and with the hitters we had that first year life could get pretty deadly—Charlie would give himself a lift by going up into the stands and tearing off a couple of solo numbers.

Everything I've done since—well, almost everything—was tried out and sharpened in Milwaukee. (Except fireworks. I couldn't use fireworks because of the wooden park.) Milwaukee was a marvelous proving grounds. Situated a little outside the big city, Chicago, its citizens probably felt a little neglected. If you give Milwaukee people a fair show for their money, they'll support you. If you give them something extra, they'll flock to you.

Understand this, I never announce any of my gags ahead of time, except in the rare case where the nature of the gag demands it. As often as not, we gave away a door prize. Anything we could think of as long as it was for laughs. I have always been a great fan of the theatre. My father covered theatrical openings before he became a sportswriter, and I loved to go backstage with him afterwards to meet the performers. I was a great fan of Olson & Johnson, whose *Helza-poppin'* was the big hit of the time. They had a running gag in the show which started with a small plant being brought out onto the

52

stage. As the show went on, the plant grew bigger and bigger, and just before the curtain they would present the by then giant plant to somebody in the audience.

It should be no secret by now that this is the kind of incongruous situation—a man standing with a big plant in the middle of a theatre—that I love. We all began to think of weird gifts we could give away as door prizes, just to see how the lucky winner would react.

One of the first giveaways was the worst swaybacked horse anybody had ever seen. Rudie borrowed it from a local dairy, confident that the lucky winner would beg us to take it off his hands. I made the mistake of asking the winner what he was going to do with it, though, and he, showing a regrettably mercenary mind, told me he was going to sell it back to me.

Actually, we always sent the winner something far more valuable than the comic prize he had won. Once, we decided to give six live squab to the most dignified man we could find in the ball park, in order to answer the burning question of how a dignified man would hold onto six live squab while watching a ball game. (On this one we had to cheat just a little. We spotted the man we wanted as he was buying his ticket, got his stub number and faked the drawing.)

For all you students of human behavior, what he does is to lose three of the squab in the early innings. He retains the other three by holding one in each fist and the third between his knees. It was a magnificent performance over the full nine-inning distance. In the morning, we sent a couple of dozen dressed squab to his home.

Another lucky fan won a couple of dozen live lobsters delivered in their cages. The lobsters spent the night trying to crawl out of the cages; the fan spent the night trying to push them back in. We delivered a 200-lb. cake of ice to one guy, and six ladders to another.

We were all one big family. During the games, I wandered around, second-guessing Grimm's strategy with the fans and inciting them against the umpires. "Look at that bum!" I'd yell. "Can you imagine anyone calling one like that against us?" Moving around the way I did, I could have the whole park ready to march by the time the game was over. Many a time in Milwaukee I had to escort the umpires off the field to keep them from being bombarded with bottles. "I don't know," I'd tell them, shaking my head sadly. "You'd better call them better next time or I won't help you get off."

Whenever I wasn't at the park, I was out speaking around the state, not to make a direct sales pitch, but just to let the people get to know me. My standing offer was that if any seven people would get together, I'd come to make up two tables of bridge and speak.

It was while I was speaking at a factory during the graveyard shift (midnight to 8 A.M.) that I came up with the idea that got us our first national publicity. A couple of the workers complained to me that with the factory on a wartime 7-days-a-week schedule it was impossible for them to come to any games. So we scheduled a special "Rosie the Riveter" morning game for the night shift, starting at 9 A.M. All women wearing their welding caps or riveting masks were admitted free. The ushers, in nightgowns and nightcaps, served breakfast: cereal and doughnuts with milk or coffee.

We really gagged it up. As the fans filed in, they found Red Smith, our coach, sleeping in the coaching box in his nightgown and nightcap. Nearby was a smoke pot and an old outhouse. Just before the game was supposed to start, an alarm bell rang. Red jumped up, lit a cigar with the smoke pot and wandered over to the top of the dugout to thumb through a Sears Roebuck catalogue.

Wartime travel being what it was, the opposition didn't arrive until noon. We had a band on hand, though—all of them tastily clad in nightgowns also—and we all had a lot of fun while we were waiting. Then we murdered the visiting team, 20–0, and everybody went home happy.

We had morning games about four more times, and the idea was copied by quite a few big-league teams.

Charlie Grimm was a great man to have in Milwaukee, as he proved again a dozen years later when he managed Milwaukee's first major-league team. Charlie and the good burghers of Milwaukee have some special rapport—the word *gemütlichkeit* has to be thrown in here someplace—born, no doubt, of their mutual love for light laughter and heavy food. Charlie knew every eating place in Milwaukee, and he planned his meals like a general planning a campaign. He is the only man I ever saw who would be anticipating his dinner while he was putting away a heavy lunch. "Ohhh, these spareribs are good," he would say, running them down his teeth like a harmonica. "But, ahhh, wait until I get my teeth into the pork shanks I'm going to have at Mader's tonight."

Charlie is a fine entertainer. He is so good that in order to get him back to his farm in Missouri with some money in his pocket after our first season, I booked him into the Wisconsin Theatre for a week as a song-and-dance man. He is also an excellent speaker, a far better speaker than I will ever be. Unhappily, Charlie never cared too much for my program of massive exposure and he kept ducking out on me. I had to do something about that. With the team about to leave on a road trip, I held him in the office until the last possible second. "Oh, Charles," I said, pushing a piece of paper toward him as he was rushing off, "don't forget to sign this."

By the time the team came back to Milwaukee I had the document blown up and waiting. It read: *I, Charlie Grimm, hereby agree to speak on any and all times I am scheduled. Failure to do so will result in a $100 fine for the first failure and $500 thereafter.*

Charlie thought it was a great gag until I fined him the $100 for turning down his first assignment. He never did take the chance of going for $500.

Unless you want to get stuffy about it, you have to say that Charlie led our league in hitting that year. I want to say it, anyway. We kept agitating Charlie to play a game and finally, to shut us all up, he put himself in as a pinch hitter in the last game of the season. And darned if he didn't hit a line drive to the right-center field fence, his old alley, and go puffing and sweating around the bases for a triple.

I think my favorite gag in Milwaukee was the one I pulled on Charlie in our third year there. With his forty-fifth birthday coming up, we decided to throw a birthday party for him. By this time we had set attendance records and were fighting for the pennant, so we could afford to present him with something more substantial than The Cup. A week or so before the ceremony, the press asked him what he wanted for his birthday. Charlie, always kidding, answered, "A left-handed pitcher."

OK, Charles, I figured, if that's what you really want . . .

I quickly ran down the list of possibilities and found a pretty good left-hander at Norfolk, named Julie Acosta. The going price on a minor-league pitcher of good caliber was in the $5,000 neighborhood. I called the Norfolk owner and told him I'd give him $7,500 for Acosta. "And," I said, "I'll also give you a $5,000 bonus providing nobody knows he's been bought."

Wild elephants could not have torn the secret from him.

A warm and touching ceremony was held for Charlie including, at what seemed to be the high point of the day, the presentation of a $1,000 war bond. Grimm, a sentimental soul, was so grateful—and so broke—that he actually wept. "I owe it all to my dear wife Lillian," he said, and to prove that this was no idle endearment he turned it over to her on the spot.

I was announcing part of the ceremony from the dugout. (I believe with my father that my place is neither on the field nor in the locker room and so I have not appeared publicly on a ball field more than two or three times in my life.) "Perhaps I should make it clear," I announced, "that this is the $1,000 war bond Charlie has been patriotically saving for out of his payroll deductions."

Charlie whirled around to get the bond back from his dear wife. Lillian, having already tucked it into her purse, made it clear that as far as she was concerned that part of the proceedings was closed. Good old sentimental Charlie, I thought he was going to kill me.

Fortunately, I still had Acosta standing close by in a 15-foot birthday cake, the first time I ever used the cake gimmick. Mickey Heath, moving into the breach nicely, announced, "And here, Charlie, to complete your day is the birthday present you said you wanted, a left-handed pitcher." Out stepped Acosta, and our friendship was saved.

I have almost never interfered with a manager's lineup—although I'll admit to having dropped some rather pointed suggestions at times —but this one I couldn't resist. "Come on, Charles," I said, back in the dugout. "Why don't you pitch him?"

Charles looked a bit dubious, so I put on my most threatening frown, a frown so menacing that it has been known to move innocent children to fits of hystercial laughter. "Charles . . .?" I growled, glowering.

"I'll pitch him," he said.

It would be nice to be able to say that Acosta put the frosting on the cake by pitching a shutout. He didn't. He lost in 13 innings, striking out 17 men. Julie won his other three starts for us, though, and helped us to the pennant.

By the time I bought Acosta, we had some real good players. At the beginning, though, we had nothing. Players came and went so rapidly that Grimm would come to the ball park without knowing his starting lineup. We had 46 different players during the year, and I made 42 separate deals. It was in Milwaukee that I started the gag, later trotted out again in St. Louis, about having three teams: "One going, one coming and one playing."

We took any player we could beg, borrow or buy, just so long as his old club didn't ask for immediate payment. My standard deal was "five hundred down and the rest when you can catch me," which was a way of saying that we'd settle up at the end of the year if I had any money.

It wasn't that we weren't drawing good crowds. The fans responded from the beginning. The way we were operating, however, the money went out as fast as it came in. Faster. To meet the bills I would run down to Chicago almost weekly and borrow a hundred dollars or two from the small loan companies. After a while, it got to be a question of borrowing from two or three companies in order to meet the monthly payments on the old loans and still hold onto enough money to keep the club operating. The loan companies were scattered all over the city (although always on the second floor) and some weeks I'd be running in and out of a dozen different places. In the end, it became a job just to keep book on who I owed, when the payments were due and which companies were still eligible to be hit for new loans.

Once you get on this kind of a treadmill, it becomes absolutely vital to keep up on the payments, because the loan companies have a "credit round table"—an exchange of information—among themselves. The moment any one of them marks you lousy, you can't borrow five cents from any of the rest. When I did get myself boxed in to the point of having to skip a payment, I'd wait until just before closing time on Saturday and borrow my money from one of the companies I had already established a good credit rating with. I knew they wouldn't be able to check until Monday morning, and by that time I'd have the weekend receipts and be able to straighten everybody out.

I made a lot of Saturday afternoon trips to Chicago. Somehow I never quite lost my credit.

Keeping our stockholder happy became something of a problem too. Arthur Vyse, it developed, was a worrier. Arthur knew nothing at all about baseball but he knew enough to become very, very concerned about his father-in-law's money when he discovered what kind of a club he had invested in. He became even more concerned when he found out he was our only real stockholder. (To discourage any feeling that we were carpetbaggers from the South, we had distributed a few shares among a handful of local people.) Fortunately, we were keeping several sets of financial reports to be used according to the challenge of the moment. We even kept an honest set to be seen only by ourselves and the Government. Needless to say, Vyse never saw that one.

To keep him happy, we held a stockholders' meeting during the season, attended by me, Rudie and Vyse. I explained to the assembled stockholder, quite truthfully, that an independent minor-league operation does not expect to make money during the season. It makes its money after the season is over by selling players to major-league clubs.

With that explanation behind me, I ran down our entire roster, calling off each player's name and the sum we expected to sell him for. Rudie was stationed across the room at an adding machine, and every time I called out a figure, he would whack it out on the keys. You know, there is nothing that sounds quite so official as the click of an adding machine.

Schmitz, $40,000 . . . *click, click; click, click, click*

Koslo, $35,000 . . . *click, click; click, click, click*

Peck, $30,000 . . . *click, click; click, click, click*

(Rudie informed me after the meeting that I had inadvertently sold Hal Peck twice, once for $30,000 and later for $20,000, which seemed to be overdoing it a bit. The weird part of it was that I eventually did sell him twice at pretty close to those sums—plus players.)

At the end of the performance Rudie hit the tabulating key, and the machine clicked away portentously and came to a halt. Silence filled the room.

"Two hundred and twenty thousand dollars," Rudie shouted, not a quaver in his voice.

Arthur was reassured.

I was so carried away myself that it seemed only decent, in my role as president, to declare a special $2,500 dividend for our stockholder, payable at the end of the year after all that money had come rolling in.

As it turned out, I was able to buy up Arthur's interest before the second anniversary came around, which meant he got back $50,000. In less than two years, he had doubled his money and received a 10-percent dividend, a return of 110 percent. His father-in-law, whom I never did meet, was so impressed that he put Arthur in charge of all his financial affairs. I am confident that Arthur continued to invest that money wisely and well, although I doubt whether he ever again realized quite the return that he earned on his shrewd, farsighted investment in the Milwaukee Brewers. Actually he was a fine partner and man, and I wasn't really kidding him that much. We had two left-handed pitchers I knew we could turn into cash at the end of that first year, Johnny Schmitz and Dave Koslo. I sold them for enough to come within a few dollars of paying off what was left of our indebtedness to the bank.

Over the winter, I put myself deep in debt again by assembling an entirely new team, for the most part on a credit basis. I bought two players from Dallas, Heinz Becker and Grey Clark, without putting up any money at all, and both of them eventually became batting champions for us.

On opening day, 1942, it looked as if we were going to start paying off on them immediately. I had spent the whole winter speaking around the area. Interest was still growing. The advance sale was tremendous. I had not a thing in the world to worry about except rain.

I woke up about three in the morning and went outside to check the weather. It looked as if it was going to be a beautiful day. As was my habit, I arrived at the park about 5 A.M. and worked until it came time to station myself at the gate. The weather still looked great. The crowd looked even greater. In our little wooden park, with a seating capacity of slightly under 9,000, we drew a crowd—I'll never forget this figure—of 15,599.

In the first inning, a few dark clouds began to drift overhead. By the second inning, they were heavy and foreboding. In the third inning, there came the darnedest rainstorm I have ever seen, a quick downpour that flooded the field, washed out the game and moved on. Here and gone. Like that. Behind the rain came the sun. Once again, it was a beautiful day.

I walked onto the field to watch the sun sparkling upon the muddy infield and the empty stands.

Weather has never since bothered me. In every area, there comes a time when you know you have lived through the worst that can possibly happen. You know that, come what may, you will survive. No matter how great the crowd or how important the game, my attitude from that day forward has been, in the words of the old song, that if it rains, I'll let it. And who knows? Maybe in the long run it will even work out for the best.

I did get a quick promotional gag out of the rain-out. The American Association gave an annual award to the city having the greatest opening-day turnout, and although our washed-out crowd had been far and away the largest, we were disqualified on the highly technical grounds that a washed-out crowd is no more official that a washed-out home run. On behalf of the citizenry of Milwaukee, I was outraged. I immediately declared Present-a-Trophy-to-Milwaukee Night, trotted out The Cup, refitted for the occasion with a new and highly emotional inscription plate, and awarded it to ourselves.

Right from the beginning, I regret to say, I had failed to make myself a leading candidate for any popularity award that my colleagues in the American Association might see fit to bestow. Since baseball rules are ridiculously and ineptly written, I have always read the rule book with an eye toward loopholes. The proof that I might have succeeded to some small extent came when the league fathers called a special meeting and passed about nine new rules, all of them directed against us. To show how contrite we were, Rudie and I walked into the league conference room wearing football helmets and fencing masks to protect ourselves against the onslaught. Oh, they were mad. Now we were not only making a travesty of the rules, we were making a travesty of their little meeting.

One of the new rules had to do with the moving of fences. Having no real players of our own when we first came to Milwaukee, we had to adjust as best we could. It was not only that our hitters couldn't hit, most of them couldn't run either. Our players were so slow, in fact, that Charlie didn't even bother to have a steal sign. The other team did have a steal sign, of course, and what was worse, they had guys who could take it and run with it.

In the interests of closer competition, we introduced a loose, sandy mixture into the base paths in such abundant quantity that the runners would sink up to their ankles as they ran, like kids running on the beach. If we couldn't run, nobody ran.

Hitting was the real problem, though. As I moved among the fans that first night, one of the questions I heard most often was, "With a right-field fence only 265 feet from the plate, how come we've got no left-handed hitter who can hit a long ball?"

An excellent question. It is a question that asks the question: "Why should all those other teams come in with their long-ball hitters and take advantage of *our* fence?" The answer was not long in coming. On top of the permanent wall I built a 60-foot chicken-wire fence which turned all those short home runs into long singles.

The next year, with hitters of our own, it became necessary to do a little maneuvering. Calling upon my Lewis Institute training. I designed a system for sliding the wire fence back and forth along the top of the wall by means of a hydraulic motor. When the visiting team had more left-handed power than we did, the fence would stay up. Otherwise, we would reel it back into the foul line.

From there, it was only a short hop to the ultimate refinement. In the best of all possible parks, the fence would be up for the opposition and down for us. We could do this without any trouble at all—and we did do it—by reeling the fence in and out between innings. That is, we did it once. They passed a rule against it the next day.

Until they passed the rule, understand, this was all perfectly legal, even if it did not necessarily qualify us for that season's Abner Doubleday Award for sportsmanship above and beyond the call of duty. It is my job, as I see it, to get my players the greatest possible advantage within the rules.

We had our difficulties on the road, too. Columbus, the top Cardinal farm, had its usual quota of hard-throwing pitchers. It also had a high mound and the worst lights in the league. This poor little club of ours didn't have anybody who could hit the ball out of the infield even when they could see what they were swinging at, and Columbus always clobbered us.

There are many ways to battle such rank injustice. Some people get together and adopt unanimous resolutions; others write letters to the editor. I did neither. Upon sober reflection, I bought my boys miners' caps—with the light in front—to wear as they groped their way to the plate. Our coaches held lanterns aloft in their respective boxes to indicate the general direction of the playing field. Packie Rogers, our second baseman, took a light meter out to the field with him and spent his odd moments taking readings.

Great anguish was visible in the Columbus front office, although not enough anguish to do anything about those lights.

At our next stop, Indianapolis, the management—still sulking over some long-forgotten and probably imaginary slight—refused to put on the lights so that we could take our batting practice. Apparently, someone had not been reading the papers, because with those lanterns still in our equipment trunk they were playing right into our hands. We hung the lanterns on either side of the batting cage and to the delight of the people already in the park, went through the motions of taking batting practice anyway.

As Charlie Grimm and I were sitting in the dugout, enjoying the fun, Donie Bush, the Indianapolis manager and owner (and a long-time major-league player and manager), came charging down the aisle toward us. Bush, of course, was entitled to get as mad as he wanted, but being a man in his fifties, he should never have allowed himself to become quite so athletic about it. Halfway down the stairs, he pulled up short with a charley horse. At that point, I decided it would be just as well to duck into the runway behind the dugout.

At length, Donie came limping down and eased himself onto the bench alongside Grimm. All the fire was out of him. "Charlie," he said, in a small, bewildered voice, "I like you. You know I've always liked you, Charlie. And they didn't make them any better than old William Veeck. But tell me, Charlie, how could such a nice man ever have had such a so-and-so for a son?"

What really brought the wrath of the mighty down upon our heads, I suppose, was a masterpiece of rules juggling—in which three rules were kept in the air at the same time—that came close to winning the pennant for us on the last day of the 1942 season.

The first team we put together at Milwaukee came down to that final day only half a game behind Kansas City, the league leader. And we were playing a doubleheader against Kansas City on our own home grounds.

Viewing a situation like this on a basis of simple mathematics, you can see that if you win the first game you don't want to have to play the second, because a second victory is meaningless and a loss will drop you right back into second place again. If you lose that first game, the second game does you not the slightest good because you're already eliminated.

By combining two rules, I could see a way of controlling that second game:

1. The decision on whether to turn the lights on during a game was left entirely to the discretion of the home team.

2. Before scheduling a night game, the home team was required to give the visiting club adequate notice. If such notice was not given, the home club was to be fined $50.

Now, follow this closely: If I could start the first game so late that it would not be completed until night was about to fall, I would be in a position to do whatever I wanted about that second game. If we won the first game, the umpires would have to call off that second game because of darkness. They could not invoke the special importance of this game to force me to put on the lights and play a night game, because they would be forcing me to break a rule and pay a fine.

If, by chance, there was enough light to start the second game, it would still be entirely up to me whether I wanted to put the lights on, after an inning or so, when darkness fell.

The first game was scheduled to start at 1:30. That meant it would be necessary for us to hold off the opening pitch for three hours.

At this point, a third rule came into play. It is up to the home team to decide whether the field is fit for play. Control of the game is not given over to the umpires until the manager of the home team hands in his lineup card.

Early in the morning, Rudie and I, along with the ground crew, went out with hoses and soaked down the infield until it was afloat. Fortunately, nature may abhor a vacuum but it has nothing against us deep thinkers. About three drops of rain fell around noon, giving us an official record of scattered showers in case of an appeal.

As the Kansas City players came out of their locker room at 12:30, our ground crew went to work on our strangely soggy infield. Working at a fine, arthritic pace, they proceeded to cover over the puddles with dirt. Shovel by shovel. An hour passed and it was time to start the game. On they worked. Once the water had been soaked up, they began to smooth down the infield. Never have so many raked and smoothed and patted an infield with such tender and loving care.

Kansas City, well aware that something was coming off even if they didn't know what, began to moan. Roy Hamey, the Kansas City general manager, was calling George Weiss (head of the Yankee farm system) in his Newark office, every fifteen minutes. Weiss was calling Trautman. Trautman was trying to get me on the phone, with no noticeable success. Weiss was trying to get Hamey back to find out how things were going.

Well, all that ringing got annoying. We informed Hamey that we couldn't get any work done if he kept tying up our phone, and poor Roy had to go running across the street to a drugstore to make his subsequent calls. They were still fixing up the field when he returned. I had been thoughtful enough to bring a hangman's noose to the park with me, since I was fairly certain the time would come when Hamey would feel in great need of one. I figured the time had come. Oh, he was flaming.

Out on the field, Johnny Neun, the Kansas City manager, was so upset that he took a vow he would never manage again—which didn't prevent him from becoming the manager of the Cincinnati Reds five years later.

At 4 o'clock, the ground crew examined the field critically, shook their heads in dismay, and went back to work.

It was 5 o'clock before the game finally started. And for awhile it looked as if we were going to get away with it. With Hy Vandenberg, who later went to the Cubs, doing the pitching, we had a lead going into the eighth inning. But Eddie Stanky booted an easy double-play ball, the only time I ever saw him blow an important play in his career. Vandenberg got mad and laid one down the middle and— Bomb—we lost it. I saw little need to put the lights on and play the second game.

It was the last time we failed to win the pennant. In my last three years at Milwaukee we won three straight pennants.

Getting the players that took us from last place to a first-place tie in a single season wasn't quite as easy it may have sounded. The war hadn't yet started in June, 1941, when we came to Milwaukee, but the draft was on. Good players were already scarce, especially for operators who couldn't pay cash for them.

I did get one good player immediately. Jim Gallagher did me the kindness of sending up Lou Novikoff, known in the sports pages as "The Mad Russian," for our opening night. Novikoff had been a great minor-league hitter in the Pacific Coast League and an unbelievably bad one for the Cubs.

I have always felt that Novikoff would have been a great hitter if he had come up to the Cubs while Grimm was managing, because Charlie wouldn't have bothered him with signs in the majors any more than he did at Milwaukee. Lou was never one of baseball's great thinkers. He would sometimes drive us crazy by bunting with the bases loaded or by hitting away when a bunt was clearly called for. But he could hit. And hitting can cover a multitude of sins.

Lou hit so well for us that on the last day of the season he was tied with Lou Klein for the batting championship. Since we were still firmly in last place, Novikoff's run for the batting title was about the only thing our fans had to root for, and we were naturally anxious for them to have one victory to look back on through the long winter months. Novikoff himself approached this thrilling stretch run with an enthusiasm bordering upon indifference. He had won batting championships out on the Coast and he had found that they really hadn't changed his life at all.

With our final-day doubleheader about to start, Charlie called the office to tell me that Novikoff hadn't yet appeared. I called his hotel room. No answer. I tried to track him down at his known haunts. No success. Finally, I called the hotel back and asked the bell captain to send someone to his room. They found him there laid out on his bed, sleeping peacefully.

"Get him under a shower and get him dressed," I said. "I'll send a gateman to drive him out."

To stall long enough to give Lou a chance to reach the park, I closed up all except two of the ticket windows. Then I went down and told the umpires that we had such a surprisingly large late crowd beating on our doors that the game would have to be delayed. The umpires, looking up and seeing three guys wandering into the park, scratching themselves placidly, were not completely convinced but there wasn't very much they could do about it. I had to stall for about 30 minutes before word reached me that Novikoff had been delivered to the locker room, relatively intact. As I came in, he was being hustled into his uniform. Grimm was leaning over him saying, "Look, you got to get a few base hits today. A few base hits today and you win the batting title."

Lou, still unfocused, looked unhappy about having his sleep disturbed.

So Novikoff went out and got 5 hits in 8 times at bat—including a double and a triple—to win the title.

Gallagher was very helpful. In addition to Novikoff, he sent me Billy Myers, who had been shortstop for the Cincinnati Reds pennant winners of 1939–40. Billy had slowed down on the field, if not off it, but he was still better than anything we had.

We had a lot of drinkers on the team. The roistering player is one type who is always considered expendable, which means—looking at it from the other point of view—always available. The player who drinks and gets around is looked upon as a bad influence. His career, according to folklore, is brief and tragic. I had seen a few things in my young, impressionable days that did not quite sort with what I had heard. I had seen Hack Wilson arise from a tub of ice and hit 3 home runs. I had wandered around Chicago with the 1939 Cubs and had seen them run away from the field. As long as they didn't start buddying up with the young kids, the drunks didn't bother me at all.

My first purchase, as a matter of fact, was Vallie Eaves, an Indian from one of the Texas-Louisiana reservations. To show how quickly these characters are moved around, I had seen Eaves shut out the Cubs for the White Sox with 3 hits during spring training. Vallie still belonged to Shreveport at that time, and the day before the White Sox were going to buy him, he had gotten himself into a jam by stealing a case of eggs. Harry Grabiner had called off the deal and shipped him right back to Shreveport. Shreveport, in turn, had sold him to Toronto. I bought him from Toronto for $3,500, on the usual $500-down-and-the-rest-when-you-catch-me deal.

I bought him at a time when we were even more desperate than usual. I had weeded out my pitching staff with a little too much enthusiasm, and between the violin player, the pitchers who couldn't throw and the pitchers I had shipped away, Charlie's staff was down to two able-bodied men. A condition of the Eaves purchase was that he was to be put on a train for Toledo immediately so that he could pitch for us the next night.

He didn't show up at the hotel, and he didn't show up at the ball park. Grimm had to pitch little Jess Dobernick, and Dobernick went out and pitched the best game of his career. Our hitters were in their usual grand form, too, so we lost in 15 innings, 1–0.

We were still left with the problem of finding Eaves. The Toronto general manager had told me, in answer to my frantic call, that he had personally put Eaves on a train that had been due in Toledo at 10 o'clock that morning. That meant that unless Eaves had jumped the train, he was wandering around in Toledo. We had a midnight train waiting to take us to Columbus. If we didn't find him before we left, it was possible that he would never be heard of again.

65

The station manager agreed to hold the train until 4 A.M. Charlie wasn't interested in joining the search, so I had to go it alone. Neither the police stations nor the hospitals had picked up anybody answering his description. That made it a matter of checking the joints, bar by bar, on a Saturday night against a 4-o'clock deadline. The cabdriver would pull up to the curb, I'd jump out, run in, look around, jump back into the cab and off we'd go to the next bar. There are a lot of bars in Toledo. There have to be at least forty-five, because I'm sure I checked that many before I found him. You've heard of guys being paralyzed? Vallie was propped up in a corner, absolutely stiff. The cabdriver grabbed his legs, I took him under the arms and he didn't even bend.

After we deposited him in the train, I went to Charlie's room to try to figure out what to do about Eaves. Every club he'd ever played for had fined him. That obviously didn't do any good. "Let's try something different," I said. "I won't tell him you know anything about this. We'll give him a raise in salary for reporting and see where he takes it from there."

The next morning in Columbus, I had him sign a new contract with, if I remember, a $200-a-month raise and my heartfelt thanks for making it safely to Toledo.

Grimm pitched him that afternoon in the first game of the double-header. It was hot. Ohhh, it was hot. Poor Eaves was just beginning to sober up about the time the game started, and the sweat was pouring out of him.

Our hitters were still hot too, and Eaves lost, 1–0. Charlie threw him back in the fifth inning of the second game, and he was the losing pitcher in that one, too, 3–2.

(We didn't win a game in Columbus for almost two years. I came to the conclusion that we were too tense, that we were trying too hard, and so after we had lost a Saturday afternoon game I threw a party for the boys at the Deshler Hotel. I ordered half-a-dozen cases of bourbon and half-a-dozen cases of Scotch and invited some of the girls in to join the celebration. The next day we had a doubleheader and half our team was missing. Charlie had pitchers playing everywhere. The boys came staggering in, one by one, during the afternoon and if Charlie could see the whites of their eyes, into the game they'd go. We had to put out an announcement afterwards that the team had been stricken by an epidemic of ptomaine poisoning from eating tainted oysters. Oh yes, we won two games that afternoon. We didn't lose another game in Columbus until halfway through the following season.)

66

Eaves pitched well for us that year, so well that I sold him to the Cubs at a time when I was in desperate need of money. But Vallie's heart wasn't in the big leagues. He kept calling us from Chicago—where, you will remember, they play only day games—asking if we wanted him to come up and pitch for us at night.

"Vallie," I'd tell him, "you don't belong to us anymore. You can only pitch for the Cubs."

"But I like you," Vallie would say. "You and Charlie were so nice to me up there, giving me a raise and everything. I want to help you."

He liked us. He liked us so much he came up to Milwaukee twice, determined to pitch for us. We almost had to use force to keep him from putting on a uniform.

We got him back again the next year, on option, after a typical foul-up. That was the year Judge Landis issued wartime orders against traveling to the regular training camps. Vallie, who apparently didn't bother to read either the newspapers or his mail, reported to Catalina Island. This was little help to the Cubs, who were training in French Lick Springs, Indiana. The Cubs' road secretary, Bob Lewis, who may be the only living saint I know, lost his temper for one of the rare times in his life and sent Vallie a ticket for a slow bus between Los Angeles and French Lick.

Vallie had a good heart. Once you understood that he really couldn't help himself, he was no great problem. I had sent word around to all the Milwaukee bartenders, for instance, that I would buy back any knives they took away from him. Vallie had a friendly little habit of pulling a knife when they shut him off. He wouldn't have hurt a fly, though. All the bartender had to do was talk to him sympathetically, and Vallie would turn the knife over.

In those first couple of years in Milwaukee, we picked up a swinging group. Bill Norman, who came to me as a player insisting he was thirty, was a booze man then, although he subsequently became a beer man, like me. "Willie Card" remained with me, except for his year and a half as manager of the Detroit Tigers, until his death this spring. You can't find a better baseball man. Merv Connors, Sammy Hale, Vance Page, Roxie Lawson, they could all hold their own with the Chicago Cub gang of blessed memory.

Murray "Red" Howell, an outfielder from Georgia, spent a brief but memorable tenure with us. Murray was a real good hitter, and I had paid a pretty price to get him. He arrived at our training camp in Ocala, Florida, with a fourteen-year-old wife, an unquenchable thirst and an unprecedented talent for getting his head lumped up.

During spring training, a call came to me at about 3 o'clock one morning, and a little feminine voice said: "We've got your player here at the Sunset Inn. Come and get him."

When I got there, Murray was out cold on the floor and this little bit of a barmaid, about 4'11", was sitting alongside him with a bottle in her hand. Every time he'd so much as quiver, she'd belt him over the head. Poor Murray, I've never seen a man with so many lumps on him.

On opening day in Milwaukee, we won by some ridiculous score. That night, while we were celebrating our victory, I got another call about Howell. Only this time it was to inform me that they had him down in the jail. "Fine," I said. "Hold on to him until morning and I'll be down."

This child-wife of his, it developed, was just full of talent. They had spent the night touring the bars, with Murray doing the ordering and his wife, a sweet-faced little girl, carrying the gun, according to the police blotter. When he reached the stage where the bars refused to serve him, she would slip him the gun—which, thank goodness, was defective. As had to happen, he eventually found a bartender who hit him over the head with a bungstop and knocked him cold. Murray was being held in the jug on a long list of charges.

Well, Charlie and I talked to the judge. We explained that Murray was just a big, playful boy who, given one more chance, could become a credit to his country and his community and, to get right down to it, the Milwaukee ball club. The judge was willing enough to go along. As a matter of routine, however, he had to go through the formality of a trial in order to protect the arresting officer from any possible suit for false arrest. Fine.

Howell was taken from the lockup, and I went up to explain the ground rules to him. All he had to do, I told him, was admit the gun was his and then we would all go home.

Murray was not completely sobered up, but he kept nodding his head and saying, "Sure, Bill, sure."

Back I went to the judge's chambers to rejoin Charlie. Murray was brought in almost immediately. "Mr. Howell," asked the judge, "is this your gun?"

And Murray jumped up and yelled, "What are you trying to do, you dirty so-and-so, frame me?"

Back to the jug goes Howell.

The judge is so mad now that he's pacing back and forth across his chambers. Charlie and I fall into step beside him, one on either side, and we're pacing along with him, trying to calm him down enough to be able to remind him that Murray had, after all, been drinking rather heavily the night before and had obviously not completely understood what I had told him.

It took awhile for the judge to run down. He finally stopped walking, though, and in his best judicial language, he told me, "Okay, your guy made a mistake because he's still half-loaded. Go up and explain it to him again, and this time, by heaven, make sure he understands!"

With great patience, I went over the whole routine with Howell again, emphasizing as strongly as humanly possible that the whole hearing was a mere formality, that the decision was in and that he was going to be released. All he had to do, I told him, was to say yes to anything the judge asked him, and if that was too much of a strain, he could look at Charlie or me and we would slip him the sign.

Murray not only understood now, he was filled with remorse at all the trouble he had caused us. We had a good cry together and, in due time, we assembled once again in the judge's chambers.

This time, the judge smiles at him helpfully and picks up the gun. "Now, this is just a matter of formality, Howell," he says. "Don't worry about it. Just tell me whether this is your gun."

And Howell squints at him and says, "Why, you dirty so-and-so! Ain't you the same dirty so-and-so who tried to frame me a few minutes ago?"

Milwaukee justice is swift. The judge bangs his desk with both fists and yells, "Five hundred dollars and six months at Waupan! And get him out of here!"

Back to the jug goes Howell. The judge is waving away all our explanations, and the next thing we know the three of us are walking again. Back and forth we go, walking and talking. Charlie talks for awhile and I talk for awhile and the judge just keeps on walking.

In the end, he agreed to suspend the sentence on condition that I got Howell out of town before sundown. The fine stuck.

So I paid the fine and put in a quick call to Edgar Allen at Knoxville, the only operator I knew who would buy a player on such short notice.

Howell went home to pack. Late in the afternoon, he and his bride were driving southward, with me following closely behind. As soon as he passed the city limits, I called the judge to tell him that the mission had been accomplished.

I had lost $1,500 on the forced sale—after getting one day's action out of Howell—and, needless to say, I wrote off the $500 fine as a complete loss. But it wasn't. During the summer, I kept getting checks for sums like $62, $132, $34, until the $500 was completely paid off. He never enclosed a note or anything, just the checks.

It wasn't a bad deal for Edgar Allen, either. Howell led the Knoxville Smokies in hitting that year.

I couldn't complain. We had the three top hitters in our league: Eddie Stanky, Heinz Becker and Hal Peck. Stanky was always one of my favorite players. I had gone to Macon the previous year to buy a pitcher named Frankie Marino, who had won 13 straight games. Stanky was playing shortstop for Macon, and I had seen a very favorable Cub report on him. I offered the Macon owner, Doc Williams, $7,500 for Marino provided he would sell me Stanky for $2,500. After the deal was set, Williams, who was a drugstore owner, told me, rather gleefully, that I could have had Stanky for nothing if I was willing to pay $7,500 for Marino.

"That's all right," I told him. "I'm delighted with the deal. I'm glad you are, too."

At the end of the year, after I had sold Stanky to the Cubs for $40,000, I received a wire from Williams saying: I SEE WHAT YOU MEAN.

I felt that Stanky should be playing second base, not shortstop. At spring training, we had four other shortstops in camp and only one other second baseman. On the first day of training, I got to the park a little late and saw all five shortstops huddled together behind second base. When the conference broke up, Stanky trotted over to shortstop and the others went off in assorted directions. "Gentlemen," Stanky had told them, "if you want to stay on this club you had better find yourselves another position." That was the end of that.

Eddie was a tough little man in uniform, but he has always been a complete gentleman off the field. At Macon, he had fallen in love with the manager's daughter, Dickie Stock, a spectacularly beautiful and intelligent girl. We were scheduled to play exhibition games in Nashville and Chattanooga, and before we left, Eddie asked me if he was going to make the club. Well, there was no question about that. In that case, he said, he wondered if he could have the two days off while we were down South so that he could go to Macon and get married. I told him he could have all the time off he wanted, but that if he was going to get married I had better raise his salary.

Eddie was rooming with Greek George, a catcher, and the Greek began to ride him about Dickie. The Greek had a rather broad and colorful vocabulary and Eddie, who doesn't go for that kind of talk at all, kept warning him to cut it out.

This was 1942, remember, during the early days of rationing.

70

Eddie had driven to camp with nothing except his clothes, four extra tires for his beat-up old car and—for reasons I never thought to inquire about—a revolver. As George kept after him with his pungent banter, Eddie took out the revolver and warned him not to say one more word about Dickie.

Greek found the word, and Eddie fired. I came dashing into their room about three seconds after the shot, and there was George standing against the wall with a bullet hole no more than six inches above his head. I never had the courage to ask Eddie whether he was that good or that bad a shot.

Eddie put his four tires and his revolver into his car and drove off to get married. The Greek did not seem too upset when we put him in with another roommate.

Eddie was a tremendous competitor for us. I remember one night when the Toledo catcher came into second and spiked Eddie so badly that he ripped the sock completely off his foot. Eddie didn't so much as stoop over to rub it.

In baseball, let me say, there is a code that says, "Big-leaguers don't rub." You may have noticed that after a batter is hit by a pitch he may flex his shoulder or twist his neck a little but he will never rub the spot where he has been hit. If you ask any of them about it, they will always say, "Why should I give him the satisfaction of showing he hurt me?" This may sound rather naïve, since a pitcher who has just hit a batter behind the ear with a baseball traveling 80 mph has a mighty strong suspicion that it might have stung a little. What the players really mean is that there has somehow developed a code of honor which forbids them to make a display of any physical injury caused by an opponent. There are those, I'm sure, who would call it nothing more than the code of adolescence. I'm not among them. I would even dignify it, I think, by calling it not so much a code but a tradition—for any profession worth the name develops its own traditions. Courage and honor are not such commonplace commodities, now or ever, that they should be scorned.

At any rate, Stanky took care of the Toledo catcher on a play at the plate before the game was over. I dropped into the clubhouse after the game—something I rarely do—to see how badly he had been cut. A gash about six inches long ran down his leg. To get him to the hospital was bad enough. To get him to submit to the routine tetanus shot was almost impossible. Eddie somehow felt that to accept medication would dishonor him. The only way I could get him to take the shot was by picking up the phone and giving him the choice between yielding or going back to Macon immediately.

Our season at Milwaukee didn't start until a day after the major-league opener, so Charlie and I were able to go down to Chicago to see Eddie's big-league debut in 1943. Eddie was the Cubs' lead-off man, and the first pitch thrown to him as a big-leaguer hit him right on the head and cold-cocked him. Eddie got up and sort of wandered around in little circles, as if his feet weren't hitting the ground. Charlie and I were in a front box on the first-base side of the field. He came wandering over to our box, still dazed and wobbly, and said, "Charles, is that the way they play the game in this league?"

"That's what I've been telling you," said Charlie.

"OK," Stanky said. "I'll take care of it."

Waving everybody away, Eddie staggered over to first base. The next batter swung at the first pitch and hit a slow ground ball to the Pittsburgh second baseman. The second baseman threw the ball to his shortstop, Huck Geary. Stanky hit Geary right around the knees and knocked him into center field and out of the ball game. For awhile, they didn't think Geary would ever play another game. As it was, he retired at the end of the year. Word gets around fast. The word, to paraphrase the Lone Ranger joke, was: "Don't fool around with Eddie Stanky."

Greek George, of course, could have told them that.

The Greek was one of my all-time favorites. One of the reasons we got along so well was that we had a common love for amusement parks. Another reason was that I knew that any time I wandered around with him, something was going to happen. Once while we were riding the Ferris wheel at an amusement park in Indianapolis, Greek spotted a line of baldheads in the seats a little below us. The Greek happened to have his pockets stuffed with Eskimo pies (what's the matter, you've never seen a man with his pockets full of Eskimo pies before?) and every time we came around to the top of the circuit he'd yell "Bombs away" and try to zero in on the baldheads. He is splattering ice cream bombs onto everybody down the line, and there is nothing I can do to stop him. Now, there are times when you go out into the world expecting or even courting danger. But to have to fight your way off a Ferris wheel is ridiculous. And that's what we had to do. We had to get out of our booth running and battle our way through a bitter and ugly crowd, a crowd reeking of vengeance and ice cream.

The screwiest thing George ever did, in the furtherance of his base-ball career, was to rig himself up as a human slingshot. The Greek was our regular catcher until he hurt his arm so badly that he couldn't

72

throw. A catcher with a bad arm is like a baritone with bad tonsils. Forget him. My boy wasn't going to be forgotten that easily, though. The Greek figured out a way to lend Nature a helping hand—and arm, and shoulder—by rigging himself up in a goofy contraption made out of two strips of inner tubing. One strip was tied around his wrist and looped around the back of his neck; the other ran between his wrist and upper waist. It was George's considered opinion that he now had only to pull the arm back as far as it would go, exhale, and let the rubber bands come snapping back, converting his wounded arm into a thing of thunder and lightning.

He was rather hurt when Charlie still wouldn't let him catch.

Toward the end of 1942, while we were in the stretch of that pennant race that ended in a tie, we suddenly began to run out of outfielders. We were in such desperate straits that when our left fielder, Ted Gullic, was injured we had to replace him with a sore-armed third baseman, Sammy Hale. Sammy had been on the bench because his arm was so bad that he couldn't make the throw across the infield. Every time a ball was hit to left field, Stanky had to run out and practically take the ball out of his hand.

A week or so later, we lost our right fielder Hal Peck, for reasons I will go into presently. There we were with nobody left to put in his place except Greek George and his Elastic Arm.

His slingshot hypothesis did not work out at all when put to the test. George would crank that arm way back and the ball would come blooping in toward the infield like a dying bird. So now we had both our second baseman and our shortstop running out every time a ball was hit either to left or to right field. We played one series in the big Columbus ball park while both our nonthrowing outfielders were doing their stuff, and the Columbus hitters established a record for two-base hits that will never be touched.

While we were in Columbus, during that same series, I made a quick trip to Detroit to sell the Tigers one of our pitchers, Hank Oana. Boarding the bus for the trip back, I slipped into an empty seat beside a blond young fellow. We got to talking and it developed that he was, of all things, an outfielder who had just been released by some club in the Sally League. His name was Cotton Goodell and he was going home, his dreams of glory behind him.

Well, I had not read the complete works of Charles Van Loan as a boy for nothing. Here, I knew, was no chance meeting. Fate, moving in its strange, mysterious way, had dumped my outfielder right into my lap. It didn't bother me for one second that he had been unable to make a Class-B league. Fate had dealt Goodell these dark moments merely to heighten the drama. I knew how these stories ended.

When I got off the bus in Columbus, Cotton Goodell got off with me. He played right field for us through the remaining games of the road trip while Greek George sulked in his tent and made a few minor adjustments in the tensile strength of his arm.

In the first game he played for us, Goodell came to bat in the late innings with the bases loaded and two men out and hit a moderately high pop fly just behind the pitcher's mound. The ball dropped right in the middle of the four infielders and the pitcher while they all stood around in a tight little circle staring at each other. With two out, our runners had been going, of course, so Goodell had batted in three runs and won the ball game.

Something happened like that in every game. Goodell never hit a ball out of the infield, and yet in every game he would get an important base hit. He would top a little twisting grounder ten feet down the base line and it would die right on the foul line; an infielder would fall down coming in for a ground ball; a ball would bounce off a pebble. I never saw anybody look so lousy on a ball field and still look so good in the box scores.

After all the work I had done building up a respectable baseball team for Milwaukee, I certainly had no intention of insulting our fans by bringing him back with us. I gave Goodell his release, and he resumed that briefly interrupted bus trip home. When we took the field again in Milwaukee, Greek George and his Magic Wand were back in right field.

For the next few days, the fans at Borchert Field gave me a terrible time. Everybody I sat with wanted to know how come I had let go of that sensational new outfielder, Cotton Goodell.

As fond as I was of players like Stanky and George, my favorite player—the one I always felt was my good-luck charm—was Hal Peck. Hal was a good all-around player who had developed remarkably as a hitter in that second year in Milwaukee. By midsummer, half a dozen major-league clubs were interested in him. I had agreed to sell him to the White Sox for $40,000 late in the season, and the contract was on my desk waiting to be signed. I needed that money. We were operating on a day-to-day basis again, holding out for the year-end player sales that were finally going to put us in the black.

To get Peck himself a little extra money, I had arranged for various base-running contests that night, because I knew:

1. He could easily outrun anybody on either team.
2. I was holding the stopwatch.

Late in the afternoon, I was sitting comfortably in the office in a pair of swimming trunks—having just helped the ground crew water the outfield—when the phone rang. A slightly hysterical Betty Peck shouted into my ear, "Hal just shot his leg off. What will I do?"

I had visited the Pecks often enough up in their home in Genesee Depot to know that there was a doctor right across the street. "Get him over quick," I told her, "but don't let him administer anything except first aid. Then go to the hospital in Waukesha, and I'll meet you there."

I called up two Milwaukee orthopedists, picked them up in my car and drove the 15 miles to Waukesha. I'm not known by the state police of the nation as the most conservative of drivers, but this time I broke all my own speed records.

What had happened was that Hal had gone to his hen house to shoot some rats, had stumbled as he entered and shot off the second and third toes of his left foot.

At the hospital, we met with nothing but complications. The first complication arose because the country doctor did not want to give up the case, which meant I had to wrestle with him and medical ethics for awhile before I could get my orthopedists in to inspect the damage and decide what kind of an operation had to be performed. In the meantime, the doctor had given Hal a shot of tetanus, and Hal was showing every symptom of being spectacularly allergic to it.

By the time I entered his room, he was delirious and calling, not for his wife, but for me (although I am attributing no cause-and-effect relationship there). While we were watching, he began to break out in blisters, the biggest blisters I have ever seen. Blisters the size of pancakes. They would bubble up before our eyes in a matter of seconds.

The specific for this kind of allergy reaction was a loose, watery oatmeal, not taken internally but patted on the blisters themselves. For the rest of the night—12 solid hours—Betty and I sat on opposite sides of the bed, dabbing the oatmeal on the blisters as they came up.

All through the night Hal was delirious. And all through the night he kept calling for me.

The orthopedists performed two operations to trim the stubs of the lost toes. Unfortunately, they were in complete disagreement on whether their patient would be able to play baseball again. One of them stated positively that since Hal still had his big toe, little toe and heel—the three points of contact between the foot and the ground—

his balance and his speed of foot would be virtually unaffected. The other flatly disagreed. I called in half a dozen other experts, and they split right down the middle on me too. I had each of them write out a full report of their findings in affidavit form, then I dropped the four unfavorable reports in the wastebasket. Finally I had the hospital make me up a full set of X-rays.

Now all I had to do was figure out who I could sell a three-toed outfielder to.

There was only one operator in all of baseball, I decided, who had the guts to take that kind of a chance. That was Larry MacPhail, the brightest, most imaginative man who has ever been in our business.

We were so broke at that moment that I was just barely able to scrape together enough money for a one-way train ticket to New York. If I didn't sell Peck to MacPhail I had no idea how I was going to get back.

In old Ebbets Field, there was an elevator not far from the main entrance to take you up to the press room and the club offices. As the elevator door opened to let me out, it opened upon the beefy, welcome figure of Larry MacPhail. "Get away from me," he roared. "You're here to sell me that one-legged outfielder of yours and you're not going to get away with it."

I recoiled at the thought of such a thing. "No, I'm not," I said. "I came down to see you clinch the pennant."

I sat with MacPhail in his private box, rooted hard for the Dodgers and never mentioned Peck. About halfway through the game he said, "You're not going to sell him to me, you know."

"Who?" I said.

"You know who. Peck. Your one-legged outfielder."

"Larry," I said. "Will you stop talking about Peck and let me watch the ball game."

The next day I sat with him again and never mentioned Peck. Every now and again, he would look over at me under his eyelids, suspiciously.

The third day, I said, "Listen, you know you're the only guy in baseball with enough guts and imagination to gamble on this guy. You know what his potential is, and I know he's all right. Look, I'll show you the X-rays and medical reports I've got here."

"Aha," he said, "I knew it. I knew it. Didn't I tell you I knew it?"

I tried to hand him the reports.

"Get away from me," he said. "What am I supposed to be, your lamb or something?"

I had to sell Peck or I would have no money to get back to Milwaukee. After the game, I hung around the press room, staying close enough to MacPhail to pick up any helpful bit of information he might drop. Eavesdropping, I think they call it. I heard him invite a couple of the writers to be his guests at the race track the next day, an open date.

Although I never bet the horses myself, I was overcome by a sudden desire to spend an afternoon at the track. MacPhail and the writers were in his private box. I was down on the open concourse, keeping him under close surveillance. I had a plan. My plan was to wait until he left the box fairly soon after the finish of a race, and then hope and pray that he was leaving to cash a winning ticket. Hope and prayer, in fact, were playing a very large role in my plans at this point. After the fourth race, MacPhail made his move. I made my move at the same time.

Somehow our paths happened to cross.

"Larry!" I said, clearly astonished. "I didn't know you were a horse man, too."

"Oh boy," he said, "you again. Just tell me one thing. Have you ever been to a race track before in your life?"

"The truth of the matter," I told him, "is that I have to win enough money to get me back to Milwaukee."

"You can go home," he said. "I'll buy your one-legged outfielder."

We made the deal right where we stood. I was to get $5,000 immediately and another $18,000 if the Dodgers kept Peck after opening day, a reasonable enough qualification under the circumstances. I was also to get Charley Brewster, a good-looking young shortstop from their farm system who, I figured, would replace Stanky for me the following year.

My only stipulation was that Brewster wouldn't be turned over to me until after the major-league draft meetings were held in Cincinnati in November. Otherwise, I'd be running the risk of having him drafted off my list before I ever got a chance to see him.

Our business complete, Larry was eager to talk about his system for handicapping the horses. He had a fistful of winning tickets. While I had been sweating him out on the concourse, MacPhail had been winning three of those first four races; he just hadn't bothered to go cash the tickets. He was in a marvelous mood. I have never really been able to decide whether I'd ever have been able to sell him Peck if he had been having a bad day.

The deal had ramifications. MacPhail left the Dodgers to join the Army, and Branch Rickey was brought in to run the club. MacPhail, as an honorable man, phoned to let me know that he had explained our Brewster agreement to Rickey. Rickey got on the extension and we had a three-way conversation.

On the day of the draft, Sam Levy called me from his paper to tell me I had lost Brewster.

"That can't be," I said. "He isn't on my list."

"He isn't now," Sam said, "but he was. Because Rickey turned him over to you just before the draft. And who do you think drafted him but his great friend, Warren Giles." (Giles, the current National League president, was then general manager of the Cincinnati Reds.)

I think Branch Rickey is a remarkable man. He does things; he has ideas; he shakes the game up. But this is one of the things I can't stand. I called Rickey in Cincinnati, and I was flaming. Rickey claimed there never was such a conversation, of course. He was grieved that I was so upset, he said, but, as much as he hated to be abrupt with me, he had all sorts of important matters clamoring for his attention.

"Oh?" I said. "Where are you?" Before it occurred to him that I had to know perfectly well where he was since I had just put in a call to him, he was saying, "In Cincinnati."

"That's what I figured," I said, "because I've always heard it said that the thieves get together to split up the loot."

As much as Papa Branch hated to be abrupt with me, he hung up.

Understand that I got the $7,500 draft price from Cincinnati for Brewster, which brought the total price for Peck up to $30,500. I was upset because Brewster was worth more than that to me.

By spring, however, the boot was on the other foot. Rickey telephoned me at our camp at Waukesha, a call, I must say, that was not completely unexpected. I knew he had been asking for waivers on Peck so that he could return him to me before he had to pay that $18,000.

Mr. Rickey opened the conversation by telling me that Peck's foot was still so bad he could hardly run. I had spent a lot of time with Peck over the winter, and I knew all about his foot. I knew very well that he was going to have some trouble in spring training, because there was a growth at the point of amputation—what they call a plantar's wart—a not unusual development in that kind of healing process. The orthopedists had assured me that the removal of the growth was the most minor kind of operation. Peck's recovery, they said, had been everything they could possibly have hoped for.

The real reason for Rickey's call was that he had been unable to get the waivers. "Isn't it strange," he said, "that the only people who claim him are your great friends in Chicago?"

78

"There's nothing strange about it to me," I said. "It shows they've done a better scouting job than I thought. But if you're accusing me of doing something illegal, let's just go down to the Commissioner's office and find out."

"Well," he said, "I don't like the looks of it."

"I couldn't care less whether you like the looks of it or not. We made a deal. You've maneuvered your way out of part of it, but you can take my word for it that you're not getting out of this part."

"All right," he snapped. "But as far as trading with me, you're dead."

Well, Papa Branch, in my opinion, had been initiating the new Philadelphia owner, Bill Cox, into the league by trading him a pound of hamburger for a pound of prime sirloin. "I'll tell you something," I told him. "I'd rather be dead than getting a hosing like you're giving that live one of yours, poor Cox."

Rickey had to turn Peck over to the Cubs for the $7,500 waiver price and then pay me the $18,000 he still owed. I bled for him all the way to the bank. The Cubs kept Peck for awhile and eventually sold him back to me. I had the growth cut out and after he had another great season at Milwaukee a year later, I sold him to Connie Mack.

I was living up on a farm outside West Bend, a very friendly little community. We had about ten other people on our party line, and they were all very faithful about listening in on our phone calls to make sure they had the latest dope about the team. Sometimes there would be so many people on the line that I couldn't hear the guy at the other end. I'd have to ask a couple of my fellow subscribers to hang up and call me back later to find out what had happened.

Mr. Mack called me at the farm late in the year to find out what I wanted for Peck. I asked for $20,000 and a couple of ballplayers.

One of the guys on my line, who was quite a fan, said, "Oh, Will, he's worth more than that."

"You think so?" I said, lowering my voice.

"Sure he is. You don't want to let him go for that."

All the while, Connie was saying, "There's interference on the line, Bill. . . . We have a bad connection. . . . How much did you say?"

I raised my voice. "I said thirty thousand dollars, Mr. Mack."

"My goodness," he said, "I thought I heard something else."

"No, no. I said thirty thousand dollars. We have a very bad connection. I can hardly hear you at all."

"All right," Mr. Mack said. "You'll send him to me as soon as your playoffs are over, won't you?"

I would and I did. I also sent my neighbor a few cases of Scotch.

Eventually Mr. Mack sold Peck to the Yankees, and I got him back with me once again when I operated at Cleveland. That was a fairly complicated deal, too, and I'll save it for its own time and place.

Milwaukee was the great time of my life. What can you say about a city after you have said that? Milwaukee was my proving grounds. It was the place where I tried out all my ideas, the good and the bad, without the terrible pressure to succeed that comes with a major-league franchise. Milwaukee was all fun, even when I was running around from loan company to loan company. It was all light, all laughter.

I sold, not because I wanted a capital-gains deal or because I wanted to move on to the major leagues. I would have been content to remain in Milwaukee for the rest of my life. I sold because it had come down to a choice between the club and my marriage. It is impossible to operate the way I operate and have any kind of a home life unless—as later, with Mary Frances—your wife is a part of the operation too.

I had left to join the Marines at the end of the third season, missed the next season and returned, on crutches, for the last six weeks of 1945. My marriage had been breaking up before I went into the service. We had three children by that time and both of us—Eleanor and I—wanted to give the marriage a fighting chance. We both knew I couldn't do that and still operate my ball club. Eleanor was a fine horsewoman. She loved the outdoors. We agreed that I would sell the club and use the money to buy a guest ranch in Arizona.

I sold the club with ridiculous ease; without, really, any negotiations. While I was in Chicago for the World Series at the end of the season, I ran across Rogers Hornsby. Knowing that Hornsby had once tried to buy the Milwaukee ball club, I offered the information that the club was for sale. "If you're really serious," he said. "I know a fellow who wants to buy one."

The next night Oscar Salinger, a Chicago attorney, came to my room. "Rogers tells me you want to sell your club," he said. "What do you want for it?"

I told him I wanted to come out with $250,000 after taxes.

"That's fair enough," he said. "Draw up the papers and we'll sign."

That was that. In less than a minute, I had sold the Milwaukee Brewers.

The end came fast, but it was not without pain. How I loved that ball club.

A Universal-International Production | 5.

THE Arizona experiment didn't take. Eleanor and I had already grown too far apart. As far as our marriage was concerned the ship had sailed. The fault, as I will make abundantly clear later, was mine. It was mine from the beginning and it was mine at the end.

I couldn't take the quiet. I couldn't take the inactivity. And most of all, when it came right down to it, I couldn't take the complete separation from baseball. There are people who find a grandeur in a sunset or in the Grand Canyon. Fine. To me, there is nothing more beautiful than a stadium or an amusement park filled with people. Anything filled with people. I have spent most of my life in a ball park. In Cleveland, I was all set to build myself an apartment in one of the stadium towers until somebody discovered that I would be violating a city ordinance. Later, in St. Louis, Mary Frances and I and our son, Mike, who was then a baby, were able to live right in Sportsman's Park by converting the old offices into an 8-room, 3-bedroom apartment.

When I'm in operation, I get to the park early in the morning and make four complete tours before the game starts, checking everything from the concessions to the men's rooms. I watch every game and not from the owner's box. I have *never*—never means not once—sat in a box in my own park. I move around the park, inning by inning, and always end up in the press box. It is among the fans and the writers that you find the real rooting, the real excitement.

Eleanor, who had been an equestrian in the Ringling Brothers circus, loved ranch life. I like riding too, and I had done quite a bit of it at the Ranch School. But my legs were giving me so much trouble—the right leg was being held together by bone grafts and the left leg was still recovering from a bad case of jungle rot—that I really couldn't sit comfortably on a horse. That left me to sit and watch the cactus grow. Cactus grows an inch a year, which makes an afternoon of cactus watching rather unrewarding.

Our guest ranch was called The Lazy Vee. We had some delightful people out there, people I still bump into now and then. I could

81

have enjoyed them all tremendously if they had not been paying me, as it were, to be charming to them. I have to be on the giving, not the receiving, end. If you give me a woolen muffler, I've got to send you back a herd of sheep. I'm not bragging or complaining or looking for any psychological interpretations. I'm stating a fact. That's the way I am, and that's the way I have always been.

On top of it all, the timing was all wrong. I had spent the previous 18 months in various hospitals and it was not the time of my life to retreat into the desert to meditate and to fast. It was a time to be up and doing.

I cannot say that my romance with the cacti ever really got off the ground.

Spring came, finally, and with it the old itch to get back into baseball. During 1946's spring training, the Cubs and White Sox came through Tucson to play an exhibition game. I invited all the Chicago newspapermen to the ranch for dinner and pounced upon them hungrily for news of the great world beyond.

In the course of the bull session that always develops when good baseball people get together, I started a wonderful argument by putting forth the proposition (which I still firmly believe) that it is far easier to run a major-league club than a minor-league one. In the majors, I kept insisting, you had enough money to cover over all your mistakes, while in the minors you were always operating so close to the bone that ingenuity had to take the place of money, and every mistake became a major catastrophe.

Ed Burns, of the Chicago *Tribune,* the last of my father's contemporaries, took me to the mat on it. He not only disagreed with me, he had the telling point that I didn't know what I was talking about because I had never had the prime responsibility for running a major-league club.

"Well," I said finally, "I'm gonna prove it to you one of these days."

"I'd be delighted to have you prove it," he said. "But until you do, I reserve the right to remain totally unconvinced."

That started me thinking about what I had been telling myself all winter I hadn't been thinking about.

Harry Grabiner, one of my heroes, had just retired from baseball after years with the Chicago White Sox, and we had been talking to each other almost weekly over the phone. I would say, "How do you like this retirement? Boy, this is the life, huh?" And Harry would say, "Nothing like it. Let those other fools go out and break their backs."

And each of us knew the other was lying in his teeth.

So I called Harry and told him the time had come to stop kidding

82

ourselves and get back into business. "Fine," he said. "What will we use for money?"

"Don't worry," I said. "We'll find it. One of these days I'll come knocking on your door. Boy, this retirement is for the birds, isn't it?"

Harry was my kind of baseball man. He had started selling score-cards around Comiskey Field as a kid and had been picked up and more or less adopted by old Charles Comiskey, the original owner of the White Sox. Through the years he had worked his way up to vice-president, a title which, in this case, meant that he was running the club.

When I was knocking around in my early days with the Cubs, I could always go to Harry, when the White Sox were in town, and make some extra money as a ticket seller. Later, as I moved up in the Cubs' front office, he and I organized the vendors' union in Chicago, so that the vendors would be guaranteed a living wage and the clubs would be guaranteed a professional working force.

What distinguished Harry Grabiner above everything else, however, was his incredible ability with figures. He was, to put it simply, a human adding machine. Before each season, the Cubs and White Sox played a City Series. Harry and I, as representatives of our teams, would meet in the ticket office to tote up the receipts from all the ticket sellers. I would sit at a Monroe calculator and run the figures through at a fairly good clip. Harry would come strolling in while I was banging away, run his finger down the six-figure columns and tote them all up in his head. On a good crowd, it would take me perhaps fifty minutes on the machine. Harry would do it mentally in ten. Whenever there was a discrepancy, it would be me and the machine who had made it.

He was remarkable. He used to play around with a dozen or so penny stocks for kicks. None of them was worth anything, they were all cats and dogs, but he had some magic formula for turning over a steady profit just on the mathematics of it.

Under the Comiskeys the White Sox were a pinch-penny operation. I always marveled at the way Harry Grabiner was able to keep the team going against the kind of operation Wrigley, with an unlimited supply of money, was running across town. Harry was always unpopular with the White Sox fans, though, because any time there was an unpleasant announcement to make, it was Harry who would stand up and make it. If there was good news tonight, Lou Comiskey—who had inherited the club from his father—would step into the spotlight and make it himself.

It was Harry, nonetheless, who saved the franchise for the Comiskeys first by convincing them that they had to install lights and then by working out the bank loan to pay for them. And I knew something that only a handful of people knew. Harry had saved the franchise for the family in 1941 after Lou Comiskey had died and left an almost bankrupt club to his widow. Nobody was in a better position to know about that one, because I was the guy he saved it from.

When I first began to look around for my own club after Boots Weber retired, I set my sights on the White Sox. Getting the backing I needed to buy a big-league team was nothing like the trouble I had finding one measly stockholder for Milwaukee. A syndicate of Chicago bankers was ready to put up all the money I needed. But I couldn't buy the White Sox because Mrs. Grace Comiskey went into court to prevent the bank from selling the club out from under her.

Lou Comiskey had provided in his will that Harry was to be retained for ten years at $25,000 a year, and although Harry could have had a better deal from me, he was loyal to Mrs. Comiskey. Then, five years after Lou Comiskey's death, word got to Harry that Mrs. Comiskey was unhappy with the provision that kept him at the head of the club. And so Grabiner, who had saved that franchise for the Comiskeys just as sure as God made little apples, said, "Gee, then I'd better leave." He packed up and left without asking for a penny of the $125,000 he was legally entitled to.

I have never found that kind of honor and loyalty to be in any great supply. This was the man I wanted with me as I set out to find myself a big-league team.

I had promised Oscar Salinger, the new owner of the Brewers, that I would put in an appearance in Milwaukee on opening day. With that as an excuse, I left the ranch in April and headed east. Actually, I was on the prowl for my team.

Taking first things first, I had to find out what teams might be available. For this information, I called on Louie Jacobs, who had run the concessions for me in Milwaukee. Louie has had a tremendous influence upon my subsequent career.

When I took over the Brewers, the club owed Louie something like $20,000. Trautman, in trying to help me get started, had asked Jacobs to cancel the debt, and Louis had done even more than that. Knowing that I had operated the concessions myself at Wrigley Field, he volunteered to cancel his contract.

I called Louie, whom I knew only casually, and asked if he really wanted to waive the debt and give up the concessions.

"Of course I don't want to," he said. "But I do want to see you make a go of this. Put it this way: I'm willing to."

84

"Well," I said, "that's nice of you but it's also a little silly. I'm not looking to run out on any debts, all I want is a little time. So if you'll give me time, I'll reinstate the debt and extend the contract."

Louie and I became close friends. And when Louie is your friend, he's your friend for life.

Because his concession business is the largest in baseball, Louie probably knows more about the internal struggles within clubs than anybody else in the country. He told me that Bill Benswanger of Pittsburgh wanted to sell, which came as no surprise. He also advised me that Cleveland could be had, and that *was* a surprise. Most people, even people close to baseball, were under the impression that Alva Bradley, the Indians' president, owned the club. He didn't. Bradley owned only a small percentage. The rest of the stock was owned by John and Francis Sherwin. This made for a most interesting situation, although not necessarily for Bradley.

I went to Chicago to let Harry Grabiner know I had a couple of possibilities staked out and, more to the point, that I had been very serious about wanting him in with me. "There's nothing I'd like better," he said. And then he added wistfully—and I'll never forget this—"I'd like to show the people in Chicago that I'm a good operator. You know, Bill, they don't think much of me in this town."

The next step was to get some financial backing. I went to see Phil Clarke, the president of the City National Bank of Chicago, the man who had been willing to put together a syndicate for me back when I had been trying to buy the White Sox.

Here was another case where I was cashing in on that legacy of affection everybody had for my father. Phil Clarke had been one of my daddy's closest friends, so close that the first thing I had done upon going to work for the Cubs had been to call Clarke and ask him to buy my father's old box. "I'd rather have you sitting in it," I told him, with absolute truth, "than anybody else." He still has that box to this day.

The other members of that shadow syndicate had been Phil Swift and Lester Armour of the meat-packing families. My Swift and Armour were both bankers.

At the same time, I was well aware that in the changing tax structure brought on by the war, men in their tax brackets were no longer interested in investments that brought them only dividends. Dividends are income and therefore taxable up to 91 percent. On the plane from Tucson, I had been trying to figure out some system of financing that would let them take their profits some other way.

This is one of the headaches of buying a ball club when you are always short-bankrolled, like me. It is also part of the fun. I enjoy the financial maneuvering and the backstage intrigue of putting a deal together. In my purchase of the Indians there was not one routine moment from the time Louie Jacobs tipped me off until the moment the deal was closed.

The stock plan I had worked out on the plane is what I call a debenture-common stock group. Instead of taking their investment solely in stock, my backers would get it 85 percent in debentures and 15 percent in stock.

A debenture is little more than a note. It is a loan which pays interest and is callable after a specified period of time. I was not proposing, let it be understood, the usual *convertible* debenture, which gives the holder the right to buy more stock at a later date at something close to the original price of issue. Quite the contrary. The attractiveness of my plan was based entirely upon the opportunity to put as little as possible into the stock and as much as possible into the debentures.

Suppose, now, you were investing $100,000 with me. By getting $85,000 of your investment in debentures, you would be paying only $15,000 for your stock. And yet, since everybody else was investing the same way, you would own just as great a percentage of the company as if you had received the whole $100,000 in stock. In effect, then, you would be buying $100,000 worth of stock for $15,000, a leverage of better than 6–1. (By means of a bank loan, as we shall see later, that leverage can be doubled.)

Now obviously, if we went bankrupt, you would lose your $100,000 and you wouldn't care less whether you had lost it as a loan or as an investment in stock. But if we succeeded, as we hoped to succeed, the debenture (the loan) would be bought up, you would have recovered almost all of your original investment and your $15,000 worth of stock would actually now be worth the full $100,000 on the open market. Assuming a real success, it would be worth even more. And if you sold that stock, your $85,000 profit would be taxed not as regular earnings, at a rate of up to 91 percent, but as a capital gain at a flat 25 percent rate.

I think there is one final point worth making here. The papers almost always refer to "my capital-gains bankers from Chicago," which implies they are in with me for a quick stock sale. I think you can see from this that the opposite is true; it's on the sale of the stock that the system begins to catch up with you. If you had invested $100,000 entirely in stock and had eventually sold the stock for $200,000, you would be paying 25 percent of a $100,000 profit, or

$25,000. By selling $15,000 worth of stock for $200,000, you show a profit of $185,000 and you have a tax bill of $46,250.

The debenture-stock grouping does not encourage you to sell, it encourages you to hold.

The first question you would ask, after I outlined this form of financing to you, would be, "Yeah, but will the Internal Revenue Bureau let you do it that way?"

That, at least, is the question my bankers asked. They had never heard of that kind of financing before either.

The lawyer I had hired to represent me was Sidney Schiff, who had been my father-in-law's attorney. Sidney, it developed, was also the attorney for the City National Bank, which made it all very cozy. Schiff had never heard of this kind of debenture-common stock grouping either—but upon careful study he gave us the opinion that it was perfectly legal and legitimate. The Bureau of Internal Revenue, in due time, agreed.

I still don't know whether I invented a financial gimmick or not. I do know that at the time, none of the bankers or lawyers in my group had ever heard of it. Today, it is in common use.

In addition to Swift and Armour, Clarke brought in Art Allyn, Sr., an investment broker who became not only a member of our syndicate but a close friend and benefactor. These were the men, along with Sidney Schiff and Newt Frye, another Chicago broker, who became the bulwark of every other baseball deal I have ever been in.

There was one other member of the syndicate, too: Bob Goldstein, who was then vice-president of Universal-International Pictures and is now head of 20th-Century Fox's international operation. Goldstein came in for $50,000 himself, but he also had a man—whose name I won't mention for reasons that will become apparent—who wanted in for $150,000.

All right, I'm faded. I had all the outside money I had been looking for, because I wanted to keep 30 percent of the club for myself, plus another 10 to 15 percent to distribute around among a dozen or so local people in either Cleveland or Pittsburgh. I am a strong believer in local representation in any enterprise, and particularly in one where you are dealing so directly with the public.

I could have bought Pittsburgh for something like $1,600,000. I toured around the city, I had Cliff Westcott come in to look over the park, I spoke to Benswanger's attorney. I found nothing to indicate that Pittsburgh had any particular potential at that time. When I moved on to Cleveland, I had already written Pittsburgh off.

I spent four days wandering around Cleveland. Most people, inter-

87

ested in a city's potential, go to the Chamber of Commerce and receive a lot of figures about hotel facilities and suburban growth. Which is fine if you want to open another hotel or grow some more suburbs.

I talk to cabdrivers and bartenders because these are the people who deal in conversation, the way a butcher deals in veal chops. They know how the average guy in town really feels about baseball, about the team and about the current operator. I would get into a cab, drive around for awhile talking to the driver and have him let me out at a tavern. I'd stand at the bar for awhile and talk some more. Then I'd get another cab to drive me to another tavern. I made from 100 to 150 stops this way in four days. I found there was enthusiasm about the team and utter disillusionment about the operation. I am telling quite a bit about Bradley's operation when I say that he was still not broadcasting his games because he felt, despite a mountain of evidence to the contrary, that radio would hurt his attendance. When I say that the Cleveland management still demanded that balls hit into stands be thrown back onto the field, I am saying it all.

As it happened, the National Open was being held at the Canterbury Club in Cleveland that same week. A playoff had to be held among Lloyd Mangrum, Vic Ghezzi and Byron Nelson on Sunday, and with the taverns all closed I went out, sat under a tree, and talked to anybody who happened along.

There was some risk in that. I was still in a walking cast and on crutches, which meant that to anyone who knew me I was readily identifiable at a distance of 50 yards. And I didn't want it known—particularly by newspapermen—that I was interested in buying the Indians. I didn't even want them to know I was in town.

We are back again to the intrigue of buying a club, and beyond that, to the special need for intrigue and secrecy in Cleveland. Ideally, both the buyer and the seller conduct the entire negotiations through representatives so that when the inevitable leak appears, both principals can say in all honesty, "I have not discussed the sale of the club with anyone."

The seller wants this protection so that he will not be placed in an embarrassing position—with almost everyone—if the deal falls through. The buyer wants it until he has been given an option and, in my special case, until he is sure he has enough money behind him to exercise the option.

There was a more pressing reason why I was just as happy if nobody on the sports beat knew I was in town. In Cleveland, I was confronted with the weird situation where Alva Bradley, the president, didn't know his club was for sale. I had a hunch I would be just as well off to let him wallow in happy ignorance until the last possible minute. Thus, upon coming to Cleveland, I registered in the hotel as Louis Edwards. Louis is my middle name, theoretically, although it usually comes as some surprise to me when I read about it. Edwards was just a name that came to the end of the pen as I was signing.

To complicate the Cleveland situation just a little more, Ben Fiery, the attorney for the Sherwins, was also the attorney for the American League.

Fiery quoted me a figure of $2,200,000.

"I'll buy it," I told him. "Now, will you give me an option, because I still have to straighten a few things out with my syndicate."

After Fiery consulted with the Sherwins, I put up $30,000 "earnest money" and was given a 30-day option.

Now we go back to the final lesson in purchasing a ball club on a short bankroll. My syndicate was not putting up the entire amount; I did not *want* them to put up the entire amount. To raise the full total, I had to borrow an even million dollars from the bank. Not a million dollars for me to invest personally in the club, understand, but a million dollars that the ball club itself—our company—would owe the bank.

Look at it from my point of view. I had around $250,000 to invest, every penny I could beg or borrow. I have always put up dollar-for-dollar with my backers, because I don't believe in asking a man to risk his money unless I'm willing to risk my own. Here is why the bank loan is so valuable, even though it means you are going to have to pay interest on a million dollars for awhile. If I had put up my $250,000 against the total purchase price of $2,200,000, I would own less than 12 percent of the company. But by borrowing a million, I am giving myself $250,000 of a $1,200,000 syndicate, and I have a fraction more than 20 percent.

Actually, I did better than that. For the work I do in putting together the syndicate, finding the club, borrowing the money and closing the deal, I take what amounts to a 10-percent finder's fee, *not* in the debentures but in the stock. Here, again, the debenture-stock grouping becomes important. Anybody with any capital-gains blood coursing through his veins should have already figured out that between the bank loan and the debentures, we had only $180,000 worth of stock in our new company. My finder's fee was not 10 percent of the whole deal, which would have been $220,000, but 10 percent of the stock, which is only $18,000. But as part of that same finder's fee, I was allowed to use that $18,000 to buy stock. Which meant that I invested a grand total of $268,000 and ended up with a fraction more than 30 percent of the stock.

I still had to borrow the million dollars. I couldn't borrow it from Phil Clarke's bank or from Armour's or Swift's banks, because it would be highly unethical for them to recommend a loan on a deal in which they were themselves financially involved. Bob Goldstein had a good friend, Chick Fisher, who was president of the National Bank of Detroit. Fisher, as the son-in-law of the Detroit Tiger's owner, Walter Briggs, had a working knowledge of the finances of a major-league baseball operation. Few bankers did.

Since I wanted to borrow the money from a Cleveland bank, if it were at all possible, I made it clear to Chick Fisher that I had come to him only to have somebody to fall back upon in the event the Cleveland banks got stuffy. Chick couldn't give me a definite answer. All he could do was tell me that he thought there was a good chance his bank would be willing to go for half the loan.

I went back to Cleveland—registering again as Louis Edwards—picked up the classified phone book and glanced down the bank listings. The nearest one to the hotel seemed to be the City National Bank. By dropping Phil Clarke's name nimbly into the conversation, I set up an appointment with the bank president for the same afternoon.

To set the scene as I walked into the City National Bank, I have to remind you that during this entire period I could get around—even with the crutches—only by wearing a walking cast on my leg. A walking cast differs from a regular light cast in that it has a metal support running up the leg. My great problem, without going into the medical details, was that I had an open infection underneath the cast. The odor of decay seeping out of that cast would get so bad that I could have hired myself out to clear any room within fifteen seconds.

I like people. I am a gregarious man. In order to maintain some kind of contract with my fellow man, I would walk around with little bottles of cologne in all my pockets. Having cut little holes into the knee of the cast I could empty the bottle of cologne down into the leg itself.

Out in the street, of course, this technique was a little more difficult, especially since the cast was so thick that the pant leg couldn't be pulled above the knee. When the situation showed signs of really becoming desperate, I would just flick the cologne down the side of my pants.

Remember also that I had been on the road for almost two months,

90

shuttling around between Pittsburgh, Cleveland, Detroit, Chicago, Buffalo and New York, living out of one little bag and flopping down in hotel rooms or trains. Under the best of circumstances, I am a casual dresser. Mary Frances, putting it a little more pungently, says that when I really get dressed up I look as if I've forgotten my pants.

Now you have the picture of what I looked like as I swung into the bank on my crutches—one leg bulging from the walking cast, the side of my rumpled pants slightly moist from the cologne.

I informed the secretary, a neatly groomed, pretty but rather stiff-faced young lady seated in front of the president's door, that I had an appointment. As she stared at me, in my rumpled clothes and somewhat frazzled open-necked sport shirt, it became readily apparent that she was one of those secretaries who identifies herself completely with her boss's position and status. If a kangaroo had hopped up to her desk and asked to see the president she could not have been more incredulous.

"I'm sure," she said, "you have made a mistake."

"Well, no," I said. "I think this is the right bank. Mr. Sidney Congden."

She weakened enough to ask me my name.

"Veeck," I said, rhyming it—accurately in all possible regards here —with "wreck."

Her whole world brightened. "No," she said, glancing up from her appointment book, "I knew you didn't have an appointment. He has an appointment with Mr. Veeck"—rhyming it, with visible pleasure, with "sleek."

"That's me," I said.

For a while there, I didn't think she was going to announce me, appointment or no. She turned out to be a very nice girl, though, and, in the end, quite helpful.

In the taxi, on the way to the bank, I had jotted a few figures down on the back of an envelope to show how much more business I was going to do with my aggressive and imaginative promoting. Since the Indians had almost broken even the previous year with an attendance of less than 400,000, I had projected the profits from this marvelous attendance to show how quickly I would be able to repay the loan.

It was all pretty general and pretty vague. In addition to the figures on my envelope, plus my non-negotiable hopes and dreams, I had only my experience as a successful minor-league operator and the solid financial backgrounds of my backers to recommend me. I was also able to pass on the information, for what it was worth, that there was a good chance Chick Fisher up in Detroit would be willing to take half the loan.

My backers proved to be a mixed blessing. Congden wanted to know if I could give him, as a reference, the name of any banker I had ever actually done business with, preferably one who wasn't going to be a partner.

There was only Mr. Weinhold up in Milwaukee.

Congden asked me if I wanted to step out of the room while he talked to him.

"Look," I said, "there's no reason for me to leave. I know what you're going to ask him. Mr. Weinhold is a nice, honorable man; he'll tell you the truth as he sees it. If he doesn't give me a good count, I'll get up and leave quietly."

Congden got him on the phone, and all at once I'm wondering what Weinhold did think of me and my Milwaukee operation. Most especially, I am wondering whether he knew anything at all about my broken-field running among the Chicago loan companies.

When Congden hung up he looked a little bewildered. What Mr. Weinhold had told him, as passed on to me, was roughly this: "Five years ago, this fellow came to me with a harebrained scheme. If he's in there with another of his harebrained schemes, I'd like to get in on it again. We're just a little bank up here but I'll go as far as the bank can go with him and if there's anything left over I'd like to take a piece of his play myself." Speaking for himself, Congden went on, "I suppose I should have told you that I know Weinhold. Weinhold is a *very* conservative banker. Even for Milwaukee he's a conservative banker. I can't imagine Weinhold lending any money on a thing like this, let alone taking . . . 'a piece of your play.'"

Checking with Chick Fisher, he became slightly more bewildered. Chick had asked him to pass the word to me that his loan committee had approved the full million. He had then told Congden that he knew I wanted to borrow the money in Cleveland but that if Congden didn't want it all he'd like to have half of it up in Detroit.

Congden studied the figures on the back of my envelope for awhile, drumming his fingers on the desk. "Mr. Veeck," he said, finally. "If these figures are right, we'll go along with you. I think we can manage the whole loan ourselves." And then, bubbling over, he chuckled, "You know, I think it will be kind of fun."

I have never worried about bankers since. I may occasionally find it difficult to borrow a thousand or two for myself but I know I'll never have any trouble borrowing a million or two to buy a ball club.

Congden had access to the Cleveland books right there in the bank.

He called his loan committee into session on the spot. Two hours after I walked into the bank with my envelope, I walked out with my million dollars.

I had all the money I needed to exercise my option. It would have been easy . . . if it had been that easy.

Until I had the bank loan, I had maintained a rather uneasy anonymity. On my second trip into Cleveland, I had let the hotel manager know I was registered under a false name, just so he'd have some prior knowledge in the event I was breaking a law. I was. He was quite upset about it, but he agreed, when I explained the reason, to go along with me. The same afternoon, though, a New York sportswriter called the hotel, asked for Bill Veeck and was put right through to my room.

"No," I said, "if you check the register, you'll see my name is Louis Edwards, and I'm in the farm machinery business. I've come for the convention here."

"Well, we think you're Bill Veeck," he said.

"The baseball man Veeck? Hey, that's wonderful. It will give me something to tell everyone when I get home. This stuff is too high, the farm machinery, and I'm not buying any. But it will be wonderful to be able to go home and tell this story."

Nothing was printed, and I never heard from New York again.

Alva Bradley's early denials were even more convincing since he, of course, really believed them. Now, with the bank loan secured, I wasn't worried about secrecy any more. It seemed a good idea, in fact, to let the publicity start building until the day I exercised the option and took over officially.

Bradley was furious when he learned about the option. To his dying day, he felt I had betrayed him, an attitude I found rather curious since I hardly even knew him.

Our option gave us until 11 A.M., June 22, to raise the money. With the City National Bank now guaranteeing a million of it, it was agreed that the full amount would be deposited with them. Bradley promptly formed a syndicate of his own and was given an option to buy the Indians at 11:01 A.M. if, for some reason, I didn't exercise mine.

Nothing to worry about there. All the Chicago people had already deposited their certified checks. Bob Goldstein was coming in personally with his $50,000 and his friend's $150,000.

One of the stipulations Ben Fiery had made, in giving me the option, was that I was to submit my list of stockholders for approval. At five o'clock on the evening of June 21, 18 hours before the option ran out, Ben called to tell me that his $150,000 friend was a man of questionable character and therefore not acceptable. To this day, I don't know whether Fiery was calling as attorney for the Sherwins or for the league. At the time, it couldn't have mattered less. I had to go out and raise $150,000, one way or the other, by eleven the next morning and I was in the ridiculous position where, in the literal sense of the old cliché, I didn't have one minute to spare.

I called Louie Jacobs in Buffalo and told him the predicament I was in. Because Louie runs the concessions for so many clubs, he had a standing rule—and a wise and necessary one—against investing in any ball club. "Anyway," he said, "I know I wouldn't be able to transmit the money from my bank to yours that fast. You're going to have to get the money in Cleveland."

That gave him an idea. Through his race track concessions, he knew a wealthy Cleveland attorney named Sammy Haas who he thought would help me. "The only thing," Louie said, "is that he's kind of a character. He's represented all the hoodlums and gamblers in Cleveland. I'm sure he can't show on this thing. If they didn't approve the other guy, you can bet they won't approve him. The only way he can do it is to lend the money to you."

"Louie," I said, "I don't have eight cents' worth of security. I've already hocked everything I could lay my hands on to get up my end of the money."

Louie gave me Haas' address, anyway, and told me to get into a cab and go right out there. I was let out in front of a small mansion in Shaker Heights. Haas was a small, thin man, small enough, probably, to have been a jockey. He was handsome for such a little man, though, with a thick, well-groomed head of graying hair. In my years in Cleveland, I would learn that he was a brilliant lawyer and, as Louie had said, a notorious and controversial figure. If Sammy Haas sneezed in public, the papers reported a raging hurricane.

"I know why you're here," Sammy Haas told me. "Louie asked me to call him back as soon as you arrived."

Once again I found myself listening in on the silent side of a phone conversation. This was a brief one. "Louie says you're OK," Haas said. "That's good enough for me."

He was lending me $150,000 for forty-eight hours; no security, no interest, no questions, no nothing.

I arrived at Haas' bank at nine the next morning, as he had instructed, and found him waiting there. He drew a cashier's check for $150,000. "My advice," he said, "is to take this into another bank, cash it, and draw another cashier's check on that bank. Then go to a third bank and do the same thing. That way, there won't be any chance of having the money traced back to me."

While I was going into the second bank, Hal Lebovitz, who was then with the Cleveland *News,* spotted me and tagged along. Lebovitz became a sportswriter soon afterwards but he was then, I think, just a general reporter. He walked the rest of the way with me, along the wet sidewalk of a cool, clearing morning, wondering what in the world I was doing running in and out of banks.

I had other things to worry about. I still didn't have all my money.

Right after Fiery had given me his happy news, I had called Bob Goldstein in New York. Bob immediately began to assure me that he was flying into Cleveland first thing in the morning with his $150,000 friend's check and his own. I told him to forget his guy but to be sure to get in early because we had no leeway at all on our option.

Early in the morning, Goldstein had called from the New York airport to tell me the morning flights to Cleveland had been canceled. The Cleveland airport was socked in. "But don't worry," he said. "I've got a flight to Detroit, and I'm arranging to charter a plane there to get into Cleveland. If the airport opens up at all, I'll be there."

At about 10 o'clock, I arrived at the City National Bank, bade Lebovitz good-bye and went in. No Goldstein. I deposited my $150,-000 and sat down to sweat it out.

Although Bradley wasn't at the bank himself, he had a couple of his lawyers stationed there as observers. They were standing by, in a bored, routine way, waiting for me to exercise my option so they could get back to work.

All at once, there was a quickening of tension, so sharp you could feel it, as they became aware that I was still short a lousy $50,000 and quite obviously waiting for it to arrive. The clock on the wall suddenly became very popular.

I can remember watching that clock until about 10:30 when someone called from the airport—the pilot, I suppose—to say that Goldstein was on his way. After that? I tell you, Judge, everything went black.

If Goldstein didn't make it on time, I was not only going to lose the Indians, I was going to look like the world's biggest jerk. The sportswriters were already in Ben Fiery's office, just across the street, waiting for the routine announcement that I had bought the team, a story they had been printing for three days. If Bradley walked into that room as the new owner instead of me and explained that, after all the publicity, I didn't really have the money, I would be marked as a fourflusher for the rest of my life. To make my morning complete,

95

I would also forfeit my $30,000 "earnest money," all the cash I happened to have in the world.

I was brought out of these gentle reveries, I suppose, by the sound of a cavalry charge from a Universal sound track, as Bob Goldstein—in a scene any of his movie companies would have been ashamed to use—came galloping into the office at five minutes to eleven. I could hear the bugles sound as he turned a black satchel over on Congden's desk; I could see the flag whipping gloriously in the breeze as $50,000 in American-type cash money—nicely greened—came pouring out. There had been a delay in chartering the plane out of Detroit and, to play it safe, Bob had dashed into Chick Fisher's bank to have his check cashed.

We strolled across to Ben Fiery's office in the Union Commerce Building and made the announcement everyone had known was coming.

"Well," I said, after all the questions had been asked, "let's go to the ball yard."

Ed McAuley of the *Cleveland News* drove Harry Grabiner and me to League Park. I started up toward the second deck to mingle with the fans, and a steady wave of applause moved behind me. One big guy jumped up and slapped me on the back. "This is the best darned thing," he yelled, "that has ever happened to this town."

That's how it went in Cleveland from Day One. A crowd of 19,000 came out to see the game the next night. The night and Sunday games were played in the big Municipal Stadium (capacity 78,000) and on our first Sunday we drew 57,720, the second largest Cleveland crowd in five years.

Sammy Haas was in no hurry to get back his $150,000. The problem of piecing together a neat, workmanlike cross-section of the business community seemed to intrigue him. Since he knew the city about as well as anybody, he recommended a few of the people he thought I should approach. That was as far as he would go, though. He wouldn't even arrange the introductions, because he felt that any involvement with him could only hurt me.

I used to stop off in his office every once in awhile just to talk, because he had a brilliant mind. He was probably the best-read man I ever knew, and he loved to discuss literature. One day, as we broke off some discussion that had us both excited, I said, "Why don't you have dinner with me tonight and come down and watch the ball game?"

And he said something that seemed very sad to me. "Look," he said. "I wouldn't want to hurt you. I'm *persona non grata* with the

96

people of this town. I've associated with hoodlums and I've got their mark on me. That's all right. I knew what I was doing and why I was doing it, and I'll live with the consequences. But I'm not coming down there with you and louse up your action."

Well, if there's one thing I'll do, I'll pick my own friends. I associated with a lot of hoodlums in Cleveland myself before I was through. But nothing I could say could change Sammy's mind. If he ever came to see a game, he must have bought his ticket at the window and sat off by himself.

Dinner with Boudreau | 6.

WE HAD two great players at Cleveland, Bob Feller, the best pitcher in baseball, and Lou Boudreau, the best shortstop. Problems we had aplenty. My first problem was that the best shortstop in baseball was, in my opinion, not the best manager, an opinion that was not greatly altered by a close, intimate and—as it turned out—unbreakable association in Cleveland.

There were never any personal difficulties between Lou and me, to set that matter straight. I liked Louie. I still like Louie. Louie was a nice, amiable boy who had walked into the Cleveland front office at the age of twenty-four and asked if he could become their new manager. At twenty-eight, he was still a faintly bewildered Boy Manager. The team I inherited was in sixth place; I thought Lou should have had them higher.

My main objection to Lou was that he managed by hunch and desperation. You ask Casey Stengel why he made a certain move and he will tell you about a roommate he had in 1919 who had demonstrated some principle Casey was now putting into effect. You ask Lou and he will say, "The way we're going, we had to do *something*." If there is a better formula for making a bad situation worse, I have never heard of it.

I particularly wanted to get Louie out of the manager's office because I had Casey Stengel waiting in the wings, ready to sign.

My past relationship with Casey, such as it was, went back to Milwaukee. This is a story I can sometimes tell, if I have had a particularly good day, without blushing.

Before I left for the Marines, at the end of the 1943 season, I talked to Jim Gallagher about hiring Charlie Grimm back as manager of the Cubs. Charlie had just won a pennant for us, and I felt that maybe he was back in fashion. Jim didn't think Phil Wrigley would even consider it, though, and so when I went into the service Charlie was still my manager.

I had given my power of attorney to both Rudie Schaffer and Louie Jacobs and, with ballplayers becoming extinct, had asked Jim Gallagher to keep an eye on the roster and help us out where he could.

The scene now shifts to a naval hospital on Guadalcanal, the following summer. There comes to my bed one loose page ripped from the overseas edition of *Time* magazine. As I glance down the items I am brought up sharply by one little paragraph—one little sentence really —which says that Charlie Grimm has just lost his first game as manager of the Chicago Cubs.

My mental processes from that point are almost impossible to explain logically because, after all, I had asked the Cubs to hire Charlie and I am sure I must have been happy to learn that he was back in the big leagues. I can only point out that I was flat on my back, with one leg so badly injured that the doctors were trying to get my permission to amputate and the other leg being slowly eaten away by jungle fungus. Back in the States, I had a wife and three children. Take away my ball club and I was a pauper. I was frightened and doing my best not to show it.

All my fears, all of that bottled-up rage about what had happened to me, focused at that moment—I suppose—upon that notice in the magazine. To lie in bed and cry out against fate isn't very satisfactory. The historical events that had dumped me there were impersonal and imponderable. What is fate to me or me to fate? But to ask what Jim Gallagher was doing to me . . . ahh, that's getting it down to where it can be handled.

Gallagher had told me he wasn't going to take Charlie, hadn't he? Then as soon as my back was turned he had grabbed him. Who was managing my ball team? I don't know how close you can come to the narrow edge without falling off, but I swung awful close. I saw a plot to ruin me.

Thinking these things was bad enough. I went ahead and did what I regret more than anything I have ever done in baseball. I wrote Jim Gallagher a cruel and stupid letter, which opened: "I asked you as a friend to help me. If you think you are helping me by stealing my manager, then I am now asking you to stop helping me forthwith. . . ."

It was a letter filled with nicely rounded insults and sarcasms. If there were intimations that I was writing as one of the fighting troops

98

overseas who had been betrayed by civilians, so much the better. It was an injudicious letter, a most unfair, unkind and unforgivable letter.

Jim never answered. He is such an honest, conscientious guy that he was wounded very deeply. I know that he still had that letter in his desk when I got home.

When my mail caught up to me, there was a letter from Rudie explaining that Charlie had been given a chance to go back up with the Cubs and that our new manager was Casey Stengel. In the same mail were letters from both Red Smith and Mickey Heath telling me that Stengel was a bum.

Naturally, I whipped off another letter, accusing Rudie of being in on the plot. I wrote him that Stengel was an incompetent and a clown, and that I didn't want him around any team of mine. I wrote that Stengel was a second-division manager who was entirely satisfied to have a losing ball club as long as Stengel and his wit were appreciated. "If you have given him an iron-clad contract," I wrote, "I suppose you'll have to keep him. But next year I want him out."

I did hear from Rudie. He wrote me a sharp, angry letter, letting me know that Stengel had come to Milwaukee only as a personal favor to Grimm, because Charlie had not wanted to leave unless they found a replacement—like Stengel—who would fit into our free-and-easy, clowning operation. He wrote that I was not only being unfair but that I was being stupid because Stengel was doing the greatest job of managing he had ever seen and was undoubtedly on his way to winning a pennant for me and setting an attendance record.

Before the season ended, I was shipped to the naval hospital at Corona, California. I set up an office beside my bed, had a telephone installed—which took some doing—and swung back into action. Immediately, it became apparent even to me that Stengel was doing a remarkable job. He not only won a pennant for me, he sold 15 players, undoubtedly a record in itself, and for outrageously high prices.

At the end of the season, Rudie called to tell me that Casey wasn't going to return the next season because he felt he was in an impossible situation. Great. Now I wanted Casey and he apparently didn't want any part of me.

Casey lives in Glendale, which is not too far from Corona. I asked him to come down to see me before he signed with anybody else. I admitted that I had written a most unfortunate letter in which I had said some very unkind things about him, but that I wanted him to know that I was well aware how wrong I had been.

The first thing Casey told me when he appeared was that my letter had nothing to do with his decision. He was leaving, he said, partly because there were a couple of guys who were sharpshooting—meaning Red Smith and Mickey Heath—but mostly because he just couldn't seem to get along with Sam Levy. I said, "Casey, I'll square Sam Levy, and the others don't make any difference. I'd appreciate it if you'd reconsider."

But Casey wanted out. Nevertheless, he visited me a couple of times afterwards, just to try to cheer me up. His own leg had been broken a couple of years earlier when he was hit by a taxi in Boston, and he would roll up his pants and show me how well he was able to manipulate his knee and ankle.

My first action after getting the option on the Indians had been to call Stengel in Oakland to offer him a job. "You can be a vice-president," I said, "or you can stay in the wings ready to take over as manager, or maybe we can work out something with Boudreau and you'll be able to take over as manager right away."

Casey didn't want anything to do with the front office and he didn't want to be put in the position of breathing over Boudreau's shoulder. "But," he said, "if you can work it out so I come in as manager right away; well, you know, there's still nothing like the big leagues."

The night after I took over the Indians, Lou had dinner with Harry and me at our suite in the Cleveland Hotel. In those 24 hours, I had already managed to lose all the initiative by letting the writers know that we were thinking about a new manager. (Harry had a candidate of his own, Jimmy Dykes.) It was made clear to me, in short order, that Lou was so popular in Cleveland that if I traded him away, I would have the whole city down on my neck.

There is almost no such a thing, I have found, as an untouchable player. When you trade a long-time favorite, the writers find kind words for such forgotten virtues as sentiment and loyalty and speak most darkly about front-office ingratitude. Three days later, they are back to telling the manager how to run the ball club. The fans vow never to enter the park again; a few zealots even picket the park carrying banners proclaiming their unyielding purpose. The next time the Yankees are in town for a Sunday doubleheader, they're all there pleading for two tickets behind first base.

But trading as popular a player as Boudreau as my first move in a new town would be something else again. Ill-will, created at the very beginning of any operation, is ruinous. Long after everybody had forgotten Boudreau, that first hostile impression would persist. I would be running the risk, in other words, of being perennially attacked for other reasons, on other grounds.

100

The only thing we could hope to do was to get Louie to step down voluntarily. Fat chance. Louie was holding all the cards and he knew it. He knew that if I came right out and said, "You can play for us but not manage," I'd be running the risk of his answering, "If I'm not going to manage, I won't play for you." He knew as well as I did that I couldn't afford to put either myself or the club in that position.

Let me put one story to rest. I never offered him more money if he would step down; that would have been the ultimate insult. I must admit, however, that Lou could have made me very happy by coming up with that kind of proposition himself.

It was funny, in a bumbling sort of way. I somehow managed to swing the dinner conversation to the mixed feelings baseball men seemed to have about how great a strain was placed upon a player-manager, pitching the whole discussion, needless to say, on a high philosophical plane. Most experts, I felt called upon to point out, seemed to feel that a fellow couldn't really play his best when he was managing. Harry, out of his long experience in the league, observed—purely in the spirit of scientific inquiry—that, yes, he had to go along with the majority on that one. I, citing my own meager experience in the minors, had to agree that, yes, the strain did tell. "And you're the greatest shortstop I've ever seen," I told Lou, as if the thought had just occurred to me. "It would be a shame, you know, if your duties as a manager diminished that." The last thing in the world I wanted, you know, was to see his playing hurt.

And all the time I was chattering away, all of us knew that Louie was making incredible plays at shortstop every day. The trouble, as far as I was concerned, was that his incredible playing wasn't doing a thing for his managing.

Lou was willing enough to play it our way. If philosophy was what we wanted, philosophy was what we would get. Lou observed thoughtfully that while he himself hadn't found managing to be any great strain —had in fact found it to be quite stimulating—yes, he could see where there were *some* playing managers who might be affected.

I have always believed that once you see you are going to lose, it is just as well to lose gracefully. About the time dessert was being served, I was saying, "Well, I want you to know that we certainly want you to stay on as our manager. We've got all the confidence in the world in you, Louie old boy."

That mission neatly unaccomplished, I remained on for the big Sunday doubleheader the following day and then went to Lakeside Hospital to get the infection in my leg cleaned up.

For the next week, the hospital room became my office. We shined and polished the ball park. We set up the speaking engagements. We started to promote. Will Harridge, upon welcoming me into the American League, had let me know he expected great things in Cleveland, "But, of course, you're going to cut out the gags." My backers were, frankly, quite pleased that I had Harry Grabiner at my side as a restraining influence.

Everybody agreed that "the bush stuff" I had pulled in Milwaukee, like giving away livestock, would never go in Cleveland. So I gave away livestock in Cleveland and the fans were delighted. All the theories and the stunts that had been tested in Milwaukee were put to work in Cleveland and proved to be just as successful.

People are people. Coca-Cola doesn't change its advertising from town to town. I don't change my promotion. Housewives don't protest violently if their butcher throws in a soupbone with a pound of chuck. It's possible that they are even pleased. Nor do students stone the park and chant anti-baseball slogans because you throw in some free entertainment with the ball game.

There were a few front-office details that had to be taken care of. I don't believe in firing anybody. Given no evidence to the contrary, I am always willing to assume that the man who has been doing the job knows at least as much about it as anyone I could bring in to replace him. Instead, I raised everybody's salary 10 percent.

The doors came off my office. I put in a direct telephone line—and advertised the number—so that anyone who wanted to call could get me direct without any nonsense about switchboards or screenings. The fans and the press were informed that there would never be a D.A. (Don't Disturb) on my home phone. Day or night. I always knew where I could get the press if I wanted them; I could never see why they weren't entitled to the same privilege. If a drunk or two called in the early-morning hours, well, that was one of the occupational risks. A drunk has to be pretty interested in the team to call at three in the morning.

There was the matter, too, of wrenching Cleveland baseball out of the Harding era. Ladies' Day was reinstated. There being no radio contract, I invited all the stations to broadcast any of our games, in part or *in toto*. "If you get them sponsored," I told them, "pay me what you think a fair proportion."

Players came and went on the familiar three-team shuttle. Having assumed control a week after the trading deadline, there were no important deals I could make. I could make good, however, on promises I had made to eight of my old Milwaukee players to give them a shot at the majors.

To show how flexible our roster was, one of my old Milwaukee pitchers, Joe Berry, landed at the Cleveland airport well after the game had started, came to the park, put on his uniform, went in to pitch in extra innings and got the hit that won the game.

With a sixth-place team, our only publicity asset was Bob Feller. I wanted Bob to make a run at the strikeout record, which meant he would have to start every fourth day and remain in the game even when he was being hit very hard. Bob was more than willing. He broke the record on the last day of the season by starting with only two days' rest. While he was at it, he won 26 games for a team that won only 68 games all season.

When we took over the Indians with the season almost half over, the club had drawn only 289,000 people. At the end of the season, in a city that had never reached a million attendance in its history, the figure was 1,052,289.

At the end of the year, the Cleveland baseball writers voted me Man of the Year for their Ribs and Roast banquet—the first of what was to become an annual award. Excerpts from a couple of the skits will pretty well explain both the operation and its impact. In this first skit, the writer portraying me was Jack Clowser:

McAULEY: Oh, hello, Mr. Veeck. We were just wondering about a big story for tomorrow.

VEECK: Just call me Bill. Or Old Will. I've got a great story for you. I also have sandwiches and something to drink in the press room.

ALL: What's the story?

VEECK: I've traded Bob Feller.

ALL: Traded Feller!

COBBLEDICK: What did you get for him, Bill? Williams, Hughson and Ferris?

VEECK: Better than that! What a trade! Best I ever made. You fellows got your typewriters hot?

ALL: (*poised at typewriters*) Go ahead. Shoot.

VEECK: (*triumphantly, after dramatic pause*) I have traded Feller for the biggest damned cannon cracker in the world.

The other skit went like this:

DOYLE: What's the battery tonight, Barnum and Bailey?

LEWIS: I thought Feller was going to pitch.

DOYLE: He goes Sunday. Feller starts against the Tigers in the first. We play a herd of elephants in the second.

Every Day Was Mardi Gras... | 7.

THE second year in Cleveland, the Indians moved up to fourth place and drew 1,521,978 people. In 1948, we won the pennant and drew 2,620,627, still the all-time attendance record despite the Dodgers' move to Los Angeles with a ready-made team and a coliseum which could accommodate over 100,000 people. And in 1949, my last year in Cleveland, we drew 2,333,871.

The best way to tell you what we did to draw these crowds is to tell you what we did not do. We did not open the ticket windows and expect the citizenry to come rushing up with their money in their fists. We have never operated on the theory that a city owes anything to the owner of a baseball franchise, out of civic pride, patriotic fervor or compelling national interest. Baseball has sold itself as a civic monument for so long that it has come to believe its own propaganda. *There is nothing owed to you.* A baseball team is a commercial venture, operating for a profit. The idea that you don't have to package your product as attractively as General Motors packages its product, and hustle your product the way General Motors hustles its product, is baseball's most pernicious enemy.

Look at Horace Stoneham. Stoneham had the best franchise in the National League. He had, potentially, the best drawing card in Willie Mays. He was in New York, the center of the communications industry. What did he do about it? He not only refused to go two steps out of his way to sell his team, he resisted the publicity that was being thrust upon him. In the end, he picked up his franchise and moved to San Francisco, indignant because his attendance had fallen.

The feudal barons of old used to throw their garbage on the floor and keep covering it over until the stench became so unbearable that they had to move on to another castle. The feudal barons of baseball are becoming castle-hoppers. When the Polo Grounds began to fall apart, Stoneham moved on to his new windblown castle by the sea. And Stoneham is one of the few owners in baseball who has no outside interests and therefore might be expected to pay more attention to the only wheel he has spinning for him.

104

In Cleveland, we did not open the windows and wait. We drew our crowds in the following unheroic, sweaty ways:

1. We gave them a lot of fun and a lot of entertainment.
2. I hit the chautauqua trail, making as many as 500 speeches a year.
3. We built a winning team.

Between doubleheaders, we had shows featuring colorful and dramatic fireworks displays and circus acts. The philosophy behind this is simple. I have always loved fireworks and circus acts. My tastes, I have found, are so average that anything that appeals strongly to me is probably going to appeal to most of the customers. The first night game after we got our license, we had fireworks displays showing a flame-eating pelican, two planes in a dogfight and, finally, a plane sinking a battleship in a thrilling encounter at sea. At least, the plane was supposed to sink the battleship. Something got fouled up in the inner working and—this is the truth—the battleship pulled a complete upset on us and knocked down the plane. Ah well, the fortunes of war.

The next week, we had a night for Lefty Weisman, the Indians' long-time and very popular trainer. To show our affection and high regard for Lefty we presented him with five thousand silver dollars in a wheelbarrow. The highlight of the evening came when we wished him godspeed and told him to pick up his loot and take it away. Lefty grabbed the handles eagerly and shoved. The wheelbarrow shoved right back. Five thousand silver dollars, as we well knew, have about the same tonnage as a light destroyer. A tow truck was under the stands, waiting for the signal to come out and take it away.

We had something going almost every day, for in our three and a half years in Cleveland every day was Mardi Gras and every fan was king. We even had two "house acts," Max Patkin and Jackie Price, both of them ex-players of mine. Patkin had been a pretty good pitcher for Green Bay when it was a farm club of Milwaukee. It is easy enough to describe Max. He is a hawk-faced, long-nosed, crane-necked, rubber-boned scarecrow. Describing his act is something else again; you had to be there. The best way to start is to come right out and admit that Max's bones were not attached to his body. Max had undoubtedly come in one of those put-it-together-yourself cartons, like a kid's bicycle, and someone had misread the diagram and neglected to put a few of those washers (A) and locknuts (B) into screw (C).

The first time I saw Max he was pitching for Green Bay. As a matter of fact, he pitched a shutout that day. All of a sudden, as he was winding up, his arms began to twist around like pretzels, his front shoulder shot up so high into the atmosphere that his head was completely obliterated and, in strict defiance of all laws of anatomy and maybe even of gravity, his hips went jutting out halfway to third base. Everybody roared, the players included, and you could see that this was what they had been waiting for. When he got on base, he really went into his act. It began with a sort of stiff-jointed eccentric dance as he took his lead off the base. When the pitcher tried to pick him off, Max rose up on his toes, his neck came rising out of his body in a gentle swanlike curve and, with his elbows pressed in against his skinny body, he went pitter-pattering back to the base in quick, tiny steps. Once back on the base, he took another hitch on his spinal column and dropped his head over the umpire's shoulder to read the decision. It was the funniest thing I had ever seen on a ball field.

At the time I was buying the Indians, Max was just getting out of the Navy. He had broken his pitching arm before he went in, and he really couldn't pitch any more, but I sent him down to our farm club in Wilkes-Barre, ostensibly as a pitcher but actually with instructions to polish up his act, the only time a clown was ever sent to the minors for seasoning.

Max would coach an inning or two for us, when we finally brought him up. The keener intellects among the Old Guard were naturally enraged at having a clown actually appear on the field during the play of the game—although Max's qualifications to coach first were as good as anybody else's. After all, the only thing a first-base coach has to do is . . . let's see, there must be *something* he has to do.

The one thing that bothered me about Max was that he had a touch of the gutter in him. If he wasn't getting the laughter he expected, his contortions would begin to border on the obscene. The first season we had him with us, I'd always watch him like a hawk. As soon as he began to drift toward bad taste, I'd bellow out: "Noooooooo, Max, noooooo!"

The umpires viewed him with mixed emotions. They couldn't stop themselves from laughing at him, and yet they had to keep an eye on him because he was the only man who could dispute a call with a twitch of a muscle. After one of our boys had been called out on strikes, Max would sometimes topple over on his back, as rigidly as a falling tree, as if he were fainting from the shock of it all. He once arose to find big Cal Hubbard bearing down on him to throw him out of the game, and that can be a shock. What made it tough for Max was that the umpire on first base would sometimes be saying, "Come on, Max, do that backward fall before you go," while the umpire-in-chief was scowling down to warn him off—one of the rare instances of dissension among that tightly knit brotherhood of blue-suited trade unionists.

Patkin and Jackie Price are usually associated together in the public mind because I brought them to Cleveland at about the same time and frequently used them, you might say, on the same bill. There is no similarity. Patkin is a comic, and Price is an artist.

Jackie Price was playing shortstop for Milwaukee when I came out of the service. I would get to the park early in the morning, look out the window and there would be Jackie practicing the most phenomenal kind of tricks. Not tricks really, either; feats of skill. Jackie would be playing catch—catching and throwing—while standing on his head. He would install a portable trapeze set in the batter's box, hang down by his knees and hit a pitched ball. He could place two catchers side by side and, in one motion, throw a fast ball to one of them and a curve to the other. He could stand at home plate and, again in the same motion, throw one ball to the pitcher's mound and the other to second base. He could stagger three fellows a few feet apart and, in that one motion, throw a different ball to each of them.

Sometimes he would be bouncing over the outfield in a jeep. Jackie would shoot a baseball out of a pneumatic tube, go driving after it and with split-second timing, reach out and catch it backhanded while the jeep was somehow looking out for itself.

Like all artists, he sacrificed all to his art. With all the incredible things he could do, Jackie's hands were always so badly bruised and battered from that constant practicing that he had trouble doing the one thing he was getting paid for, fielding simple ground balls cleanly.

I was so impressed with Price from the first that I tried to get Detroit to hire him to perform in the 1945 World Series. Hank Oana, whom I had sold to the Tigers, had got them into the Series with his pinch-hitting and I was naïve enough to think that entitled me to ask for a favor. Instead, the Tigers hired Al Schacht, known as "The Clown Prince of Baseball." Baseball is soaked in tradition—I might even say it is pickled in tradition—and one of the most inviolate of these traditions seems to be that baseball humor has to be unfunny. This has enabled Schacht to last a long time.

I promised Jackie then that I'd get him into the big leagues as a player and a World Series performer both. That, at least, was one promise I kept. At the end of that first season at Cleveland, I brought him up and asked Lou to let him play our last few games at short. Jackie even managed a couple of base hits.

Like Patkin, Jackie had his idiosyncracies. One of them brought his playing career with the Indians to a slithering halt. Everybody needs relaxation, right? Some people like golf; Jackie Price liked snakes. He liked his snakes so much that he used to wear them around his waist like a belt. Jackie was one of the most identifiable men I have ever known; I mean, he was the one with the snake around his waist.

Joe Gordon came to us in 1947, and Joe has to be on anybody's all-time, all-star team of agitators. If I had to put in time on a desert island I can think of no one I'd rather have along than Joe, because even on a desert island he would always find a few ways to keep the hours dancing along.

Well, Joe could see at once that there were untapped potentialities in a man who wore snakes as an accessory to his wardrobe. Right from the beginning of spring training, they became fast friends. And just as well, too, because Jackie didn't remain in camp forever. The club was on a train to make an exhibition game in California. In the diner with them were some women bowlers. Jackie was eating his grapefruit happily; the snake around his waist was resting comfortably, content with his life of usefulness and ease and the knowledge that he was loved. The women bowlers were chattering about nudging the 7 pin into the 10 pin and such other matters as delight the feminine heart.

All that peace was too much for Gordon to take. He suggested to Jackie that it might be interesting to let the snake loose down the aisle. Which Jackie did. Women bowlers began to leap onto the tables and race screaming down the aisle. Men, to put it delicately, lost their appetites. The conductor, following the snake back to its source, grabbed Jackie and demanded to know his name. Jackie quite naturally told him his name was Lou Boudreau and politely requested that he be unhanded.

At the next station, Louie's peaceful card game was interrupted by a couple of beefy detectives who informed him they were about to throw him off the train. The secret word, of course, was "snakes." Once that word was uttered, Lou was able to convince them he was not their man. The next thing I knew, I had received a wire from Lou that he was sending Price and his pets home. I shipped Jackie down to South America, a far happier climate—for the snakes if not for Jackie—while Lou cooled off.

Many of the best gags come out of some purely external situation. Once you're thinking along those lines it becomes easy to latch on to them. By the second year in Cleveland, we had moved all our games into Municipal Stadium, which had been a huge white elephant to the city from the time of its construction. Just as the season was getting

108

underway, the stadium was also leased to a politically strong group which was going to promote midget auto racing. I began to scream. The reason I gave for not wanting the midget racers in there was that the track they were building cut right across the outfielders' positions in both left field and right field and directly behind the catcher's box at home plate. An even more compelling reason was that I knew the sponsoring group was stronger politically than I was at the time, which meant they were going to get the choice dates whether I wanted to play a night game on those dates or not.

Despite my screams of anguish, construction of the track began the moment our club went out on the road. On our return we were to play a Friday night game against the St. Louis Browns, our first night game of the season. And I got lucky. For six straight days before our return, it rained. The rains had started just after the contractor laid down the soft bottom, and by the third or fourth day the track was just one foot of solid mud.

Now I put on the pressure. I threatened to cancel the lease and move the team back to League Park. I threatened to sue the city for the loss of revenue on our 30,000 advance sale. I called Will Harridge in Chicago and asked him to help me along by issuing a statement that if the game couldn't be played because of something as extraneous as a track for midget autos, Cleveland would forfeit the game.

I walked out onto the field, followed by a cordon of photographers, and sank one of my crutches almost up to the crotch as the bulbs flashed.

On Thursday afternoon it stopped raining, and work was renewed on the track. The contractor kept telling me not to worry. As soon as he laid down the top layer, he kept saying, the track would be hard as cement. I immediately made it clear to the assembled newspapermen that the thought of my outfielders running over cement did not comfort me at all. I volunteered to fix the track myself so that it would be suitable for play—and also permanently unsuitable for midget auto racing.

The pressure had been building on Mayor Tom Burke (later U. S. Senator Burke), who was really a wonderful guy. Burke, caught in the middle, had to make some kind of statement, so he announced that he was going to come down and personally inspect the track.

Great. I grabbed a couple of guys from the ground crew and we dug a deep hole in front of one of the little gates opening onto the field, right where the track curved close to the grandstand. We filled the hole with loose dirt, which we watered down. And we watered it and

109

we watered it and we watered it. We watered it right up to the time the mayor arrived.

I had my crony Larry Atkins, the Cleveland fight promoter, waiting outside to greet the mayor and conduct him onto the field with full ceremony, for we were most anxious, in that critical moment, to observe correct protocol, show the mayor the courtesy his position deserved and make certain that he came down the right aisle and through the right gate.

As Mayor Burke reached the bottom of the steps, I came toward him to extend a fond greeting. The mayor took one step through the gate, opened his mouth to return my greeting and, his mouth still open, sank like a stone to his thighs. He was so deep in mud that we had to call for help to pull him out, commiserating with him all the while about our mutual misfortune at having gotten ourselves involved in such a deplorable situation.

Burke never said a word. He went marching back up the stairs, stomping down hard here and there to knock the mud off his pants, shaking one foot as he ascended and then the other. To all intents and purposes, the midget racing promotion went stomping and shaking out of Municipal Stadium with him.

By this time, the controversy was all over the front pages of the Cleveland papers, and I suddenly thought, *Now, wait a minute. Let's see what we can make out of this.*

I put in another call to Will Harridge and, just to keep the publicity going, had him announce that he was sending his chief umpire down to inspect the field and make sure the track was not a hazard to life and limb. Then I sat down and tried to figure out what I could work up that would entertain the fans, make a laughingstock of midget racing and end the whole controversy on a light and pleasant note for everybody—especially me.

You ask the question and the answer comes bouncing back. If midget auto racing was what they wanted, we would get some midgets and have them race in autos. I called Marty Caine and put in an order for as many midgets as he could ship in on such short notice—the first time I ever used midgets, incidentally.

I kept moaning about the track, and the publicity keep booming. We didn't only have the front pages now, we had the headlines. The afternoon headline of the Cleveland *News* read:

"SOME KIND OF BALL GAME" DUE
IN STADIUM TONIGHT, VEECK SAYS

Despite threatening weather (it did begin to rain again immediately after the game ended), 61,288 fans turned out, half of them to see the ball game and the other half to see the track.

We gave them a show. For the early arrivers we had a fireworks display, climaxed by a return bout between the battleship and the plane. After the superiority of air power had reasserted itself, Van Patrick, our radio broadcaster, took the field mike and announced that as a special attraction, Bill Veeck was going to present the first midget race at the stadium.

Down from the left-field exit came six midgets racing madly for six kiddie cars that had been planted at the edge of the track. There were five men midgets and one woman midget (the woman was there only because Caine hadn't been able to find another guy, but her presence seemed to lend exactly the right tone of nuttiness to the event). The six of them jumped into the cars and began to pedal madly across the field toward home plate. Waiting at the plate, we had a huge lollipop to present to the winner.

And then we got a terrific break. While a barbershop quartet was bringing the proceedings to a close, Bob Hope came strolling onto the field. Bob, who dropped in on us occasionally, unannounced, had been reading about the battle and he had come down to see what all the shouting was about. He received a solid 5-minute ovation and then delivered himself of a hilarious 15-minute monologue—pausing only to leap away from the mike every now and then and shriek, "Whoops, one of those midgets almost got me."

The track? Well, the contractor had been right all along. By the time the fans started to arrive, there was not a puddle to be seen. It was rather embarrassing. It seemed only decent after all that moaning to at least have a damp spot or two to show them. Everybody seemed to think the whole thing had been a publicity gag all along. There were some people unkind enough to accuse me of fixing the weather. Ridiculous. I mean you can fix the weather for a day maybe, but for a whole week?

That's what happens, though. I have found that once you get a reputation for being a man who is willing to meet a good story halfway, you begin to get credit for anything that happens on your own side of the horizon.

When I was operating in Chicago in 1959, Hoyt Wilhelm was pitching against us. At the time he was the hottest pitcher in baseball. In the first inning a swarm of gnats descended upon him, thick as locusts, just as he was winding up.

Wilhelm backed off. The umpires, reinforced by our coaches, bat

111

boy, trainer and grounds keepers, came out with towels and Flit guns to beat them away. Back stepped Wilhelm. Just as he wound up, the gnats descended on him again. This time we smoked them off with torches. Back they came. Every time Wilhelm went into his windup, it was like a signal for them to return. Finally, I got one of the fire bombs from the fireworks crew and ignited it in their midst. They disappeared in a suffocating screen of white smoke and were never heard from again.

I was curious enough to call the Natural Museum in the morning to find out if they had any explanation. They did. The gnats were in their mating season. They had selected this particular place, the mound, earlier and a certain odor was given off that kept attracting them back. The fire bomb had not only killed off half of them, it had changed the odor. The fact that they kept coming back just as Wilhelm started his windup was apparently an accident of timing. It took him just about the same time to compose himself and step back on the mound as it took the gnats to regroup and swoop down again.

You can't expect sportswriters sitting up in the press box to be students of the mating habits of the gnat. (It's almost too much to ask the gnats themselves to show more than a cursory interest.) Returning to the roof, I became aware that I was being looked upon with suspicion, indulgence or amusement, depending upon the mood, loyalities and dispositions of the individual looker. I couldn't find it in myself to disappoint my public. "It takes all winter to train them," I shouted, throwing up my hands in disgust, "and now ... pouf ... one lousy bomb and they're all blown up."

The gag that got us the most publicity during my four years in Cleveland came out of a fan's Letter to the Editor. Joe Early, a night watchman at a Chevrolet plant, wrote the editor of the *Press* to ask why ball clubs were always giving special "days" and "nights" for highly paid players who didn't need the loot, instead of to fans, like him, who did. He signed it GOOD OLD JOE EARLY.

Why not indeed? There was a basic truth there which I think all fans have thought about at some time or other. Besides, our record-breaking season was coming to an end and it seemed like an excellent idea to honor one fan as a symbol of all fans.

We really didn't want to publicize Good Old Joe Early Night ahead of time. Rudie had to get his address from the *Press,* though, so that we could call Joe and tell him to be at the stadium. Except for that one call, we did nothing at all with him. The *Press* latched onto it, as might have been expected, and they publicized it. We would have lost all faith in journalistic enterprise if it hadn't.

112

We gave a lot of gifts away to other fans, too. Among other things, we had 20,000 Princess Aloha orchids—all beautifully packaged—flown in from Hawaii in a special temperature-controlled plane. They were presented to the first 20,000 women to come through the turnstiles.

We had a lot of fun with Joe Early. We started by announcing that we were giving Good Old Joe a house, done in Early American architecture. The crowd gasped at such largesse. Out came an outhouse. With suitable fanfare, we announced the presentation of an automobile, fully equipped. Out came one of those old Model-T cars, filled to the scuppers with gorgeous women. This one was a circus car, one of those trick cars that explode, backfire, shed their fenders, rear up on their back tires, etc. We gave him all manner of livestock including the inevitable swaybacked horse.

After the fun was over, the real gifts came. We gave him a new Ford convertible, followed by a truck completely filled with gifts: refrigerator, washing machine, luggage, wristwatch, clothes, console, everything any quiz show subsequently thought of—Everything, to be frank, we could talk the local merchants into contributing to the cause.

Joe Early became a celebrity for a time and was booked on radio and TV. The funny thing was that his luck seemed to change from that day on. The last I heard of him he had become quite successful.

My favorite gag in Cleveland came a year later, and it came not on another note of triumph but as a concession of defeat. I proposed that on the day we were mathematically eliminated from the pennant race we take down the pennant flying so proudly from our flagpole and bury it with full military honors. Neither Bob Fishel nor Rudie Schaffer liked the idea at all. Bob felt very strongly that funerals were not a subject to be kidded. Rudie thought it was not only in poor taste but just a little too cute. I thought it would be hilarious. It seemed to me that we would be showing that we could kid ourselves just as readily as we could anybody else. I also felt that by accepting the blame for failure ourselves, we would be taking the heat off the players and the manager.

Rudie picked up a horse-drawn hearse somewhere, and the day before the season ended we conducted an old-time funeral. I cast myself as the mortician, a role for which I was undoubtedly fitted. Rudie, as the parson, wore a top hat and frock coat, and carried a copy of the *Sporting News* (the *Sporting News* being known as "the Bible of Baseball"). I was resplendent in a high silk hat and a low sense of humor.

To the accompaniment of a funeral dirge, the flag was lowered and folded sadly into a pine coffin. The pallbearers, who included Boudreau, the coaches and the rest of the front-office executive staff, slid the coffin into the hearse. I climbed back onto the driver's seat, took the reins and drove slowly around the field, dabbing at my eyes with a well-soaked handkerchief. As we passed the Cleveland dugout, the players joined the procession. We made our mournful way around the field, all of us, and back to the flagpole in center field where a grave had been carefully prepared.

I thought it was a funny gag. And no one could say that it wasn't original. The Old Guard disagreed, of course. I was now making a travesty of losing. But no, it was not only the Old Guard. On this one, my instinct deserted me. Those who liked it thought it was great; those who didn't thought it was in atrocious taste.

I had hoped to combine the funeral ceremony with a rescue mission. Early in the season, when we had dropped to seventh place, a delicatessen owner named Charlie Lupica, a true and faithful Cleveland rooter, had climbed to the top of a flagpole and vowed to remain there until we recaptured first place. That left Charlie with plenty of time on his hands for the next 117 days, for, although we came close a couple of times, we were never quite able to grab the lead. A child was born to him, his fourth, and still Charlie held to his stated purpose and his lonely vigil. A magnificent and dedicated human being, Charlie.

Unfortunately, we were unable to get him and his flagpole to the park in time for the funeral ceremonies. The flagpole was higher than the bus wires, which meant, we discovered too late, that we needed a special license to move him through the city, and even then we had to devise a long, circuitous route. We were able to work things out in time, happily, to carry him to the park in triumph for the final day.

While the band played "Charlie, My Boy," Charlie slowly descended to rejoin his waiting family. It had to be a slow descent because the photographers, never known for any overabundance of sentiment, kept shouting at him to slow down so they could get their pictures. Charlie, who did not seem to have anything against getting his picture in the paper, was nothing if not obliging.

We had a new car for Charlie, too. We had gifts for his wife and for the children. We had also planted a four-poster bed under the flagpole, plus a bathtub, drawn and ready—which was not only to clean up Charlie but also to clean up the old joke about the homecoming soldier. Which would Charlie go for first, the bathtub or his wife? That was the tantalizing question we were posing.

114

There were those who were willing to give me credit for thinking up Charlie's gag, too; patently unfair to Charlie. Flagpole sitters, like .300 hitters, are born not made.

From a purely promotional standpoint, I have one rule I think is vitally important. If you are going to give something away, only give away the best. If the nature of a promotion demands that it be announced beforehand, make sure it is tied to the best possible attraction.

Five days before we honored Good Old Joe Early, as an instance, we had a night for one of our pitchers, Don Black, who had injured himself badly in a weird way. While fouling off a pitch, Don had fallen to his knees and then passed out cold. A weakened blood vessel had burst in his brain, and for three weeks he was in a semi-coma. The doctors told me that anything might have brought it on, even a cough or a sneeze.

Don's background made it particularly tragic. I had bought him from Milwaukee the previous year, knowing he was an alcoholic and that he was deeply in debt. To keep him from drinking, I had held back his salary for the rest of the year, using half of it to pay off his debts and sending the other half to his wife. Don himself was put on a dollar-a-day allowance and forced to come to the office to collect even that. The reason I wanted him in the office was that I had contacted Alcoholics Anonymous and asked them to station a man there. Every day, while Don was waiting for me to come out with his dollar, the man from AA would talk to him. Don joined. By the time he was injured, his bills were all paid off, he had stopped drinking and he was doing just beautifully.

We wanted to raise some money for him. By a quirk of the schedule the Red Sox, the team we were battling for the pennant, were coming to town for only one game, the last game we would play against them all season. The advance sale was already 30,000.

I asked the Red Sox for permission to play the game at night, so that we could contribute our share of all subsequent receipts, above the advance, to Black. Tom Yawkey not only agreed, he offered to contribute the Red Sox' share of those receipts too. I didn't want that. I wanted Black to know that the money represented the city of Cleveland's high regard for him.

The attendance was 76,772, and we were able to give Don's wife a check for better than $40,000. We also won the game and went into a tie for first place.

Now, people are not fools. If we said we were anxious to raise

115

some money for Don Black and named a Tuesday afternoon game against the St. Louis Browns for that purpose, they would know darn well that it was they who were making the contribution, not us.

The same principle had applied a month earlier when we held a Thank U Night for the entire state in appreciation of their support through the season. I particularly wanted to show the people from the small northern cities that we were well aware how important they were to us. It being patently impossible to invite them all to the park, I invited every mayor in the state to attend a pre-game garden party and to bring along his wife and a friend. Mayor Burke of Cleveland was my co-host.

In the open section between the bleachers and the temporary wire fence we had constructed, we erected 20 colorful tents. Inside the tents, refreshments were served. Outside, amidst a forest of potted palms, were banquet tables under gaily colored umbrellas. Wandering troubadours weaved in and out among our 2,000 guests, entertaining them as they feasted. At the same time, a vaudeville show was being presented on a special stage we had constructed in center field.

The game itself was against the last-place White Sox, which might, at first glance, make it look like a second-rate attraction. No. The mayors were invited for the night Satchel Paige was going to start his first game at home, and Satch was, at that moment, the greatest attraction in the history of baseball. He was in the midst of a streak in which he was to break five night attendance records in five straight starts.

Our paid attendance was 78,382, the all-time night record. The 2,000 grandstand seats we had roped off for our guests were seats we could easily have sold.

Don Black Night and Thank U Night were, each in its own way, the two most important games we had to offer all season.

I now have to add one footnote. There was one exception to the rule of presenting the best possible attraction when I had to advertise a promotion. I always tried to get the Philadelphia Athletics in on something. Mr. Mack was a boyhood idol of mine, and I was extremely fond of him until the day he died.

Mr. Mack, alone among the Old Guard, never screamed that I was making a mockery of the grand old game, even though Mr. Mack himself was always the personification of dignity in his old-fashioned high-collar shirts and his precise and rigid bearing. The others, like Clark Griffith, looked upon my little entertainments as a disgrace to the game and insult to their own persons—although I never noticed

116

any of them, Mr. Griffith in particular, looking quite that insulted when I handed them their share of the receipts.

And they were so wrong. My philosophy as a baseball operator could not be more simple. It is to create the greatest enjoyment for the greatest number of people. Not by detracting from the ball game but by adding a few moments of fairly simple pleasure. My intention was always to draw people to the park and make baseball fans out of them.

When I first began to present fireworks displays, the Old Guard screamed that I was cheapening baseball by trying to lure the fans in with other attractions. The fact that I never advertised fireworks was always overlooked. I almost always did have fireworks after a night game in Cleveland, but I always reserved the right *not* to have them. The baseball game was still the main attraction.

In what way does a fireworks display intrude upon a baseball game? It seems to me that they blend together perfectly. Baseball loves to wrap itself in that phrase "The National Game," but what's so un-American about fireworks? To me, fireworks bring on the memory of an old Fourth of July celebration, of a pleasant afternoon in a small Midwestern town or an exciting night at a carnival.

Dan Levin, in writing an article on Cleveland for *Holiday* years ago, expressed it perfectly and beautifully:

> I remember one night game in the Cleveland Stadium, the summer of the pennant-winning year. The massed dots that were 30,000 people, lighted queerly by the arc lights, against the backdrop of the night. The wail of a train behind the crack of bat against ball. The forlorn bleat of an ore freighter on Lake Erie. A night plane, lights flicking brightly, homing toward the airport. The crowd relaxed and then taut, mostly with jackets on, because it was not the warmest of summer evenings. Loneliness and the vastness of this amphitheatre.
>
> Then, as the last batter ground out, the fireworks began. Great balls of flame spiraled upward. A pinwheel of colors coruscated in the deepening night. One display had the shape of a tank, and from its nozzle fire sprayed toward the darkened scoreboard. Showers of sparks burst and trickled into nothingness before us. Enthralled, we sat among the thousands who watched quietly, not wanting this fairy spectacle to end.
>
> On what night, and in what place, will we ever be closer to the heart of America, I thought, than on this summer night, in the Cleveland Stadium?

Yes, that's it. Yes.

...and Every Fan Was King | 8.

WE DID NOT draw crowds simply by putting on a show. Cleveland had been without a pennant winner for 26 years, the longest of any American League city, and we communicated our determination to produce one. I agree completely with the conservative opposition that you cannot continue to draw people with a losing team by giving them bread and circuses. All I have ever said—and, I think, proved—is that you can draw more people with a losing team plus bread and circuses than with a losing team and a long, still silence.

We are in the entertainment business, competing for the entertainment dollar. Competition is tougher. In 1902, there wasn't much else you could do unless you wanted to stay home and sing along with the player piano. We are now competing directly with horse racing and harness racing. (At the time I was surveying Pittsburgh, the team's greatest asset, to my way of thinking, was that there was no race track in the area.) Like everybody else, we are competing with television. Golf has become a mass sport. There has been an upsurge in individual sports like boating and sailing, fishing and hunting. Indirectly, we are competing with pro football and pro basketball and I suspect that one day we will be competing with soccer. It is only a historical accident, after all, that baseball is our national game instead of, say, soccer, which is the national game in almost every other country in the world.

It has been baseball's great good fortune that its growth in this country coincided with the great periods of immigration. The immigrant parents—and the children of the immigrants—did not want to associate themselves with an "old country" sport but with what they were assured was the great American game.

Don't misunderstand me. I am not saying that baseball is not a great game. It has to be a great game to have survived what we have done to it. I believe that baseball as played in the major leagues is the best entertainment buy, dollar for dollar, in the country. I also believe that it should be sold on that basis. Baseball did not become our national game because of some divine plan and it will not neces-

118

sarily remain the national game because of some divine protection.

I have already pointed out that it was Mr. Phil Wrigley who first charted how precisely attendance followed the won-lost column. But why should that be? The game is the same, whether the home team wins 4–3 or loses 4–3. All major-league teams are reasonably well matched. Even the team finishing in last place wins one-third of its games.

You do, of course, have a small, loyal cadre of perhaps 83 technicians who will come out, regardless of the standings, to watch the geometric pattern of the game unfold in all its beautiful precision and balance. To them, the game's the thing. You will generally find them sitting in the bleachers. I have discovered, in 20 years of moving around a ball park, that the knowledge of the game is usually in inverse proportion to the price of the seats.

If you depend solely on people who know and love the game, you will be out of business by Mother's Day.

With the casual fan, then, it is not the game, it is the winning or losing. The average fan identifies himself completely with the home team. If the home team wins, he wins. If the home team loses, he loses. It is not pleasant to lose; we spend too much of our life losing our own galling little battles. You cannot expect a man to pay good money to come into your park and be humiliated when it is so easy to stay home.

It is this unconscious fear of losing, of subjecting himself to a personal humiliation, that keeps the fan from going to the park, just as it is the unconscious anticipation of winning, of scoring a personal triumph, that brings him rushing in.

Entertainment, beyond its more obvious purpose, softens the blow of losing. It gives the fan something else to think and talk about as he is leaving the park. Instead of the pain of another loss, he can think, with pleasure, of the fireworks or the circus acts or the band or the Harlem Globetrotters. And remembering that visit with pleasure, he will not have quite that moment of doubt, of hesitation, the next time he thinks about coming to the park. Entertainment lives for the present but it also looks to the future.

This theory of pleasure and pain and personal identification may sound highly fanciful but it can be proved, in dollars and cents, in the concession receipts. If the home team wins, you will do twice as much business during the concession blowoff; that is, in the amount of money the customers spend as they are leaving the park. Being happy, they are twice as willing to leave some money behind.

It is shown even more dramatically when you combine the concession blowoff with a fireworks display at the end of the game. I began to use fireworks, as I say, because I love fireworks. I became aware very quickly, however, that fireworks pay for themself many times over.

For one thing, a fireworks display is the simplest possible method of traffic control. If people all leave the park at the same time, your concession blowoff is necessarily of limited duration. With fireworks, that blowoff period is extended. Some people leave immediately after the game, some drift out while the fireworks are still on, and some stay to the very end.

All right. If you lose a game and have no fireworks you will have a minimum amount of business. Let's have X stand for this minimum, with the understanding that all these ratios are on a per capita basis.

Lose game; no fireworks	X
Lose game; fireworks	1.4 X
Win game; no fireworks	2 X
Win game; fireworks	3 X

The first thing to notice is that more money is spent when you win than when you lose, under any circumstances. Even by staggering their departure and giving them the pleasant afterglow of the fireworks, the fans are not in the same happy, spending mood they would be in if they had won.

The second thing to notice is that a fireworks display after a victory helps more than the same display after a defeat. Following a victory the receipts go up 50 percent, following a defeat only 40 percent.

There is no known substitute for winning, and no known cure for losing. We are dealing here only with remedial action. It has always been my belief that you have three years to produce a winning team after you come to town. If after that time you haven't come through, I suspect that the value of entertainment and publicity and promotion will fall off very substantially.

Many of the club owners who accused me of making a travesty of the game when I first began to use fireworks as an innocent form of entertainment now feel called upon to entertain their customers with frequent and full-blown postgame fireworks displays themselves. Any questions?

How important are concessions to a major-league operation? This important: for most clubs, it is the difference between finishing in the red and finishing in the black. (Take away both the concessions and the radio-TV receipts, and there isn't a club that would operate in the black.)

120

Let's stay with concessions as long as we're on them because, as you know, this is a subject that has always intrigued me. And let me use Chicago as my example, instead of Cleveland, since Chicago is fresher in my mind and since we did more business per capita while we were winning the pennant in 1959 than any club had ever done before. On the standard deal with a concessionaire, the club takes 20 percent of the gross receipts. Over the year, each person who came into Comiskey Park spent more than $1.20. On our paid attendance of roughly 1,420,000—plus the women, kids and various special groups—the concessions grossed some $3,250,000, out of which our cut was $650,000.

The point I am making, to apply these figures to the original text, is that the baseball fan, identifying himself so closely with the home team, is moved not only by the excitement and color of a pennant-winning team but by the sense of personal triumph.

This identification of the rooter with his team is most clearly seen in college football where the direct and personal identification of the rooter lives on in that classic figure of American humor, the Old Grad. Football is the college man's sport (with the exception of Notre Dame's huge rooting section among working Catholics, who are tied by a strong religious identification). One of the reasons for pro football's increased popularity in the past decade has been the huge leap in the college population since the war.

Baseball is the workingman's game. A baseball crowd is a beer-drinking crowd, not a mixed-drink crowd. This is why a pennant-winning team can galvanize an entire city the way a football team, with its more limited audience, cannot. (With the exception, again, of Green Bay, which is utterly unique.) A pennant-winning team makes an enormous contribution to the morale of a city. Everybody suddenly becomes friendly. There is a feeling of common purpose that never fails to remind me of a city after a disaster. Have you ever noticed the camaraderie that comes over a city that is digging itself out of a bad snowstorm? People who normally wouldn't nod as they pass, talk to each other. Involved as they all are in a common experience, they know they can speak to each other without being rebuffed. Just as important, perhaps, they have a common ground on which they can feel superior. They have survived and they are digging themselves out, and so when they talk about how bad it was they are really congratulating each other on their fortitude. Just as with a snowstorm, there is that feeling of reflected glory in a successful baseball team. Cleveland is winning the pennant. The eyes of the whole country are upon Cleveland, upon us, upon me and you. *We're looking pretty good, aren't we, Mac?*

Since nothing is more contagious than the desire to be part of some great victory, the whole city begins to rally. Before long, the woman upstairs who was aware of baseball only as some minor nuisance that took up valuable time on the radio becomes aware that something is in the air. Pretty soon, she is asking the kid downstairs, the one she used to bawl out for throwing a rubber ball against the staircase, "How did the Indians make out?" Before the season is over, she will get her husband to take her to a game if only to see exactly who and what she is rooting for.

The only thing that makes life a little difficult is that only one team can win. Which means that just so long as baseball insists upon selling baseball on the won-lost column, only one team in each league is sure to prosper.

On a day-to-day basis, the baseball fan wants to be able to identify not only with a winning team, but with one colorful, bigger-than-life player, so that *he* will be hitting the home run, *he* will be making the game-saving catch, *he* will be the hero of the multitudes. The slugger's the man they all want to be. A Dempsey will always catch the imagination more than a Tunney.

We don't have the colorful, bigger-than-life character in our society any more, and I find that a worrisome thing. We don't have him in baseball, we don't have him in boxing, we don't have him anywhere. This country used to spew forth colorful trial lawyers: the Bill Fallons, the Clarence Darrows, the Earl Rogers, the Sam Leibowitzes. You'd have as much trouble naming a trial lawyer today as you would an English tennis player. (At any rate, you would have before Louis Nizer wrote a best seller.) Today, you have the corporate lawyer and the team player, both of whom serve a necessary purpose and both of whom are rather dull. Texas is the last stronghold of the individual, and while we make a lot of jokes about the big, blowhard, ten-gallon Texans, nevertheless they command our attention.

I know I'm laying myself open to the accusation that I'm going back to my own "1902," but it is a fact that baseball used to have the Ruths, the Foxxes, the Greenbergs, the Hack Wilsons, to command our attention. There was a sharpness to their personalities and a swagger to their movements. Even Joe DiMaggio. DiMaggio was not colorful in himself, and yet there was a color to the way he stood at bat, positioned himself in the field, raced after a fly ball. The tempo of the game swung with these players, the eyes of the fans moved with them. They dominated any game they were in.

122

Ted Williams was the last player to bring the color of sheer individualism to the game because he, like Dizzy Dean, was both a great player and a great character. Williams told off all authority, as we would all secretly love to tell off authority. The fans either cheered him because he was doing what they knew in their hearts they wanted to do, or they booed him because he was daring to do—and managing to get away with—what they wouldn't admit they also wanted to do. Either way, nobody ignored Ted Williams when he stepped onto a baseball field.

How many active players will people make a special effort to see or to read about? Yogi Berra, yes. Nellie Fox, a little bit. Minoso, maybe. Piersall, if the moon is right. But what slugger, what new Ruth? Mantle? No. It should have been Mantle, but no.

Maris's run for Ruth's record—abetted by Mantle—was a godsend to the American League. It saved us all from a disastrous year. Yet with it all, with the enormous spotlight of the enormous communications industry trained upon him, Maris's personal impact was unbelievably slight. His great desire seemed to be to submerge himself.

There's no doubt it's all a part of the conformity that has dropped over the country. I suspect that, in great part, it is the result of the regimentation of education. I suspect it goes back even further, to the feeling that we are no longer a new country, with open frontiers, but a world power which has to operate carefully according to carefully planned policies and procedures.

In baseball, it gets back to the baseball moguls' preoccupation with dignity and control. The businessman has taken over the game. The businessman, quite naturally, has an organization manager. The organization manager's slogan is, "We don't have no stars on this team. They're all just one of twenty-five." You don't have no stars, Managers, and you don't win no pennants.

Color is the thing they have done everything in their power to get rid of. As soon as a boy is signed, a carefully planned program of brainwashing sets in. There are rules of behavior for the new boy as soon as he reports to his first minor-league team. When he comes to spring training for the first time, a public relations man grabs him before he even dons his suit and brainwashes him with more rules of proper behavior, of proper dress, of the proper amount to tip. There is even somebody, usually the wife of one of the older, respected players, to lecture the rookie's wife on what is expected of her and to guide her to the proper hairdresser. Being two scared kids, possibly in a big city for the first time in their lives, they drop into the mold without a struggle.

123

"Behave yourself and keep out of trouble," the young player is told, "and you'll make a lot of money. Remember, this is a business and you're a businessman."

And so this young fellow who had dreamed from the cradle of playing in the big leagues tells the sportswriters who are looking for something to make him come alive to their readers, "It's a business with me. I'm just in it for the money."

After he's said it three times he believes it, and he would no more think of doing anything to hurt his business prospects than would any rising young junior executive at DuPont.

And so Roger Maris, with all the publicity upon him in 1961, says, "It's a business. If I could make more money down in the zinc mines, I'd be mining zinc." What an inspiring message to pass on to the kids who are panting to identify with Roger Maris and go chasing after Babe Ruth's record with him.

The sad part of it, of course, is that if he could make more money in the zinc mines, Roger Maris would still be playing baseball and admitting to himself that he is playing because he enjoys it more than anything else in the world. Maybe he'd be colorful and maybe he wouldn't, but at least he'd be himself.

It's all of a piece. The resistance to "cheap" entertainment and the bleaching of the players' personalities both arise out of the baseball moguls' fond belief that people come to a ball park to enjoy the finer technical points of baseball. Since I cannot believe they are losing money on purpose, they must truly believe that all their fans are scholars of the game who would resent having their concentration on the great pageant about to be played out before their very eyes distracted by anything as dull as, say, fun and laughter. I find this theory particularly prevalent among owners who cannot watch a game for three consecutive innings without leaning over to their companion to ask how the last two batters went out.

A baseball team can do more for a city than lift its morale. Not only doesn't the city owe the operator of the franchise anything, but the ball club, as an organization which depends in many ways on the facilities of the city and is totally dependent on the good will of its citizens, has certain responsibilities toward the city.

On the final day of our first year in Cleveland, we threw the gates open and let everybody in free. In subsequent years, our receipts for the last game went to the Community Fund, totaling $100,633, which made us the largest contributor in the city for our corporate size.

By playing home-and-home exhibition games with the Brooklyn Dodgers, with the total receipts going to the sandlot programs of our

124

respective cities, we were able to turn over $149,534 to the Cleveland program, a sum which put a rocky program on a sound and solvent footing.

Most of all, we showed the fans that we weren't just out for their money, that we cared about them and wanted them to have a good time. I can remember looking out the window after a game had been rained out and seeing a couple of hundred out-of-towners waiting disconsolately for their train at the Pennsylvania Railroad depot. I called down to the locker room and asked Boudreau and Feller to dash over and barber with them until the train came. Another time, about 700 school kids from the Mahoning Valley were invited to a game as my guests. That game was rained out too, and I sent them all to a show so that they wouldn't go home completely disappointed.

We didn't have to be geniuses in either Chicago or St. Louis to know that the people of the neighborhood weren't going to be over-joyed at having fireworks exploding all around them, night after night, so we held "Good Neighbor Night" and had them all to the game, on the theory that nobody is as upset when that noisy party in the apartment upstairs is being thrown by friends as he would be if the people upstairs were strangers. More than that—again—we were letting them know we were well aware that we were imposing on their—we hoped—good nature.

We had special nights where 'A' students and their teachers were admitted free, because nobody else seemed to give them any recognition. We had special nights for bartenders and cabdrivers, always our prime sources of information. We had special days and nights for Boy Scouts and all youth groups. We had nights in which everybody who had worked for the Community Chest came as our guests, we had nights for the workers of Mayor's Youth Groups, we had nights for everybody who had contributed to the Combined Jewish Appeal. In many of these cases it wasn't the price of the ticket that was important, it was the knowledge that their work or their contributions were being recognized.

We wooed women shamelessly. We gave Cleveland women orchids and nylons at a time when orchids were still considered exotic and nylons were almost impossible to get. You can't get much more personal with women than that without meeting the family. Ten years later, while I was stopping off at a Cleveland hotel overnight, my chambermaid came in with another chambermaid, pointed to me fondly and said, "That's the man. He gave me my first orchid."

The first thing we always have had to do in any park is to fix up the ladies' room. Baseball always seems to operate on the principle

125

that women customers are just men customers in dresses. Ladies' rooms in most baseball parks are a shame and a disgrace. At Comiskey Park, the facilities were so bad that I forbade Mary Frances to use them until I was able to get them fixed up. By the time I was through, we had individual vanity tables and flattering fluorescent lighting. (I'd learned about that the hard way.) There were full-length mirrors so that the ladies could look themselves over and check the seams of their stockings before they went back out to face the world. Every now and then, we'd give out cosmetic kits as presents to everybody who entered. (I might as well say here that men's rooms are nothing to rave about in ball parks either. We've always had to make them fit for human beings too.)

In Cleveland, we didn't have the refinement of the full-length mirror—you keep getting ideas as you go along—but we fixed the powder rooms up quite attractively.

In every possible way we treated women as women. We knew they were not familiar with the seating plans of a ball park, and so we had special ushers to look for women who seemed bewildered and show them to their seats. We assumed they had not played sandlot ball as girls, and so we held baseball clinics to teach them something about the game. Our entertainment was occasionally pitched to what we thought would appeal to their artistic natures. Before one night game, we covered some bats, balls and gloves with phosphorescent paint, put out the park lights and trained a black fluorescent light on the infield. Since black light, as it is called, will pick up only phosphorescent material, nothing was visible except the ball, the bat and the gloves. It went over very well.

Once a woman becomes a fan, she is the best fan in the world. A woman fan focuses her interest, not surprisingly, on one individual player and follows him with a fierce and commendable loyalty. Most fan clubs are started by girls. To show how personal the feminine mind is, one woman asked me, on what I suppose was her first visit to the park, why we didn't let her know what the first names of the players were, a point which had never occurred to me before. The next day, we added the first names to the scoreboard listings. Not a bad idea, when you come right down to it.

There are other mild differences between the sexes. For one thing, women bear babies and have to spend a certain amount of time rearing them. After we had begun to operate in high gear, a registered nurse phoned to ask me why we didn't install a nursery school so that mothers could come out more often. And so we converted one of the towers into a nursery, with special sleeping quarters for babies.

126

We had a dozen registered nurses in attendance and about a hundred copies of every toy. The nursery wasn't a money-making proposition, as anyone can see. We couldn't get back enough money on the sale of tickets to pay for the nurses, let alone recoup our $40,000 investment. We were just creating the feeling that we wanted the mothers to come and have a good time. On Ladies' Days, when they paid only a small service charge, we'd have up to 500 kids. On doubleheaders the profits were blown on milk and cookies.

The nursery was a big hit with the ladies of our neighborhood. They worked out a shrewd system where one of the women would buy a ticket and bring in a whole mob of kids for us to take care of during the day while their mothers went shopping or played cards or maybe just took a nap. Fine. We had the facilities, we wanted to be Good Neighbors, and I have always had a boundless admiration for opportunists of either sex.

The nursery idea gave birth to other ideas, as these things will. A couple of times for door prizes, we gave away tickets to a night game complete with baby-sitting service. During my last year in Chicago, we were trying to work out some kind of a system under which parents who wanted to come to the game could call us for a baby-sitter. We wouldn't be paying the sitter, mind you; we'd get a cheaper price by dealing wholesale and we'd guarantee a responsible person.

The best thing that can be said about catering to the needs and whimsies of women is that it works. In 1948, we had an unbelievably high ratio of women customers. In fact, if you add the number of women who came in on Ladies' Day and the kids' groups and the special nights, our total attendance that year was close to 4,000,000.

In the face of that imposing figure, I am going to say something that will probably sound paradoxical. I do not believe in giving away tickets. Tickets are the one thing I have to sell. To give them away is to cheapen the product I am selling. If an organization writes me for tickets to auction off as part of a fund-raising program, I'll send a cash donation instead. If they write for a couple of tickets to give away as a door prize, I'll send something that will serve the purpose at least as well. No tickets.

I'll take care of 25,000 at a clip as our guests, yes. I'll give large groups of tickets to organizations like the Boy Scouts, yes. But always to a particular group for a particular reason at a particular time. Because here the effect is precisely the opposite. When a whole group is given tickets, the day at the park becomes a great event to be anticipated and remembered. When you give tickets to the workers of a charitable organization, the tickets become a reward, a mark of

127

recognition. These things don't cheapen your tickets, they enhance them.

Nor will I give tickets to anybody else to give away. I have always turned down these supermarket deals, where the store gives away a ticket with every $50 purchase of merchandise. If the store wants to buy tickets at box-office prices and use them as a premium, well, it's a free country. But nobody can give away one of my tickets unless it says on the front of that ticket that it was bought from the ball club at the face-value price.

As a major part of our promotion I moved around and met people. If the attendant in the men's room wanted to talk baseball for half an hour, we talked baseball for half an hour. Hank Greenberg could never understand it. "If you spent half the time charming the other owners in this league that you spend charming men's-room attendants," he'd say, "you'd be able to get all the rules changes you're always talking about pushed right through." What Big Henry could never understand was that I enjoyed talking to fans. George Weiss, on the other hand, never quite brought out the best in me.

I spoke in every hamlet in Ohio, and I missed darned few places in Missouri, Iowa, Indiana, Wisconsin and Illinois. I spoke from church pulpits and I spoke standing on a bar, and I once went down into a coal mine. On a year-round basis I averaged better than a speech a night. There were days when I made as many as 15 separate appearances.

I always traveled light. I would buy a toothbrush and a tube of toothpaste wherever I was stopping and that would be about it. I must have left thousands of toothbrushes and tubes scattered around the various states where I've operated. I'd sometimes stop off to invite a friend for a ride, and the next thing he knew he was on a 3-day jaunt to the hinterlands. I liked to have someone with me, not only for company but because I don't carry money. Occasionally, I'd run into one of those embarrassing situations where an innkeeper either didn't know me or *did* know me and wouldn't take a check. That's something that will deflate you when you get to thinking that you're riding the top of the world.

It's hard work, traveling around like that. Sometimes it's grinding work. Although I must say that no matter how tired I was, I always enjoyed myself. But look at the opportunity that is being handed to you. You are invited to spread your gospel before an audience that is not only captive but grateful to you for appearing; that, in fact, thinks you are doing *them* a favor. If General Motors could get that

128

kind of an audience under those conditions, it would have speakers blanketing the country. The reluctance of other baseball operators to appear before small gatherings of potential customers would bewilder me if I didn't know them so well. When you start with the premise that the world owes you a sellout every Sunday, you look upon these requests not as an opportunity but as an imposition.

Sure, I'm hustling tickets. But it's the most subtle kind of hustling possible. I have never mentioned tickets during a talk. I have never suggested that we want to sell tickets. I have never asked them to drop in at the park when they come to the city. They are there, I know, to be entertained. They want to hear something they ordinarily wouldn't hear about our players, about our team, about the backscene maneuverings of baseball. I don't think it would be right—or even smart—to break in with even the most gentle sales pitch.

The message is there. The message is that I care enough about their good will to make the trip and meet them and speak. The message is that it is exactly as far from Hamilton to Cleveland as it is from Cleveland to Hamilton. Our surveys showed that 85 percent of the groups I spoke before came to the park in one way or another.

There was once, I must admit, that I claimed a better return than we got. During a big doubleheader in Cleveland, while I had Frank Lane up on the roof with me admiring the crowd, I sent word to the guy at the public-address system to announce that the special train for Detroit people was leaving from a certain track at a certain time. Naturally, Lane was vastly impressed, because Detroit played at home the same time we did. It wasn't Lane I was after, though. It was Billy Evans, the Detroit general manager. Evans couldn't run into me in a hotel lobby without trying to reform me. Not that I was the apple of his eye, or anything like that. Billy, having known my father, simply couldn't believe the apple had fallen that far from the tree. At the major-league meetings that winter, I waited for Evans to begin one of his stirring lectures about the dignity of the game. "I don't know, Billy," I said. "I must be doing something right because I was running special trains in from Detroit all year, taking your fans right out from under you."

This was hitting Evans where he lived. He bristled and he blustered. He expressed complete disbelief. "OK," I said, making it clear that this kind of discussion was distasteful to me, "just ask Lane." That is what we economists call long-range planning.

One thing I have no egotism about at all is my ability as a speaker. A professor of speech once stood at the back of the hall and graded my performance. He reported that I did everything wrong, that my voice was weak, my delivery pitiful and my organization impossible. I also, I learned, had the lamentable habit of twisting my finger through my hair as I talked, and scratching my wrist. "If you were a student of mine," he said, "I'd have to flunk you. The only thing I can say for you is that you seem to be completely effective."

I may not be good but I'm cheap. I never charge for an appearance, either a fee or expenses, and you can't get speakers any cheaper than that. So despite my deficiencies I was usually booked a year in advance and had to turn down thousands of invitations—literally, thousands—because of the physical impossibility of being in five places at the same time. It has always seemed to me that once you have accepted a booking that far in advance, you are obligated to appear. I had to cancel a few dates when my leg was amputated; outside of that, I can't think of any appearances I either missed or canceled during my entire stay in Cleveland. Occasionally, I'd be delayed by an automobile accident or by the weather, but sooner or later I'd get there.

The same thing was true in St. Louis and Chicago. I remember one time with the Browns, I was scheduled to speak at a banquet in Springfield, Illinois, with France Laux, a St. Louis radio broadcaster, and then come back to St. Louis to address a luncheon at the Chase Hotel—where I happened to be living—the following noon. The Springfield affair broke up at about 10 P.M. It had started to snow about 7:30, and by the time Franz and I started back, a heavy, driving snow had traffic slowed down to a crawl. The driving conditions were so bad that we had to stop off at a little town along Route 66 and have chains put on the tires. As we hit the outskirts of St. Louis in the morning, cars were abandoned all over the road, for we had been driving through the worst blizzard in St. Louis history. A mile and a half from the hotel, the car quit cold. I jumped out and began to walk. Now, I have never worn an overcoat or a hat within my memory. I don't wear ties. I had to push my sport jacket into a cold wind and battle my way through the snowdrifts on crutches. I made it, though. At exactly 12 noon, I came puffing into the Chase Hotel ballroom.

No one else was there. Just me and a couple of waiters. I had been so intent upon making my appointment that it had never occurred to me in all that time that nobody else was going to be crazy enough to come out in a blizzard to listen to me talk.

The most difficult period for me was the winter of 1960, in Chicago, when I was already quite ill and well aware that I might have to

130

leave baseball for awhile. For the first time, the constant traveling from place to place became a chore.

Well, it was more serious than that. I had been blacking out quite regularly, and I was afraid to drive a car. Dizzy Trout was chauffeuring me around.

I stayed with it to the bitter end, though. The day before I was to go to the Mayo Clinic, Dizzy drove me to the Medinah Golf Club, west of Chicago, in a bad rainstorm. After I was introduced, I said, "I'm glad I'm here now because I'm going to be in Mayo Clinic tomorrow."

That got a big laugh, because of course they thought it was just a gag. (I'll have to remember to use it again when I get back into action.) The next day, of course, the story was in all the papers that I had gone to Mayo. Within the week, I got a card signed by everybody who had been there at Medinah. *We thought you were just kidding,* the card said, *and we want to thank you for taking the trouble to come out.*

I received more than 3,000 cards at Mayo's, most of them from people who had heard me speak.

In Cleveland, I hit the chautauqua circuit with Governor Frank Lausche, now a U. S. Senator. Frank and I got to be great friends. For a time we lived in the same apartment building on 30th Street. Lausche, a minor-league ballplayer in his youth, is the greatest vote collector I have ever seen. In Ohio, he is an independent force. Lausche doesn't run under the banner of the Democratic Party; the Democratic Party just hopes that Lausche supports it.

I myself am bi-partisan, tri-partisan and quatri-partisan. I may not agree with what you say, sir, but I will fight to the death for your right to buy a ticket at my box office. I agree wholeheartedly with J. Edgar Hoover that it would be folly to drive Communist baseball fans underground.

In later days, I had a chance to become a political power in the state of Ohio myself. Just before I sold the Indians, I was offered a tremendous sum of money to run for the U. S. Senate against Robert A. Taft. To clear up any misunderstanding, the money wasn't offered as a campaign contribution; it was a quarter of a million for the safety-deposit box. And to clear up any doubts about how solid an offer it was, it was brought to me by an absolutely reliable man who was very much involved in politics and known to be a close friend of mine.

Since I was not born the day before yesterday, I was perfectly aware

131

that, had I accepted their kind offer and been elected, I would have been expected to follow orders. I know myself well enough to know that would have led to all kinds of interesting troubles. Besides, I was a great admirer of Robert Taft. He was one guy who knew how to say no, a rare talent in politics.

Before anyone laughs at me for even speculating about the possibility that I could have beaten Taft, let me say that I believe I would have been elected. Anyhow, I don't think the Republican Party was laughing.

You still don't think I'd have had a chance against Taft? Well then, you weren't in Cleveland during those three and a half years when the Indians pushed the world news from the front pages. You weren't in Cleveland in those years when the Indians brought the people of the city so close together that it was as if everybody was living in everybody else's parlor. You weren't in Cleveland in those days of cheer and triumph when every day was Mardi Gras and every fan a king.

One $200,000 Dog for Two $100,000 Cats — 9.

IF I COULD have picked my own place in the game of baseball, I would have been out there on the field, making stunning plays at shortstop like Lou Boudreau, or turning casually at the crack of the bat to make one of those brilliant over-the-shoulder catches of Joe DiMaggio. ("Yay, Veeck!") As a kid in high school, I showed nothing more breathtaking than a stunning inability to hit a curve ball, and so I have done the next best thing. I'm like a book publisher who, unable to write the great American novel himself, passes judgment upon the manuscripts of his betters.

The old adolescent dream has left its mark, though. As all ballplayers can tell you, I am a hero worshiper. Wherever players of taste gather together, I am spoken of fondly as the ballplayer's lamb. There is almost nothing I won't do for a player who is putting out for me. Harry Lowrey came to me in Milwaukee at a time his baby was quite sick and neither he nor his wife had the energy or the inclination to look for an apartment. I turned my own house and car over to them and sent Eleanor and my own kids back to her mother's. After a couple of weeks, Harry left the club and took the baby home to the Coast. I understood perfectly how he felt. Instead of telling him that he would play for me or nobody, I was happy to give him permission to play in the Pacific Coast League.

I have never had a serious holdout. As far as salaries are concerned, I would just as soon give a player what he thinks he deserves if I can afford it. I have always found the ballplayers' demands quite reasonable. At St. Louis, I once had half-a-dozen of my players sign blank contracts and let me fill in the salary myself. There was a little gamesmanship (or contractmanship) involved on their part, of course, since I was putting an onus on myself to be more than fair. But gamesmanship apart, they knew Ole Will would give them a fair shake.

We did have a few publicity holdouts just to get some ink during the off-season, one of the more harmless winter sports. In Cleveland, Bob Feller would drop in to see me from time to time for widely heralded contract negotiations. Bob and I would chat awhile about everything under the sun except salary, then release a statement that we were still fairly wide apart but had every confidence our differences could be settled amicably. At last, with the weather turning warm, I'd say, "Hey Roberto, maybe we ought to sign."

The actual signing couldn't have been quicker or easier. Bob and I would each write a figure for his basic salary on a piece of paper and split the difference. The first year, he wrote down $60,000 and I wrote $65,000, so he cost himself $2,500. The next year he wrote down my original $65,000 but my figure was $62,500, which meant he recouped half his loss. He did a lot better than that, actually. I had Feller on an attendance-bonus clause those first two years, and in that record-breaking second year he earned himself an extra $27,500.

The most fun I ever had in a publicity holdout was with Johnny Berardino, a utility infielder I had bought from St. Louis for $50,000, for reasons I will go into shortly. John had landed a couple of bit parts in the movies, hired an agent and, in order that his acting career would not go completely unnoticed, had been threatening to quit baseball and devote himself to his art.

So when I bought Berardino I got myself a built-in publicity gimmick to fool around with. John announced that he was going to bring his agent along to negotiate his baseball contract for him, another first in the wonderful world of sports.

John is a delightful fellow and we had some very pleasant conversations for about a week, although the agent, who suffered under some strange delusion that we were really there to talk contract, proved to be a distracting influence. Especially after he got carried away by all the publicity and seemed to think he had to justify his presence by talking in upper-bracket figures.

I knew what I was going to pay John, John knew I knew what I was going to pay him. I mean that agent never got into the spirit of a contract negotiation at all. . . .

Finally, I told John: "I think we've pushed this about as far as it will go. We'd better sign something."

John turned to his agent and said, "All right, you better leave now. You're not very practical and you'll end up getting Bill so mad that you'll cost me money."

Just to keep the gag going, we thought it prudent to protect John's future by taking out an insurance policy on his face. If Johnny Berardino had been hit on the face by a batted ball that year and left so disfigured that he was no longer able to pursue his career as an actor, he would have been compensated to the amount of one million dollars. This policy cost me something like 78¢ a month (I was covering him both home *and* away) but, as I always say, nothing is too good for one of my boys.

Having, through incredible good fortune, preserved his features, Berardino has gone on to a fairly successful acting career. You see him on television all the time now. For awhile, I always seemed to see him being gunned down by one of Al Capone's boys—for this, I had to protect his features?—although he has now straightened himself out and has been rewarded with the second lead in *The New Breed*.

The kick I can get out of baseball, my limitations as a player having been what they were, is in the back-scene, front-office maneuvering. The trading and the dealing. The one way I can put myself on the field, if only vicariously, is by assembling a team that represents my ability as a scout, a trader and a psychologist.

Building a ball team is like dealing yourself a poker hand. You have all winter to rummage around through the deck for the best possible combination of cards. The season itself becomes little more than the laydown of the hand you've dealt yourself. With one exception. You still have that brief period between mid-April and June 15 to try to pick up that one key player or make that one key trade that will plug your most glaring weakness. To hold to the poker analogy, you still have a chance to fill an inside straight.

And here is the essential conflict that arises in my relationship with the players. The ballplayers are my friends and heroes, and yet as a part of my job—the most difficult part of all—I find myself depersonalizing them, maybe even dehumanizing them. I find myself looking upon them, of necessity, as currency, as a means of exchange. If there were a Mann Act to prohibit the shipping of ballplayers over state borders, I'd be in just about as much trouble as any reasonably civilized man in this hemisphere.

Trading in the player market can be fascinating and exciting. There are times you can even declare yourself in on somebody else's card game just by being alert. And lucky.

In 1943, as a minor-league operator, I came close to pulling off a $100,000 coup (essentially, I did pull it off) just by glancing at the Western Union ticker. I had come back to the office in my swimming trunks after helping the ground crew water the outfield. Before I changed, I looked over the news on the ticker and saw a notice that the Philadelphia Phillies had received permission to put their bullpen coach on the active list because their lone catcher had just broken a finger.

Catchers are always in short supply. In the war years, they were like gold. I knew the Phils had been down to their last catcher and I had tried to help them out by selling them my own, Hank Helf— at an appropriate price, of course. Bill Cox, the Phils' owner, had been wildly disinterested.

Quickly, I ran through the catchers who might be available in the high minors. The only possibility was Andy Seminick at Knoxville. Knoxville, as you'll remember, was operated by Edgar Allen, that quick-draw artist who had taken Murray Howell off my hands at such short notice. Allen's secretary informed me that I might be able to reach him in New York, but that if I couldn't he was definitely going to be in Philadelphia to see Mr. Cox the next morning. All right, Allen was obviously going to Philadelphia to sell Seminick. And that wasn't necessarily bad. Since Cox knew that he was going to see Allen in the morning, he might not bother to try to track him down in New York today. And since Allen was not in his own office, looking over the ticker tape himself, he might not find out about the injury to the Phillies' lone catcher until he picked up the morning paper. All the pieces were falling neatly into place. What had started as an idle fancy was beginning to be exciting.

The Giants were playing at night, and I was able to catch Allen at his hotel. "You've got a catcher I'll buy for $15,000," I told him, "and I'll send you a player on option next year. The only thing is that this offer is only open until nine o'clock tonight because I need a catcher desperately."

Under ordinary conditions, I was offering him a very good deal.

So good a deal that if he didn't hear about the injury to the Phillies' catcher before the deadline he had to take it. At five of nine, Edgar Allen called back to tell me I had myself a catcher. "OK," I said, "send me a wire."

The next morning, the wire on my desk, I called Cox and told him I wanted to sell him a catcher. "No," he said, "I'm not that desperate. You got nothing but bums up there, Helf and the rest. I'm gonna buy a catcher from Knoxville. Mr. Allen is coming up to see me today."

"Oh?" I said. "Fine. I'm sorry you have such a low opinion of my catchers, but everybody's entitled to his opinion. That's what our boys are fighting for, isn't it?"

An hour later, Cox called back and said, "How come you didn't tell me you bought Seminick?"

"Well," I said, "you told me right off the bat that my catchers were a lot of bums. I wouldn't want to sell you a bum."

"Seminick is the guy I want," he said.

"He's not for sale," I said.

"Yeah, I know. But what will you take for him?"

"I'll tell you what I'll take," I said, getting down to business. I told him I'd take Coaker Triplett, an outfielder who had always hit well in our league, plus a pitcher by the name of Newt Kimball, another good Triple-A player. "And," I said, "you've got a fellow by the name of Ennis in the Inter-State League. I'll take him. And," I said, "I'll take $30,000."

He screamed. Ohh, how he screamed.

"I'm sorry you feel that way about it," I said. "But I told you I didn't want to sell him. Let's just forget about it."

An hour or so later, he was back on the line to tell me he had arranged to send me Kimball but that he hadn't been able to get waivers on Triplett.

I told him I was willing to take $15,000 instead of Triplett.

"On this guy Ennis," Cox said. "I'll bring him up and start getting him ready for delivery."

The delivery of Ennis was going to be a little complicated. Ennis being on option, the Phils had to bring him up to their own roster before they could send him away. Once he was on their roster, though, they had to get waivers from the other clubs in the National League before they could ship him back to the minors.

"If you can't get waivers," I told Cox, "I want the right to designate where he's going to go, right? You'll sell him at the waiver price to whatever team I stipulate."

Ennis, at that time, was in his first year of professional ball in a

136

Class-C league. I had first heard about him from Jack Doyle, the old Cubs scout who had recommended most of the players on my father's championship teams. I had seen Ennis earlier in the year myself while I was scouting the Inter-State League and had been vastly impressed. (George Kell was in the league at the same time and I had tried unsuccessfully to buy him.)

Seminick was already packing to leave for Milwaukee when I called the club. I was so delighted at the way everything had turned out that, after telling them he was going to the majors instead of the minors, I added that I'd send Andy a $250 bonus for all the inconvenience I was causing him. I wonder if Seminick ever figured out why he was given a bonus for reporting to the majors. I know I haven't.

I never did get Ennis, of course. Casey Stengel was managing at Boston and the night before I made the deal with Cox, Casey—by the luck of the draw—had dropped in at Trenton and seen Ennis play. When the waiver list came through shortly afterwards with Ennis's name on it, Casey put in a claim. Stengel was fired at the end of the year, but by that time Ennis had entered the service and the wartime rules said you couldn't transfer a serviceman.

As soon as Cox let me know he couldn't get the waivers, I called Jim Gallagher and filled him in. "I'll stipulate he's to go to the Cubs," I told him. "You'll get him for the $7,500 waiver price and you'll pay me $42,500. For $50,000, it's the best deal you've ever made."

For an outlay of $15,000 plus an option, I now had $45,000, plus the prospective $42,500 on Ennis plus a useful pitcher. And all from watching a ticker.

It didn't work out that way, because I was crossed. Cox was thrown out of baseball for betting on his team, and in came Bob Carpenter, the scion of the DuPonts. More to the point, in came Herb Pennock to run the team for him. I lost no time getting Cox on the phone to make sure the Ennis deal was made known to the new owners. Cox put Pennock on his extension and then I put Rudie on mine. With the four of us on the line, Cox explained the deal to Pennock, and Pennock agreed to it.

When Ennis came out of the service in 1946 and was the sensation of the spring-training camps, Pennock refused to turn him over to the Cubs.

Pennock always ducked me after that. Not because his conscience was bothering him but because whenever I'd see him in the hotel lobby at any of the meetings, I'd shout out at the top of my lungs: "Hey, Herb, you still owe me $50,000!"

137

My last memories of Pennock are of a thin, crouched man scampering around a corner.

Sometimes, in making a trade, it is the interplay of personalities that either works with you or against you. The best deal I ever made came about because I knew that Clark Griffith looked upon me with no great affection. Washington had two players I wanted very badly for the big push in 1948, Early Wynn and Mickey Vernon. Griffith wouldn't deal with me. I kept after him constantly anyway, offering him bales of money, in addition to players, because I knew that Griffith did not have any great resistance to money. If I had been able to sit down alongside Griff and show him, say, $100,000 in cash, I had no doubt that—once he had been revived—he would have reached automatically for a pen. Unable to sit with him and discuss the matter like two reasonable adults, I did the next best thing. I kept waving the money at him regularly in the public prints. (It would be impossible to get anywhere with Boston with those tactics. Tom Yawkey isn't interested in money and he likes to deal in absolute confidence. With Yawkey, a premature leak can kill a deal and blatant publicity is fatal.)

After the season was over, I got lucky. Joe Haynes, a pitcher for the Chicago White Sox, had married Griffith's adopted daughter during an earlier tour of duty at Washington. Haynes, a fair sort of pitcher, had been out with a sore arm at the end of the year. Two weeks before the winter meetings, I read that he was going to have to go under the knife to try to get the calcium taken out. Under those conditions, his market value was zero.

Frank Lane had just taken over in Chicago. I offered him our second-string catcher, Joe Tipton, for Haynes, dead or alive. Needless to say, Lane jumped at the deal.

To put it in the most delicate possible way, I had Joe Haynes stashed out in an abandoned mine shack and I was holding him for ransom. Griffith, I knew, wouldn't be able to stand the thought of having any son-in-law of his playing for that goofball in Cleveland.

Clark Griffith didn't come to Chicago for the meeting himself. He sent his nephew Calvin. I was at the Blackstone, and Cal was at the Palmer House. I called and said: "I've got Mr. Haynes and you've got Mr. Wynn, does that suggest anything to you?"

The deal I proposed was Joe Haynes for Early Wynn, and Eddie Robinson for Mickey Vernon. Cal being somewhat balky, I threw in a relief pitcher, Ed Kleiman, and promised to pay for Haynes' operation, which seemed the only decent thing to do—especially since I had already made the same promise to Haynes.

At 2 in the morning, he called back to tell me that Uncle Clark had agreed. I wasn't going to give Unc a chance to have any second thoughts in the morning. "I'll come right over and we'll close the deal," I told Cal. "We might as well give the newspaper boys something to write about today." The deal was announced at 4:45 A.M., a ridiculous hour.

Haynes hung on with the Senators for four years, winning 10 games. Wynn won 163 games for Cleveland, then was traded to Chicago where he has won 59 more. In my first year in Chicago, he won 22 games and pitched us to the pennant.

There are reasons why you sometimes think a player will perform better for you than for the club he's with. Usually it has to do with architecture of your park. With Wynn, it was our pitching coach, Mel Harder. Early had been a fast-ball pitcher up to then with a history of running out of gas at the end of the ball game. Harder, a great curve-baller himself, had shown that he could pass his technique on to others. Our only miscalculation was that it took Wynn half a season to perfect his curve. By the time he began to win for us, we were already too far back.

An interesting footnote to this trade is the part played by Joe Tipton, a nondescript catcher. Joe started my best trade for me by going to Chicago for Haynes. Lane then sent him to Philadelphia for Nellie Fox, the best trade Lane ever made. Fox, of course, was waiting for me along with Wynn when I arrived in Chicago. Nellie won the Most Valuable Player award in our league, and Wynn won the Cy Young award as the best pitcher in baseball. Which would seem to make Tipton, by transfusion, the most expensive nondescript catcher of all time.

Then sometimes, in making a trade, you have to take the long way around. At Chicago, I had my eyes on Juan Pizzaro of Milwaukee and a couple of their other second-line pitchers, Joey Jay and Carlton Willey. I had scouted Pizzaro myself in Jacksonville years earlier and had never been able to figure out why he couldn't win in the majors. Both Jay and Willey were good-looking pitchers who had never really been given much of a chance. Milwaukee was willing to talk but they wanted to talk mostly about Luis Aparicio, the surest way at that time to put a chill on the conversation. I got together with Bill DeWitt, who had just became general manager at Cincinnati, and learned that he was willing to trade his good shortstop, Roy McMillan.

My proposition was for him to make any kind of a deal he wanted as long as Pizzaro was in it. He would then turn Pizzaro over to me along with Cal McLish from his own staff and I would send him Gene Freese, our third baseman.

All I had to do after that was sit back and let William O. carry the ball. It was a wonderful way to make a trade, especially because Al Lopez had already served notice that I might as well get rid of Freese because he wasn't going to play him.

I thought I was being cute about McLish. After being very effective at Cleveland, Cal had flopped with Cincinnati. I had shrewdly deduced that as a control pitcher, Cal had been unable to pitch in the small Cincinnati park but would snap right back to form in our big Chicago park. I now have to admit that I was wrong—but Pizzaro came on fast over the second half of the season, under Lopez, and became one of the top pitchers in the league. Cincinnati did even better. With Jay winning 21 games for them and Freese knocking in a lot of runs, the deal won them the 1961 pennant.

And yet, you cannot say that it was a bad trade for Milwaukee; this is the great misconception most fans have about trading. But, you say, if Jay had won his 21 games for Milwaukee and Pizzaro his 14, the Braves would certainly have won the pennant. Ah, but you can't play the trading game that way; a trade is not reversible. There is no way of knowing what Jay and Pizzaro would have done if they had not been traded. There is no way of knowing what they would have done if DeWitt had kept Pizzaro and given us Jay. There are too many variables. That's what makes life in the player market so much fun.

As a rule, trades are not nearly as complicated as the ones I've cited. Nobody fools anybody. You know what you want; you know what the other man needs; and you know what you can offer. It is always wise, I think, to trade different positions. If I have a surplus of outfielders and am weak at third, my best bet is to find a team that has a surplus at third base and needs an outfielder. In that kind of a trade, both of us know we are doing ourselves some good. If I offered a man one of my outfielders for one of his outfielders, his automatic reaction would be to ask himself what I know about one of them that he doesn't.

Generally, I have always found that if I want to deal I have to go out and propose one myself. Except for Frank Lane, nobody ever offers me anything. Frank, of course, is round-heeled when it comes to a trade. I don't mean that you can take advantage of him; he's built too many teams up from the ground with his trades. I mean that if

140

you come to Frank with a proposition, he can't say no. When I was in St. Louis, I'd call Frank up and say, "Things are dull around here. Let's do something." That's all it took. We had our good-field, no-hit shortstops—Willie Miranda and Joe DeMaestri, players of roughly equal ability—shuttling back and forth between St. Louis and Chicago like commuters. This is the kind of deal made just to whip up a little excitement. To try to make it look as if big things are happening. It's like trading a $200,000 dog for two $100,000 cats; who has a better right to put a value on our players than us?

But Frank will also trade *good* players just to whip up excitement, and that's something I seldom do. Frank is a bright man and a very good judge of ballplayers. He's good for baseball because he's a man who does things. He typifies activity and progress. I know they accuse him of lousing up baseball in some of the towns where he has operated, but the record shows that he has always improved the team and increased the attendance. Until Frank gets back in operation, baseball will be the poorer. But Frank's weakness as a trader is that he will deal just to deal. Frank will trade a Colavito for a Kuenn as much, I think, for the joy of trading the home-run champion for the batting champion as out of the needs of his team. When it comes to trading for newspaper space, I'll stick to my cats and dogs.

Hank Greenberg, another of my closest friends in baseball, was exactly the opposite. The next trade I make with Hank will be my first.

I brought Henry into the executive end of baseball at the end of 1947 after he had been released by Pittsburgh. Well, it wasn't quite that simple. I claimed Hank from Pittsburgh for $1. We were the only team to put in a claim, possibly because he had let it be known that he was retiring and possibly because he carried a salary of something around $60,000. I felt that baseball would be foolish to let a man of Henry's class and intelligence and background get away, and so I met with him at the World Series in New York. I was hoping, frankly, that he'd be a part-time player while he was learning the operating side of the game, but I told him we'd be happy to have him in any capacity he wished. Hank wasn't the least bit interested in playing or coaching. For that matter, he didn't exactly leap at the opportunity of working in the front office.

I have been told by some of my best friends that persistence is one of my finer qualities; in other words, I can be an awful pest. Henry went to Phoenix with his wife after the Series to relax and play some tennis. I flew in right behind him to remind him that he belonged in baseball, not on a tennis court. The Greenbergs went on to the Coast;

I went on to the Coast too. In the end, I was able to talk him into joining us, and by the time I left Cleveland he was ready to take over as the Indians' general manager.

When I landed in St. Louis a year later, Hank and I would talk over the phone almost every day. I would be under the impression that I was calling to propose a trade but somehow it always ended up as a social call. Hank knew exactly what we needed in St. Louis and he could spend hours telling me about it. I knew what we needed too. We needed players. Advice Hank would give me; players, no.

In my final year in St. Louis, when I was hanging on by selling some of my older players, I kept trying to help both myself and Cleveland. (That's my story, and I'm sticking to it.) Cleveland had a contending team, and so I offered some of my players for some of their nice, round figures. Henry was so cool to my nice, round figures that the air would turn to gelatin just about the time he was hanging up on me. I had a good starting pitcher, Virgil Trucks, who I knew would help him. "Henry," I'd say, "you can have Trucks for $100,000 and—" SLAM! Henry never did hang on long enough to find out what player he wasn't going to give me in addition to not giving me the $100,000.

I tried everything. At one point, Hank was flying to Rome. I found out what time he was due to arrive and put in a person-to-person call to catch him stepping off the plane. "Henry," I said, "do you realize that we are in an unprecedented position to consummate baseball's first intercontinental trade? You'll give me Doby and—" SLAM!

Another time I called him in New York, right on the trading deadline. "Let's make a deal while we still have the chance," I said.

"Bill," he said, "what are you bothering me for at this time of night? The deadline's past. It's one-thirty in the morning."

"It's one-thirty in New York," I said, "but it's eleven-thirty here in St. Louis. We'll make a deal St. Louis time. I'll give you—" SLAM!

Henry got his revenge, though. I had decided that Cleveland was in desperate need of my first baseman, Hank Arft, for several good and compelling reasons that I can't for the life of me think of. I kept hammering Arft at him, and he kept pointing out that he already had a far superior first baseman in Luke Easter—as I well knew since I had signed Easter for Cleveland by advertising for him over the radio during a quick trip to Puerto Rico.

Hank never did hang up on me, though, which seemed to indicate a basic interest. Just before the trading deadline, I decided I had indulged him long enough. I sat down at the teletype machine in our office and typed out a message to Hank in Cleveland, warning him that this was the last opportunity I was going to give him to buy Arft.

After a slight delay, the machine began to click away. It said:

ARFARFARFARFARFARFARFARFARFARFARFARFARFARFARFARFARFARF

Well, the teletypes, being rather sensitive machines, would occasionally become stuck. I kept waiting for someone to bring the runaway machine under control, but for line after line there was nothing but ARFARFARF.

At last, the machine ground to a halt. I leaned forward to read his answer. It was:

I CAN'T STOP LAUGHING. KEEP THAT DOG IN ST. LOUIS.

He couldn't hang up on me, though. All he could do was turn off his machine.

The trades that built Cleveland from a sixth-place team to a pennant winner in the space of two years are worth going into, because they show how a team is pieced together. They also illustrate my basic philosophy. I don't believe in trading for the All-Time Futurity; I trade for players who are going to help me in the here and now, not in some Great-Come-and-Get-It Day. It has been my experience that the Youth Plans and Five-Year Plans lead not to pennants but only to new Five-Year Plans. For further details, please consult the Philadelphia Phillies.

The first deal I made was for Joe Gordon, who, with Lou Boudreau, gave us what was probably the greatest second-base combination of all time. The trade, which was made almost as soon as the trading restrictions were lifted at the end of the 1946 season, is pretty typical. Gordon had just finished the worst season of his career. There were rumors around that he and Larry MacPhail had almost come to blows in the Yankee locker room after the final game. The Yankees had Snuffy Stirnweiss, a good second baseman, sitting on the bench. Joe, something told me, was eminently available. The Yankees needed a pitcher. I could offer Allie Reynolds, a solid right-hander, or Red Embree, who had been beating the Yankees all year.

MacPhail was another operator who was always willing to come to me with a proposition. At Fenway Park, during the World Series, he came walking by my seat and said, "Let's make a deal." I said, "Fine. I'll be over in a couple of innings."

Larry was sitting in an aisle box just behind the walkaway, to the home-plate side of the Red Sox dugout. I settled down on the step below him. "Tell you what I'll do," I said. "I'll give you Reynolds for Gordon and Bockman or I'll give you Embree for Gordon."

143

Bockman was a minor-league third baseman who'd had a good year at Kansas City.

MacPhail was just about to take Embree, which was the deal I was hoping he'd go for. Just as he was teetering on the edge, he said, "Let me ask DiMaggio. I'll come back and tell you before the game is over."

DiMaggio was sitting in the second row of boxes, a little to the first-base side of the screen. I went back to my own seat and watched while MacPhail huddled over Joe between innings. At the end of the next inning, I went back to MacPhail's box. "Joe says there's no choice," Larry said. "He says I'm off my rocker if I don't take Reynolds."

We went back to the concession stand and wrote the deal out on a paper napkin, sealed it with a red hot, and came back down and watched the rest of the game.

The Gordon-Reynolds trade was one of those rare deals that won pennants for each side. You can't ask for anything fairer than that.

It also gave birth to a second deal, which is interesting in that it shows how the throw-in players can turn out to be more important in the long run than the guys you each set out to get. The Yankees had come into possession of my old good-luck charm, Hal Peck. I wanted him. The Yankees, having traded away Gordon, needed another infielder. I had Roy Mack, a player MacPhail had always liked. So we start with the standard trade. Each of us has a player the other wants. Each of us knows it. Each is ready to trade. I shook the bottle up a little by saying, "Now Peck for Mack wouldn't be a fair deal, so I think I should be entitled to something more." From there we went back and forth, shuffling things around until it was agreed that Larry would give me Al Gettel, one of his second-line pitchers, plus a choice from a list of half-a-dozen of his good minor-league pitchers. In return, I gave him a promising minor-league catcher, Sherman Lollar.

The wild card here was the anonymous minor-league pitcher. One of the pitchers on his list was Gene Bearden, who was of special interest only because he had not played on a Yankee farm but had been on option to Oakland. Casey Stengel was managing at Oakland, and I knew I could count on Casey for an honest appraisal. "If MacPhail's crazy enough to give him up," Casey said, "grab him."

I'm not going to say that I thought Bearden was going to be anything special. He was the biggest surprise I've ever had in baseball. The first year we had him, we sent him back to the minors. In 1948, though, he exploded. He won 20 games for us, including the playoff

144

game against the Red Sox, and he pitched a shutout for us in the World Series and also came in to save the final game.

It was the only good year Gene ever had. I wonder if anybody has ever made the connection between Gene's quick decline in 1949 and the fact that Casey Stengel, his old manager at Oakland, came up to manage the Yankees that same year. Casey knew something about Gene—or at least suspected something—that he had been warming over in the back of that craggy mind of his. Bearden was a knuckle-ball pitcher, the only pitch he needed when he was right. Most knuckle-ballers, to be effective, have to keep the ball low. Gene's knuckle ball was especially effective because it broke down very sharply, which made it impossible to hit for any distance. From watching him as often as he had, Casey had the distinct impression that Gene's knuckler usually dipped below the strike zone after it broke, which meant that Gene was totally dependent upon getting the batter to swing. He instructed Yankee hitters to lay off Bearden's knuckle ball until there were 2 strikes against them. He was right. Bearden would fall behind the hitter and have to come in with his very ordinary fast ball or curve or, even worse, start his knuckler up high. That kind of information gets around the league with the speed of light, and Bearden was through. Casey giveth and Casey taketh away.

Lollar, the throw-in on the Yankees' side, took much longer to develop. I had him come around to me again in St. Louis, and I traded him once again, this time to Chicago in a cat-and-dog deal with Lane. Fortunately, Lollar was still there when I came to the White Sox in 1959 and he was by then a solid man for us.

My boy Peck was a good player for us at Cleveland. He had the best batting average of any of our outfielders the first year, and he was our best pinch hitter the year we won the pennant.

In addition to trades, we filled in our team from our own roster. Eddie Robinson had come out of the service and was having a big year in the minors when I bought the club. Eddie was playing, however, with a dropped foot; the nerves had somehow weakened so that he couldn't control it. We paid for an operation over the winter, and wrote him off for the better part of the next season. By 1948, Robinson was ready to step in and take over at first base, one of our weak spots.

There was mental rehabilitation of a sort too. Ken Keltner, our third baseman and one-time power hitter, had a miserable season in 1946. There seemed little doubt that he was on the downgrade. Still, when I signed him for the next year, I gave him the same amount of money and told him that if he had what I considered a good year I'd give him a bonus of $5,000.

"What do you consider a good year?" he asked.

I said, "Oh, if you hit .280 and drive in 80 runs, that's a good year."

The next year, Kenny hit the ball better than anybody on our club, with less luck than anybody in the league. If you walked into the park late and saw somebody making a sensational leaping, diving backhanded catch, you could bet that Keltner had hit the ball.

On the last day of the season, he was hitting under .260 and had driven in around 75 runs. I called down to the locker room, got him on the phone and said, "Hey, where have you been? Weren't you supposed to come up and see me at the end of the season?"

"I didn't win anything," he said. "I'm having a lousy season."

I suggested that he wander up anyway. As he came through the door I said, "I've got $5,000 for you."

And he said, "I didn't earn it, Bill." And he started to weep.

"You hit the ball better than anybody else on this club," I told him. "It wasn't your fault they kept catching it."

He took the check and walked out still sniffling and mumbling.

Kenny, no man to concern himself too much about training rules normally, spent all winter getting into shape. In 1948 he led us to our great start, with 10 home runs in the first three weeks, and he went on to the best season of his life. His final home run—number 31—was the big blow in the winning playoff game.

As we left for spring training in 1948, there was one glaring weakness I knew I would have to fill. Joe Page of the Yankees had just shown how valuable a relief pitcher could be. We had nobody who could be counted upon to come in and stop a rally. Nobody at all.

The Athletics had the man I thought could help us in Russ Christopher, a tall, cadaverous right-hander who pitched with a swooping, almost underhanded motion. Christopher's ball would come from down under and then dip as it neared the plate, which meant that the hitters almost had to beat it into the ground. And that is precisely what a relief pitcher wants to make them do.

Christopher was a medical freak. He had a hole in his heart, which leaked some of the used-up blood back into his bloodstream instead of into the lungs for a fresh supply of oxygen. He was, in short, a blue baby grown up. I don't know how many blue babies survive to a ripe old age without an operation, but I would be inclined to doubt that many of them grow up to be big-league pitchers. Christopher had been pitching in the big leagues for six years, and pitching well.

146

That wasn't all. Christopher had come down with pneumonia that spring while the Athletics were playing an exhibition game against the Senators in Orlando, and Mr. Mack had left him behind to recuperate.

I was still willing to take a chance on him. I arrived in Orlando the day before the Athletics were coming back to play the Senators again, because I wanted a day to try to talk Griffith out of Early Wynn. No rapport there at all.

I had made an appointment to have breakfast with Gordon Cobbledick of the *Plain Dealer* at St. Petersburg the next morning, the day Mr. Mack was due. I flew to St. Pete, had breakfast with Cobby and told him, "Come on, let's go."

"Where are we going?"

"I've got to see Mr. Mack at Orlando. I've got to talk him out of a pitcher."

"But," Cobby said, "I thought you just came from Orlando."

"I did," I told him. "I couldn't break a breakfast appointment with you, could I?"

Cobby and I grabbed a cab to drive us the 120 miles back to Orlando. Mr. Mack, of course, told me he couldn't sell Christopher to me because of his bad heart. I told him I knew all about that.

"But he's in bed now with pneumonia," Mr. Mack said. "I'm afraid this may be the final blow to the poor boy."

"I'll give you twenty-five for him," I said, "if I can talk to him first."

Mr. Mack was shocked. "That would be a terrible thing for me to do to you. He's a sick man. He can't play."

"That's not your problem, Mr. Mack. I'm willing to give you the $25,000 if you'll give me permission to talk to him."

Russ was lying in bed, with his head peeking out from a mountain of blankets. At best, Russ was gaunt and hollow-cheeked. Sick as he was, he was all nose and ears. Around his eyes there was that sickly bluish cast. I hadn't expected him to look as if he could run a marathon but to be truthful, the sight of him gave me pause.

"Hey, Russ," I said cheerfully. "Do you think you can pitch?"

He was so weak he could hardly talk. "I don't know," he whispered.

"Do you want to?"

"Sure I want to. I'm a pitcher, and I want to pitch. But I don't know . . . Look at me."

"I'm going to go down and buy your contract," I told him. "I'll take a gamble on you."

"Bill," he said, "I think you're crazy but you have my word on one thing. I'll do the best I can for you."

Russ was a tremendous asset. Although his record showed only 3 wins against 2 losses, he must have saved more than a dozen games for us. In one spell at midseason, he practically kept us in the race.

Still, there were times he frightened the death out of us. Russ couldn't throw more than a couple of pitches warming up in the bullpen because after a little exertion he would have trouble breathing. If he had to throw more than a dozen pitches after he entered the game, his lips would turn purple. Boudreau only used him against a batter or two as a rule and rarely for more than one inning. Afterwards Russ would take a hot shower to stimulate the flow of blood, and be quickly swathed in warm blankets.

His record is one of the strangest you will ever see. He appeared in 45 games, which looks like a lot of work, especially since he grew progressively weaker as the season wore on and was scarcely used at all the final month. In those 45 games, though, he worked only 59 innings. And I'm sure he set an all-time record for getting the most outs on the fewest number of pitches. In four ball games, he threw only one pitch. Each time, the pitch resulted in a double-play.

By late summer, we were saying, "Look, Russ, you've done your share. If you want to go home ..."

"No," he'd say. "The doctors know what's wrong with me and they say it doesn't matter. I told you the first time you asked me—I'm a pitcher. If I die, I might as well die pitching."

It was his last year, though. For the remaining six years of his life he stayed in the warm, sunny climate of San Diego, his home. We helped him, from time to time, wherever we could. No one ever had a stronger claim on our help than Russ Christopher, a thin, jug-eared and gallant man. A pitcher.

There were other minor deals and purchases getting ready for the big 1948 push. I paid $50,000 for Johnny Berardino, whom we didn't need, just to keep Detroit from getting him. A week before the trading deadline, we picked up Bob Kennedy in a trade with the White Sox. We wanted Kennedy for only one reason. We had a weak-throwing outfield and Bob had perhaps the strongest throwing arm in the league. If, during the season, a situation arose where Boudreau needed a strong arm out in right field, he could reach into the dugout and Kennedy would be there. Kennedy did save one game for us under precisely those circumstances. Since we ended in a flat tie and won the pennant in a playoff, he could claim, with justification, that he had won the pennant for us with that throw.

Little by little the team was pieced together, both the team on the field and the team on the bench. With the June 15 deadline coming on, we were in first place and I was getting ready to draw to that inside straight. The only left-handed pitcher on our staff was Gene Bearden, and we needed another one, somebody who could just win an occasional game for us in the second game of a doubleheader and take a few turns in relief. The only left-hander available was Sam Zoldak of the St. Louis Browns. In St. Louis, where Bill DeWitt was holding his franchise together by selling off his players, everybody was available.

Zoldak had a fairly unimpressive record. In five years he had won 23 games and lost 27. His principal recommendation was that he was the best and, unless I am mistaken, only left-hander St. Louis had.

At 10 P.M., two hours before the trading deadline, I called DeWitt and held as abrupt a negotiation as I have ever held with Frank Lane.

"What," I asked "will you take for Zoldak?"

"$100,000," he said.

"It's a deal," I said.

This is the kind of a deal, I say, that you have to make. Zoldak wasn't worth $100,000 or even $50,000 to a team fighting for third place. He wasn't worth $20,000 to a team in the second division. But at that moment, with that team I had in Cleveland, he was worth whatever I had to pay.

Zoldak won his first two starts for us, and shortly afterward he won a very valuable game by beating the Yankees to prevent them from sweeping a 4-game series in our home park. Over the year he won 9 big games for us and saved a few others in relief.

Sam, a short, chubby, good-natured guy, delighted in his identification as "the $100,000 pitcher." Sitting in the clubhouse after a game, sipping his beer or pop, he would lean back happily and ask one of the bigger stars, "And how much did they pay for you?"

After we won the playoff game in Boston, I threw a gala victory party for the players at the Kenmore Hotel. The champagne flowed like Burgundy, and the Burgundy flowed like champagne. As the evening was coming to an end, I toasted each of the 25 players individually, with a passing mention of their more remarkable attributes and contributions. When I got to Zoldak, I lifted my glass and said, "And here's to our $100,000 pitcher."

Big, round tears began to topple down Sam's chubby face—remember, we were all pretty well along by that time. He threw his arms

149

around me and still sobbing, he said, "Bill, this is the nicest thing that ever happened to me. But I've got to tell you something, Bill. I'm not really worth $100,000."

He was, of course. To ask what a player is worth to you is like asking what the deuce of clubs is worth to you in a poker game. Generally, it's the worst card in the deck. But if you need the deuce of clubs to fill a straight flush, it's worth everything in the pot.

Since, as sportswriters are always saying, footballs and baseball executives take funny bounces, Bill DeWitt, who had sold me Zoldak, was faced with that identical decision in 1961 at Cincinnati. This time, the prospective seller was, technically, me. William O. is perhaps the best trader in baseball today. He made fantastic trades when he was dealing his St. Louis players away, always getting the absolute top dollar and then something else besides. We were associated in St. Louis after I bought the Browns, and my respect for him increased. Before he moved to Cincinnati, he had put together the Detroit team which jumped into contention in 1961. In Cincinnati, of course, he made the key trades that won the Reds their first pennant in 21 years.

Cincinnati, however, had a terrible catching staff. I can't think of any pennant winner I have ever seen with such a raggedy lot of catchers. We had the catcher in Chicago Hank Greenberg felt he could use, my old friend Sherman Lollar. Hank offered Lollar at an admittedly high price—not in cash but in players. The key was a fancy-fielding shortstop the Reds had at Indianapolis, Chico Ruiz. In addition, Hank wanted one of their relief pitchers, Brosnan or Henry. DeWitt was in the classic bind. He had to decide whether to trade away a piece of the future for an aging catcher coming to the end of the line. But still, I would insist, a catcher who was worth more to Cincinnati at that particular moment than he had ever been worth to anybody in his prime. Although I was still president of the White Sox, I was already out of action, and DeWitt out of our long friendship, asked me what I thought. I told him I'd make the deal in a second. He had no guarantee, I said, that with or without Ruiz, Cincinnati would ever be that close to a pennant again. When William O. turned the deal down, I was flabbergasted.

In August, after I had sold my interests in Chicago, the White Sox got waivers on Lollar and offered DeWitt the same deal again. Again DeWitt felt the price was too high. He got away with it, because he won the pennant with what he had. You couldn't have convinced me it was the right decision when he made it, though. If Cincinnati had lost the pennant, they would have lost it because DeWitt wouldn't pay the price for Sherm Lollar.

150

It will be noticed that I have not mentioned two of the most important—and certainly the most publicized—additions to the pennant-winning Indian team, Larry Doby and Satchel Paige. I have omitted them because each deserves a special chapter for himself.

The Name of the Game Is Gamesmanship

10.

As the 1948 season opened, the professional odds-makers had us 20–1 in the pennant race. Oddsmakers are cold statisticians, who train themselves to be deaf to the background music of local enthusiasm. Being businessmen, not gamblers, they give no points to the gamblers' feeling of rising expectancy that tells you in your bones that the dice are going to fall right, that the cards are coming, that this is the year.

If the oddsmakers paid any attention to the optimism running through the streets of Cleveland, it was only to write it off as a particularly nasty case of spring fever.

In Cleveland, we knew. From the opening day, when a record crowd of 73,163 turned out to see us against the Browns, to the closing day when 74,181 came to see us lose the final game to Detroit, we knew.

After I have made the best possible case for the proposition that I won the pennant with my brilliant trading, I then have to level and admit that the main reason we won was because I had been unable to get rid of Lou Boudreau, the best deal, as the saying goes, I never made.

As the previous season came to an end, Boudreau's contract ended too. We had finished fourth; I thought we should have done better. By this time I felt secure enough to think I could trade Louie away without having blood flow through the streets of Cleveland. I had discussed a trade with DeWitt before the season ended. I had started to prepare the ground for Lou's departure even earlier by trading Gene Woodling to Pittsburgh for Al Lopez in the winter of 1946. To my mind, Lopez was the best managerial prospect in baseball and I wanted him on our roster where he would be ready to take over on short notice.

During the 1947 World Series between Brooklyn and the Yankees,

DeWitt and I got down to business. The Indians were going to give up Boudreau and two outfielders, George Metkovich and Dick Kokos, plus something in excess of $100,000 (any time you dealt with St. Louis it was understood that you were going to contribute a certain amount toward the upkeep) for Vern Stephens, a hard-hitting short-stop who would replace Boudreau for us; Jack Kramer and Ellis Kinder, two good pitchers; and Don Lehner, a center fielder.

The deal was so close to being made that I had Al Lopez sitting downstairs in the lobby of the Savoy-Plaza waiting to be introduced to the press as the new Cleveland manager. It collapsed at the water's edge because DeWitt came up with a last-minute rider that would have had me paying the difference between Boudreau's salary and the St. Louis manager's salary for three years, a matter of $90,000, all of the money to be put up ahead of time. DeWitt had a certain amount of logic on his side. He would be inheriting the managing end of Lou's salary as well as the playing end, and it is never considered good form to greet a new player—especially a star like Boudreau—with a cut in salary. A player's morale was low enough when he reported to the St. Louis Browns.

I might have sympathized with Bill's cruel dilemma a little more if I hadn't been so certain that he was going to sell Boudreau as soon as he got his hands on him. My only misgivings in negotiating the deal, in fact, was that DeWitt would sell him to Boston. With Boudreau at shortstop, the Red Sox would have been awfully hard to beat.

DeWitt sold the Red Sox the same players I had been negotiating for, in two separate packages, for $250,000 and some players.

In accordance with my operating philosophy, I had let the Cleveland writers in on the negotiations from the beginning. A couple of them had been advising me on the St. Louis players. As soon as the deal collapsed, I notified them all.

The story broke all over the headlines of the Cleveland newspapers. But a funny thing had happened. It broke not as a deal that had collapsed but as a deal that was still under active consideration. The World Series was almost ignored in the Cleveland papers in the outcry against what seemed to be the imminent departure of their beloved boy manager.

The *News* printed a ballot on the front page to give the fans a chance to be heard. More than 100,000 ballots were mailed in, and the vote was 90 percent for returning Boudreau to the manager's office. Booths were set up in parking lots all over the city to distribute form letters demanding that I retain him.

I first learned how badly I had transgressed when the first of the

152

telegrams was delivered to my room in New York the next morning. It read: IF BOUDREAU DOESN'T RETURN TO CLEVELAND, DON'T YOU BOTHER TO RETURN EITHER. It was signed by a minister, whose theology evidently admitted no nonsense about cheek-turning or prodigal-son-welcoming. Other communications from the aroused citizenry followed, many of them uninhibited by the strictures of the cloth.

It may not throw anybody into a state of shock at this point, but I have nothing against front-page publicity, even when the front-page publicity is directed against me. I was, let us say, disillusioned but not displeased. Luckily, I was at the Series with Bud Silverman, a close personal friend, a good baseball fan and also the political reporter for the *Plain Dealer*. Bud could see the situation not as a publicity windfall but, in his own terms, as a political boner that could ruin me with my constituency. "You've still got a chance to control the publicity," he said, "but only if you go right back to Cleveland and explain in person that the deal is off."

I was all in favor of that. As I have said, once you see you're not going to win, the smart thing to do is to make yourself a graceful loser. Far better to retire to a previously prepared position than to let the defeat develop into a rout. Since I had been unable to trade Lou anyway, I told Bud, I would go back to Cleveland, listen to the voice of the people and bow to the will of the fans. As soon as the Series was over.

Bud straightened me out on that one quickly, "When the time comes for a politician to run home and mend his fences," he told me, "the time has come for him to do it right now. Tonight you'll be able to accept defeat gracefully. Two days from now it will be too late."

I reserved two tickets for a flight which would land in Cleveland at 8 P.M. that night. I had a taxi stationed outside Ebbets Field so that we'd be able to see as much of the game as possible before we had to leave. It turned out to be the game in which Floyd Bevans pitched a no-hitter for 8 2/3 innings.

In the eighth inning, Bud was saying, "We got to go, we got to go." I was saying, "I'm not leaving. This is history being made. Tomorrow, we'll go." Somehow Bud got me up from the seat and we retreated slowly up the aisle, stopping at every step. He got me to the back of the grandstand, near the exit. I couldn't leave. With two out and two men on, Lavagetto came in to pinch-hit, and when his drive bounced against the right-field wall, Bud and I went charging out to the taxi. We made the plane with only minutes to spare.

Bud was right. Mass meetings for the protection and preservation of Lou Boudreau were being held in downtown Cleveland that night. Another day might have been too late. Bud helped me to extricate myself from what could have developed into an impossible situation.

The news that I was returning had traveled ahead of me, and the more devoted Boudreau supporters were waiting at the airport. From the tone of their devotion, I could see that the best I could hope for was that they would rip off my epaulets and hold a court-martial proceeding before they hung me.

Tony Pianowski, from our office, had come down to the airport, thank goodness, to pick me up. With a little help, I was able to rise above disaster by climbing on top of the car. From that position of relative safety, I proceeded to rise above truth. But not, understand, above principle; I have no principles against rising above such petty truths. I announced that I had returned to hearken unto the voice of the people. "If I find that the people of this city are against trading Lou Boudreau," I shouted fervently, "then you can be certain he won't be traded."

They cheered me to the echo, which beats getting lynched any time.

Tony drove me down to Euclid Avenue and Ninth Street, the main intersection of town. It was mobbed. There must have been 3,000 to 4,000 people milling around the downtown streets. I walked into a group of about two dozen angry people and asked them how they felt about trading Boudreau. It was made crystal-clear to me that they didn't like it at all. I assured them that if they were that much against the trade, it wouldn't be made. As I started across the street, the groups descended on me from all sides. Somehow as I began to talk, a stepladder appeared at my side. I climbed up, in the middle of the street, and said: "Look, Boudreau is going to remain in Cleveland and manage the club. I'm not going to trade him. Because of his importance, as demonstrated here tonight, and because the fans in the last analysis run the ball club, I am bowing to their will. I was stupid even to think about it."

I swung up the center of the street from block to block, making my speech. The guy with the ladder—whoever he was—kept hustling behind me. All automobile traffic, by this time, had disappeared. As soon as a new crowd surrounded me, I'd climb up the ladder so that they could all see who they were yelling at. We were there, after all, in a common purpose. They were there to yell and I was there to let them yell.

After everybody had gone home—even the guy with the ladder—I toured the taverns and discussed the trade with little knots of people at the bars. Early in the morning, I was still hitting joints in the back

154

alleys, startling drunks in their maunderings so that I could listen to their voices and bow to their wills. The spirit of repentance was upon me, and nobody who strayed outdoors that night was safe from having his temper carefully surveyed and his will appeased.

There was still the matter of answering the thousands of letters that came pouring into our office. One woman, summing up the general tone neatly, wrote only two words: *Drop Dead.*

I answered them all, explaining carefully that having heeded the voices of the people, I was bowing to the will of the fans. The woman wrote back: *Drop Dead, twice.* I saw little reason to pursue that correspondence any further since she was obviously a lady of strong views and limited vocabulary.

Boudreau was sitting pretty once again. He had me over a barrel and he knew it. He refused the one-year contract I offered him and insisted—being no fool—on a two-year contract. Being no fool myself, I gave it to him. I did get one concession written into the contract, the right to name his coaches. The two he had, Oscar Melillo and George Susce, were nice guys and good friends of his but they were little help to him, to my way of thinking, in running a ball club. Having some sense of the fastidious left in me, I didn't hide my feeling that I thought he needed a wee bit of help.

Lou ended up with what might be called "a humiliation of coaches" (the opposite of a pride of lions). And high-paid coaches too. I had hired Bill McKechnie at the end of 1946, as soon as I read he had been fired as manager of the Reds. (I got to Bill before anybody else by tracking him down at the Cincinnati railroad station as he was leaving town.) McKechnie was a great handler of pitchers and a man I hoped Louie would lean on. The funny thing was that although Louie may not have wanted him around at first, they developed an extremely close relationship. When Lou became manager of the Red Sox later, the first thing he did was to hire McKechnie in the same capacity.

To make sure I got McKechnie, I had offered him $20,000 plus a bonus based on our home attendance. For every 100,000 people we drew after the first 1,500,000, Bill was to get $2,500. I thought he might make himself an extra $5,000 in bonus money or, if everything went well, even $7,500. He did slightly better than that. In 1948, he collected on 1,100,000 people, a bonus of $27,500. His total salary, as a coach was therefore $47,500 at a time when the average coach was getting from $6,000 to $7,000.

I had also hired Tris Speaker. It has always been my feeling that baseball throws its greatest asset—its heroes—down the drain. Tris Speaker was working as a steel salesman around Cleveland. I hired him as a part-time batting coach and good-will ambassador at something around $15,000.

To allow McKechnie to devote full time to being an assistant manager in 1948, I made Mel Harder our pitching coach at his old pitching salary of $20,000.

Muddy Ruel, who had left as manager at St. Louis, replaced Melillo. Muddy was hired at his old managing salary of $30,000, although, in truth, we paid him only a nominal sum that first year because he was still collecting on the final year of his St. Louis contract. Anything we paid him would only have been deducted from what he was getting from DeWitt. The agreement was that he would continue to receive his $30,000 in subsequent years, though, and he did.

Ruel was the only one of the coaches Boudreau resented, possibly because Muddy had replaced Lou's close friend, Melillo. The next year, I brought Ruel up to the front office. To replace him, I hired Steve O'Neill, who had just been fired as manager of the Detroit Tigers. Steve had been Louie's first manager in the minor leagues, and they were quite fond of each other. Steve was so delighted to come with us—his home was just outside Cleveland—that he told me to send him a blank contract. I filled it in afterwards for something in the $10,000 to $15,000 bracket.

Never has a team had so many coaches, and never have coaches received so much pay.

Shortly after I signed Lou to that 2-year contract, he was awarded the Man of the Year trophy. In his acceptance speech at the Ribs and Roast banquet the following spring he volunteered, in effect, to step down into the playing ranks if I was not satisfied with the way he managed. He was never put to the test. In 1948, Lou had the greatest season any player has ever had. It was an incredible year. When we needed a base hit, Louie gave it to us. If we needed an impossible play, Louie made it for us. He dominated the season so completely that most people, looking back, are under the impression he won the batting title. He didn't. Ted Williams beat him out. Lou, however, won all the awards. My opinion of his ability as a manager remained more or less unchanged. Lou is the best manager who ever hit .355.

At the end of the year I burned the old contract, to suitable photographic coverage, and gave him a new 2-year contract at $75,000 a year. "Lou was determined to prove I was a jerk," I said. "I was. He did."

It was just as well for Louie that he had the new contract. After surviving our four turbulent years, Lou was fired by the new owners.

Next to winning the pennant, my great ambition that year was to

156

break the Yankees' record for attendance in a single game—81,841. Our target date was Sunday, May 23, a big Sunday doubleheader against the Yankees. Rudie Schaffer and I went all out on our promotion. We arranged for special excursion trains all over Ohio and the surrounding states. For kids under twelve we offered a $1 package that included admission (60¢), a Cleveland Indian sketchbook (50¢), and a cloth replica of our club insignia, the Smiling Indian (25¢). With the big day coming on, we had an advance sale of 57,000 and we had no doubt that the record was at our mercy. Nothing could stop us short of rain or a sudden outbreak of diphtheria.

On Sunday, there was a driving rain. It was still raining at game time.

I had delayed having another operation on my leg in order to see the promotion through to the finish. The day before the game, with nothing left to do except pick up the chips, I had rushed to the hospital and the operation had been performed. I was supposed to lie back comfortably and watch the games from a television set in my hospital room; instead, I was on the phone all morning talking to Rudie. We were getting an amazing turnout in that kind of weather, Rudie told me, but, he thought, short of the record. We wanted to get the games in anyway. The rain was letting up, and after an hour's delay, the first game began at last.

Once that game started, nothing in the world could have kept me in the hospital. I had to get to the park to look at all those people. I asked the nurse to bring me my clothes. Consternation. Flat refusal. Nurses and doctors running around. Lectures. "I'm going," I said.

Larry Atkins was there with me. "OK, Larry," I said finally, "I guess we'll have to do it the hard way. Go back to my apartment and get me some clothes."

The hospital authorities surrendered and gave up my clothes on my promise that I'd stay for only one game.

When I got up to the press box in the third inning, we were leading 4–0. I stayed through the cold, blustery day to watch Joe DiMaggio hit 3 tremendous home runs to knock in 6 runs and beat us 6–5, as we left the bases loaded in the ninth inning.

By then, the crowd figures had already come in. We had 78,431 on an impossible day. But still below the record.

I went back to the hospital and sulked. We did win the second game. Consolation for a disappointing day.

A month later, on June 20, we had a Sunday doubleheader against the Athletics, who were surprising everyone by staying close to the lead. It was a good attraction and we promoted it. We had a moderate advance and no thoughts at all of coming close to a record crowd. The Sunday turned out nice and sunny. Half an hour before the game we could see we were going to have a better crowd than we had anticipated. And they kept coming in. It was one of those crazy things that sometimes happen where by some common impulse everybody decides at the last minute to go to the game. Many of them, I suppose, because they felt they wouldn't have to buck one of the enormous Sunday crowds. As the game started, they were still pouring in heavier than ever, and we could see we were going to come close to the record. They were standing three deep in back of the grandstand, they were sitting on the bleacher steps, they filled the space between the wire fence and the old bleachers.

At the end of the fifth inning, word was passed to me that we had 82,781, a new record. This was an announcement I had to make myself. I swung down to the box alongside our dugout and asked the public-address man for the mike. All the way down, the customers, guessing the reason, applauded. I made the announcement brief and to the point, thanked them all and started back up. The applause was enormous. Another proof that the people at the park identified themselves not only with the victories on the field but with our victories at the box office. Here they had taken a personal part. Every person in the park that day could look at the record attendance figure and see himself as that final "1."

We won both games.

We went on to win the pennant by resorting to gamesmanship— the art of winning without really cheating—as never before in the long and sometimes devious history of baseball. Gamesmanship has always been a part of baseball. Back in 1890, the Baltimore Orioles' catching star, Dashing Jack Doyle, was severely censured for tossing pebbles into the shoes of the hitters as he crouched behind the plate. If the hitters, being slightly uncomfortable, were thrown off their stride or if they were somewhat slower running down the base lines . . . well, there wasn't anything against it in the rules at the time. And every grounds keeper is well stocked with pebbles.

During my days with the Cubs, we had a great third baseman, Smiling Stan Hack. I well recall that in 1935, the sale of "Smile-with-Stan-Hack" mirrors was exceptionally brisk to the bleacherites. Now that I think of it, it was rather strange how often the makeup of female bleacherites seemed to need attention when the opposition was hitting. . . . But then, the vanity of the female has always been a strange and incalculable thing. And if a beam of light occasionally

158

shone in the batter's eye on a particularly important pitch . . . well, what better pitch to choose? Unladylike? Of course. Unsporting? Perhaps. Ineffective? Oh no. Awfully, awfully effective. And, until it happened too often, perfectly legal.

In Cleveland, I used much of the same gamesmanship as I had in Milwaukee, albeit with a little more finesse as befitted my new station.

The playing field at Cleveland Stadium was the biggest in the majors. There was so much pastureland in the outfield when I arrived that I expected warfare between the sheepmen and the cattlemen to be renewed momentarily. Because the home players tend to become discouraged after they have hit a few balls 450 feet and seen them caught, I installed a temporary wire fence around the field, measuring 320 feet along the foul lines and curving out symmetrically to 410 feet in center. (There is an interesting psychological effect in bringing fences within reach. After we put up the wire fence there were almost six times as many balls hit over the wire fence and *into the old stands*.)

The majors had no rule at that time against moving a fence—that didn't come until Frank Lane threatened to construct a portable fence in Chicago and move it between innings as we had in Milwaukee. Still, having learned in Milwaukee that movable fences bring swift action from the rulesmakers, we knew better than to talk about portable fences in Cleveland.

As far as anyone knew, our fence was permanent. Sleeves were driven into the ground and the fence poles were inserted, at regular intervals, into the sleeves. Actually, we had five or six sets of sleeves, nicely spaced so that we could move the fence in and out as much as 15 feet. We didn't buy television time to make a public announcement of what we were doing because we didn't want to disturb the Commissioner's office or upset the opposition. We moved the fence stealthily, in the dark of night.

Before the Yankees came in with all those big strong healthy boys of theirs, the fence would be moved back just as far as it would go. When our little friends from St. Louis paid us a visit, we would move the left-field fence in as far as we could and keep the right-field fence as deep as we could. The Brownies had no right-handed power, but they did have a couple of left-handers who could hit the ball out.

It was a most obliging and adaptable fence.

There was also the matter of our infield. We had, in Cleveland, the Michelangelo of the grounds keepers, Emil Bossard. A grounds keeper can be an invaluable member of a ball team. The infield, for instance, is not flat, it is turtle-backed. (The rule book says: "The infield shall be graded so that the base lines and home plate are level with a gradual slope from the base lines up to the pitcher's plate, which shall be 15 inches above the base-line level.") Suppose, though, that you have a couple of very good bunters on your team. It is to your advantage, as anyone can see, to put a little curl at the end of that turtleback. It is to your advantage to have the ground just along the base line slope *back,* almost imperceptibly, toward the playing field, not only so that fair bunts won't roll foul but that foul bunts can roll fair. And it is to your advantage to have that part of the infield grass nearest to the plate soft and perhaps even soggy so that the bunts will come to a quick halt. If, on the other hand, you have nobody who can bunt, the ground should be hard and swift and the infield even more turtle-backed than it normally is.

There was also the matter of that pitcher's mound. The rule in this regard has been tightened up in recent years, but in those days the theoretical 15 inches from the base-line level to the top of the pitcher's mound was almost impossible to measure, leaving a great deal of latitude for native ingenuity. Our mound at Cleveland always changed according to the pitcher of the day. Bob Feller always liked to pitch from a mountaintop so that he could come down with that great leverage of his and stuff the ball down the batter's throat. Ed Lopat of the Yankees liked a wide, flat mound. When Lopat was pitching against Feller, we'd make it so high that if he had fallen off he'd have broken a leg.

An artist like Bossard takes both starting pitchers into considera-tion and keeps sculpting and shaping the mound daily to give the greatest possible advantage to the home team. But where Bossard's wizardry really shone through was in the way he tailored our diamond to the individual needs of our infielders. We did not have one infield at Cleveland; we had an infield segmented into four sections.

Boudreau, you know, had very bad ankles. His ankles were always so weak that he never played a game without having them tightly wrapped. Lou wasn't fast afoot at all. He played shortstop by antici-pation, by instinct, by knowing what each opposing batter was likely to do against the pitcher working against him at the time. Bossard therefore kept the grass in front of shortstop high and well watered to slow the ball down.

At second base, our needs were entirely different. Joe Gordon was an acrobat, swift of foot and sure of hand. Joe could make plays on hard-hit balls that no other second baseman in the league could touch. The grass toward second, then, was clipped to the nubbin and the base paths between first and second were kept as hard as a rock.

Ken Keltner, at third base, was nearing the end of the line. Kenny's

160

legs were creaking on him all year. Bossard had an answer for that, too. The area around third was soaked down daily to reduce the shock and strain on Keltner's legs to a minimum. Third base at Cleveland was such a bog that if alligators had poked their heads up along the coaching box, none of us would have been at all surprised. With the strain taken off his legs, Ken could still make the plays, so the grass was left at the normal height.

Our first baseman, Eddie Robinson, was an average fielder. The first-base segment was therefore maintained in a normal way.

We ended the season with a burst of sign-stealing, one of the oldest tricks in baseball and one of the few parts of the game which unfortunately goes unobserved in the stands. Signs are stolen in many ways. Coaches steal the sign from the catcher or, even more often, pick up some giveaway from the pitcher's movements. This kind of sign-stealing takes a great amount of talent and is approved by all right-thinking baseball people. Charley Dressen is reputed to be the world's greatest expert, especially if you're listening to Charley. I have my doubts. Not about Charley's skill but about his effectiveness. The coach who picks up a giveaway has to pass his information to the hitter and pass it fast. Dressen does it by whistling. The trouble is that once Charley gets to whistling, there is the natural suspicion that he ain't just whistling "Dixie." As a result, a pitcher who is about to throw a curve ball might well decide to throw a fast ball just to see what happens. A batter who finds a fast ball coming at his head after he has heard the chirping for a curve can get quite a thrill.

At Milwaukee, we had a marvelous sign-stealer in Roxie Lawson, who also passed the pitch on by whistling. Roxie, being a man who would steal a sign and let the glory go, could whistle away all afternoon without drawing anything except admiration. I have a feeling that the best sign-stealers in baseball today are equally unknown.

Throughout the history of baseball, going back to the first time Abner Doubleday crawled out of a cave and lit a fire, information has been passed on to the hitter by less intellectual and less sportsmanlike means.

McGraw used to station a man with a pair of binoculars in the window of the Polo Grounds clubhouse, which was in that cutout in deep center field. The clubhouse man had only to lower or raise the shutter to signal the upcoming pitch.

In most parks, the clubhouse is under the stands, and the man with the binoculars is out in the scoreboard. Two years ago we had Dizzy Trout out in the scoreboard at Comiskey Park. One of our pitchers, Red Worthington, a very religious man, left the club and quit baseball because he thought we were playing unfair. And yet I doubt if there is one club that hasn't tried it at one time or another in recent years. There is absolutely nothing in the rules against it.

Cleveland had a long tradition of scoreboard espionage, with rather indifferent success. As we returned home for the final month of 1948, following a disastrous road trip that had dropped us out of the lead, we were in third place, 4½ games off the lead with only 21 games left. With figures like that, there is nothing to do, normally, except watch the Magic Numbers go by. Desperate measures were called for. Boudreau and some of the boys decided to take another shot at sign-stealing—and this time with more modern methods. Instead of binoculars, they bought a spotting scope, the kind of portable telescope used on rifle ranges. The spotting scope put the scoreboard observer right in the catcher's lap.

Our man in the scoreboard was Marshall Bossard, son of Emil. Occasionally, he was spelled by another of the Bossard boys, Harold.

The sign was passed on by covering one of the scoreboard openings with either a white or a dark card, depending on whether the pitch was going to be a fast ball or a curve.

Now, understand that the sign isn't passed on with every pitch. If it were, the opposition would spot it in about two minutes. Nor would it be possible to pass on every pitch even if you wanted to. A big-league catcher usually gives his signs in a fairly complex pattern with any number of built-in switches. The first thing the spotter has to do is to break the code and stay alert for every switch. This is why I say that sign-stealing, even when it is done from the scoreboard, is part of the real byplay of baseball, part of the battle of wits. Once he has broken the code, the spotter has to pick a few key moments in the game to pass the sign on. And he has to be right 100 percent of the time. As soon as your team has the slightest misgiving about the accuracy of the signs, you can fold up the spotting scope, throw away the binoculars and go home.

But here's where the next complication arises. If the sign-stealing is effective, the opposition is going to suspect what is happening. They are going to be sure of it as soon as a hitter steps into a pitch he has no right to expect and belts it halfway into the stands. In one game against the Yankees, Joe Page threw a curve ball to Joe Gordon on a 3–0 pitch. Gordon hit it into the bleachers and before the ball had landed, everybody from the Yankee bench was out on the field, pointing up to the scoreboard and screaming. Now the opposition has a mission in life. They are going to do their best to cross you up and make it hurt.

162

Marshall Bossard was great. He picked his spots masterfully and he never missed.

Not all batters want to know what is coming. Generally, the power hitter, the man who takes a big swing, wants the sign. The punch hitter, the man who wants to be ready on every pitch, doesn't.

In Cleveland, Boudreau himself didn't want the signs. Neither did Dale Mitchell. Doby went by fits and starts. He'd take the signs on pitchers he had trouble with but he didn't want them on pitchers he felt he could hit. Keltner, Gordon and Robinson, our other home-run hitters, were happy to get them. And they hit a couple in this way to win us a few of those games. Especially Keltner and Gordon.

There was one final bit of gamesmanship I came very close to using, something that would have brought about rioting in Boston, a beating of editorial breasts throughout the nation and a change in the rules, all within 24 hours.

Our magnificently written rules read that "the manager of the home team shall be the sole judge as to whether a game shall not be started because of unsuitable weather conditions or the unfit conditions of the playing field."

The manager, in this instance, means the front office.

Clubs through history have called off relatively meaningless games because of bad weather even though to the eyes of the casual observer the sun seemed to be shining brightly. Out of a decent respect for the opinion of mankind, it is customary to give such excuses as "threatening weather" or "wet field." There is nothing in the world, though, to prevent me from saying the field is unfit because I had a nosebleed behind first base.

I had always dreamed of the day when a pennant race would come down to the last day and I would be faced with a situation where it was to my benefit *not* to play that final game. In 1948, that was exactly the situation confronting me.

We were one game ahead of the Red Sox and scheduled to end the season against the Detroit Tigers. The Tigers had their best pitcher, Hal Newhouser, ready to go against us. The Red Sox were playing the Yankees. If the Red Sox won and we lost, there would be a tie for first place, which would necessitate a playoff game. If we did not play, we would win the championship no matter what the Red Sox did. It had already been determined, in a special drawing, that if a playoff game became necessary it would be played at Fenway Park where the Red Sox were practically unbeatable.

In short, we had nothing to gain by playing the game and the world and all to lose. I called the weather bureau, and the forecast was "possible showers."

I looked this situation squarely in the eye—and I quavered. A voice within me—let us call it, for lack of a better word, conscience—said, "You can't do it. It isn't fair to the players to brand them forever as the team that won the pennant by ducking out on the final game." A contending voice within me—let us call it, for lack of a better name, Bill Veeck—answered, "Come on, you jerk, this is what you've been waiting for."

I didn't trust myself. I hastily put in a call to the league president—let us call him, for the sake of accuracy, Will Harridge—and I told him, "Under the rules, I can determine what the weather is and how the field looks. I can call off the game without giving any reason."

"You wouldn't do that," Will said. Will spent the best years of his life telling me I wouldn't do things I went right out and did.

"Will," I said, "I have a strange feeling that if a cloud crosses the sun tomorrow morning, I am going to call off the game. I am willing to surrender my prerogative to your office. You'd better come down here or send a representative from your office."

There was a long pause. Will was trying to figure out what my angle was. You send out a cry for help along the leased wires of the American Telephone and Telegraph Company and they sit there and wonder what your angle is.

"Come on, Bill," he said. "You're going to have a full house. You wouldn't throw 80,000 people away."

"We've already drawn all the people anybody could want," I told him. "What's another 80,000? Especially when I'm sure of at least two World Series games if I don't play."

Harridge sent down Tommy Connolly and Cal Hubbard to rule on the weather. It was a beautiful day and we lost the game. "You see, Veeck," I kept muttering, "that's what you get for being honorable."

In all my years in baseball, there has been only one game I have been sure—absolutely sure—of winning. That was the playoff game in Boston. All through the year, Lou Boudreau had given us the play we needed to stay alive or the hit we needed to win. I knew absolutely that, whatever had to be done to win this one, Lou would do it. Before the game, crossing from the third-base dugout to our first-base box, I asked Larry Atkins to make arrangements for a victory party at the Kenmore.

Lou had called Hank Greenberg and me down to the dugout before the game to ask our advice on his lineup, something he had never

164

done before. He wanted to know if it was all right with us if he played Allie Clark, a utility outfielder, at first base. I said, "Louie, you've managed the ball club without aid all year. I'm certainly not going to be looking over your shoulder in the most important game of all."

It was a daring move. With the Red Sox starting Denny Galehouse, an old-timer who had control but no particular speed or breaking stuff, Lou had decided to forego the lefty-righty percentage. Instead, he was playing the other percentage, Fenway Park's looming left-field wall, by packing his lineup with right-handers from top to bottom. Including Clark. The only thing about it was that Clark had never played an inning of first base in the major leagues.

First base is not the most difficult position in the world. But if Clark made an error which cost us the game and the pennant, Lou would be attacked from coast to coast for taking that kind of a chance in such a climactic game. If, on the other hand, Allie won the game for us with a dramatic home run, Lou would be hailed nationally for his courage, his imagination and his intellectual honesty.

As it was, Allie Clark was the most inconspicuous player on the field. He was the only man in our lineup who failed to get a base hit. Not a ball was hit anywhere near him all day. Boudreau's great gamble went unmarked and unremarked upon. It was as if the South had fired on Fort Sumter and missed.

The victory party was an action party aimed, among other things, at releasing the tension that had been building up through the season. There was another reason. I like parties. This one was restricted to our players and our writers. The only outsider was a little fellow who had come down from Cleveland for the game and had been invited, on the spur of the moment, by Keltner and Tipton. As the evening wore on and tempers began to flow . . . I mean *flare,* either Tipton or Keltner—things were getting a bit kaleidoscopic at that point— decided their guest was really an intruder so he picked up the little guy and threw him out. The other, feeling his duties as a host more keenly, ran out to the hall, picked him up and threw him back in. Joe Gordon, finding the situation of interest, was willing to lend them both a hand. It was almost like calisthenics with the poor guy being heaved in and out by the numbers. One thing led to another—with Gordon perhaps doing the leading—until Tipton and Keltner pulled off their jackets to have at each other. Over to break it up ran Hank Greenberg and myself. Hank, showing the quick reactions that were to gain him election into the Hall of Fame, arrived in time to almost get belted in the nose with the only punch thrown. Kenny and Joe, apparently feeling that their point had been made, put their jackets back on and became buddies again.

The party ended, for me, wandering around Boston with Joe Gordon until about seven in the morning. At noon, I was awakened by the sound of somebody beating upon either my head or the door. It was a fellow from *Sport* Magazine, and he seemed to be in some trouble. What had happened was that *Sport* was holding a luncheon downstairs to announce the launching of its first issue, and Ted Williams, booked as the principal speaker, had failed to show up. Good Ole Will, as everybody knows, is always available.

"I'll stand under the shower for a couple of hours," I told him, "and be down."

"You can't," he said. "You've got to come down in the next fifteen or twenty minutes."

"I'll stand under a cold shower for fifteen or twenty minutes," I said, "and be down."

So I stood under a cold shower and went down and delivered one of my brilliant addresses. It couldn't have been too bad. The next year, at *Sport's* first annual banquet, I was invited to be the featured speaker.

After the luncheon was over, I was informed that one of our troop was still missing. Gene Bearden, who had pitched the playoff victory, was apparently still celebrating somewhere in Boston, in midafternoon. We organized a search party and finally found him. Three days later, he shut out the Braves in the third game of the World Series.

In Cleveland—and again in Chicago—I can say, without fear of contradiction by my worst enemy, I did my darnedest to get the World Series tickets to the fans who had supported us through the year.

As soon as we got the go-ahead to accept World Series orders, which was before we had the pennant clinched, I told Larry Atkins to take care of any of "our" people who wanted tickets: busboys, bartenders, men's-room attendants, cabdrivers, waitresses, shoeshine boys and the telephone operators at the hotel and at the hospital.

"Anybody?" he said. "You're crazy. It will be everybody!"

Anybody or everybody, I told him. These were the people who had supported us from the beginning and had helped us from day to day and they deserved to be in on the victory. I gave away 250 sets of tickets to that strata of Cleveland society and I paid for them all myself. For the Boston games, the waitresses at the Kenmore Hotel all received tickets out of our allotment, too, although I suspect that they still rooted for the Braves.

The distribution of tickets in Cleveland brought on an argument

166

with Commissioner Happy Chandler, the first of two World Series arguments we had. It had always been standard procedure to sell each customer a ticket for each of the home games, so we quite naturally had the tickets made up in strips of three. Since people don't like to go to games alone, we allowed each applicant to order two strips.

When it came time to open the ticket sale, we set a mail deadline for midnight and had the office staff come in to start processing the tickets. Around midnight, I received a call to come down to the post office. The mailmen had a room full of bags for us, bag after bag after bag. "And," I was told, "the letters are still pouring in."

I went right back to the office and told Rudie we had to change the system and allot the tickets by the individual game to take care of three times as many people.

I hired a Brink's truck to take the tickets back to the printing company to be cut. The post office started dumping the bags on us, and the Brink's truck started bringing back the tickets. We began to stuff the envelopes. A group of my friends—known throughout Cleveland as the Jolly Set—came over from a party to help us out. We worked through the night and through the morning, the women of the Jolly Set in their evening gowns, and we stayed with it until we finished the job.

It was a lot of work. In addition to stuffing three times as many envelopes, we had to make out a refund to send back with every ticket.

For my efforts, I was rewarded by a call from Chandler. "You can't do that," he said. "You've got to sell your tickets in sets of three."

"Oh?" I said. "And just why do I got to?"

"Because if you don't," he said in ringing tones, *"you will establish a precedent!"*

"Happy," I said, "I couldn't care less about precedents. I'm going to sell my tickets my way, unless you can figure out a way I think is better."

This is the kind of thing that gripes me beyond words. My only crime was that I had been trying to spread the tickets around to as many of our fans as possible, at a cost to nobody but our own club. By being as fair as humanly possible, I could only be helping all of baseball. It was inconceivable to me that anyone could object. And yet, it always happens. Anything you try to do for the customer, whether it be for his enjoyment or his good will, is sure to bring on some pompous and silly protest.

I had one final controversy with Chandler before we played the first World Series game in Cleveland. If you remember, there were no radio broadcasts in Cleveland when we arrived. I had simply offered the rights to everybody. The next year, the rights were bought by WGAR, the leading station in Cleveland. WGAR, however, wasn't able to clear unlimited time for us and we found our games being cut off amidship for such things as the Friday night fight—a grand way to cheapen baseball. The next year, I went around to every station and found only one—WJW—which would guarantee to take every inning of every game.

Before the playoff game in Boston, a meeting was held to sign the necessary papers for the radio and TV broadcasts of the World Series and, under those special circumstances, for the playoff game itself. Mr. Spang, the head of Gillette, was there to represent the sponsor and there was also a representative from the Mutual Broadcasting System.

I very quickly became aware that WJW was not going to be allowed to carry the World Series, and that neither of our regular announcers was going to be hired to broadcast the games.

"Now wait a minute," I said. "This is patently unfair. These are the guys who helped us draw our crowds all year. Now comes the day of rewards and they're getting cut out. What does it matter to you if they carry the Series, as long as your Mutual affiliate carries it too?"

WJW was owned by Bill O'Neil, of the General Tire family. He had just started his first little station in those days and while I'm sure he wasn't starving, that wasn't the point. It just wasn't right.

I called O'Neil from the conference room and found he was willing to agree to carry the broadcast on whatever terms were laid down, either sponsored by Gillette or the regular sponsors or, if Gillette preferred, not sponsored at all.

Mutual and Gillette remained adamant. I turned to Chandler for help. "Well," Chandler said, "you can't expect me to take any part in this. We have a contract, and we're going to live up to the contract."

I said, "Happy, are you representing me and baseball or are you representing Gillette and Mutual?"

He was as indignant as only a politician can be. "That's a terrible thing to say," he said. "I take that as a personal slap in the face."

"That's the way it sounds to me," I said. "But I can assure you of one thing. Since you say we're going to abide by the contract, I can assure you we are going to. Just exactly as the contract is written."

The first thing I did was to refuse permission for the playoff game to be broadcast to Cleveland over the Mutual affiliate. The next thing I did was to study the contract.

The first two games were played in Boston. The train back to Cleveland for the third game arrived two and a half hours late, which fouled up a lot of things but not this particular project. I arrived at the park, flanked by my attorneys, an hour before the game, just as the Mutual crew was beginning to set up its equipment in the regular broadcasting booths. "Gentlemen," I said, "of course you realize this is going to be conducted under the exact terms of the contract, which means that you can't use this booth to broadcast from. The contract says you will use any booth in which there are facilities designated by the management. The management is designating the football press box up on top."

It was as if I had hit them with a sledgehammer. From the football press box, halfway down the foul line, it was impossible to see home plate.

"That *is* unfortunate," I said. "But that's what you're going to use." And I added, "I also want to inform you that you're entitled to one hundred admissions for your technical people by the terms of the contract. The contract, it says that. It also says they will be seats obscuring no one's view. Now, there is only one place in the ball park where you won't obscure anyone's view. I have directed that one hundred seats be set up beyond the wire fence up against the bleacher wall."

With the fans already filling in the space between the fence and the bleachers, the seats were worthless.

"If you want to take it to court," I told them, "fine. My attorneys here tell me I'm within my rights. Mr. Chandler informed me we were going to observe the contract in scrupulous detail and this is what we are doing."

The Mutual representative, Paul Jonas, was a little fellow, and he was so mad I thought he was going to jump right out of the booth.

"I'll tell you what *we'll* do," he said. "We'll go on the air and tell the whole country why we can't broadcast the play-by-play to them."

"Perfectly all right with me," I said. "You can do anything you want to. I'm sure you're well acquainted with the laws of libel. If you aren't you can consult your attorney. I am going to have your broadcast taped, so I suggest that you be very careful what you say. If you imply for a moment that this isn't being carried out within the terms of the contract, I will haul you through every court in the country."

I said, "You can call Spang"—and I suspect they did—"and you can call Chandler"—and I know they did—"and it will make no difference what they say. I'll do only what the contract says I have to do."

I don't know to this day what I'd have done at the last minute. I

169

often wonder. O'Neil brought the impasse to an end by calling me about 15 minutes before the game to ask me to let them go ahead.

I said, "Send me a wire stating that you have asked me to let Mutual broadcast and that you feel everything has been done to satisfy you that could be done. And put in one other thing and see that they agree to it. Put in that in the future, the station that carries the broadcasting for the club during the year will carry the Series and will be permitted to use at least one of the regular announcers."

Those were the rules that went into effect the following year, and those are the rules in effect today.

It Only Takes One Leg to Walk Away | 11.

WHEN I signed Larry Doby, the first Negro player in the American League, we received 20,000 letters, most of them in violent and sometimes obscene protest. Over a period of time I answered all. In each answer, I included a paragraph congratulating them on being wise enough to have chosen parents so obviously to their liking. If everyone knew their precious secret, I told them, I was sure everyone would conform to the majority. Until that happy day, I wrote, I was sure they would agree that any man should be judged on his personal merit and allowed to exploit his talents to the fullest, whether he happened to be black, green, or blue with pink dots.

I am afraid irony is lost on these people, but that's not the point I want to make here. A year later, I was a collector for what is now called the Combined Jewish Appeal. This time I got something close to 5,000 violent and sometimes obscene letters. In answering, something very interesting happened. The names began to have a familiar ring. I became curious enough to check our files and I found they were to an astonishing degree—about 95 percent—the same people. A year after that, I converted to Catholicism. About 2,000 anti-Catholics were concerned enough about my soul to write me violent and again often obscene letters. All but a handful of them were already in our anti-Negro and anti-Semitic files.

So I am one man who has documentary proof that prejudice is indivisible. The jackal, after all, doesn't care what kind of animal he sinks his teeth into.

170

I have always had a strong feeling for minority groups. The pat curbstone explanation would be that having lost a leg myself, I can very easily identify myself with the deprived. Right? Wrong. I had tried to buy the Philadelphia Phillies and stock it with Negro players well before I went into the service. I think we live in a time when we psychoanalyze everybody's motives too much and that it is entirely possible to look at something which is ugly and say "This is ugly" without regard to conditioning, environment or social status. My only personal experience with discrimination is that I am a left-hander in a right-handed world, a subject on which I can become violent.

Thinking about it, it seems to me that all my life I have been fighting against the status quo, against the tyranny of the fossilized majority rule. I would suppose that whatever impels me to battle the old fossils of baseball also draws me to the side of the underdog. I would prefer to think of it as an essential decency. If someone wants to argue the point I won't object, although we'd have a better chance to be friends if he didn't.

Let me make it plain that my Philadelphia adventure was no idle dream. I had made my offer to Gerry Nugent, the president of the fast-sinking club, and he had expressed a willingness to accept it. As far as I knew I was the only bidder. The players were going to be assembled for me by Abe Saperstein and Doc Young, the sports editor of the Chicago *Defender,* two of the most knowledgeable men in the country on the subject of Negro baseball. With Satchel Paige, Roy Campanella, Luke Easter, Monte Irvin, and countless others in action and available, I had not the slightest doubt that in 1944, a war year, the Phils would have leaped from seventh place to the pennant.

I made one bad mistake. Out of my long respect for Judge Landis I felt he was entitled to prior notification of what I intended to do. I was aware of the risk I was taking although, to be honest, I could not see how he could stop me. The color line was a "gentleman's agreement" only. The only way the Commissioner could bar me from using Negroes would be to rule, officially and publicly, that they were "detrimental to baseball." With Negroes fighting in the war, such a ruling was unthinkable.

Judge Landis wan't exactly shocked but he wasn't exactly overjoyed either. His first reaction, in fact, was that I was kidding him.

The next thing I knew I was informed that Nugent, being in bankruptcy, had turned the team back to the league and that I would therefore have to deal with the National League president, Ford Frick. Frick promptly informed me that the club had already been sold to William Cox, a lumber dealer, and that my agreement with Nugent

171

was worthless. The Phillies were sold to Cox by Frick for about half what I had been willing to pay.

Word reached me soon enough that Frick was bragging all over the baseball world—strictly off the record, of course—about how he had stopped me from contaminating the league. That was my first direct encounter with Mr. Frick.

There is a suspicion, I suppose, that if I tried to buy the Phillies and stock it with Negro players, it was only because, showman that I am—promoter, con man, knave—I was grabbing for the quick and easy publicity and for the quick and easy way to rebuild a hopeless team. I am not going to suggest that I was innocent on either count.

On the other hand, I had no particular feeling about making it either an all-Negro team or not an all-Negro team. The one thing I did know was that I was not going to set up any quota system—a principle which cost me my original backer. As always, I was operating from a short bankroll. The most obvious backer, it seemed to me, was the CIO, which had just begun a campaign to organize Negro workers in the South.

The CIO was ready and eager to give me all the financing I needed. The money, in fact, was already escrowed when the CIO official I was dealing with asked for my assurance that there would always be a mixed team on the field. (I don't like to duck names, but there was a promise from the beginning of the negotiations that his name would not enter into any of the publicity.) The only assurance I am willing to give anybody, ever, is that I will try to put the best possible team on the field.

I had another potential—and logical—backer, Phillies Cigars, who had already indicated a willingness to bankroll me. Ford Frick lowered the boom.

What offends me about prejudice, I think, is that it assumes a totally unwarranted superiority. For as long as I can remember I have felt vaguely uneasy when anybody tells me an anti-Negro or anti-Semitic or anti-Catholic joke. It only takes one leg, you know, to walk away.

When Eleanor and I first invested in our guest ranch, our partner was going to be an old Chicago friend. Since he had previously operated his own guest ranch in Arizona, our agreement was that I was going to put up the money, he was going to operate the ranch, and we were going to split the profits. The partnership broke up as soon as I picked up his brochure and read that our ranch was to be restricted. For the benefit of those not familiar with the vocabulary of prejudice, restricted means No Jews. I told him that the people who had helped me most up to then were Jewish and that, in any case, I absolutely wouldn't go along with that kind of silliness. I told him, further, that I didn't want to be in business with anyone whose mind ran the way his obviously did. Eleanor and I bought him out that same day, even though it cost us almost all the money we had left from the sale of the Brewers.

As it turned out, the whole Arizona resort area was restricted, something that had never filtered through my thick head. The Lazy Vee became one of the few completely open ranches in the state.

I ran into the "restrictive branch" of anti-Semitism again during my first weeks in Cleveland, after Harry Grabiner decided to travel back and forth between Cleveland and his farm in Allegon, Michigan. I hardly needed a full suite for myself, so I moved out of the Cleveland Hotel and into a private club. The first time Harry came back to stay for a few days, I stopped at the desk to tell the room clerk to reserve a room for Mr. Grabiner.

"I'm sorry," he said. "I don't think we have a room for Mr. Grabiner."

"You have no what?" I said, astonished.

"I'm sorry," he said. "Mr. Grabiner is Jewish. We can't allow him in the club."

"That's fine," I said. "Send the boy up in ten minutes to get my bags."

Before I leave this subject, I should say that my ultimate ambition —that thing you are going to do some day to make your life worthwhile—has been to become a lawyer and devote myself to legal aid of the American Indians. To date, I've talked a good fight and done nothing beyond buying a law library to enable me to "read law" on my own. The one thing that gave me pause about settling in Maryland, in my current retirement, is that Maryland is not one of the states which allow you to take the bar examination without a degree from a school of law. The Negroes have made their greatest advances through the courts, largely through the work of Negro lawyers. The Indians have been so deprived of education that they do not even have their own lawyers to throw into the battle.

I first became interested in the Indians and their lore back in my days at the Ranch School in Los Alamos. Later, as a resident of both Arizona and New Mexico, I became very much interested in their arts. For years, I have collected Indian rugs, pottery and paintings.

The Indians in the Southwest are the most underprivileged, mistreated and neglected of our citizens. When you drive through that area and come upon land that looks absolutely valueless, you know

173

you're on an Indian reservation. When, as a final irony, it turns out that there is uranium or oil under the reservation, the Government breaks the treaty and takes the land away.

Most prejudice, I believe, is reducible to basic economics. We steal the Indians' land and to justify what we are secretly ashamed of doing, we say that they are a savage, backward people—which is a way of saying that the land is too good for them anyway.

With the Negroes, there is nothing to take away except their right to make a living. We justify that by saying they are a backward, ignorant people—which is a way of saying that they couldn't compete anyway. We push them into slums and we say, smugly, "How can people live like that?" as if they were there by choice.

After I became established in Cleveland, I was invited to address the graduating class at a Negro high school. I leap to that kind of invitation, white or Negro. I try not to give the usual pablum talk about entering into the bright and beckoning world, hearing enough of those while I'm waiting to get in my licks. If you think the typical graduation address at a white high school is pap, ask yourself how that same address probably sounds to a bunch of Negro kids. The speaker ahead of me was a politician who made one of those innocuous speeches in which one bids for the Negro vote without saying anything that might jeopardize white votes. Pure pablum.

I got up and I said: "I want to address my opening remarks to all of you who still think the Constitution of the United States applies to you. The part that says all people are created free and equal. You have wasted this part of your education. You are living in a dream world. Since I don't know what I could say at this stage of your life to get through to you, you might as well stop listening to me right now. Obviously, those of you I am still talking to do not believe that. . . ."

I went on to point out that the only way they could amount to anything in that brave, beckoning world they were being told about was to educate themselves so thoroughly and become so capable in their work that they would impress their ability on white people and therefore be able to fight more intelligently for their rights. Like it or not, I told them, they had to be not only as good as the white man in whatever they chose to do but better, because the world had imposed upon them the burden of proving that the Negro had been backward not because he was unintelligent but because he was uneducated.

The speech was given a big play in the Negro paper, the *Call-Post,*
174

and I don't suppose there were many Negro high schools in Cleveland where I was not subsequently invited to speak.

All this is background, a presentation of credentials to the signing of Larry Doby and Satchel Paige. When I came to Cleveland, I was almost sure I was going to sign a Negro player. We had four or five Negro friends sending us reports from the beginning. At the start of the 1947 season, I hired a Negro public relations man, Lou Jones, so that he could familiarize himself with the league ahead of time and serve as a companion and a buffer to the player we signed. I spoke to the Negro leaders of the city and told them I was going to hold them responsible for policing their own people in case of trouble. (There was nothing for them to be responsible for, of course. We never had one fight in Cleveland in which a Negro was involved.)

I moved slowly and carefully, perhaps even timidly. It is usually overlooked, but if Jackie Robinson was the ideal man to break the color line, Brooklyn was also the ideal place. I wasn't that sure about Cleveland. Being unsure, I wanted to narrow the target areas as much as possible; I wanted to force the critics to make their attacks on the basis of pure prejudice—if they dared—and not on other grounds. To give them no opportunity to accuse us of signing a Negro as a publicity gimmick, I had informed the scouts that I wasn't necessarily looking for the best player in the Negro leagues but for a young player with the best long-term potential. And I only wanted to sign one Negro because, despite those glowing credentials I have given myself, I felt that I had to be in a position to extricate the club fairly easily in case we ran into too many problems.

The player whose name kept floating to the top was Larry Doby, the second baseman of the Newark Eagles. Still moving with great caution, I told Rudie to have Bill Killifer follow Doby for a few games without leaking what he was doing. Rudie followed instructions so well that he didn't even leak word to Killifer. He just told Bill to go down to Atlanta over the weekend, scout Newark and call us back with a rundown of all their players. Bill, logically enough, arrived in Atlanta under the impression that he was supposed to scout the Newark team in the International League. Upon looking through the paper and seeing that Newark wasn't in town, he did what any sensible man would do at the end of a wild-goose chase. He got stiff.

By the time Rudie tracked him down two days later, the Newark Eagles were in New Orleans. Bill eventually turned in a favorable report on Doby, and I scouted him myself, back in Newark, just before we bought him.

175

I had always felt that Mr. Rickey had been wrong in taking Jackie Robinson from a Negro club without paying for him. Contract or no, the owner of a Negro club could not possibly refuse to let a player go to the major leagues. It meant too much to the whole race. For anyone to take advantage of that situation, particularly while talking about equal rights, was terribly unfair.

I offered Mrs. Effa Manley, the owner of the Newark club, $10,000 for Doby's contract, plus an additional $10,000 if he made our team. Effa was so pleased that she told me I could have the contract of her shortstop, who she thought was just as good, for $1,000. Our reports on the shortstop were good too. We had eliminated him because we thought he was too old. To show how smart I am, the shortstop was Monte Irvin.

To make it as easy as possible for Doby, I had decided to make the announcement on the road. Lou Jones picked him up in Newark and brought him to the Congress Hotel in Chicago to meet me and the press. In the taxi, on the way to the park, I told Larry, "If you have any troubles, come and talk them over with me. This is not the usual con, I mean this. It will take some time for the other fellows to get used to you. You have to accept that. You may have to go it alone for awhile. That's why Lou Jones is here."

A couple of the players made their objections known; I found faraway places to send them. Predictably, they were players of little talent and therefore the most threatened economically. Joe Gordon, a club leader, was the player who welcomed Doby with the most open heart and became his friend and confidant. That didn't surprise me at all. Some of the writers disapproved, although not in print and not to me personally. That did surprise me.

In his first day in uniform, July 3, 1947, Doby saw action as a pinch hitter and struck out. During that whole first year, he was a complete bust. The next year, however, when Tris Speaker and Bill McKechnie converted him into a center fielder, Larry began to hit and one of our weak positions suddenly became one of our strongest.

Some of the players who had not seemed overjoyed at having Larry on the team became increasingly fond of him as it became apparent that he was going to help them slice a cut of that World Series money. The economics of prejudice, as I have discovered many times, cuts both ways.

And when Doby hit a tremendous home run to put us ahead in the fourth game of the World Series, it could be observed that none of the 81,000 people who were on their feet cheering seemed at all concerned about—or even conscious of—his color.

176

Doby was as close to me as any player I have ever known, although it took awhile before he would stop in the office to talk over his troubles. I am extremely fond of Larry and of his wife, Helyn, and their children. After all that is said, I have to add, in all honesty, that he was not the best man we could have picked for the first Negro player in the league. I don't say that from the club's point of view, since we could not have won without him, but from his.

Larry had been an all-sports star in Paterson, New Jersey. A local hero. He had never come face-to-face with prejudice until he became a big-leaguer. Prejudice was something he knew existed, something which he had accommodated himself to in his youth if only in the knowledge that it was going to keep him out of organized baseball. He had not been bruised as a human being, though; he had not had his nose rubbed in it. It hit him late in life; it hit him at a time he thought he had it licked; and it hit him hard.

We did not train in Florida. I had moved our training quarters to Arizona, not so much in preparation for Doby as out of an unpleasant experience with the Milwaukee Brewers. The Brewers' regular training headquarters were in Ocala, Florida. Our clubhouse was way out in left field, and the Jim Crow section was between the clubhouse and the edge of the stands. I was rather naïve about segregation. In those day it wasn't really publicized that much, as I suppose many Northern soldiers who took back seats in buses found out.

Being much the same age as most of my players, I would pitch batting practice, go to the clubhouse for a shower and then come out to watch the game. I emerged one day after the game had started, saw a few Negroes sitting in the bleachers and sat down with them, as is my custom, to barber a little as we watched the game.

Within a few minutes, the sheriff came running over to tell me I couldn't sit there.

I said, "I can't? I am ... Why can't I?"

He told me it was for Negroes only.

I may have been naïve but I wasn't so naïve that I couldn't understand the meaning of a simple declarative sentence. Still, I continued to play it innocently. I said, "I'm not bothering them. I'm enjoying our talk and they don't seem to resent me too much. They won't mind if I stay here."

He kept trying to explain that the rules hadn't been laid down for their benefit, while the people around me, who seemed to be fairly well informed on that point, kept snickering gleefully.

"Well," I said finally, "then you'd better get your deputy and throw me out, because that's the only way I'm going to leave."

177

"You'd better get out," he said, "or I'll get the mayor."

There was a threat to make the blood run cold.

The mayor came bustling over, in short order. "You read our contract," I told him. "Our contract says we're leasing the ball park and we have sole control over it. As such, I may throw you out."

I got the usual stuff then about a violation of a city ordinance taking precedence over all private contracts.

"I don't know anything about that," I told him. "What I do know is that if you bother me any more we'll move our club out of Ocala tonight. And we'll tell everybody in the country why."

Here *was* a threat to make his blood run cold. We had taken over a little hotel, the Ocala House, for six weeks; if we left, the hotel and the town would both be hurt.

I sat there every day, just to annoy them, without ever being bothered again. Nevertheless, I had already made up my mind to get out of Florida. By arranging for the Giants to come to Arizona with us, I was able to move the next team I had down South, the 1947 Indians, to Tucson.

At Tucson, I discovered, the bleachers weren't segregated but the hotel was. We weren't able to talk the management into allowing Larry to stay with us his first year, although we did make it clear— and they agreed—that in the future they would take all of our players, regardless of race, creed or previous condition of servitude. It was easy enough for me to tell Larry that these things took time. It was true enough to say that we had, after all, broken through one color barrier even if he was going to have to wait a year. It was easy for me, because it was he who was being told to be patient and to wait.

For Larry, it was a bad spring for him all around. In addition to everything else, he wasn't hitting at all. Toward the end of training, Boudreau was beginning to mutter out loud that it might be a good idea to have him spend a year in the minors.

Doby made the team in Houston, our first exhibition game after we broke camp. But that was not a very happy day for him either.

The Giants and Indians were traveling north together, through Texas, with exhibition games scheduled for Houston, Dallas, Fort Worth and a couple of other cities. Knowing that Texas had a law against mixed participation on the field, we protected ourselves—and gave ourselves the leverage we needed to battle back—by booking an alternative schedule through New Mexico and Nevada.

The Texas games were all sellouts long before we arrived, due in some part at least to the attraction of a colored player. Still, as we had anticipated, the state officials threatened to cancel our games if we put Doby on the field. "Fine," we said. "We had a feeling you might say that, so we made an alternative schedule."

Once again, we found little disposition on the part of the promoters to let their racial theories keep them from making a few dollars. The games went on. We had even brought along a couple of extra colored boys from our minor-league teams to make it clear that we intended to play whom we wished.

We'd have done better, I suppose, to have taken the alternative route. It's hard to say. Doby was treated very badly in Houston, beginning with when he couldn't get a cabdriver to take him to the park. When he came to the plate for the first time, he was roundly booed. Larry took one pitch and then he hit what may very well be the longest ball I have ever seen hit in my life and was certainly the longest ball ever hit in Houston. Everybody in the park stood up and cheered as he rounded the bases. Larry hit two home runs, two doubles and a triple that day and made a couple of sensational catches in center field. In every succeeding year, he was greeted in Houston like a favorite son.

But Larry was not a man to shake off those earlier slights and insults that easily. He was always very sensitive. If he wanted to dispute an umpire's call, he would back off and point to the back of his hand, as if to say, "You called that on me because I'm colored."

When he was knocked down, he would sometimes throw his bat out to the mound. There was no doubt, understand, that he was right in thinking he was being thrown at because he was colored. All colored players were thrown at for years, a practice arising from an old coach's tale that Negroes didn't have the guts to come up off the ground and dig back in. It is usually called, with a delicacy unusual in baseball, "taking their power away." (Here, again, notice the rationalization of an economic prejudice. Having drawn the color line, we had to tell ourselves that the Negro, after all, didn't have it in him to make the grade anyway.) Some of them, like Luke Easter, would get up laughing and, as often as not, knock the next pitch out of the park. Larry may have hit the next pitch out of the park, but he wasn't laughing.

It was a very real and bitter and gnawing battle for Larry all the way. He had suffered such a shock that he was possessed by the idea that he had to fight the battle for integration for his kids, Larry Jr. and Christine, so that they would never be bruised as badly as he had been.

Knowing how he felt about it, I'd make sure that when I took him and his family to dinner we would go to a high-class white restaurant

—to a far better place, in fact, than I would normally care to go myself.

Unless I'm very much mistaken, it was Larry who broke the color line in the Miami restaurants in the spring of 1955 when I was operating the Miami ball club. Clure Mosher, a television sportscaster, had called to ask me to appear on his show. Doby happened to be in the city for the ballplayers' golf tournament, and so I agreed on condition that all the Dobys would appear with me and that the station would find a good place for us to eat afterwards. Mosher, an ex-All-American football player, was all for it. He reserved a table for us at a very expensive restaurant named "Out of This World." Just in case we ran into any trouble, the station manager, Big Ed Little, who was about 6 foot 6, came along with us. As we entered the restaurant, he was protecting our rear. I was carrying the baby.

We couldn't have spent a more delightful evening. The owner greeted us himself and seated us at a table where we were not overly conspicuous but still visible to everybody in the room. Six or eight parties stopped by as they were leaving, the women as well as the men, just to tell Larry they had enjoyed seeing him play—an indirect way, really, of telling him they were delighted to see him in the restaurant. In every way, we were left with the unmistakable impression that the owner and the customers had been waiting for someone to do what Larry was doing.

It was important to Larry to make this kind of breakthrough, because the problem was always on his mind. Speaking purely about his career as a ballplayer, it was too much on his mind. Not that he wasn't a very good player. He led the league in home runs twice. In 1954, when the Indians won the pennant, he led in both home runs and runs batted in.

With all that, his inner turmoil was such a constant drain on him that he was never able to realize his full potential. Not to my mind, at any rate. If Larry had come up just a little later, when things were just a little better, he might very well have become one of the greatest players of all time.

Leroy Had Been There Before | **12.**

SATCHEL PAIGE could not have been more different than Larry Doby. Satchel is above race and beyond prejudice. It has been interesting to me to notice that when the great Negro players are listed, Satch is sometimes completely forgotten. He's interracial and universal.

Larry and Satch represent different eras of American history. Satch never appeared to be interested in fighting battles, changing social patterns or winning acceptance beyond what seems to come to him naturally as a legendary American folk hero. Satch wouldn't have been at all upset at not being allowed to stay in our hotel in Tucson that first year. He would not only have expected to stay across town, he would have preferred it. He doesn't want to go to white restaurants with you and he doesn't want you to go to Negro restaurants with him.

Satchel Paige is a skinny Paul Bunyan, born to be everybody's most memorable character. For 20 years, he pitched every day of the year, night and day, summer and winter, following the cry of the wild dollar all over the United States, the Caribbean and South America; a different city every day, a different team every night. He pitched in the fancy big-league parks and he pitched in scrubby sandlots in such small towns as Lost Woman, North Dakota. He barnstormed against All-Star big-league teams, greater himself than the greatest stars, and he pitched his guaranteed three innings against sandlotters, a giant among pygmies.

Completely uneducated, he has picked up a tremendous range of knowledge in his travels. Satch can hold forth, with equal ease, on baseball, dictators or mules. "I've majored," he likes to say, "in geography, transportation and people. Ah been a travelin' man." When Satch got on the train—the times he made the train—he would always sit down alone. Pretty soon the whole team would be gathered around, listening to him spin his yarns. Satch doesn't hold conversations, he holds court.

You will never find a better example of the unlettered man of great natural wit. I once went with him to the Friars Club in Hollywood, where he was being presented with some kind of an award. The head

181

table was, as they say, distinguished. You couldn't throw a straight line three feet without having it ricochet off six comedians. After Satch finished breaking up the joint, nobody would go on except the singers. "You think I'm crazy?" the comedians all said. "I'm not going to follow him."

His is a sly, offbeat wit that depends in great part upon a slight twisting of the words. All of our players, as an example, were given personal questionnaires to fill out. Sometimes Satch would write that he was married, other times that he wasn't. Every day, though, he was leaving a ticket at the box office for Mrs. Paige, and every day a different woman was picking it up. At length, we cited this phenomenon to him to try to get his marital status straightened out for our records.

"Well," he said, "it's like this. I'm not married, but I'm in great demand."

After the final 1948 World Series game in Boston, Satch flew back to Cleveland with, I believe, Gene Bearden and Kenny Keltner instead of coming on the train with the rest of the club. Skinny as he is, Satch is an enormous eater. After he had finished two complete meals, the stewardess, as a gag, offered him a third. Satch downed it with no difficulty. The stewardess, no quitter she, came back with another full meal. Satch declined with thanks.

"Aaaaaaah, Mr. Paige," she said, "you're full."

"No, miss," Satch drawled, "I'm not full. I'm just tired from all that eating."

I go way back with Paige. When I was a kid, I used to see him pitch for the Homestead Grays and the Kansas City Monarchs in the old American Giants' park right across the street from Comiskey Park. I was in the Hollywood park in 1934 when he pitched that famous 13-inning, 1–0 victory against Dizzy Dean, the greatest pitchers' battle I have ever seen.

In his younger days he had blinding speed, but only a little wrinkle of a curve. Satch, in fact, didn't develop a good curve until he was fifty-four years old. But even in those early days he had all kinds of different deliveries. He'd hesitate before he'd throw. He'd wiggle the fingers of his glove. He'd wind up three times. Satch was always a practicing psychologist. He'd get the hitters overanxious, then he'd get them mad, and by the time the ball was there at the plate to be swung at, he'd have them way off balance.

His great asset, though, was his control. One of his barnstorming gags was to set up a one-by-two plank behind home plate and stick four tenpenny nails into it. Then he'd drive the nails into the board

182

by pitching from the mound. And never take more than ten pitches. That's control, man. One of my own unfulfilled ambitions is to start a game with an entire team of midgets and let them go a couple of times around the batting order, walking endlessly. Another of my unfulfilled ambitions is to pitch Satchel Paige against that same team of midgets. Satch, I think, is the only pitcher alive who could get the ball consistently into that tiny strike zone.

I had come to know Paige fairly well by running across him on the barnstorming trail, and I got to know him even better through our mutual friendship with Abe Saperstein. In addition to running the Harlem Globetrotters, Abe has always had a couple of teams in the Negro leagues.

One of the first things I did after taking over in Cleveland was to check with Abe Saperstein to find out whether Satch still had it. I didn't want to sign him as the first Negro in the American League, though, because I knew that would be giving the Old Guard a chance to muddy up the waters by charging that my interest in Negro players was entirely promotional and mercenary.

Satch heard about those inquiries, all right. The day after I signed Doby, a wire arrived from him saying: IS IT TIME FOR ME TO COME?

I wired back: ALL THINGS IN DUE TIME.

In 1948, after I bought Zoldak, the time had come. Feller wasn't going well. Christopher was beginning to weaken. We were desperately in need of a pitcher who could make an occasional start and go a few innings in relief. I had already discussed Satch with Boudreau. Lou wasn't interested. He had heard somewhere that Satch had very little left. Well, if there was one thing I knew about Satch, it was that he could be counted upon to rise to any occasion. I called Abe Saperstein and asked him to get in touch with Satch and bring him to Cleveland.

They were supposed to arrive the night of July 5, and I had a room reserved for them under a fictitious name. One of Satch's more prominent characteristics is that he is bound by neither the clock nor the calendar, and they didn't fly in until early the next morning. I told Abe to take Satch right from the airport to the park. Then I called Lou and asked him how he'd like a little extra batting practice against a young pitcher I thought might help us—by no means an unusual request. Lou was in the habit of looking over pitching prospects by batting against them.

With the scene so neatly set, Hank Greenberg and I went out to the park to watch the final act unfold. "Satch," I said, "it's important to me that you look good against this guy. I've been telling everybody for lo these many years that you're the greatest pitcher in baseball. Now's the chance to prove it."

Satch has a cute little grin, not unlike Floyd Patterson's, with the bottom lip puckering out and curling. "Man," he said, "I'm not ready for this. But you know Old Satch. He don't need anything extra." I must have looked a little jumpy, because Satch let his eyes go out to the pitching mound. "Don't worry, Mr. Will," he said softly. "Ah been there before."

Lou came out through the dugout in his uniform, ready to indulge me. "Where's the kid?" he asked.

I pointed to Satch, who was sitting with Saperstein in the other dugout. Lou almost dropped.

Satch hadn't been pitching very much at Kansas City, and he was still a little stiff from the plane ride. To loosen himself up, he allowed that he'd run around the park "a few times." He jogged out to the outfield, thought better of it, and jogged right back. You could see he was a little winded from all that exercise. As I shall demonstrate in a few moments, Satch was a minimum of forty-eight years old at that moment, an age when prudent men have long since stopped running for buses.

Normally, Satch throws about three pitches to warm up. This time, either because he was rusty or because he wanted to make extra sure he was sharp, he threw to Boudreau for about 15 minutes. He was, I was happy to see, throwing as easily as ever.

As ridiculous as it was for Satchel Paige to be on trial, that was precisely the situation as he went out to the mound to throw to Boudreau who, at that moment, was leading both leagues with a batting average of almost .400. Against Paige, he batted .000. Satch threw twenty pitches. Nineteen of them were strikes. Lou swung nineteen times and he had nothing that looked like a base hit. After a final pop fly, Lou dropped his bat, came over to us and said, "Don't let him get away, Will. We can use him."

I had foolishly believed that nobody could possibly accuse me of signing Paige for a gag. Not when we were in the middle of a four-way pennant fight. But my talent for underestimating the Old Guard's resistance to reason and logic remained unimpaired. The cry went out that I was—yes—making a travesty of the game and—yes—cruelly exploiting an old man's reputation in his declining years.

We were, at that moment, sitting in first place. We had already drawn over a million people and our advance sale alone assured us of reaching two million. In the face of all that, an astonishing number of presumably intelligent and literate writers saw the signing of Paige

184

not only as a—yes—"cheap and tawdry" box-office stunt but as an admission that I was writing off our pennant chances. I welcome all publicity—good, bad or psychopathic—but there are times, you know, when I am left just a wee bit puzzled.

I think I was most disappointed by the reaction of J. G. Taylor Spink, the publisher of the *Sporting News,* the remarkably good baseball weekly. Taylor had always been the only rockbound conservative who had been able to understand what I was trying to do in using entertainment to build up interest while I was surreptitiously building up the team. He had always gone out of his way to encourage and support me. With the signing of Paige, he wrote, "Veeck has gone too far in his quest for publicity." Indirectly, he criticized Harridge for approving the contract.

In his editorial, Spink wrote:

> To bring in a pitching "rookie" of Paige's age casts a reflection on the entire scheme of operation in the major leagues. To sign a hurler at Paige's age is to demean the standards of baseball in the big circuits. Further complicating the situation is the suspicion that if Satchel were white, he would not have drawn a second thought from Veeck.

(If Satch were white, of course, he would have been in the majors twenty-five years earlier, and the question would not have been before the House.)

Satch demeaned the standards of baseball with five big victories over the remainder of the season, plus some valuable relief work. After every Paige victory I would send Spink a telegram:

NINE INNINGS. FOUR HITS, FIVE STRIKEOUTS. WINNING
PITCHER: PAIGE. DEFINITELY IN LINE FOR THE SPORTING
NEWS AWARD AS ROOKIE OF THE YEAR.

Spink did have the integrity to print the last of the telegrams and concede that he had been a bit hasty. He did not have quite the grace to go all the way:

> The *Sporting News* will make no change in its original editorial, except to express its admiration for any pitcher—white or colored—who at Paige's age can gain credit for five victories over a period of six weeks in any league, major or minor. But it cannot express any admiration for the present-day standard of major-league ball that makes such a showing possible.

185

It now seemed that Satch wasn't demeaning the standards of baseball as much as the standards of baseball were demeaning Satch.

The big-league debut of Satchel Paige took place three days after he came to town, a 2-inning relief appearance against the St. Louis Browns. As Satch came strolling in from the bullpen, a tall, thin (6'5") man with incredibly skinny legs and incredibly large feet, the park erupted. There is an electricity just in the sight of the Old Man walking lazily across the grass toward the pitching mound, an excitement and anticipation that justifies the trip to the park.

The first batter, Chuck Stevens, lined a single into center field. The leadoff man in the next inning opened with a single and went to second when the ball was kicked around in center field. They were the only hitters to get on base. As time went on, I found that Satch liked to have the first batter get on. He'd sometimes walk the first man or sometimes even the first two, and I would have been willing to take an oath that he did it on purpose.

In the course of setting his string of attendance records, Satch drew—according to the book—51,013 people in Chicago, a night attendance record at Comiskey Park, and only a thousand-odd below the all-time Chicago record. That figure is wildly low. Nobody will ever know how many people were in the park that night. My own guess would be about 70,000.

It was the only time in my life I have ever been frightened by a baseball crowd. The mob began to converge on the park so early that it took Bob Fishel and me about an hour and a half to drive out from downtown, a trip that usually takes about 15 minutes. A few blocks away, with all traffic at a complete standstill, Bob and I got out of the cab. Almost immediately, we were torn apart in the swirling mob. By the time I reached the park itself, there was such a solid crush around the gates that it had become impossible to move. The night was hot and the mood was ugly. Fortunately for me, I'm fairly conspicuous with my bare head, sports jacket and crutches. Someone up in the White Sox office spotted me out the window and sent down a couple of special cops to pluck me out.

I pleaded with Mrs. Comiskey to throw the gates open and let everybody in—a rather indecent proposal for me to make to a nice lady about to draw her first sellout crowd in years. By the time she recovered enough to assure me that the police could handle the situation quite adequately, the mob was breaking down the gates.

In the mad rush into the park, one of the turnstiles was ripped clean out of the floor and sent flying through the air, missing a customer's head by about this much. Well, not really a customer. Only a freebie. The man who was almost killed was, by a weird coincidence, Bob Fishel, my erstwhile companion of the evening. Bob, having been swept along with the mob, was within a foot of the turnstile when it went.

Everybody came pouring in. There was not a place in the park that was not covered by human, sweating flesh. I am not talking only about the seats and the aisles and the standing room in back of the grandstand. There was not even loose standing room *underneath* the stands. People were jammed there, shoulder to shoulder, with nothing to look at except the hot dog stands and each other.

Just before the game, I went down to the bench and told Satch, "Leroy, this one is very important to me. Really give it to them tonight."

Satch reacts to excitement and crisis. He gave them everything: the hesitation pitches, the eephus, the submarine pitch and the crossfire. He shut them out on five singles, and four of them were bloopers.

Any time I told Satch that it was important to me that he bear down, he would come through like that. He did it for me again in Miami, in 1951, while I was running the Miami Marlins for a couple of friends on a purely volunteer basis.

On opening day in Miami, I worked out a gag for Paige to drop in on us in a helicopter. Satch threw only 2 or 3 pitches, for he had not thrown a ball all winter, then he strolled out to the bullpen and reclined comfortably in a contour chair as befitted one of the nation's more distinguished senior citizens. Nobody had known he was coming except me, and the crowd got a big kick out of it.

The next day while I was having lunch with the Miami manager, Don Osborn, he was still chuckling about it. "You know," he said, "I'll bet the Old Man could still go out and throw an inning or two on the exhibition trail."

"The exhibition trail?" I said. "He didn't come down here for a gag. He came down to pitch for us."

Osborn had been a minor-league pitcher himself for many years. "Oh, come on," he said. "I was too old to pitch five years ago and I'm at least ten years younger than Satch. He can't pitch in this league."

"Tell you what we'll do, Donald," I said. "You just line up your nine best hitters, and you tell them you're going to give them ten dollars for every base hit they get off him."

"And you're paying?" he said.

"I'm paying."

I grabbed Paige. "Leroy," I said, "this is important. I want you to show these guys a little something. No base hits."

Satch struck out nine men in a row. From the top to the bottom.

Osborn fell in love with him on the spot. It was Don Osborn who taught Satch how to throw a good curve in Satch's fifty-fourth year.

Satch's age has always been a subject of lively debate, a debate he did not go out of his way to discourage. It could even be said that he dished out his age the way he dished out his pitches, mixing his figures up nicely and always keeping his interviewers off balance.

After we signed him, a magazine dug up a birth certificate showing he had been born on July 7, 1906. The keepers of the baseball records accepted that as the official date. Nobody else, least of all Satch himself, paid the slightest attention to it.

In between Cleveland and Miami, Satch had played for me in St. Louis. There was the usual moaning and meowing when I signed him that I was making a mockery of the game, no small accomplishment in St. Louis. All Satch was, of course, was the best pitcher on our club. The next year, he was our only representative on the All-Star squad. He won 12 games, appeared in 46 games, only one less than the league leader, and was the best relief pitcher in baseball. I would sit along some old-timer in the stands, and he would tell me, "That Satch is sure a marvel. I played against him in Columbus, you know, in 1906."

I knew, within reasonable limits, how old Satch was. I knew because it had become important for me, at one point, to find out. In his early days in Cleveland, Satch was so wounded by the accusations that he was slightly older than the Parthenon that he stated positively and for the record that he was ready to reveal at last that he had not pitched his first game in professional baseball until 1927. To show his good faith, he offered $500 to anybody who could prove he had been pitching earlier. The operative word there, of course, was "prove." Otherwise, I was ready to claim the $500 myself. A few days later, a guy walked into the office with a clipping from a Memphis paper which showed that Satch had pitched for Chattanooga in 1926.

Oh yeah, Satch said, that was that other Satchel Paige. "Now that I recollect," said Satch, "I did once hear there was a Satchell Paige pitched around Chattanooga when I was just a boy. Spelled his name with two L's. A local fellow."

Somehow, an independent fact-finding committee set up on the spot rejected his explanation. I thought it was a great joke on Satch until I discovered he had made his $500 offer on my behalf. Under pressure, Satch thinks fast.

Under those conditions, it seemed like a good idea to find out just how old he really was before he youthened me out of any more $500 bills. I quickly came to two decisions:

1 The worst thing I could possibly do was ask Paige.
2 The only other person who really knew was his mother.

After a great deal of difficulty, I was able to reach Mrs. Paige at her local general store in Mobile, Alabama, which had the only phone in the neighborhood. I found out quickly enough the source of Satch's humor. "I can't rightly recall whether Leroy was my firstborn," she said, "or my fifteenth." Having had her joke, she told me she really couldn't remember what year he had been born, but that she could guarantee he wasn't her oldest.

Well, it was a start. I hired a private detective to check the birth records at the city hall in Mobile. Here's what he reported: The Mobile records did not go back any farther than mid-1900, and while there was no record of Satch himself, one of his younger brothers was in the 1901 list. My detective reported, further, that the birth certificate dated July 7, 1906, had not been made out for Leroy Paige but for Leroy *Page*. Since the names of all Satch's brothers and sisters had been spelled correctly, he said, and since the Mobile records were filled with Leroys, he felt confident that we could scratch that date.

This could only mean, then, that Satch could not possibly have been born any later than the early part of 1900. Satch himself always gave his birthday as September 18. Assuming that a man has a sentimental attachment to his actual birthday, Satch could not have been born any later than September 18, 1899.

What makes the debate so intriguing is that Satch is amazingly youthful-looking. And quite vain about it. One of the great days of his life came when a St. Louis railroad station detective put the arm on him because he answered the description of a young guy who had held up a liquor store. Bill Durney, our traveling secretary, straightened things out quickly enough, but as the detective was walking away, Satch called out, "That holdup man, how old did you say he was?"

The cop looked down at his flier and said, "It says here twenty-four or twenty-five."

For the next few weeks, Satch would pretend to be incensed at this latest example of police brutality. At the end, he would never fail to call out loudly, "Hey, Bill, how old did that detective-man say that no-good holdup man who looks like me is?"

Satch didn't often get to the railroad station. He had spent so much of his life hopping from town to town by himself that he had a rather cavalier attitude toward communal travel. It can be said of Satch that he missed countless trains but no scheduled games. He had the plane schedules committed to memory. When the game was due to start, Satch and the umpires would be there. It was a mark of the special esteem in which he was held that the other players permitted him this special privilege.

His effect upon people is best shown, I think, in his relationship with Clint Courtney, the Browns' hard-nosed catcher. Clint came from a poor farm district of Alabama, and the racial question was very strong with him. Word was brought to me, in Clint's first year with the club, that he had served notice that he wouldn't catch Satch. I liked Courtney because he was a rough, tough little man who played the game for all it was worth. I felt very strongly that this was a matter entirely of environment and upbringing. Once Clint got to know Satch, I was sure, he'd come around—even though I was perfectly aware that Satch would do nothing to appease him. Satch, in fact, did precisely the opposite. He'd needle Courtney, in his sly way, just sharply enough to let Clint know he was ready for him any time Clint wanted to make something of it.

In the beginning, Courtney wouldn't even catch Satch in the bullpen. Then, I began to see him warming Satch up. Shortly afterwards, I could see them sitting side by side in the bullpen, talking. At last, Clint came up to the office and said, "I'd like to catch Paige."

"Oh," I said. "Why the change?"

"I like the guy," he said. "That Satch, he's quite a fellow. Just sitting out there talking to him, I've learned more about calling a game than I ever knew in my life."

"Yeah," I said. "But what about this business that he's black?"

"I guess that's right," he said. "But this is different."

"So? What are you telling me for? Tell Hornsby."

"You know how it is with Hornsby," Clint said. "He don't like Satch."

Later in the season, I dropped into an interracial joint I used to go to in Detroit—The Flame—and there, sitting at a table together, were Paige and Courtney.

"You know," Courtney said as I sat down, "it's a funny thing. My daddy is coming up when we get back to St. Louis. He's going to see me sitting in the bullpen talking to this Paige and he's gonna jump right over the fence and try to give me a whupping. But Satch and I
190

have it figured out that the two of us can whup him no matter what happens."

This is the way Satch, just by being Satch, can affect a guy who didn't even want to warm him up.

As far as the opposition went, Satch was so impersonal that he never knew their names. I don't think he even looked at their faces. He had pitched against so many players in so many towns that they were nothing more than batting stances to him. Batting stances he remembered.

"Hey," he'd say, on seeing Phil Rizzuto swing in batting practice, "I pitched against that little fellow when I was touring with Bob Rapid. Don't wanna throw him my little curve low and away. Last time I did that was in Fargo and the outfielder's still chasing it. . . ." And then would come the final indignity. "Didn't have no people there either." Bob Rapid? That was his private nickname for Bob Feller.

Mickey Mantle, as a switch-hitter, played havoc with Satch's identification system. Mickey hit one out of Sportsman's Park right-handed to beat us in a night game. When he went to the plate the next night against Satch, he was naturally swinging left-handed. This time Mickey hit a screaming line drive to the center fielder. "Geez," Satch said, back in the dugout, "them Yankees sure get them great kids. Last night a kid busts up the game and tonight this other kid hits one like that off the old man. Where they come up with two kids like that?"

There developed one of those crazy situations in which some of the players, not quite sure that Satch wasn't pulling their leg, tried to explain that it was the same kid, and Satch, absolutely convinced that *they* were pulling *his* leg, didn't believe them.

He was always at his best against the Yankees. Joe DiMaggio, for one, couldn't touch him. Satch handled Joe with such ease that he'd drive us all nuts by deliberately walking a man to get to him. The only time I ever really got furious enough to seriously consider throttling a manager came while Satch was pitching against the Yankees shortly after he had joined me in St. Louis. For seven innings, Paige had a no-hitter going. On the last out in the seventh, Rizzuto stepped on Satch's toe as he was covering first base, spiking him badly enough so that Satch was limping as he went back to the dugout.

I'm out in the bleachers and right away I'm seeing the headlines. Right away I'm writing the glorious climactic chapter to the saga of Satchel Paige. Satchel Paige, after all those years behind the color line, has finally made the majors in his old age and here, in the twilight of his career, he has pitched a no-hitter against the New

York Yankees. Because, don't you see, the spiked toe has given us a perfect excuse to get him out of there, the no-hitter intact, without anybody ever being able to accuse us of protecting him.

I looked down to the bullpen and I saw that Zack Taylor wasn't warming anybody up. If ever I cursed those crutches, that was the time. I went swinging and skipping around the park, praying that we'd put on enough of a rally to give me time to get down to the dugout. Naturally, our little Brownies are going out like lambs— 1, 2, 3. With the third man at bat, I'm shouting from the back of the grandstand, "Get him out of there, Zack! Get him out of there!"

Paige went back to the mound, still limping. The Yankees got a couple of hits in the eighth, and another dream went up in smoke. If I'd have had a cannon, I'd have blown Zack's head off.

An Epitaph for Harry Grabiner | 13.

ONE of the great joys of our quick success at Cleveland was watching the fun Harry Grabiner was having. After all the years of scrimping at Chicago, Harry was showing them all how he could operate when he had a chance to go first class. As a man, he had always traveled first class. Harry had a wonderful family. His daughter was June Travis, a Hollywood actress of some note before her marriage. His wife, Dottie, was a woman of such beauty that if you placed her and June side by side you could not tell which was the mother and which the daughter.

Reserved as Harry normally was, he was a wild and uninhibited rooter. During the course of a game he would keep jumping out of the office to run to the top of the stairs and cheer our boys through every rally. Harry was a hitter. Early in our association, I learned to stay away from those stairs during my tours around the park because Harry could pound you black and blue. In Cleveland, he was finally getting a chance to root home a winner.

He was a tremendous asset in running the business end of the club because he was always practical. When it came to paying $100,000 for a Zoldak, he'd say, "Great." But when it came to some of my wilder promotional fancies, he would suggest some alternative that would serve the same purpose at about half the price.

192

I have said before that Harry was an honorable man. Let me give another example. I had dealt with Harry quite a bit in Milwaukee, in both the buying and selling of players, and out of our old friendship in Chicago we always leveled with each other. I had a forty-year-old pitcher named Earl Caldwell, whom I had bought from the Texas League, a side-arm, almost underhanded pitcher who had been up with the Athletics fourteen years earlier and had later put in time with the Browns. By the time he reached us, he was a fussy old guy, who always wore rubbers and carried an umbrella. The rest of the players called him "Grandmother."

When I got Caldwell, I promised him I'd do my best to get him another shot at the majors, a promise I made to almost all my players. Although he had only a middling sort of year, I called Harry and told him I thought Caldwell might be able to help the White Sox in relief. Harry didn't want him, and nobody else was even interested enough to draft him. The next year, though, Caldwell had a pretty good season. I was operating the club out of the Corona hospital as the year ended, and this time I told Harry I was sure Caldwell would help him.

"But he's nine hundred years old," Harry said. "I wouldn't have any idea what to offer you for him and—I don't have to tell you—I don't have any money to fool around with."

I said, "Harry, pay me $5,000, then pay me what he's worth to you after you have him. If you don't think he's worth anything, send him back on June 15 and I'll give back the $5,000, and at least I've got him into the majors again like I promised."

Caldwell surprised even me. He pitched brilliantly for the White Sox from the start, far better than he had ever pitched before in his life. In the middle of May, Harry sent us $10,000. I immediately called to thank him and to let him know I was very well pleased with the price. Caldwell continued to pitch well, and in mid-August another $10,000 arrived.

That was the kind of fellow Harry was. He had agreed to pay me what the man was worth to him and he was scrupulous about keeping his word. To my immense delight, Grandmother Caldwell was an even better pitcher for Harry the next year, far and away the best relief pitcher in the American League.

Now let's go back to Cleveland. Before the 1948 season, we had set an attendance goal of 2,000,000 people. As the season progressed, it became increasingly evident that we were going to roll right over our goal and go on to smash all records. Harry had a paper schedule

193

of our home games on which he kept track of the attendance. He had three columns of figures. In the first column were the figures he had projected at the beginning of the year to show the attendance we would have to have, game by game, in order to reach our 2,000,000 goal. In the second column, he would write down the actual attendance of each game as the season progressed. In the third column, he kept adjusting his original projection, game by game, to show what he now estimated our final figures would be, based upon our advance, our position in the race, and the constantly rising enthusiasm. It was all pretty complicated.

Harry and I shared the same office, and it became a sort of ritual for him to stop off at the desk every day to fill in the previous day's attendance and perhaps make a new projection. He kept the schedule in the inside pocket of his jacket, folded in three parts, and by the time we entered our last home stand of the season it had been folded and unfolded so often that it had come completely apart. Harry would have to hold the frazzled, dirty pieces together on my desk while he ran down the attendance column, adding in his head, as always, because with his machinelike mind he never bothered to make a footing and write down a total.

We had been home on that last home stand for about a week when Harry stopped by at about 5 o'clock to go through the usual routine. He was in marvelous spirits. Our attendance was already half a million over his original estimate and, more important, we had started the winning streak that was to carry us back into first place. I was sitting at the desk, as usual. Harry, as usual, seated himself on the very edge of the desk itself, leaning down over the tattered schedule. All things as usual. In a minute or two, we would each get up and go our separate ways. I would step out into the stadium and begin to mix with the early customers. Harry would go up to the press room to sip his usual cup of tea and act as host to the writers.

And all of a sudden I heard him say, "I can't add. I can't add."

I looked up, startled. In his eyes, I could see . . . what? No, not fear, but a sort of dull shock. For Harry not to be able to add was like me not being able to talk.

"Harry," I said, "what's the matter?"

"I can't add." The same incomprehension. The same dull shock.

"You're just tired," I said automatically. I was frightened to death. "You're tired, Harry," I said. "Come on over to the couch and sit down."

But he reached out for my hand and in that same quiet voice he said, "I can't think. Bill, hold my hand. I can't think."

194

I knew at that moment that it was something serious, something more than a stroke. Harry Grabiner was spilled there across my desk, grabbing onto my hand, the three sections of his schedule spread out around him, broken and awry. And Harry Grabiner was saying that he couldn't think. Harry Grabiner. I knew this was it, that it was over, that from one second to the next he had died there on my desk. No question about it. No question.

While we were waiting for the doctor, I brought Harry over to the couch and held him in my arms like a frightened child. The moment anyone came into the office, he would huddle closer to me in terror and whimper, "Don't let him get near me, Bill. Don't let him get near me." The only other person he wasn't afraid of was Ada Ireland, our telephone operator.

The doctor took one look at him and told me there was nothing he could do. "I could cut open his head, look in and sew it back up," he told me. "All that would do would make him die a little sooner. I know what I'd see without cutting him open."

I left Harry huddled in Ada's arms and went out front to put in a rush call to a psychiatrist I knew quite well. A last, forlorn hope. I introduced him to Harry not as a psychiatrist but as a friend who had dropped in to say hello. He didn't have to ask Harry more than three or four questions before he knew it was out of his field. "Something inside his head has been eaten away," he told me. "His mind is about gone."

I had called June immediately, and she had quickly flown in from Chicago with her husband, Fred Friedlob. Harry was taken back to Allegan where, through some hidden reservoir of strength and will, he held on until we won that playoff game in Boston. He wanted so badly to win that pennant, his first pennant after all those years. He walked around outside the house all during the game listening to the radio broadcast, and the moment it was over and we had won he walked back into the house and collapsed.

Harry had always wanted to show them that he was a good operator.

The Jolly Set | **14.**

In Cleveland, I was on the town. While technically I was still married, my marriage had ended the day I boarded the plane in Tucson to fly East, a vulture in search of a dying ball club.

I had first known Eleanor Raymond when I was a little boy. Her father was the owner of the Federal-Huber Company, a leading manufacturer of plumbing fixtures. He was also owner of Lorraine Headlights, a name most old-timers will remember. There was a time in this country when if you did not have Lorraine headlights on your car you didn't have lights. The Raymonds owned a big farm in Hinsdale. Eleanor and I went to the same kindergarten class and attended the first couple of grades together before she was sent away to private school.

Mr. Raymond sold Lorraine Headlights just in time to have his entire profit wiped out in the 1929 crash, and thereafter his life became a series of ups and downs. Eleanor and I moved in with her parents during one particularly low period of our life and it turned out they were just about as broke as we were. With Mr. Raymond, there was no way of telling. Riding high or scraping bottom, he was always the same cheerful, confident man, and I developed a tremendous admiration for him. I have been up and down so often myself that I sometimes have the feeling I've spent my life in the front seat of a rollercoaster. I have been busted and I have been affluent and I have been busted again, and I don't think anybody has been able to tell the difference.

Eleanor had her father's guts and resilience. Feeling that she was a drain on his suddenly limited funds, she left her private school in Nebraska and joined the circus. She had come to know the Ringling family through the years because the Raymonds, like the circus, had their winter headquarters in Sarasota. In the flush days, they had always gone down to Sarasota in a private railroad car, but Eleanor came from Nebraska, looking for a job, on a day coach. In addition to performing as an equestrian, she worked the Wild West and ran the elephants.

196

She was with the circus and I was an office boy for the Cubs when we met again. Wooing a girl out of town on $18 a week isn't easy. There was no chance of seeing her at all unless the Cubs were on the road and the circus was playing within a reasonable radius—Louisville, Cincinnati, Rockford, Milwaukee, Peoria, Pittsburgh. I'd run over to Comiskey Park to pick up a few dollars selling tickets or working the concessions, then grab an overnight train and, in effect, join the circus for a few days.

When Eleanor and I were finally married I was making $22 a week, and, in recognition of my new responsibilities, Mr. Wrigley raised my salary to $25. Maddened by such wealth, we honeymooned at French Lick Springs, Indiana, a resort area where the Cubs later trained during the wartime restriction on travel. Honeymooners are supposed to yearn for privacy, and we sure found it; it was ridiculously out of season. The only two other guests in the whole hotel were Colonel Jacob Ruppert and Joe McCarthy, who had apparently come down to discuss the Yankees' problems in utter secrecy. It made for a very festive atmosphere. They would sit at one end of the tremendous dining room ignoring us, we would sit at the other end ignoring them, and the full band would play on faithfully until the four of us had left.

At the end of the week, we had to hand the dining room and the band over to the exclusive use of Ruppert and McCarthy. I had been quoted a price of $16 for the room, which I had taken to mean $16 a week. It turned out to be $16 a day, a financial disaster that brought our honeymoon to an abrupt end. I had to send a collect wire to the Cubs' office, telling them that if they wanted their boy back they would do well to send money. We returned, via Greyhound bus, to an apartment that was completely bare except for a couple of mattresses on the floor. That was how we started our married life.

I bring all this up to show that Eleanor was willing to share hard times without a whimper or a complaint. Then and always.

By the time I left the Cubs to go to Milwaukee, I had just been made treasurer at a substantial salary. We had been married six years and had had two children. But there was not a word of caution or complaint from Eleanor. "If that's what you want to do," she said, "let's do it." And when we bought a farmhouse in West Bend, fifty miles north of Milwaukee, and found out too late that it had been built for summer, not winter, living, there were no recriminations because the place was so uncomfortable or because the kids were always coming down with colds from playing on the bare floor. We didn't buy the farm until the Brewers had begun to show a profit, of course, but we

197

still didn't have enough money to buy the furniture we needed or to put down rugs.

The farm was a great mistake all around. The way I operated, hustling around until the early morning hours, it never seemed logical to drive fifty miles for a couple of hours of sleep and then turn right around and come back. More often than not I didn't get home, and *that,* quite understandably, Eleanor did object to.

She could understand my philosophy of mixing with the fans, she could go along with the speechmaking and even the late stops in the taverns and bowling alleys. It was the time I spent with the sportswriters, whom she considered the least important part of a baseball operation, that she most resented. To her, they came to symbolize all that was going wrong with us and she couldn't stand the sight of them. Being a strong-minded woman, with little talent for hypocrisy, she would inevitably be riding in the hills when they came to the house. When later, in Tucson, I invited the Chicago writers to the ranch for that bull session, Eleanor wasn't there. She had walked out before they arrived.

After my first season in Cleveland, we made one final attempt to get back together. I had chartered a plane for the Red Sox-Cardinals series and had invited all the Cleveland writers and their wives to come along with me. I hadn't set that up especially for Eleanor. We always tried to include wives because it seemed to me that everybody had a better time when the girls were around. We even had a coed press room, in addition to the regular press room at the stadium, to give the girls a place where they could relax and have a drink while they were waiting for their husbands. It goes without saying that the writers did more of their work in the mixed room than in the regular press room, and I did not notice that their copy suffered.

I had to make a speech at the Peabody Hotel in Memphis just before the series. She joined me there, and we flew to St. Louis for the first two games. The reconciliation didn't last as long as the Series. Her attitude was that since I was spending all my time with newspapermen and baseball people anyway, why had I bothered to have her come up? Not, certainly, to see a couple of baseball games. On the flight from St. Louis to Boston, we loaded the Cleveland contingent aboard, along with a few old friends like Sam Levy and Vincent X. Flaherty. Eleanor wasn't happy about that at all. When we made an intermediate landing in Chicago to refuel, she picked up her bag, looked me in the eye and said, "I still don't like the people you associate with." She walked off the plane and I didn't see her again until
198

we were divorced three years later. A sad way for a marriage to come to an end, on a five-minute refueling stop between St. Louis and Boston.

All right, in Cleveland I was on the town. I lived three separate lives after hours, none of them completely independent of my life as a baseball operator and yet each of them having its own flavor and its own cast of characters. There was, first of all, my usual after-hours wanderings, the speeches and the appearances. There was a group of congenial people who became widely known in Cleveland as "the Jolly Set," with whom I spent what might be called the normal night-time hours. And there was, finally, the fascinating world of the "night people," the citizens whose social lives don't begin until everybody else has closed up his shutters and gone to bed. I have always hated to go to bed for fear I'll miss something.

The difficulty in living on both the day and the night side of life is that you have to have more than a native curiosity and basic liking for people. You have to be born with a strong constitution and you have to cultivate an ability to function without much sleep. In Cleveland, I had little enough to fear. I operated, day after day, on two hours' sleep. Oh, I'd spend a full day in bed occasionally to catch up, but those days were far and few between. As part of my regular routine, I would leave my final stop at six in the morning, go right to the ball park and maybe sleep on the rubbing table or on the couch I kept in the office.

I lived out of an apartment in the Hollenden Hotel downtown, but the apartment was little more than an extension of the office. If I was home, the door was always open. Anybody who wanted to come in and talk to me didn't even have to knock. It was always open house, and people were always streaming in and out. My friends would tell their out-of-town friends, "When you come to Cleveland, stay at Bill's." The out-of-town friends began to tell their out-of-town friends and I finally had to put in a couple of extra beds to handle the overflow.

I even had my own Man Who Came to Dinner. I had come back from the hospital after one of the operations on my leg at about 8 in the morning. I called Atkins to come have breakfast with me, then went into the bathroom to soak the stump of my leg. When I came out, Larry was there on the davenport with Alex Zirin of the *Plain Dealer* and another guy. Naturally I had four breakfasts sent up. Larry's friend stayed with us all day, had dinner with us and selected a bed

199

to his liking. He stayed on for a week, sometimes coming with me to an opening or some such function, sometimes staying home. But whenever I dropped in, there he was, ready to put down his knife and fork and talk baseball. After about a week, it occurred to me that Larry was imposing just a little by dumping his hungry friend on me like that when he himself had plenty of room right next door. I banged on his door and said, "I wouldn't want you to think I was hinting, Lawrence, but is this friend of yours ever going home or have I adopted him?"

To which Larry answered—just like the old joke—"What do you mean *my* friend? I thought he was *your* friend. He was sitting right there when I came in with Alex."

It turned out that he was a salesman from upstate. "I just dropped in to meet you," he said, "and, gee, everybody was so nice to me and I was having such a wonderful time I thought I'd stay around awhile. I don't have to get back to my home office until the end of the month."

That will give you an idea of the way I was living in Cleveland.

One of the best ways to meet a lot of people and spread good will, I have found, is to go to openings. Any openings. I made every opening in Cleveland, whether it was a hamburger joint or a plush lounge or a filling station. I came uninvited and unannounced and I spent money. I was a most welcome guest because, modesty aside, I was an attraction. I remember one saloon that advertised a gala 3-day opening. When I arrived at 7:30, with my usual promptness, the place was deserted. In fifteen minutes there were more people clamoring to get inside than we had at some of our games in my final year in St. Louis.

It was, in fact, my passion for openings that brought the Jolly Set together. Shortly after I came to Cleveland, Sammy Haas asked me if I'd help out a friend of his named Max Gruber, who was opening a restaurant in a new shopping center. Sammy had more than a friendly interest in the project now that I think of it; he just happened to own the real estate on which the shopping center was being built.

I'd have done anything for Sammy, but this was no favor. Tipping me about an opening was like giving a long shot to a horseplayer. To make sure nothing went wrong, I dropped over the next day, which was Sunday, introduced myself to Max and Ruth Gruber as an old concessionaire and stayed through the night helping them get the place ready.

I was at Gruber's for 100 straight nights. The opening night was for Sammy Haas. The next 99 were for myself. I'd hit all my other
200

stops first, of course, but I was always sure to end up at Gruber's and stay until it closed. Whitey Lewis, the columnist from the *Press,* lived nearby and he and his wife, Virginia, began to drop by. Before long, some of the other writers and their wives began to make it a regular stop: Gordon and Doris Cobbledick, Frank and Frances Gibbons and Ed and Genevieve McAuley among others. Joining us also was Winsor French, a sort of high-class gossip columnist for the *Press,* and Bud and Phyl Silverman. There were non-newspaper people in our group too: Johnny Lindheim, who owned a record shop, was a charter member, along with his wife Lois; so were Dick Haber, a sweater manufacturer and his wife, and Bud and Gert Rand. Bud was a lawyer and, later, head of the group that bought the Cleveland Arena. And, of course, Marsh and Mary Ann Samuel, Spud and Wyn Goldstein, Larry Atkins, Marty Caine, Dr. Bill Neville and the Grubers themselves. Plus some other part-timers and floaters.

Gruber's became the acknowledged headquarters for the Jolly Set, a name tagged on us by Bill Roberts, a *Press* cartoonist who loved to draw us in his strip.

It does a restaurant no harm to have, as a regular clientele, people who get their names in the paper. Some of the biggest restaurants and saloons hire press agents to implant that impression on the public. Almost overnight, we made Gruber's the best-known restaurant in Cleveland and one of the most successful in the country.

In the Jolly Set we had parties. We had parties to celebrate our birthdays and our anniversaries. We had parties to celebrate a Cleveland victory. I threw a coming-out party in the Hollenden ballroom for my wooden leg the day it arrived, danced every dance, split the stump open and ended crawling back to my room on hands and knees. And like Don Marquis' king we had parties just because nobody could think of any good reason *not* to have a party. After the Jolly Set had spent the night at our office helping us mail out the World Series tickets, we celebrated by holding a dance at high noon.

There were some beauts. Dick Haber, a superior party thrower, had a Come-as-the-Name-of-a-Moving-Picture party on the back lawn of his rather sumptuous home. Through great good luck, the Veterans of Foreign Wars were holding their convention in Cleveland at the time and, through even greater good luck, one of the candidates for National Commander had brought a 20-mule team along with him to publicize his campaign. I made a deal with him. I let him go around the ball park with signs urging his candidacy, and in return he lent me the 20-mule team so I could go to the party as *The Covered Wagon.*

I was one of the few unattached men in the Jolly Set, an oversight which was easily corrected. I know of no town that has more charming young ladies.

After the Jolly Set closed shop for the night, I'd take a deep breath and go on to the night people. The night people are the people you meet in the after-hour clubs after the theatre has let out or the last show in the night clubs has ended. Many of the night people are entertainers themselves, which made it nice because I've always had a lot of friends in show business—probably because I'd like to have been an entertainer myself if I'd had any talent. My closest friends in show business were—and are—Gene and Peg Sheldon. Gene is one of the world's greatest banjo players and one of the world's best pantomimists. Not because he's a friend of mine, but because he is. I toured around the country with them a couple of times working as straight man in their act.

Peg, Gene and I were part of a permanent established floating charades group, along with Mitzi Green and her husband Joe Pevney, and Skitch Henderson. If a couple of them found themselves in, say, Chicago, they'd call around and the rest of us would fly in. More often than not, the game was convened in New York. I used to catch a plane out of Cleveland—I know this sounds silly—and get into New York at 11 at night. Whoever was working would finish at about 12:30, and we'd all go to somebody's apartment—the regulars plus a couple of floaters—and play charades until about 5 in the morning. Then I'd catch the 6 o'clock plane out of New York and be back in Cleveland in time to start another day's work.

Mitzi and Joe once had to leave from Chicago right after the charades game to appear on the Eddie Cantor radio show in Peoria, the sponsor's home office. Peg, Gene and I went to the station with them, carrying along a tray of martinis to toast them on their way. As soon as the train pulled out, we dashed to the airport, chartered a plane to Peoria and had a car waiting to drive us to the station. Then we mixed some martinis at our leisure and were waiting for them, with the same tray, at the platform.

Elsa Maxwell once threw us a party that brought the Jolly Set and the charades group together in a head-on collision with New York café society. Elsa had been caught up in the excitement of the pennant race while lecturing in Cleveland and had become one of our biggest eastern rooters. With the major league's winter meetings being held in New York shortly after the World Series, she lost her head completely and threw us a victory party at the swankiest of the New York restaurants, Le Pavillon. *Life* and *Harper's Bazaar* were supposed to

202

have been picking up the tab in the hope of getting a picture story out of this meeting between the barbarians of the West and the cream of eastern aristocracy.

At the table with me, to give you idea, were Mrs. Norman Winston, wearing her diamonds wrapped around her like a shawl, and Salvador Dali and his surrealistic wax mustache. (Look, I don't claim to know anything about mustaches; I just know what I like.)

Lou Boudreau was there for our side along with Bob and Virginia Feller and Hank and Carol Greenberg. All the sportswriters from the Jolly Set were in town for the meetings, of course, and so was Bud Silverman. Gene and Peg Sheldon and Mitzi Green represented the charades group. Mitzi was appearing at the Copa and she kept running back and forth, between shows. The East countered by having Novotna come over from the Metropolitan Opera to deal out a couple of folk songs.

I had sworn off hard liquor shortly after I left Kenyon, due to the unfortunate experiences of a night wherein I had to call the Evanston chief of police three separate times to get me out of three separate suburban jails. I settled thereafter for beer and "Polish pop" (sparkling Burgundy wine). I used to drink a lot of beer and Polish pop. And as the night wore on and the bubbles dwindled, I had a fondness for picking people up over my head like barbells, an exercise which endeared me—or something—to all my friends. So, as I departed the Pavillon at the end of the evening, I picked Elsa up and carried her out the door with me, the best possible proof that the party had been a success. Social note: Elsa is no lightweight.

For the most part, though, the night people are a mixture of the racket men and the guys and girls who work at the regular night spots. In Cleveland, all the bartenders and all the waitresses and all the operators of the joints went to the Ten-Eleven Club, an after-hour cheat-joint run by Shondor Birns. These are great people for a fellow operating a ball club because they are, let me say again, conversationalists. They are the town criers of our civilization; the carriers of the word.

Another place at which I sometimes ended my rounds was the Alhambra. Shortly after I sold the Indians, the cashier of the Alhambra came to Chicago to plead with me to be a witness for Shondor Birns who, as I knew, had been indicted for a bombing murder growing out of a fight for control of a numbers territory. The cashier was the girlfriend of Birns' chief lieutenant, who had also been indicted. She had with her a check I had signed at the Alhambra. "You were in the night he was supposed to have bombed this car and killed this fellow," she told me, "and Shondor says he came to your table and was with you until you left."

It was true. I could remember the night so distinctly only because it had been a Sunday night. I had been to dinner at Janet Garfield's, the daughter of former President James Garfield. A whole group of us had left her house in a heavy rainstorm and had headed for the Alhambra because it opened at 12:01 on Monday morning. Shondor had come to sit with us, and he had not been out of my sight for three or four hours.

The others at the table, she said, all remembered he had been there too, but none of them, for obvious reasons, was willing to appear as a witness.

I said, "I was there that night. I saw him. I'll come over and testify."

So I went back to Cleveland to give a deposition and the big black headlines ran: VEECK ALIBI WITNESS FOR BIRNS.

My attitude is this. Although I never made it my business to know what Birns did, I have not the slightest doubt that if the police say he's Public Enemy No. 1, they know what they are talking about. If he's guilty of something, fair enough. Put him in jail. That's their business. I wouldn't sign a document saying that his reputation was unblemished. But my association with him had always been good. And on that particular night, for better or for worse, he was with me. (Incidentally, he was acquitted.)

I am no moralist in this respect, probably because I've always found the so-called hoodlums to be colorful people. And good customers of a ball club. Happy Chandler summoned me into a private conference before the first major-league meeting I ever attended to warn me he had received reports that I was consorting with known racketeers. I asked Happy to define the word "consort" and it turned out that it meant I was sitting with gamblers as I moved around the park. "Look," I said. "You can tell me who to hire on my ball club, but you can't tell me who to sell tickets to."

Actually, I never sat with the gamblers in Cleveland, because they used to sit in box seats and I won't sit in a box seat in my home park. I knew they were there, though, and I knew that money was being passed back and forth pretty much out in the open. Soon afterwards, Chandler sent around a circular warning us that the FBI was going to check gambling in all the parks. I had the word passed around that I wanted the money kept in their pockets.

A month later, the FBI issued a report stating that Cleveland was the cleanest town in the league. Virtually no gambling at all.

Frick gave me a similar order in Chicago. There is a group of gamblers who have been sitting in the bleachers at Comiskey Park for twenty years. I used to enjoy sitting among them for an inning or so because they were men who really knew baseball and always seemed to be having a good time.

I told Frick, "I'm sorry. They're customers. They pay their way in. I'm not going to have them arrested as long as they don't bother anybody else."

And that's precisely the way I feel about it. If the police want to evict them or arrest them, that's their business. As the operator of a ball park, I worry only about the people who create a disturbance.

Baseball attacks the problem of gambling from the wrong end. Understand this: the gambling on big-league baseball is tremendous; more money is bet on baseball, I think, than on any other sport, horse racing included. It is a worrisome thing. But only an infinitesimal portion of it takes place in the park. Nothing is accomplished by throwing anybody out.

We're not going to stop the gambling, so that means we had better watch it as closely as possible. The one place it can be watched is from the bookmakers' end. That's what I was doing in Cleveland while Chandler was sending people around to count how many dollars changed hands in 16 ball parks. The bookmakers are happy to cooperate with a baseball operator because their interests happen to coincide with his. The bookmakers don't want fixes any more than we do; they're the guys the fixers are betting against.

The baseball odds for the entire country come out of Minneapolis. Every morning I would handicap the Indian game, figuring out what I thought the odds should be. Then I'd get the syndicate's morning line from the Cleveland representative of the Minneapolis syndicate, and later, the closing line. If the betting odds had ever been significantly out of line with my own, or if there had been a significant shift in the closing odds, I would have been able to order a change of pitcher before the game started and to begin investigating at once.

I used the syndicate representative in other ways. To make sure they always have the best and the latest information, these guys subscribe to newspapers all over the country. He once stopped me in the hallway, for instance, to ask me what I knew about "this tremendous hitter Zernial in Burlington." I not only hadn't heard of Zernial, I wasn't sure I had heard of Burlington. Checking through our scouting files I found we had no report on him. I got curious and started to follow him, and as a result we drafted him at the end of the year. If these people have better information than my scouting force, I'm not proud. I'll use them.

OK, then. Cleveland was a ball. Around the clock. Laughs and parties, fun and games, attendance records falling and a World's Championship coming up.

There is a verse that has run around in my head since I was a boy: "Run, run as fast as you can. You can't catch me, I'm the Gingerbread Man." But the time comes when you either stop running of your own account or you run up your own heels and trip yourself.

I don't know how to say this without sounding pretentious, so I'll just say it as directly as possible: When I stop running I can be a serious man. I had very little religion in my. upbringing, and I felt there was something lacking in my life. In previous years, I had read up a little on Judaism, since so many of my friends were Jewish, and for a time I had fairly serious thoughts of converting. By 1948, I had moved out of the Hollenden to the 30th Street apartment, and every day in driving to the park I passed St. John's Cathedral, a beautiful edifice on Ninth Street. One day, in August, I found myself going inside, on sudden impulse, to find out what I could about Catholicism.

I don't want there to be any misunderstanding. I had no burning desire to renounce my past life of sin and folly and retire to a monastery. Fun and games and a bottle of beer are part of the joy of life. I believe life abounds in joy for those who will take it, and I have always reached out with both hands to take my share. I wasn't looking for something different, I was looking for something more.

Inside the Cathedral, I spoke to the rector, Monsignor Richard Walsh. He was very sympathetic. He gave me a lot of books to read, and I began to take instruction.

Then Msgr. Walsh went on his vacation and a young priest took over my instruction. He was a good fellow, a hail-fellow-well-met. The only thing wrong with him was that he had no answers for my questions. He kept saying, "Don't worry, everything will be all right, that's not your problem." I don't like to be treated like a child, especially at a time I am asking for answers to deeply troubling questions. So I stopped taking instruction.

It all closed in on me as the World Series was coming to an end. I have found, in my experience, that there is a basic rule of life, a good rule probably. Let us call it Veeck's Law of Enforced Humility: When you've run as fast as you can up the highest mountain you can find, you will find something or somebody waiting at the top to deflate you.

We went into the last Series game in Cleveland, on a Sunday, leading 3 games to 1. We had 86,288 paid attendance in the park, the greatest crowd in the history of organized baseball. I had my oldest son, Will, who was then eleven years old, up to see the Series. Will had never shown interest in baseball—possibly as a reaction to me—which bothered me not at all because I don't believe in dynasties. He's a marvelous boy. Eventually he went to MIT and is now teaching. I'm an admirer of his, unfortunately from a distance.

Will's seat was at the end of the aisle. Since I didn't have a seat of my own I was sitting on a newspaper on the step alongside him, and I guess I was a little overenthusiastic for a grown man. But this is what I am, an overenthusiastic grown man, and this is my life, putting people into ball parks, and this was my crowning moment, a championship ball team playing to a record crowd. And it is good at the crowning moment of your life to have your oldest son there to see it. I was saying, "Isn't this great, Will? Did you ever see such a tremendous crowd? Did you ever in your life see anything like this?"

He looked down at me and he said, "How come you couldn't have been a scientist or something I could have been proud of?"

Boy, kids can cut you down to size.

We lost that one, which meant we had to go back to Boston to end it. The train ride home from Boston was something. It being our intention to celebrate our victory in a modest sort of way, we loaded champagne and sparkling Burgundy onto the train the way the old-time firemen loaded coal. Eddie Robinson's wife, Elaine, was a lovely-looking girl, cool and imperturbable. She is one of these girls who leaves the impression that she has spent her entire day grooming herself. Never a hair out of place all year. I thought to myself, *Gee, I wonder if just once she can become ruffled?*

I shook up the half-filled bottle of wine I held in my hand and just sprayed it gently toward her. Mrs. Robinson turned around, cocked an eye at me in her cool and imperturbable manner, shook up her own full bottle and gave it back to me full blast. From there on into Cleveland, it rained champagne in the diner. At one stage of the festivities, I remember talking to the stewards to find out how much a diner cost because there seemed little doubt that I would have to buy the railroad a new one. We got off cheaply. The railroad was able to fix up the diner as good as new for not much more than $6,000.

As the train pulled into Cleveland in the morning, fresh from that blowout, we found a motorcade of open cars waiting at Union Terminal to carry us in triumph through the city. Lou Boudreau, his wife and I rode in the back seat of the mayor's car, right behind the band-wagon. The mayor having declared a holiday, there must have been half a million people lining our route as we made our way down Euclid Avenue to University Circle. Every whistle in the city seemed to be blowing and every horn blaring.

At the end of the line, Louie and his wife went off together. The mayor went off. All the players jumped out of their cars and went off. Everybody seemed to have somewhere to go except me. If we had come home at night I would have been all right, but where, I wondered, did people go in the daytime?

It was only a couple of blocks to my apartment, and so I walked home alone. Do you know what the saddest thing in the world is? To go home to an empty apartment in a moment of triumph. Triumph has no flavor unless it can be shared.

I sat in my empty apartment, with the sunlight all around me, and I thought of my son who was something less than proud of me. And I thought of my wrecked marriage and my lost family. And I thought of Harry Grabiner in a deep coma, waiting for death. I'd had it all, everything I'd hoped for when I came to Cleveland. Everything and more.

I had never been more lonely in my life.

I knew even then that I was going to have to sell the team soon. Eleanor had begun divorce proceedings earlier in the year, but had agreed to hold off her action until the baseball season was over. Once she filed again, I'd have to sell my interest in the club because I didn't own anything else that could be turned into cash. Half the club, I had agreed, belonged to her and the kids. Her attorney had been willing enough to wait, because if we won the pennant its value would be increased. When we got off to a bad start the next year, her attorney, quite properly, reinstated the divorce suit while we still had a seller's market.

The underlying reason for the sale of the Indians was to get a good chunk of money to settle upon Eleanor and, more important to both of us, to set up trust funds for the three kids.

It was a little more complicated than that, really. Upon learning why I had to sell, Lou Seltzer, the publisher of the *Press,* offered to arrange for me to borrow the money for the trust funds so that I could remain in Cleveland.

I decided against doing it that way. I told myself at the time that the whole purpose of the trust funds—to secure the kid's futures—would be defeated if the trusts were tied to a loan. I suspect now that mixed in there, unconsciously, was the feeling that I had done everything that could be done in Cleveland and that the time had

208

come to pick myself up and wander on. It may have been, too, that some instinct for self-preservation warned me that the time had come to stop running and take a little rest. You can't have your gingerbread and eat it too.

All my original stockholders got back $20 for every dollar they had invested. For one minute, I held a check for $1,000,000 in my hands, made out in my name, the end product of the $1 I had started out with in Milwaukee. That million dwindled fast. To begin with, the tax bite took 25 percent of the profits off the top. In addition to turning over half of what was left to Eleanor, I also bought the ranch, which was in her name, from her. Add it all up—or, more to the point, subtract—and you can see that while I was unusually solvent I wasn't in any position to look any of the Rockefeller clan in the eye.

This was my status and my frame of mind and my way of life in the fall of 1949 when I met Mary Frances Ackerman. For the record, the divorce proceedings and the sale of the club were both well underway before I ever saw her.

When the Ice Capades came to town, Bud Rand, a member in good standing of the Jolly Set, pitched their publicity girl at me. I had, perforce, already heard of the young lady. The sportswriters all over the country had billed her as "The World's Most Beautiful Press Agent," and were giving her as much publicity as the Ice Capades itself. Rand kept assuring me that she was not only beautiful but intelligent and intriguing and the repository of all feminine virtues. After all this buildup, I very quickly came to the conclusion that she was exactly the type of woman I would go to the ends of the world to avoid.

During all this time, I discovered later, Bud Rand had been giving Mary Frances the same pitch about me and had been rewarded with the same massive disinterest. Bud wasn't a man to let a little thing like mutual distaste stop him. He invited each of us to his home for dinner, finally, without bothering to tell either of us that the other was going to be there.

We got off as badly as both of us would have expected. I found myself asking why a beautiful and intelligent girl like her was beating her brains out instead of getting married and raising babies.

"Oh," she said, "you think I've beaten all my brains out, is that what you're trying to say?"

"No, no," I said. "That's the trouble. You'll never be happy with a guy unless he's some super being. You make too much money and you live on expense accounts and everybody tells you how great you are. You're spoiled. No mere human could possibly satisfy you now."

I went on in that brilliant vein until all at once I realized—it may have been an insuppressible yawn that tipped me off—that every man she had ever gone out with or sat alongside at a dinner table had given her exactly that same pitch, probably word for word, and that she was just feeding me her routine answers and undoubtedly thinking: *So this is Bill Veeck. What a jerk he turned out to be.*

Mary Frances, as Rand had told me, was a practicing Catholic. Out of my continuing interest in Catholicism, I had picked up a copy of the book *American Freedom and Catholic Power,* a controversial best seller in its day. The author, Paul Blanshard, was very worried about the Catholics taking over the country. By coincidence, I had the book in my jacket pocket when I went up to the Rands'. "Gee," she said, "I haven't read it. If you're finished, I'd like to borrow it."

"All right," I said. "But nice little Catholic girls like you shouldn't read this."

"I'm not a little girl," she said, "although I like to think I'm nice. But it's also nice to know what the enemy is shooting at you."

So now I'm wondering whether she thinks I'm anti-Catholic.

After dinner, there were a series of discussions on topics on which Mary Frances and I were in complete disagreement. That was interesting. Right at the end, with the talk turning to politics, she advanced the theory that the United States should set up special graduate schools to train our diplomats and bureaucrats instead of just throwing them into their jobs cold and leaving them to bungle through. I'm sure almost everybody has experienced the sensation of hearing some perfect stranger express their own pet idea, an idea they have thought out so carefully that they have come to feel it belongs to them the way a piece of real estate belongs to them. I had long had the idea, and had committed it to paper, that the potential leaders of the country should be winnowed out and trained from childhood. My program started right at the top, with the two political parties training potential Presidential candidates from the cradle and nominating, in the end, the man who had come up through the ranks, post by post, gaining experience in all the necessary branches of government and passing highest in the final tests.

Well, the conversation did not lag from that point. I had converted a few people through the force and clarity of my rhetoric, but I had never before found anyone, as it were, to dance with. Mary Frances was staying at her sister's in Cleveland and, as the dinner party broke up, nothing would do but that I drive her home so that we could continue the discussion.

There seemed to be a basis for further conversations, and I asked her for a date the next night. She was scheduled to go on a radio program to plug the Ice Capades. I told her I'd go along with her.

I dated her the next two nights, which took me into about every radio and TV studio in town. One week to the day after we'd met, I called her in New York, early in the morning, and proposed.

The next morning I called again and proposed again. We were quietly engaged a week later and I went to Oklahoma City to meet her parents and formally ask for her hand in marriage.

I began to take instruction again, this time with Father George Halpin in Chicago, and was baptized in December, 1949. Muddy Ruel was my godfather. Mary Frances and I had asked for permission to be married under the Pauline Privilege, which means, briefly, that since I had not been baptized in any religion at the time of my first marriage, we could be married in the Church. A ruling had already come down forbidding us from seeing each other during the six months the Church court would be investigating and reviewing our case.

Well, Muddy Ruel was a good friend of Cardinal Spellman in New York. I knew Cardinal Stritch of Chicago fairly well from the days when he was Bishop Stritch of Milwaukee and I was working with the Milwaukee CYO. It has always been my belief that when you have a little weight in court you are a fool to throw it away. Right? I was going to get all this nonsense settled in a hurry.

I observed to Cardinal Stritch that in the old days the Church had been known to grant indulgences, intimating—with my well-known tact—that I was prepared to make a contribution to any deserving church establishment. "My best advice," he told me, "is to do exactly what you have been told to do. It is not up to me to intercede." Midwestern isolationism. A New York prelate, I was sure, would look upon these matters with a little more sophistication and understanding. Muddy and I arrived in New York on a rainy day and sidled into Cardinal Spellman's office across from St. Patrick's Cathedral. We emerged a few moments later with our spirits considerably more dampened than our clothes. My attempt to put the fix in with the Church ranks among my more dismal failures.

During the six months we had to remain apart, Mary Frances and I could not even be in the same city at the same time, for the Church was most desirous of avoiding publicity. That was why going to Cleveland to give the deposition for Shondor Birns was something of an inconvenience. I had to call Mary Frances to tell her I was coming, and she had to get out of town. Shortly afterwards, she had to come to Chicago on some kind of errand and I had to get out of town. After we had run each other out of a couple of more towns,

211

I went down to the ranch to sit out the rest of the six months. It was very educational. I learned that a man could spend $100,000 fixing up his house and grounds while he was just killing time.

We were married by Father Halpin at a nuptial mass in St. Francis Cathedral in Santa Fe, on April 29, 1950.

I had picked Mary Frances up at her parents' home in Oklahoma City, then driven on to Santa Fe with her mother, her father, her grandmother, her brother and her sister. As I always say, you see here a man who eloped with the whole family.

The marvelous part of our marriage, needless to say, is that Mary Frances not only participates in my baseball operations, she is an enormous help. She is a skilled publicity and idea woman. In St. Louis, for instance, she dreamed up the idea of sending a Browns' contract to every newborn boy, presentable in 16 years, along with two tickets for the parents. The parents of a girl got two tickets and a poem Mary Frances composed for the occasion.

We had a radio and TV show together in St. Louis, and we did both radio and TV shows in Chicago. She goes on my speaking tours with me, and is not only an attraction in herself but is invaluable in other ways. I have a good memory for names normally, and yet every once in awhile I'll draw a complete blank on someone I know I should remember. I'll give Mary Frances the sign, circulate around the room a little, and when I come back she will be talking to the guy. "You remember Jim Brown, don't you, Bill?" she'll say.

"Of course I know Jim," I'll say, only a slight note of reproach in my voice. "We're old friends."

And, of course, Mary Frances not only likes sportswriters, she knows them all from her days with the Ice Capades. We started out with mutual friends all over the country. There may be a writer here and there—one of those chronic malcontents—who has his doubts about me, but all of them love Mary Frances.

As a woman who knows the working of the male mind in this field, she has always felt that when she married me she surrendered her right to express an expert opinion, particularly on our TV shows. It is her theory, and there is some logic to it, that a woman who expertizes on baseball has to sound like either:

1) a complete moron
2) The Little Expert

When the newspapermen, managers, coaches and ballplayers would gather in our ball-park apartment in St. Louis to second-guess the ball game, Mary Frances could be observed in the background preparing something for them to eat or taking care of their wives.

There is something else, too. Although I have made it clear that I don't bow three times to Mecca when I enter a ball park, I am a hard loser. A silent and brooding loser. Good losers you can have. I've played a lot of tennis—with and without a wooden leg—and when I see one of these guys jumping gracefully over the net to congratulate the guy who has just beaten him, I feel like punching him in the nose. Mary Frances is aware that after a loss I am in no mood for conversation, food or human company. She will put a tray of food beside me after awhile, suffer my ungrateful scowl silently, and tiptoe away to make sure the kids keep their distance and the dog doesn't get any foolish ideas about making any friendly gesture toward me.

If she keeps up the good work, I'll keep her on.

I'm From Missouri—Momentarily 15.

MY purchase of the Browns in 1951 brought on a quick reaction in my own little world of sports, something like that of a family gathering around a loved one in time of sickness.

Grantland Rice was inspired to new heights of poetic awe:

Stalwarts have hunted the charging lion, deep in the jungle veldt.
Brave men have stood to the tiger's rush seeking his costly pelt.
Hunters have tackled the elephant, never a job for clowns.
This world is packed with its daring deeds—but Veeck has purchased the Browns.

John Lardner wrote in wonder: "Many critics were surprised to know that the Browns could be bought because they didn't know the Browns were owned."

If John had been trying to buy the Browns, that lamentable gap in his education would have been filled in a hurry. The Browns were not only owned, they were the most owned team in captivity. They were owned by the DeWitt brothers plus more than 1,400 odd-lot stockholders, and maybe you don't think that gave us a headache. On July 3, 1951, we finally amassed the amount of stock we needed, although we still had to wait until after the holiday to sign the contracts. I swung right into action on the Fourth, though, heading for the park and the bleachers to introduce myself to the customers and warm up my lungs on the umpires.

Mary Frances was supposed to join me. To my surprise, she didn't show up. On the way to the park her taxi had swerved to avoid hitting a truck, and she had been thrown against the partition and taken home, woozy. Do you suppose somebody was trying to tell me something?

Mary Frances and I got our first chance to work as a team that same night. The Browns owned a promising young outfielder, Frank Saucier, who had perhaps the best minor-league batting record in the country. (Yes, the same Saucier whom Eddie Gaedel batted for.) Saucier was not playing for the Browns though. He was working for an oil company in Okmulgee, Oklahoma. Having signed with the Browns originally for nothing, he felt he was at least as entitled to a bonus as some kid just out of high school who had yet to swing at a pitch in professional anger and would probably never rise above a Class-B league. He was talking down my alley. I had been arguing all along that the money flowing *out of baseball* in the form of bonuses should be going to the care and preservation of the slowly dying minor leagues, with the minor-league club then giving the player a percentage of the purchase price when he was sold to the majors— something I had always done in Milwaukee.

When I returned to the hotel after the game, I put in a call to Okmulgee and was told Frank was gone for the holidays. After tracking him all over the Midwest, we finally found him, at one o'clock in the morning, at his parents' home in Washington, Missouri, only forty miles away.

"Don't go to bed," I told him. "I'll be right over."

"Gee, Bill," he said, "it's kind of late, isn't it. Let's make it tomorrow."

"Stay right where you are," I said. "I'll be right over."

Mary Frances and I rented a car and arrived at 2:30. It wasn't only a question of the bonus at this point. Frank was completely disillusioned with baseball. He was expecting a draft call and he saw little sense in setting up a new home in St. Louis for half a season. I told him if he agreed to come back, he would go on the payroll immediately and could take all the time he needed to go back to Oklahoma and put his affairs in order. I kept talking to Frank. Mary Frances kept talking to his wife. We all kept drinking coffee. At about 4:30, he agreed to sign.

We got back to our own apartment at 7. I had another cup of coffee, soaked my leg and went down to the bank to sign more papers. From the bank, I toured the park to see what changes were to be made. I didn't get to bed for forty-eight hours, and it was a great feeling. I was back in action.

Because I wanted to get it clear in everybody's mind that the days at the bottom of the slag heap were over and done with, I ran a big canvas streamer across the front of Sportsman's Park announcing: OPEN FOR BUSINESS UNDER NEW OWNERSHIP. To get it up in time to meet the, let-us-hope, thrilled and expectant eyes of the first arrivals at our twi-night doubleheader, we had to hang it wet and unfinished and let the painter put on the final letters while the customers were filing in.

I also had to get the Board of Public Service to convene in special session so they could issue us a fireworks permit. I made it clear that I had no immediate plans for shooting off fireworks, because I wanted to hold to the old formula of never announcing them in advance.

We drew 10,392 people into the park that night, and between the games they were treated to a fireworks display. Just after the second game began, I took the public-address system and announced: "As a tribute to the Browns' future success, let's all have a drink on the house." Grabbing a bucketful of beer, I passed among the customers in the grandstand and had a drink with them myself. Altogether we gave out 7,596 bottles of beer and 6,041 bottles of pop, which would indicate the presence of some 3,000 switch-hitters in the park.

This toast, incidentally, was not the sudden impulse it was written up to be. You cannot distribute 13,000 bottles of anything on impulse. You have to be sure you have an adequate supply on hand and you have to hire extra help.

The rest of the operation was the same as always. The doors came off the offices; our phone numbers were publicized. I brought Ada Ireland, the world's greatest switchboard operator, down from Cleveland. Before you ask what's so important about a telephone operator, remember this: the telephone operator is your only contact with the outside world. Ada, a gray-haired fiftyish matron when we first met, can hear a man's voice once and greet him by name when he calls back again a year later. If you don't think that makes him feel as if we know him, treasure him and want his business, then you're crazy. The first time I met Ada in Cleveland, I told her, "Just call me Bill." She said, "I don't like to be that informal, darling." *Touché*. She always called me "darling" after that.

In Cleveland, Ada had assigned herself the staggering duty of keeping me presentable, if not respectable. "Darling," she would snap, "you look like a bum." She would send me rushing off to an important appointment, and when I got to the address it would turn out to be a barbershop. She sent my clothes out to be cleaned. She kept herself posted on the females in my life and, more important, she kept them apart.

Ada captivated Mary Frances, of course, at first meeting. "You little so-and-so," she said. "You married the only man I ever loved."

As much as I kid about the Browns and St. Louis, there were things about our two and a half years there that were the happiest and most satisfying of my life. My first full year in St. Louis, I will maintain to the end of my life, was the best job of promoting I have ever done. The last year was a prison sentence, compliments of the American League.

One of the things that made the first full year so ideal was that we lived in our own ball-park apartment, something I had dreamed of from my concession days in Chicago. In concessions, the only things that can go stale on you are popcorn and rolls. Uncut rolls you can return, which means that you don't start cutting until you have some idea about the weather and the crowd. Before a big doubleheader, I'd get into the park at 3 A.M. and cut from 30,000 to 35,000 rolls. Well, there wasn't much sense going home from night school when I had to be back at 3 in the morning, so I slept in the firehouse on Waveland Avenue, right across the street. The firehouse was not without its advantages—I had my own quarters, good company was always available and the taxpayers, as is their custom, picked up the tab. But Bob Dorr, the grounds keeper, had his own little house attached to Wrigley Field, and how I envied him. To me, that was the greatest thing in the world.

Upon first coming to St. Louis, I had moved the Browns' offices from the second floor of Sportsman's Park down to the street where they belonged. That left a lot of room upstairs. Mary Frances had been running around the neighborhood whenever she had any time during the season trying to find a house. With the season at an end, she still hadn't found anything. Now what could be more logical?

"She'll never go for it," Rudie Schaffer said.

"No harm trying," said I. "Boy, wouldn't it be great!"

"Great," Rudie said. "But she'll never go for it."

Normally, Mary Frances and I didn't see very much of each other during the day. We had set up separate speaking schedules in those early days to enable us to cover twice as much territory and, we hoped, work up twice as much interest for the coming season. As soon as we

216

both had a free morning, I invited her to lunch, bringing Rudie along to leap to my support and scoff at her objections.

Well, you've probably guessed it. She had the same idea herself. She had been sneaking up there for weeks, banging on walls and deciding how to break up the maze of partitioned offices into rooms. She even had a preliminary floor plan already drawn up.

It was an odd apartment in many ways, with windows in strange corners and at odd angles. We had giant pillars in places the more classically trained architects would have frowned upon—like in the middle of the kitchen and living room—because they lent a casual atmosphere so fitting to the landscape, and because the park would have fallen down without them. Mary Frances wound spirals of lights and flowerpots around them, and they were the most attractive pillars anybody ever had to live with intimately.

We had a nice little playyard for Mike, too. Just behind the left-field stands, where the concession area broke from the park itself, there was an odd architectural formation jutting out of the wall. We covered it with ivy and built a green-and-white picket fence around it and Mike—who was about a year old when we moved in—played there quite happily, oblivious to the big beer trucks grinding in and out of the driveway right alongside him.

Actually, life got to be pretty rough on Mary Frances, because she was always entertaining. She had all kinds of special diets tacked to the kitchen door. Red Rolfe was managing at Detroit and she had his special ulcer diet. Anybody who expressed a particular liking for any dish had to be sure he wasn't just being polite because Mary Frances would tack another note to the door and make sure he got it again next time he visited us. The wives of the players and the sportswriters were always telling her what *not* to feed their husbands. "I can't do anything with him at home," they'd say. "But up here they'll all be talking baseball and he's going to eat anything you shove in front of him."

The feeding would sometimes start as early as 5 o'clock if the Yankees or Tigers were in town, because Casey Stengel and Fred Hutchinson liked early dinners. That was followed by the cocktail hour and dinners for the late diners and later arrivers. On a good night the party could continue until 5 A.M. before we broke up. In the morning, the manager and the coaches would be up, along with Rudie and Bob, to have breakfast with me. Our conferences were always held in the bathroom while I sat in the tub soaking my leg. Mary Frances would get there first to leave the breakfast trays and make sure that the window was open. She was afraid that if she

217

waited until everybody was gone and tried to clear out all the cigar smoke (mainly from Rudie and Marty Marion) at once, somebody would turn in a fire alarm.

Between the members of the group, we blanketed a 250-mile radius around St. Louis, covering parts of eight different states. I averaged better than two speeches a day on a year-round basis and once made seven in one day. We developed one new technique, too. We descended in force—in what I liked to call "safaris"—upon small towns within our radius to hold a press conference for the local newspaper and radio people. We would hire the ballroom of the local hotel, throw a banquet and arrive with Mary Frances and myself, our manager, our coaches, Bill Durney, Bob Fishel and our radio announcer Bud Blattner. As an added starter, we would dragoon Charlie Grimm whenever we were within dragooning distance of his section of Missouri. The safaris were just to let the small towns know that we considered them important to us. And they were. One of the things we were never able to overcome was the Cardinals' vastly superior radio network. They had 83 stations; we had just a handful. Since the population of St. Louis was only 850,000, we had to pull customers in from out of town if we were going to succeed.

The only attraction the Browns had when we came was Ned Garver, who by mid-season had won 11 games, exactly half the team total. Just as we had pushed Feller to the strikout record in Cleveland, for its peripheral publicity value, we decided to push Garver as hard as possible to help him become the first pitcher to win 20 games with a last-place team. It was easy to do with Ned because he was also the best hitter on the team and there was never any reason to take him out for a pinch hitter in the late innings. There was almost nothing Ned could do to get knocked out of a game, as a matter of fact, short of allowing 10 runs in the first inning. (We'd take him out then so that we could start him again in a day or two.) The Browns lost 102 games, which seemed to be overdoing it a little even for a last-place team, but Garver won his 20.

The team we took over at the halfway point was already 23½ games behind the leader. I couldn't very well go around insulting the intelligence of my audiences by praising them, so I edged in through the back door by talking about the Browns as if they were the worst team that had ever existed. (If your town is destroyed by a hurricane, there's no sense having it *almost* the worst hurricane in history. There's a certain satisfaction in being with a record-breaker.) "I'm not asking you to come out and see the Browns this year," I would say. "In fact, I advise you not to. It hurts. I only go out to see them because I have to. I'm telling you, though, that we'll have a better team next season, one that you won't be ashamed to look at.

"We've got rid of half our players," I'd say fervently, "and we mean to get rid of the rest as soon as possible."

And usually, I'd start my speech by saying, "You're going to have to forgive me if I seem nervous. I'm not used to seeing so many people."

Everybody, the players included, took it for what it was: an attempt to get people into the park by playing it for laughs. Our attendance in the second half of that year was double what it had been in the first half. At the end of the season, after being in town only four months, I finished second to Stan Musial in a sportswriters-sportcasters poll to name the city's outstanding sports figure of the year.

Satchel Paige was the first player I brought in. Max Patkin and Jackie Price came back to entertain. Within the first month we had a miniature circus, featuring "Millie the Queen of the Air" sliding down a tightwire that extended from right field to third base.

Five days after we outraged the higher sensibilities and sensitivities of the baseball world by sending a midget to bat, we held a Grandstand Managers' Day in which the fans called all our strategy. It started as a promotional gag, really, for the *Globe-Democrat*. The paper was to print a ballot on which their readers would choose our opening lineup, position by position, for the game. Everybody who submitted a lineup was mailed a ticket which would entitle him to sit in the special section behind our dugout where the Grandstand Managers would gather to call the plays.

The ballot ran in only one edition before one of the more conservative editors let out a horrified gasp and killed it.

Out of that one edition we received 4,000 ballots. Since this was one of those rare gags which by its nature had to be announced beforehand, I wanted to get Connie Mack in on it. Mr. Mack was still traveling with his team, in his eighty-ninth year, although his mind was beginning to wander and he no longer sat on the bench. Whenever the Athletics came to town, we had a schedule posted in the office to make sure that someone was always assigned to sit with him during the game. I felt very strongly that he deserved that small gesture of respect. Mr. Mack sat with Mary Frances and me in the Grandstand Managers' section for a couple of innings and enjoyed himself tremendously.

The Athletics' general manager, Art Ehlers, had threatened to protest ahead of time on the grounds that we were—and I quote— making a travesty of the game. That was all right with me; it gave me a chance to observe that he was afraid my amateurs would outsmart his experts.

And the funny thing is that they did. Never has a game been called better.

The way it worked, the Grandstand Managers showed their special passes as they entered and were given large white signs with YES printed in green on one side, and NO printed in red on the other. Bob Fishel, standing at the rail just behind our dugout, had a stack of cards to cover every conceivable situation. He held up the indicated card, the managers voted a green YES or a red NO, and a circuit judge standing alongside Bob with a walkie-talkie tabulated the result. The judge relayed the decision to Johnny Berardino, who was standing in the dugout with another walkie-talkie.

Before the first inning began, Jimmy Dykes, the A's manager, informed umpire Bill Summers that he was prepared to protest to league headquarters if all this vote tabulating delayed the game. Jimmy, always a good fellow, was just trying to help the gag along. To make sure everybody knew he was protesting, he kicked up the dirt around the plate and scowled toward my tyros. My tyros scowled right back. They were fit and ready and straining to start thinking. Here again, funny thing, the game took just over two hours, despite all the tabulating, which had to make it one of the fastest games of the year.

As for our regular manager, Zack Taylor, he reclined in a rocking chair on top of the dugout, in civilian clothes and bedroom slippers, and just leaned back and puffed on a long, curved pipe. Summers told him he had to get off the field, not because of the rocking chair or the pipe but because he wasn't in uniform. So we moved Zack, the rocking chair and the pipe into a box just beside our dugout.

The fans were brilliant. To begin with, they had made two changes in our regular lineup, putting Sherm Lollar behind the plate and Hank Arft at first base. Lollar collected three of our nine hits, scored three runs and drove in three including the game-winning home run. Arft, of course, knocked in the other two runs.

To make it even more dramatic, all the key plays were squeezed into the first three innings. In the first inning, Ned Garver, the almost unanimous choice to pitch, was hit very hard. With three runs already in and runners on first and third, Fishel flashed the sign SHALL WE WARM UP PITCHER?

Well, they voted against even warming up a pitcher, presumably on the theory that Garver's feelings might be hurt. Among the naysayers was my bride, Mary Frances, which caused Mr. Mack and me

220

—who had of course voted YES—to wonder what kind of strategist I had gotten myself involved with.

Fishel then flashed the sign, INFIELD BACK?

The majority voted YES, playing for the double play rather than to cut off the run at the plate, excellent strategy at that point. Pete Suder obligingly grounded into a double play, making my experts right two times on only one play.

We did some scoring ourselves in the first. With one run in, Lollar on first and a 3–2 count on the batter, the Grandstand Managers voted against having the base runner go with the pitch. Which was fortunate because the batter took a third strike and the slow-moving Lollar would undoubtedly have been doubled up. The next batter doubled, and Hank Arft tied the score with a single.

Arft was then allowed to steal and was thrown out at second, the only bit of strategy that didn't work all day.

We won the game 5–3 to end a four-game losing streak. I retired all my amateur managers with honors, went back to my professional and lost five of the next six games.

There was another gag I really wanted to try. Before the next — season started I had hired Buddy Blattner and Dizzy Dean to broadcast our games. Buddy had retired only a couple of years earlier and he was still in pretty good shape. My plan was to sign him for one game, put a walkie-talkie on his back and have him broadcast the game for one turn at bat and maybe an inning or two in the field. You know: "Here comes the pitch . . . oooops . . . he caught the outside corner with a curve." Wouldn't that have been great?

Blattner's contract was still owned by the Phillies. I called Carpenter and told him exactly what I wanted to do, and Carpenter said, "Sure."

"OK," I said. "Why don't you give him his unconditional release? I'll sign him for a day and then you can get him back."

"Sure," Carpenter said, "I'll be glad to do it that way for $10,000."

As I was saying, "Here comes the price . . . ooooops, too high. Much, much too high."

Let me state one thing as clearly as possible. I did not buy the Browns with the intention of moving them out of St. Louis. If I did, I put on an awfully good act of working 24-hours a day for a year and a half trying to sell them.

I did come into St. Louis—and I'll make this as clear as possible too—knowing perfectly well that the city could support only one team. I had been saying for years that the only cities in the country who could support two teams were Chicago and New York.

That would seem to mean only one thing. That I had come into St. Louis to try to run the Cardinals out of town. Yes. That was precisely what I had in mind. St. Louis had, in fact, been supporting only one team for years. The Cardinals. And understandably. The Cardinals had won more pennants than any team in the previous quarter of a century except the Yankees. The Cardinals still had all the important names: Musial, Schoendienst, Slaughter, Marion. But the Cards were on the downgrade. They were on the downgrade on the field and, just as important from my point of view, they were weak in the front office. The Cardinal owner was Fred Saigh, an attorney. Saigh was wealthier than me, of course, but he did not have unlimited wealth. That meant he could be run out of town. He didn't have unlimited experience in running a baseball team, either; as I saw it, Saigh didn't have the foggiest notion of what he was doing.

I first became convinced I could take him when his radio announcer, Harry Caray, tried to stop me from acquiring the stock I needed to close the deal. It came about in this way: Bill and Charlie DeWitt owned only 56 percent of the Browns' stock. We wanted at least 75 percent. We needed that amount for tax purposes, and I wanted it from my own point of view for, one might say, the principal of it. If you're running a club with 51 percent control, you're working just as hard as if you had 100 percent but you're getting only half the profits.

The Browns had those 1,400-odd stockholders, with anywhere from one to five shares apiece, because one of the earlier owners had once had the bright idea that the team should be citizen-owned. DeWitt, in selling me an option to buy the club, had requested that the other stockholders deposit their certificates with the Mercantile Commerce Bank & Trust before July 3. I was offering $7 a share against the $3 that had originally been paid. My option allowed me to cancel the whole deal if I couldn't get the 75 percent. (Technically, it would be more accurate to say that my lawyers had bought the option from his lawyers. Bill and I never met after word came to me through—who else?—Louie Jacobs that Bill thought he could get the 75 percent.)

I went to St. Louis myself, wrote letters to the stockholders and appeared on radio shows to request that they send the certificates in. It was at this point that Harry Caray, on his own nightly sports program, began to implore the stockholders not to sell their stock to this well-known capital-gains hustler, this con man. In case there is any doubt in anybody's mind as to who hires, pays and fires the guys who broadcast the games for a big-league team, let me clear that up. Directly or indirectly, it is the owner of the team. At the same time, I should say in all fairness that Caray is an excellent announcer. He does as good a job of selling as anybody on the air.

I'm not sure whether I'd have taken the team without that minimum 75 percent. It was a decision I would have had to make at the last moment. While the St. Louis closing wasn't quite the dramatic last-minute dash of Cleveland, it was still a near thing. The stock certificates dribbled into the bank in all sizes, shapes and colors, and it was not until two days before the deadline that we hit our 75 percent. We ended with 79.9 percent.

As soon as Saigh put his announcer Caray to work on me, I knew I had read my man right. Understanding that, it was just a matter of laying the traps. Poor Saigh walked, ran or dove into every trap we set. He was such a patsy that it wasn't even much fun.

I began to work on him from Day One. The Cardinals were our tenants at Sportsman's Field at a ridiculously low rent. They had their offices on one side of the field, we had ours on the other. To give Saigh that grim persecuted feeling as quickly as possible, I painted the walls on our side of the park and left his side unwashed, unpainted and untouched. To drive home the point that he was to look upon me as an enemy, I barred him from using our special press room or our fancy private box when the Cardinals were playing at home.

In decorating the park we put up murals of old St. Louis heroes on the walls behind the concession stands. By coincidence, they were all pictures of old St. Louis Browns players. This was a detail that would have gone completely unnoticed if Saigh had not done exactly what I expected him to. I had prodded him, he had to swing back. As soon as the Cardinals were at home, he covered the murals over with bright cardinal blankets, thereby making himself look petty and ridiculous and calling attention to something nobody had particularly noticed.

One of the first things I did, as always, was to set Saturday as Ladies' Day. The Cards had no Ladies' Day and I didn't want them to have a Ladies' Day. To guarantee they didn't start now, all I had to do was challenge Saigh to throw the park open to the ladies on Saturday too. I wasn't going to push *him* into anything.

A couple of weeks later, I sent out another challenge. The Browns were in 8th place and the Cardinals were in 4th place, 12 games off the lead but not completely out of it. To cement the good feelings that had been established between us I suggested that since it was obvious that neither St. Louis team was going to be in the World Series that fall, we should immediately schedule a post-season game for the

Community Chest. Saigh somehow got the impression that I was trying to tell the people of St. Louis that they could write off the Cardinals' pennant chances.

He had to react, of course. He wrote a letter to the Community Chest—and incidentally to the press—in which he made it clear that he was far from ready to strike his team's colors. His statement read:

> Any time Mr. Veeck gives you a check for $10,000, I will match that with a Cardinal check in addition to our regular contribution. From past history, $20,000 is considerably more than would be netted from any game or post-season series. If Mr. Veeck does have the good of the Chest at heart, he will not care from whence the money came just so it got to you. . . .

This was why I loved Mr. Saigh so dearly. With a chance to take the initiative by laying his $10,000 on the table and casually brushing me aside—which would have forced me to trip over myself in my haste to match it—he had handed the initiative over to me and, to make it even better, made it sound as if he really hoped I wouldn't get up the $10,000 so that he wouldn't have to match it.

I promptly sent the check in and renewed my challenge, expressing my sharp sense of disappointment that Saigh lacked such faith in his team's ability to draw more than a paltry $20,000 in a post-season series. To end the whole incident on a pleasant note, I had Abe Saperstein bring the Harlem Globetrotters into the park at the end of the season for the first outdoor game the Globetrotters ever played. We drew 17,000 people—14,000 of whom undoubtedly came to see the Globetrotters—and we were able to turn gate receipts of better than $20,000 over to the Community Chest.

Saigh had a few rapier thrusts of his own. On the bottom of his scorecards, he printed the slogan: THE CARDINALS, A DIGNIFIED ST. LOUIS INSTITUTION. By implication we were those vulgarians from the other side of the tracks. No one had bothered to let him know, apparently, that the dignified Cardinals had seen their greatest glory as "The Gas House Gang," starring such pillars of dignity and sobriety as Frankie Frisch, Dizzy Dean, Pepper Martin, Leo Durocher and Rip Collins.

Not that I didn't want to identify with the Cardinals. In order to give Cardinal fans a rooting interest in our team, I grabbed every old Cardinal hero I could find. By the next season I was loaded down with old Cardinals.

Toward the end of the season, Saigh had sent an emissary to sound out Rogers Hornsby about replacing Marty Marion as the Cardinals' manager. His emissary was thoughtful enough to pass the information on to me.

I couldn't allow that to happen. Hornsby, according to the newspaper reports, had been barred from big-league baseball by Judge Landis, although I, to be frank, had never heard of any such ban and I had been around baseball a long time. The point, however, was that the fans believed it to be true, and an untruth that is believed to be a fact has to be treated as a fact. Hornsby was the greatest player the Cardinals had ever had. He had managed them to their first pennant. He would be returning home after what seemed an indecent period of exile. My great handicap in battling the Cards was that they already had all the big names in St. Louis. If they added Hornsby, I would be dead.

On the other hand, here were the makings of a marvelous squeeze. If Saigh wanted to hire Hornsby, it meant he was somehow dissatisfied with Marty Marion, even though Marion had his team up to 3rd place, surely as high as they had any right to be. If I could hire Hornsby out from under Saigh, I'd have the returning hero and I'd also have given Saigh something else to brood upon. If he then fired Marion anyway, I would hire Marion as a player-coach, and have two of the greatest Cardinal names on my roster.

There was no time to fool around. I called Hornsby, and signed him over the phone. Hornsby's main concern seemed to be in getting a 3-year contract, an indication he had been trying to get a multi-year contract out of Saigh without success. I gave him exactly what he wanted, a 3-year contract at $36,000 a year.

The fact that Hornsby was not only coming back to St. Louis, the scene of his greatest triumph, but that he was being brought back by the son of the man who had fired him in Chicago added an extra fillip to the true-life story of one man's triumph over petty prejudice and adversity.

Now Saigh was stuck with Marion. He wasn't going to give me the satisfaction of firing him right away and letting everybody know I had stolen Hornsby from him. No, he waited awhile. He waited almost two full months and then with his sure sense of public relations, he let Marion go on Thanksgiving Day.

I hired Marty in time to brighten up his Christmas.

Before the season opened, I had another of the great Cardinal stars on my payroll. To seduce and subvert the old Cardinal fans even further, Falstaff Brewery signed Dizzy Dean to do our radio broadcasts. Diz was a good and colorful broadcaster, although I must say that television has cramped his style. One of the great virtues of radio was that the listener could not see what was happening. The game Diz announced, while a good game and an exciting game, was not necessarily in strict accord with the game that was being played on the field. I mean when Diz felt that the drama of the game had reached the point where it was time for a man to "slud" into third base —or do any of the number of things that would call his unique and well-publicized vocabulary into play—the runner was darn well going to come into third base "sludding," even if the throw had really gone to second base and the man who was barely sludding in under a rifle-like throw, in Diz's game, had actually rounded third and gone halfway home. Diz became one of this country's foremost victims of technological obsolescence.

The signing of Dean provoked Saigh to new heights of absurdity. The motion picture of Diz's life had just been completed when he signed with us and it was having its world premiere in St. Louis on the day the Browns and Cardinals played their traditional pre-season game. To publicize the picture, 20th Century-Fox held a pre-game parade from the theatre to the park, where we were to conduct some kind of touching pre-game ceremony. A good publicity gimmick for everybody. The Cardinals were naturally invited to participate.

Saigh, stung that we had hired Hornsby, Marion and Dean, took his trenchant pen in hand again and wrote the publicity man:

> We do not want to take part in any promotion or any program or parade in which the Browns have a single person. This is not a baseball picture, it is the life of a man who spent his active playing career in the Cardinal organization. We do not feel that anyone else should muscle in.

There was little I could do as a man responsive to civic duty but deplore that kind of dog-in-the-manger attitude since, as I saw it, this was not a matter of partisan bickering between two mere baseball teams but of the city itself paying homage to one of its most beloved heroes. And there was little the fans could do but shake their heads, laugh, and wonder what in the world was eating Saigh.

Now that I had him going, I kept after him by putting in claims for everybody he wanted to send to the minors, for I was sure he would withdraw them rather than give me a chance to get another Cardinal on my roster. At last, to clear a place for one of the pitchers he couldn't get by me, the Cards retired Harry Brecheen, one of the great Cardinal pitchers of the decade and one of the handful of pitchers to have won three games in a single World Series. I learned about it when Brecheen's name came through on the next waiver list with the notation that $1 waivers were being asked on him so that he could become a coach.

This requires a brief explanation. The purpose of the $1 waivers is to permit a 10-year veteran to make the best possible deal for himself. By paying the club who owned him only $1, the team that claims him is able to offer the player the amount they would normally have paid to the club or, at the very least, apply it toward his salary. In this instance, the $1 waivers were just a technicality to permit the Cards to take him off their active list and make him a coach. And yet, technically, it also made him a free agent. If somebody else made Brecheen a better offer than the Cards, he was free to accept it. You *know* who made him a better offer.

I offered Harry a 2-year contract as a coach and, if possible, a part-time pitcher, at $20,000 for the first year and $14,000 for the second. Harry already had a $10,000 coaching contract from Saigh in his pocket when he and his wife came to the ball-park apartment to talk to me. Harry was really torn between taking that extra money or remaining with the Cardinals, the only team he had ever played for. I had to run off to make a speech, so I left him with his old roommate, Marty Marion.

Brecheen signed with us as, of course, he had to. OK, so we had signed another of the old Cardinal stars. If we were lucky he might win a few games for us. Since he had always been a smart pitcher he might be able to teach the younger pitchers something. (He turned out to be one of the best pitching coaches in baseball.) It was a matter of no particular consequence. At least, it wouldn't have been if Saigh had been able to leave it alone. But how could Saigh leave it alone? He had to explain to everybody that we hadn't really outbid him. "This is important," he said, "so the public won't get thinking we're tightwads. Our offer to Harry was as a coach; their offer was as a pitcher. And players get more. I talked to Harry this morning. I can't blame him, of course, but I question the moral aspects of it. It verges on tampering. Verges, I said."

Out of his own mouth, he had used the word "tightwad," a word nobody in the city had even thought of, because Saigh had been giving Brecheen a good-enough deal. He also managed to implant the suspicion, again out of his own mouth, that Harry had talked to him that morning to give him a chance to match our offer.

When I was called upon to comment, I had to point out, in the interests of accuracy, that the whole purpose of the $1 waiver was precisely that: to give the 10-year man the chance to make the best possible deal for himself, not to protect him for the team that wanted to get rid of him. "I suggest the Cardinals read the rules," I said, not unmindful that Saigh was a lawyer. "The whole thing is, they didn't want to pay Brecheen what he could make."

You think Saigh could leave it alone after that? Nope. He had to keep it alive by appealing the whole case to Frick. To make himself completely ridiculous he said he was protesting "in fairness to his team, to the fans or other interested parties who might have wanted to negotiate with him and didn't have a chance to. . . ."

What he was trying to do, of course, was to convince St. Louis fans that it was I who had prevented good old Harry from making as much money as he might have. What he really did, though, was to make it sound, out of his own mouth again, as if he hadn't really been interested in keeping Brecheen in a Cardinal uniform in the first place, thereby throwing away his only real bid for sympathy.

And finally, Saigh turned the whole episode into low burlesque by petitioning the Commissioner to stop me from bothering him any more by claiming players he knew I didn't really want. Everybody was picking on poor Fred Saigh.

I had judged my man right, I felt, and we had him on the run. The year before I came to St. Louis, the Browns had drawn 247,131. In 1952, we drew 518,796, more than the Browns' only pennant winner had drawn in 1944.

We had lifted our attendance almost 300,000, and the Cardinals had dropped 300,000. We had a deal brewing with the local CBS station to carry our games, an unheard-of thing. It was still a local station, of course, but it was powerful enough to reach a far greater area than we had ever reached before.

I would have run the Cardinals out of St. Louis, I'm sure of it, except for one thing. Saigh had gotten himself into income-tax trouble. He had already been indicted by mid-1952, and I had to face the possibility that he might have to sell the team.

What a lousy thing for him to do to me.

As soon as I read the verdict, I began to talk to Milwaukee—and, to a much lesser extent, Los Angeles and Baltimore—about moving my franchise.

And yet, I was only going through the motions of protecting myself. We had done so well and had come up so far and were putting together, it seemed to me, such a good team that all the momentum was with us even if I lost Fred Saigh.

At one point, I almost did have it made. In negotiating to sell his club, Saigh went down to Houston to talk to some Texas mil-

228

lionaires. The Cardinals owned the Houston club in the Texas League, so the association was close. There was no question that the money was there, it was just a matter of making the Houston park acceptable. I came that close.

And then out of nowhere—*out of nowhere*—came Gussie Busch with his full-bodied and well-foamed bankroll. When Elliot Stein, one of our stockholders, first gave me the tip that Busch was negotiating, I put it down as just another one of those rumors. I pushed it completely out of my mind because I didn't want to believe it. A few days later, Elliot called back to tell me that while the sale might not be announced for a few days, it was set.

I wasn't going to run Gussie Busch out of town. And I certainly wasn't going to run Anheuser-Busch Inc. out of town. Busch wasn't buying the club himself, the brewery was buying it.

The brewery could run the club as part of its advertising budget, lose an unlimited amount of money and just write it off the company profits.

By the time I hung up the receiver, I knew I had been knocked out of the box.

The Greatest Right-handed Hitter of All Time | 16.

IN WHAT I consider the best year of my career, I made my most monumental mistake as an operator. Inevitably, it led to my most unpleasant experience. When I hired Rogers Hornsby, I was falling into the trap of doing exactly what my worst enemies had always accused me of; I was putting publicity and promotion ahead of operations.

The manager of a major-league baseball team is first of all a personnel man. I have always maintained that you could take a good personnel manager from any company, and if you could create a fictitious baseball background for him so that the players would accept him, he would do an excellent job of managing. Any of his coaches could take care of such secondary matters as making out the lineup and calling the plays.

Baseball is not a complex game. You could find 100 fans in the stands on any given day who could call the right strategy at the right time with the exact degree of accuracy as the manager. (I refer all skeptics to the Grandstand Managers.) Most old sportswriters, having seen more ball games than most managers, could do a faultless job. There are few managers who will win even an occasional game for you by tactics or strategy. Casey Stengel and Paul Richards are the only ones who come immediately to mind.

The manager's real job is to accommodate himself to 25 different personalities; to assess the amount of talent he has within that pool of 25 men and to exact the fruits of that talent—and maybe just a little extra for treating them well, personally and professionally. You saw an example of the latter in 1961 in Ralph Houk's handling of Whitey Ford. I think that Doby, Paige, Al Smith and perhaps Roy Sievers were men who would play a little better for me than for almost anybody else. Not that they said to themselves, "I've got to go up and hit one for Good Ole Will." It's an unconscious thing that comes out of a general feeling on both sides that our relationship is something more than the usual relationship between a player and a club. I have always believed in finding some excuse to reward a player at a time when he's down in the dumps, not when he's riding high. In baseball you are dealing with a talent that is unique (if it were not for fear of offending purists, I would say "absolutely unique") and in permanently short supply. You can't put an ad in the paper for a big-league third baseman. That's why managers get fired; you can't fire the team.

Leo Durocher was able to get more out of Willie Mays than any other manager by making Willie his personal mascot, by wheedling and cajoling him, by showing Willie that he liked him and appreciated his marvelous talents. Durocher always conned and manipulated the players who could do him the most good. Once Leo had something going for him he could ride a hot streak and push and angle and whip a contending team home. Leo may sometimes lose interest in a second-division team but he is the world's greatest manager when the wind is rising and the smell of the winner's circle is in his nostrils.

Given a team of has-beens and rookies, I'd rather have Paul Richards managing for me than anybody else. Paul will take that kind of a team and with his aloof analytical approach, warmed somewhat by an occasional flash of daring, he will get them up to fourth or even third. If that team was improved to where it became a contender, there might be a better manager. Paul never won a pennant as a manager, and now that he's become a front-office man he never will.

Stengel and Lopez will both do well with a squad of established players. Lopez will do his best job if the players are also well-behaved; he is a nice man and he doesn't want any problems. Al plays a conservative, percentage game and with his kind of team he will squeeze as much out of them as can be squeezed.

If you have a couple of personalities on your team, Stengel is the man you want. Stengel was a personality himself as a player and he's still a personality as a manager. Casey gets on well with the wild ones. He needs a personality or two to play himself against.

A manager's success, then, is not divorced from his personality.

Charlie Grimm will keep everybody happy and relaxed. No rules, no discipline, but always a lot of fun. Charlie doesn't play unusually good baseball but he will always have a happy, loose ball club and, until the team gets away from him, an original success. Every team Charlie has had in the majors has gotten away from him. Being a completely honest man, he has fired himself from almost every job he's had by going to the front office and telling them the team has gotten away from him. But a major-league manager's life is limited anyway, so Charlie goes his own way, enjoying his laughs and his food and his friends.

The image of Rogers Hornsby, as developed through the years, is that of a man who brooks no outside interference and is devoted to baseball with a single-mindedness of purpose which offends less dedicated men—like, say, club owners—in these soft and decadent times. Never is it suggested that a man whose team has invariably despised him and whose bosses have been unable to live with him— even when he was the greatest hitter in the league—just might be doing something wrong. Nor is it ever pointed out that Hornsby, for all his pride and integrity, never quit a job in his life. Instead, the men who fire him are always pictured as pompous, meddling wretches and the players as whiners and malcontents and malingerers, unable to take constructive criticism from a man who—as J. Roy Stockton wrote so winsomely after I had to let Rog go—"wanted them to win so badly that he was a sourpuss about it." A man who would call Hornsby a sourpuss would wonder why everybody was complaining about Attila the Hun's table manners.

When I hired Rogers Hornsby, my mother wrote me a note saying, *What makes you think you're smarter than your daddy was?*

When I fired him before the season was two months old she wired: WHAT DID I TELL YOU?

Before I signed him, I had consulted Gordon Cobbledick in Cleveland. "Don't get involved with that guy," Cobby warned me. "You've got troubles enough already."

I hired Rog, as we all know, because I needed him against Saigh. I set out with all deliberate speed to use him and his reputation, so I had no right to cry when he ran true to form. I didn't. With luck, though, I would have never been faced with the temptation of hiring the Rajah—although I suppose that's what all we sinners say. My first choice to replace Zack Taylor was Joe Gordon, then in his first year of managing at Sacramento. Joe would have come gladly if I could have talked his wife, Dorothy, into it. But Dorothy felt he had more security in Sacramento. Joe has always told me he regretted that decision as much as any other he has ever made. We'd have had a great time in St. Louis, Joe and I. Everybody would have been happier. If Joe had signed with me, Hornsby would have later gone to the Cardinals and Saigh would have felt much better about going to jail.

I knew the risk I was taking and still, I hired him. I was confident that after fifteen years away from the big leagues he'd be so happy to return that he'd act like a human being.

Bill DeWitt, who had been in the Browns' office back in Hornsby's day, tried to warn me. "This guy will never change," Bill told me. "It will be the same here as everywhere else."

"Don't worry," I answered, with my well-known confidence, "I can handle him."

I'm not going to go into all that went wrong between Rog and the players that spring. Suffice it to say that by late May, as the team was leaving for an eastern swing, I knew I had to get rid of Hornsby as much for his own protection as for the players. I have never seen a team so tense, so ready to explode. I alerted Marty Marion to be ready to take over on short notice, informed the sportswriters what was probably going to happen and hoped for the best. If I did have to fire the Hero of '26, better to fire him on the road and give the furor a chance to die down before the team got back.

The schedule called for us to go from Washington to New York to Boston. What tore it was the stop at Washington. Bobby Young, our second baseman, lived in Baltimore. His wife was coming to the end of a very difficult pregnancy, so difficult that she had been confined to bed for months. Bobby, being a husband of normal emotions, had been waiting anxiously for the Washington series so that he could get home to see her and assure himself that she was all right.

Hornsby refused to give him permission.

It was only about half a mile farther from Bobby's home to the park, understand, than it was from the hotel to the park, but that didn't matter. That's the way Rogers does things.

Young, having had it, grabbed a bat and waited under the runway

232

for Hornsby to come out. By sheer luck, big Bill Durney, our traveling secretary, stumbled across him first. "I'm going to kill that miserable so-and-so," Young told him, "and then I'm going home to see my wife."

Durney quieted Bobby down, guaranteed him that he'd be heading home within a few minutes and managed to get the bat away from him. Then Bill called me in St. Louis.

I called Rog. "Hey," I said, "what's the matter with you? Young is worried sick about his wife. Let him go home."

"All players are alike to me," he said, another of his wise and pithy sayings. "I can't have two sets of rules."

"That's just ridiculous. If everybody lived in Baltimore and had a wife who was pregnant and in ill health, and you let some of them go and didn't let others go, then you'd have two sets of rules. You have only one player in that situation, so you let him go and you'll only have one set of rules."

"I don't see it that way," he said.

"All right, then, I'm informing you, as president of this club, that I am going to call Bill Durney as soon as I hang up and tell him to give Young permission to go home now and for the rest of the series. I'm not going to argue about it with you, I'm just telling you so you won't be able to say I did anything behind your back."

If Rog had only been the independent character his press agents say he is, he would have quit on the spot and I would have been out of a difficult situation about as cleanly as possible. I waited.

"OK," Rog said. "If that's the way you want it."

I made reservations immediately to fly to New York and fire him there. We won a couple of games in Washington, though, and since I didn't want to fire him while we were winning, I canceled the New York trip and made reservations to go to Boston.

In New York, there was an incident that was typical of Rogers and which he seized upon later, in the press and in his book, to explain why that screwball had fired him. A fan reached out of a third-base box and deflected a foul ball hit by Tommy Byrne, our pitcher. Although Gil McDougald, the Yankee third baseman, was nowhere near the ball, the umpire ruled that Byrne was out because of interference. Bill DeWitt and I were listening to the game in St. Louis. Even over the radio it was evident that the call was bad, and even from St. Louis it was obvious that the visiting team could hardly be held responsible for the behavior of the home crowd.

When Hornsby didn't bother to protest, Ned Garver, our ace pitcher, went out, protested mildly and was thrown out of the game.

233

Now, this is annoying. One of the cardinal rules of baseball is that a manager will dispute a bad call against his team, not because he expects the decision to be changed but as a matter of competitive pride and team spirit. If you're a competitor you're out there fighting for what is yours. Another cardinal rule is that a manager protects his players in the same way an officer protects his men. You will notice, when you go to the park, that as soon as a player gets into an argument with an umpire, the manager will come running out, push the player away and take over the argument himself. If anybody gets thrown out of the game, it will be him, not his player. With Hornsby, it worked the other way around.

I called Bill Durney and told him to get to Hornsby in time to lodge a protest before the next pitch. Durney didn't reach him in time, but Rogers went out at the end of the inning and protested anyway. Apparently nobody had told my tiger in all his years in the game that a protest wasn't acceptable unless it was made before the next pitch was thrown.

I called my manager at the hotel that night to tell him I was coming to Boston the following day to see him. So Rogers knew he was through before the team left New York. He probably knew he was through when we left St. Louis, because it's inconceivable to me that one of the writers hadn't carried the tidings to him.

Monday was an off-day in Boston. I got into the Kenmore about 8:30 Tuesday morning, called Hornsby to the room and said, "I'm sorry, Rog. I think the time has come for a change. I think the club should be doing better."

Hornsby wasn't dismayed or even upset. He was used to being fired. All he said was, "What about my three-year contract?"

He had reason to be worried. I had signed him to what amounted to the uniform manager contract, with no special clause inserted to make his contract irrevocable. I probably could have settled on my own terms. But I still felt I was more to blame than Rog. I had given him the contract knowing his track record. How could I blame him for running true to form?

I went to the desk and wrote out a letter on the hotel stationery guaranteeing that his contract would be honored for the full three years. Unconditionally. That was absolutely all he was interested in. Not a harsh word was spoken, not a voice was raised. Rogers left without even bothering to go through the simple courtesy of saying good-bye to his coaches. He couldn't have cared less about them.

I still felt very badly for him. I bent over backwards to be kind to Rog in my statements to the press. I was uncharacteristically

234

apologetic. "I blew one," I told them. "It isn't his fault he was fired. It's mine. What's the old aphorism? You can't change a leopard's spots. I've embarrassed him."

I said, "It was an unfair thing to Rogers. But I think if we went along with it and waited we would be hopelessly mired. I know I didn't add any stature to myself today."

I said, "I don't want to bear any malice, I don't want to say anything to jeopardize his future. I thought he had mellowed with time. He hasn't. You can have a manager and twenty-five players in a state of anarchy or you can have a team. And this is a team game."

Hornsby, still running true to form, set up shop again as a man of unswerving principle brought down by a meddling owner. He pitched his firing to the phone call I had made to New York, so that it would seem as if I had demanded that he lodge a protest—the next day or the next week or something—and he, solid oak that he was, had refused to let me tell him how to manage his team.

He had some remarkable quotes. "I think I did a good job all around, and tried to build confidence," he said. "I tried to treat players the way I wanted to be treated, see?"

He said, "When you work for a screwball, you're apt to get screwball answers. He admits he's a screwball, but I'm friendly with him."

Before the game the next day, Bill Durney told me the players wanted me to come down to the locker room. A happier group you've never seen. I made a little speech in which I apologized to them for hiring Hornsby in the first place. When I finished, Ned Garver whipped out a two-foot silver loving cup and presented it to me on behalf of the club. The inscription read:

To Bill Veeck
For the greatest play since the Emancipation Proclamation,
June 10, 1952. From the players of the St. Louis Browns.

One of the players opened the door to let the press in, and a photographer, hearing all the excitement and laughter, asked if he could take a picture. That is the whole spine-thrilling story on the presentation of the Hornsby cup.

The story that I had, in effect, presented the cup to myself did not come from Boston. It did not come from any of the writers covering the team. It came from J. Roy Stockton in St. Louis, 1,000 miles away, and it did not come until after Hornsby had returned to St. Louis the next day. Immediately, it was picked up by writers all over the country, usually with local embellishments.

Stockton, the sports editor of the *Post-Dispatch,* knew Hornsby was going to be fired; I had told him myself. He hadn't been particularly happy about it. Stockton was a close friend of Rog's and he was also writing a book about him. When I fired Rog that literary project came to an end, so Stockton was not without his own little ax to grind.

Stockton is a bright man. He could see the cup presentation as Hornsby's golden opportunity to seize the offensive and come out of his latest debacle smelling—as usual—like a bed of roses. Although Rog is not as bright as Stockton, he does have a native cunning where his own interests are at stake. Between Hornsby's story of the phone call and Stockton's story of the cup, the impression was created that Hornsby had been pushed beyond endurance and then held up to ridicule.

Stockton worked into it beautifully by saying:

> Bill Veeck and his company jester, Bill Durney, were entirely out of order when they participated in a public humiliation of Hornsby, a great baseball figure in his own right, a member of the Hall of Fame and a name that will live long after all of Bill Veeck's stunts and Bill Durney's sophomoric jokes have been forgotten.

> It was said in a club-inspired dispatch that the Brownie players chipped in and bought a loving cup that was presented to Veeck. . . .

> That was not the spontaneous humor of a bunch of ballplayers. It was the humor of Bill Durney, who knew it would please his boss, Bill Veeck. Nor was the trophy purchased by contributions from a group of ballplayers. The trophy was charged to the Browns' account at the Hotel Kenmore. It was a club project and Bill Veeck and Bill Durney should be profoundly ashamed of themselves by now. . . .

Having established this falsehood, he went on to the job of refurbishing the Hornsby image.

> There wasn't anything wrong if the boys wanted to celebrate a little and tell Marion and Veeck and each other how happy they were to get rid of a man who wanted them to win so much that he was a sourpuss about it. But it was in woefully bad taste for the Browns' club, as represented by Secretary Bill Durney and President Bill Veeck, to go through a ceremony complete with photographs that were sent to newspapers all over the country, a ceremony humiliating and insulting the greatest right-

236

handed batter the game has ever known. . . . As for the ball-players they are easily excused. Most of them couldn't be expected to know any better.

A marvelous journalistic *tour de force*. When Stockton was through, there was nothing left of the Hornsby we had known except the dimples in his cherubic cheeks and the aura of sanctity. Stockton, to give him his due, could have shown Houdini a thing or two about dissolving a man into thin air.

Virtually the only true statement in the column was that Rog was the greatest right-handed batter the game had ever known. Every time Hornsby gets into trouble, his boosters trot out his batting average as a total defense.

I first heard about the column from Elliot Stein, who called me from St. Louis. I had no way of knowing that it wasn't true. Immediately, I called Bill Durney in and told him, "Bill, if you've been a party to this, you're about to see me become very upset." Bill swore to me that the players had chipped in $50 of their own money, and that he had known nothing about it until the cup was delivered to the hotel. I checked his story out anyway, and it was correct in every detail.

The idea had originated with Bobby Young, and Ned Garver had collected the money. Young, Gene Bearden and George Schmees had found Durney in the lobby and asked if he knew where they could get something engaved in Boston. Durney, without even knowing what they wanted to have engraved, had pointed out the manager of the Kenmore, Everett Kerr, standing close by and suggested that they ask him. Kerr had then gone into his office to phone around until he found someone who could do a quick job. The cup had been delivered to Garver at the hotel and he had paid for it with his own personal check.

Meanwhile, something interesting was happening in St. Louis. Hornsby, having misread the signals from Stockton, had given out an interview in which he said he had seen the cup in my hotel room when I called him in to fire him. Ed McAuley called him from Cleveland to ask: "Did you actually see the cup?"

Well no, Rog said, having been better briefed by then. What he had seen, he said, was a "big box" which he was sure contained the cup. Now I hadn't just paid for it out of club funds, I had bought it myself.

I should point out here that even before the Stockton column, the players had gone on record, not anonymously but by name, as to their feelings about the martyred Hornsby.

Bob Neiman said: "The news was like lifting a hundred-pound sack of sand from each player's back."

Gene Bearden: "They ought to declare a national holiday in St. Louis."

George Schmees, whom Hornsby had asked me to draft from the Pacific Coast and whom I had been very disappointed with: "I would have gone to the end of the earth for that man because he gave me my chance to play in the majors but now that I know him I wouldn't go to his funeral."

It's possible, I know, to say that these were all guys who were trying to make time with the boss. Except that Earl Rapp, who had been traded to Washington the night before, said: "If Hornsby had stayed, some of the players would have tangled with him. They were getting ready to fight."

Milton Richman of the UP, an ex-Brownie farmhand who knew the players more intimately than any other newspaperman, wrote:

> Hate is a strong word . . . but St. Louis Browns players used it every day to express their feelings for hard-bitten Rogers Hornsby. They detested him thoroughly—so much that they even avoided sitting near him on the bench.

After the Stockton column came out, the players stated publicly that it was a lie. Ned Garver's exact quote was "a dirty, rotten lie," which I thought was rather well put.

It made not the slightest difference. Everybody seemed to accept the story that I had bought the cup for myself to degrade and humiliate a great and good man. And all the time, I had been breaking my back to make the firing of Hornsby as palatable as possible to the people of St. Louis.

Nobody is fairer game for the press than I. I live by publicity, and if it ends up that I die by publicity . . . well, that's the way the agate type falls. This is the only incident since I have been wandering around in which I thought I was unfairly treated. Let them say anything they want about any of the gags. A gag is a fact and they are perfectly entitled to their opinions. Entitled? I can speak plainer than that. I turn vicious only when they keep their opinions down in the wine cellar to age and cool. Vintage controversy always leaves me with heartburn. I mean I prefer the cheap domestic stuff, hot off the press. But this wasn't a fact; it was a deliberate misrepresentation.

I went to the length of gathering affidavits to disprove it. I had affidavits from Garver and Young. I was able to account for all my time on the night before the firing, because I had been speaking at Peoria with Jack Brickhouse, the Chicago announcer. I was catching a plane out of Chicago, so our driver dropped me off at the airport and then drove Brickhouse downtown. Brickhouse could testify that I had been carrying only a small bag the size of a briefcase, hardly big enough to hold a 2-foot cup. I had an affidavit from the hotel bellboy stating that I had come in with nothing except the bag. I had an affidavit from the hotel that I had called Hornsby within minutes of the time I registered. I even went so far as to get an affidavit from the chambermaid that there had been no big box or cup in the room when she checked the room that morning.

I laid all those affidavits before the editor of the *Post-Dispatch*. "I fired Hornsby, yes," I told him, "but I didn't feel there was any point in humiliating him or embarrassing him. If the players did want to humiliate and embarrass him, they were only retaliating for the way he had humiliated and embarrassed them." The editor was vaguely impressed and completely noncommittal.

Bob Burnes, the sports editor of the *Globe-Democrat,* offered to turn his column over to me for anything I wanted to write. "I'm not looking for that," I told him. "A retraction never catches up to the original story, it only revives it."

Hornsby? Hornsby was hired to manage the Cincinnati Reds less than two months after he left us. Gabe Paul, the Reds' general manager, thought Rog would provide the firm hand so lacking at their tiller. He was fired during the following season to prevent a players' insurrection. Gee, that was a surprise.

Because I had written that note guaranteeing to honor our contract unconditionally, I was paying Rog faithfully while he was managing the Reds. Since Rog had a multiyear contract with them too, he was, shortly afterwards, being paid *not* to manage both the Browns and the Reds at the same time, a feat which should put an oak-leaf cluster on his Hall of Fame plaque. If the Rajah could have tucked one more quick job in there, he would have achieved unheard of marks for the upcoming generation of managers to shoot at.

From time to time, I still see references to the cup I bought myself after I fired Hornsby. Like everything else about Hornsby, it has been repeated so often that it has become a part of the image. Mary Frances was terribly upset at him for a long time, because he and she had always got along very well. Whenever she ran across him at baseball gatherings she would shake her head and say, "Rog, you should be ashamed of yourself for spreading a story you knew wasn't true." Occasionally, Hornsby was gallant enough to blush.

And yet, in all honesty—and this is not a last sly backhanded slap at him—I always felt sorry for Rog. He goes from job to job in baseball, his lifetime batting average sitting upon his chest like a medal, and he is a stranger among his own kind. Baseball doesn't belong to the old guys spinning their tales or to the newspapermen or to the operators. Baseball is where you find it, and you find it on the field. You're never any closer to the game than you are to the players.

The Asterisk King | 17.

THE jump from Cleveland to St. Louis started what was to become the longest and the deepest dip in the roller coaster. It was in St. Louis that my real battling with the baseball brass began. I was no longer dealing from strength as I had been in Cleveland, I was dealing from weakness. As much as Clark Griffith might disapprove of me in Cleveland, he would also call and plead with me to pitch Satchel Paige in a night game in Washington. In St. Louis, Griffith smiled pleasantly and stuck a knife in my back.

Before we move on, then, let's take a look at the baseball Establishment from Ford Frick, baseball's version of the Battle of Bull Run, on down.

Let us be fair. Ford Frick does not try to do the wrong thing. Given the choice between doing something right or something wrong Frick will usually begin by doing as little as possible. It is only when he is pushed to the wall for a decision that he will almost always, with sure instinct and unerring aim, make an unholy mess of things.

Suppose that, purely as an exercise, I had put the following baseball question to you at any time during the past twenty-five years.

Suppose, starts the question, that someone comes along to challenge Babe Ruth's home-run record—which is THE record the same way that Mt. Everest is THE mountain. To make the background more interesting, let us make the new Ruth a member of the New York Yankees so that we will have a big park to fool around with and an unlimited amount of newspaper, magazine, radio and television publicity. Now, to hoke it up even more, let us say that he returns home to this big park at the end of the season for, let us say, five final games, needing one home run to tie Ruth's record and, of course, two to break it. To make the situation even more ideal, we will have him playing the final three games of the season on Friday night, Saturday afternoon and Sunday afternoon, the three best possible dates. And as a final touch—I know this is farfetched, but remember, I'm trying to dream up the best possible promotional situation—as one final touch, let us have him tie the record on the first of those five days and break it on the last day.

All right, here is my question. Given this mythical situation, I am inviting you to take part in an office pool to estimate the attendance of:

1) those final five games
2) the last game

If you know anything about baseball, you would 1) look up the official capacity of Yankee Stadium (67,000), multiply by five and add one.

When it came down to the last game, you would 2) look up the record Stadium crowd (81,841) and add one.

This dream situation, this promotional fairy tale, is exactly what fell into the laps of the Yankees in 1961. And in flat defiance of all laws of promotion and probability, it did not even cause a minor traffic problem around Yankee Stadium. Commissioner Frick had come to the aid of the Traffic Department earlier by issuing an edict that in order to break Ruth's record, Maris would have to do it in 154 games. Otherwise, said Frick, it would go into the record books hung up on an asterisk to signify it as some kind of a miscellaneous 162-game record. What he did, in that one brilliant stroke, was to build the interest up to that 154th game and throw the final 8 games out in the wash with the baby. What he did was to turn what should have been a thrilling cliff-hanger lasting over the full final week of the season into a crashing anticlimax. He did even more. By focusing all attention onto the 154th game, he turned Maris's run for the record into a defeat—another anticlimax—instead of the victory that would have left everybody, except old Babe Ruth ghost-writers like Frick, glowing in satisfaction and feeling most kindly toward baseball. Is it any wonder that under Frick's dead hand, baseball has been in a steady process of decline and decay?

And what about my office pool? My office pool would have been won by the little blond filing clerk who has never seen a game in her life and *always* wins the office pool. The crowds for those five games averaged 18,139.

At the end, there were only 23,154 in Yankee Stadium on a warm Sunday afternoon to see Babe Ruth's record broken.

I am not bleeding for the Yankees. They could have turned Frick's asterisk to their own advantage by working up a nationwide controversy, by prodding one of the news services into sending out ballots to every sportswriter in the country, by soliciting the opinion of every home-run hitter still alive, by having their own speakers go around to every banquet, club meeting and sports program within reach. The Yankees, however, had their own record to preserve—their record for doing the worst promotional job, year in and year out, of any major-league team in the country.

I am bleeding only as a craftsman, the way a good carpenter bleeds when he sees a beautiful graining butchered. Because here's the thing: Babe Ruth's record can be broken only once. Breaking Roger Maris's record will mean comparatively little. The more the home-run record is broken from here on in, in fact, the less meaning it will have.

This was the greatest single promotional opportunity in the history of baseball and they blew it! It was blow-proof and they still blew it!

One thing we will all have to concede. The year 1961 may not have been much for baseball but it was a vintage year for Vocabulary. Frick taught the schoolchildren of the nation the meaning of the word "asterisk," and the CIA taught them the meaning of the word "fiasco." The comparison is apt.

One final note on the Maris asterisk fiasco. It was perfectly obvious to anyone with any foresight that if Maris did break the record, he would eventually go down as the record holder. He hit 61 home runs; Ruth hit 60. Those figures are undebatable. If Frick's asterisk decorates either man's record block it will be Ruth's. Frick not only blew it, he blew it to no purpose.

In short, our Commissioner did just about what we might have expected from him.

Toward the end of my first year in St. Louis, a meeting was called to elect a new Commissioner. It was common knowledge even then that Frick, who had the solid backing of the National League plus the possible backing of the Yankees, who controlled most of the American League votes, was probably going to be elected. Nobody looked upon him with any enthusiasm but nobody seemed to have anybody else to offer. We advanced a candidate of our own, my old friend, Governor Frank Lausche. Frank had been a minor-league third baseman in his younger days and was a ferocious independent in the Landis mold. Obviously, he was disqualified on two counts.

242

Lausche wasn't that interested anyway, and when he took himself out of the race I didn't bother to go for the voting—having long since given up such childish pursuits as jump rope, jacks and attending baseball meetings.

I don't want to let anybody go away with the impression that there was any sectional prejudice against Lausche. William O. McKinley, another Ohio statesman, would have been eminently acceptable if it had not been for that unfortunate occurrence in a Buffalo courthouse. Baseball doesn't want a Commissioner, it wants a figurehead, preferably a live one. In Frick, baseball got what it wanted.

The Browns were represented at the meeting by Bill DeWitt, who had stayed on as vice-president after I bought the club from him. Since Bill and I were still in the feeling-out stage of our relationship, he asked me how I wanted him to vote.

"Vote however you want," I told him. "This is something you know more about than I."

"I don't think Frick's the man for the job," he said. "I like Warren Giles."

"I was hoping you'd say that," I told him. "I knew you and I were going to get along fine."

In the first balloting, Frick and Giles were deadlocked. Frick picked up 3 votes, one at a time, but the 5 votes against him held firm. At last, DeWitt called a caucus of the five dissidents, and they agreed they would go along with Frick only on condition that Giles became president of the National League. Frick knew that the Browns were the center of the opposition, though, and he never forgot it.

Under Landis, the Commissioner's office had always been in Chicago, the natural center of the country. Chandler had moved the office to New York, and part of the deal was that Frick would return to Chicago. Instead he remained in New York where he could be within walking distance of his own natural habitat, Toots Shor's saloon. The only thing on which Frick and I have been in complete accord is the excellence of Toots Shor's saloon and of its redoubtable proprietor.

Although my personal experiences with Frick have been uniformly painful, that is not—believe me—why I think he has been so disastrous to baseball. I was able to clash with Branch Rickey through the years without ever losing sight of the fact that I was clashing with a most remarkable man. Frick's reign has been so tragic because it has covered a time when baseball has been in a period of transition and has needed strong and imaginative leadership. Professional football's attendance has been going straight up in the same decade that baseball's attendance has been going straight down, because the late Bert Bell gave the NFL just such aggressive leadership.

Nor, please believe me, have I always found myself in opposition to Frick because, juvenile delinquent that I am, I automatically rebel against all authority. I never won a battle with Landis either while I was exercising my various talents in Milwaukee, and yet I had a great respect for him because he was a man of action and imagination and color. Landis once told me, "If I always seem to be leaning over backwards when I'm dealing with you, it's because your daddy helped me get here and I don't want anyone to think I'm guilty of favoritism." That was Landis. The public looked upon him as a symbol of rock-like integrity and complete impartiality, and the public was right. The baseball operators, complain as they might, feared him and respected him and, if they had anything but tin in their heads, knew he was good for them.

I'll show you how much I respected the man. Before I brought on all those rules changes in the American Association, the rule regarding light failure said only that the game would be started over again from the beginning. That's all. The loophole there should be evident to anybody with the best interests of his own team at heart. I had a disaster signal set up with the electrician out in the power box in left field. The chance to use it came while we were playing Indianapolis, with whom we were tied for first place. At the end of four and a half innings we were behind, 3–2, and a storm was blowing in. If we finished the inning with that score unchanged, it would be an official game by the time the rains came.

We were one out from losing the game and dropping into second place when I happened to take out my handkerchief and, with a wide sweep of the arm, bring it up to wipe my forehead. At that moment, would you believe it, the lights went out. Ohhhh, everybody was hopping up and down.

The umpires demanded that I take them out to the electrician's box so that they could make an on-the-spot investigation. The electrician, a good sort, saw them coming and jammed a screwdriver into the works. By the time we had groped our way to the power box, he was cowering outside the door as if in mortal fear, while behind him the sparks were jumping all around the room.

The call came from Judge Landis at about 9 the next morning. "When is the next train to Chicago?" he said.

I told him they ran every hour on the hour.

"Then there's one at ten?"

"Yes, Judge."

244

"How long does it take between Milwaukee and Chicago?"

I told him the railroad rather proudly advertised 90 miles in 90 minutes.

"How long does it take from the station to my office?"

"I guess it takes about twenty minutes."

"You be here in my office at ten of twelve," he said.

I was there.

"All right," he said. "What happened?"

"I don't know," I said, "an act of God or something."

"Well," he said, "there will be no more acts of God in Milwaukee this season."

I waited, like a schoolboy, for the rest of it. Judge Landis looked up at me impatiently, making it perfectly obvious that I had wasted enough of his time that morning. "I'm finished with you," he said. "You can go."

That was the entire conversation. I caught another taxi and went back to Milwaukee, having spent the entire morning riding on trains so that Landis could waste thirty seconds on me. But when Landis said come, I came. When Landis laid down the law there was no argument. Not only with me. With everybody. Baseball didn't want any more lawgivers, though, and so we went from Landis to Chandler to Frick. Draw that on a graph and you end up with a perpendicular line. One thing you have to say for Frick; with that talent of his for doing the impossible, he has made Chandler look good.

The baseball rules define the Commissioner's power in one sweeping paragraph which gives him the right to take any step he deems necessary "for the good of baseball," a phrase which makes him the most absolute sovereign since Charlemagne—or at least, Prince Rainier. But Frick, as far as I have been able to see, seldom uses his power to do anything that would help the game itself. Being an amateur politician, he often uses it as a tool to reward his friends and punish his enemies. As one of his earliest and proudest enemies, I could cite examples all night.

When the Chicago White Sox won the pennant in 1959, I signed to do a pre-game television show through the Series, much the same kind of show I had been doing all year. (And exactly the same kind I had done with Jack Lescoulie the previous year on the *Today* show.) These programs have never been moneymaking propositions for me, a point I bring up for reasons that will become apparent. In St. Louis, the money was donated to Boys Town. In Cleveland, it went to provide baseball equipment for orphans. The anticipated World Series fee had already gone to pay for a sailboat we had presented to Nellie Fox on a night given him at the end of the season.

Frick invoked his terrible powers to protect and preserve the good name of the game by refusing to let me go on. It was undignified, he ruled—making my personal financial affairs his business—for an owner to appear as a common television performer.

Now let us turn to Del Webb. Webb is in the construction business. Del Webb was building the Flamingo, the first of the Las Vegas luxury gambling hotels, for Bugsy Siegel in 1947 when some sorehead stuck a shotgun through a window and blew Bugsy's head off. To protect his investment, Webb took over a percentage of the hotel. Judge Landis, who disapproved of kids pitching pennies against the playground wall probably would have had Webb out of baseball by sunset. Happy Chandler, having become Landis's successor due, in great part, to Webb's support, was hardly in a position to turn right around and tell him to cash in his chips. But then something very interesting happened. Chandler and Webb began to quarrel. Chandler, according to all reports, gave him notice to get rid of his interest in the Flamingo and to cease his association with gamblers, a not unreasonable attitude since Happy had suspended Leo Durocher for a full year just for sitting with some gamblers in a box seat.

Given the choice between getting rid of his interest in a gambling casino or getting rid of Chandler, Webb consulted his conscience and decided, apparently, that Happy had to go. He and Fred Saigh, who was also having trouble with Chandler, led a palace revolt which ended with Happy's contract being bought up.

After Frick's election, there was a vague and general understanding that Webb would divest himself of his Las Vegas holdings as soon as it could be done without too great a financial sacrifice. As far as I know, he never did. It doesn't really matter whether he did nor not. In August, 1961, the Del E. Webb Corporation bought another Las Vegas gambling hotel, the Sahara. It was a corporate deal and the hotel's gambling casino was leased out.

Being a man of the world, Frick felt that it was, after all, only a real-estate deal, completely divorced from Webb's baseball interests. Privately—and maybe even publicly—he let it be known that he wasn't worried, because Del is an honorable man who could be trusted to do nothing that would embarrass baseball. Now Webb's gambling casino may be completely divorced from baseball as far as his corporate setup is concerned, and yet I observed with interest that within a few months after his real-estate deal, Del had Mantle and Ford out

246

in Las Vegas for the Sahara's biggest promotion, a pro-amateur golf tournament.

I'm not against gambling. I'm not so much a moralist that I'm even against golf. I am very much against double standards.

Nor, I must say, has Frick himself always adopted so tolerant an attitude toward gambling. When the Mack family had to sell the Philadelphia Athletics in 1954, I was very much involved in the scramble for the franchise. I was out of baseball at the time, having been booted out of St. Louis, and I wanted to buy the club and move it to Los Angeles. I came into the meeting with 3 votes, which gave me an absolute veto since nobody could get the franchise without 6 of the 8 votes. The Yankees were backing Arnold Johnson, who was going to move the franchise to Kansas City. The other serious bidder was Clint Murchison, of the Texas Murchisons, who was also out to get the Athletics for Los Angeles. When I saw I couldn't get any more votes, I dropped out rather than keep the Macks locked into Philadelphia. That left Webb's man Johnson, and Murchison.

Normally, Frick's dodge for avoiding decisions is to call any controversy "a league affair." He will usually step in only to help out one of his friends, and even then he maneuvers like a cloakroom politician, not as a Commissioner handing down an open ruling. In this instance, Frick suddenly expressed grave misgivings about Murchison's connection with the Del Mar race track and asked for an investigation of his background. Now, Murchison made every list of the nation's wealthiest men, so he had hardly come to the conference room as a mysterious stranger. Nor was his connection with Del Mar the mystery Frick tried to make it. Del Mar, as everybody knew or could easily find out, was operated by Boys Incorporated, a foundation which Murchison and his fellow oilman, Sid Richardson, had set up to combat juvenile delinquency—a project to which baseball and Frick give unending lip service.

Frick, it seemed to me, was just doing his supporter, Webb, a favor. With the Macks sinking fast and the Yankees pushing for a vote, there wasn't a great deal of time to wait for a report to come in. Murchison saved them the trouble by withdrawing his offer.

Upon recapitulation, what do we find?

1) It is detrimental to baseball for me to appear on television, where the whole country will be watching me misbehave.

2) It is not detrimental to baseball for Webb to own a gambling hotel, particularly if it is called a real-estate deal.

3) It is not all right for Murchison to buy a race track so that he can turn the profits over to charity.

It wasn't horse racing in itself that Frick objected to, understand. That could hardly be, since the Pittsburgh owner, John Galbreath, owns one of the leading stables in the country. Galbreath is a loyal Frick supporter. When asked to reconcile those positions, Frick explained that he didn't want any franchise owned by a charitable organization.

To those who are beginning to wonder what Frick's moral position on gambling really is, I can assure them that he is firmly and irrevocably against gambling by common working stiffs as well as by tax-free foundations. In one of his more compelling directives, he warned the players sternly against indulging in games of chance among themselves.

His position, as anyone can see, is a model of consistency and clarity. Let me give another quick example of how openly and flagrantly Frick employs his double standard.

Hank Greenberg and I were the principal stockholders in the purchase of the White Sox in 1959. Hank had raised his share of the money by selling all the stock he owned in the Cleveland Indians, but Hank also had a lot of money tied up in the Cleveland debentures. Frick informed Hank that he could not be an officer of the club until the debentures were sold. That would be conflict of interest and detrimental to baseball. Hank was placed in a position in which he had to sell the debentures at a sacrifice or drop out of the Chicago syndicate. He extricated himself from that squeeze without damage only because two of the other original members of our White Sox syndicate, the Baxter brothers, were good enough to buy the debentures from him and drop out of the Chicago picture themselves.

A year later, Gabe Paul moved from Cincinnati to Houston to Cleveland and was allowed to sell his Cincinnati stock in his own good time. And that was stock, not a mere loan. Branch Rickey had been given the same consideration in moving from Brooklyn to Pittsburgh.

It is interesting, is it not, that Paul and Rickey were both loyal National Leaguers, for along with many of my American League colleagues it has always seemed to me that Frick could be counted upon to throw his weight with the National League. In return, he has always been able to count upon solid National League support. Even the Yankees usually lose out when they are in conflict with the National League and most particularly when they are in conflict with Walter O'Malley—who has emerged under Frick's protective wing as the strong man of baseball. This state of affairs came into focus most dramatically in the American League Expansion meeting, a couple of

248

vears ago, when O'Malley flatly refused to permit an American League team into Los Angeles except on his own incredible conditions, after Frick had been proclaiming Los Angeles "an open city" every hour on the hour for months. On that one, I came the closest I have ever been to forcing Frick to cast his vote openly. The expansion meeting was the most fascinating and complex episode of my baseball career—and, as the golfers say, humbling. I'll go into the details of that one at length in a later chapter. It requires a full chapter.

For the moment, I'll give a briefer example of how openly Frick has made the Commissioner's office a wholly owned subsidiary of the National League.

Early in the course of that Expansion meeting, the Commissioner's office sent down the plan by which the two new teams, Washington and Los Angeles, would draft players from the eight established teams. The key section from my point of view was that our rosters were to be frozen after the new clubs made their choices. In other words, we were not allowed to leave a promising young player on a minor-league roster to protect him from the draft and then bring him up to fill in the holes left by the players who had been lost. If, however, we decided to bring him up before the special draft, it meant we would have to clear space for him by sending down a veteran player who would be eligible for the regular minor-league draft by the established teams. Once we sent these older guys down they were, of course, frozen where they were and lost to us anyway. I know it's confusing, but what it all comes down to is that we were put in a position where we were going to lose players both ways. As it turned out, the White Sox had to dispose of six players to clear their roster, and then we lost another seven players in the special draft.

I knew very well that O'Malley and the National League were not going to permit Frick to do that to them. During the regular draft meeting at Louisville, I made a speech in which I told him that everybody knew he operated under a double standard and that when it came time for the new National League teams to draft their players the rules would be entirely different. Ohhh, he was indignant. He ran around assuring everybody that the National League system would be exactly the same as the American League system. He sent around bulletins promising that there would be "complete equality and absolutely equitable treatment of all new clubs."

The next year, of course, the National League was permitted to hold its first-year men down in the minor leagues until *after* the new Houston and New York clubs had drafted their players, and then bring them up to fill out the rosters. I had sold out in Chicago by that time, and nobody in the American League uttered a word of protest except for Ed Short, the new White Sox general manager.

In pointing this out, I have just answered the question I know everybody has been wanting to ask; i.e., how can he possibly get away with it? He gets away with it because the other American League clubs—always excepting Frank Lane, wherever he may be—accept it as a fact of life.

When I stood up in Louisville and stated openly that he employed a double standard, there were many of my colleagues who were just as indignant as Frick. They couldn't understand why I was making such a big fuss about it. "Well, that's Frick," they'd say. "You know he's a National League Commissioner."

It's perfectly apparent that he is unimaginative and vacillating. (Even his National League backers should be painfully aware of that.) But they aren't about to do anything about it. You can revolt against a tyrant but it's hard to feel anything but a faint squeamish-ness about a man who has great power in any field and often uses it only in little ways to hang on to his job. It's like the Dauphin in George Bernard Shaw's *Joan of Arc*. He's a pitiful creature, all right, but there are times when he's so wistfully pitiful that you rather like him. That's Frick exactly.

Like all men who are afraid to use their power where it counts, Frick tries to look very impressive in public. In recent years, I feel his great ambition has been to look as much as possible like Judge Landis to whom he has, in fact, developed a strong resemblance as he grows older, another proof of the power of wishful thinking. For awhile his hair seemed long like Landis's and he appeared to stick out his chin whenever a camera was pointed in his direction. He could be seen at all ceremonial functions—like World Series games—wearing a mane, a battered hat and slightly bewildered air.

This is why I have always opposed Frick. Not because I dislike him but because I believe him to be inept. Because he has done almost nothing without prodding to address himself to the problems of base-ball or the structure of the game. Even here, I wouldn't rap him unless I had a program of my own to put forth.

In the 1952 winter meeting at Phoenix, a year after Frick took office, I introduced a 3-part program to make the American League decently competitive. As a direct result of such dangerous thinking, I was kicked out of baseball the following year. One plank in the program was the Unrestricted Draft which, briefly, would have made all minor-league players eligible to be drafted by any team in baseball after their first year in professional baseball. (Historically, a player could conceivably be kept in the minors up to seven years before he became eligible for the draft.)

Ten years ago, the Unrestricted Draft would have served to distribute the talent more evenly, salvage the minor leagues and put an end to the absurd and ruinous business of handing out $50,000 and $100,-000 bonuses to untried and untested kids just out of high school.

The Unrestricted Draft was finally passed this year—in a considerably watered-down form—possibly because I wasn't around to be identified with it. In the intervening nine years, speaking most conservatively, $60,000,000 had been siphoned out of baseball.

Too late, too late. They locked the barn door not only after the horse had been stolen but after the barn had burned to the ground. There is no longer an independent minor-league system to be saved, there is only a shaky collection of farm systems, almost completely (80%) subsidized by the major leagues. The bonuses will be paid anyway because all the old channels of supply have dried up. Putting 1952's solution into effect today was like putting an obsolete bomber on the production line. Today's conditions call for an entirely different approach. In line with my philosophy of don't-knock-it-if-you-can't-improve-on-it, I have a new program to advance:

There does exist in this country, organized and full-blown, a training ground for baseball players, the same training ground that feeds professional football: the colleges. Like baseball, education finds itself in a period of transition and trouble. For years, our colleges have been violating a basic law of economy by allowing their plants to remain idle for one-third of the year. With the current demand for better trained students, coupled with a lack of facilities for all the young people who want a college education, this is a luxury neither they nor the country can any longer afford. There is little doubt that American colleges are about to move into full-year operation. (Full employment would also go far toward alleviating that historic ache in teachers' salaries, a problem that is close to me because my oldest son, Will, a brilliant mathematician, brushed aside staggering offers from some of the giant corporations to go into teaching.)

When colleges move into 12-month operation, it will naturally follow that baseball will become their major summer sport, extending from April into September. Instead of playing the 17-game schedule which is now almost standard, they could easily be playing 55 to 60 games a year. Over four years, a good young player, given competent coaching, would develop at a tremendous rate.

Organized baseball can make sure that the talent and the coaching are there if it has the foresight—for once in its life—to step in and underwrite a first-class program for every college conference in the country. For unlike football, which is the moneymaking arm of college sports, college baseball operates at a solid loss. What is required at the moment—right now—is organization, imagination and money. In a word, leadership. (What isn't needed is the customary practice of appointing a committee which never meets.)

During my final year with the White Sox, I discussed precisely such a program with three or four of the Athletic directors of the Big Ten Conference, including Duffy Dougherty of Michigan State and Red Mackey of Purdue, and also with Danny Litwhiler of Florida State University, a really progressive college coach. They were all enthusiastic.

Let it be understood that in no case would an individual team be involved with either the college or the boy. The money would be disbursed through a general fund, contributed to by all 20 major-league teams but administered through the Commissioner's office. Out of this fund would come the money for scholarships and for the hiring of the best possible coaches. The major leagues would provide equipment and roving grounds keepers. We would also supply the umpires and, in the process, be training new umpires for ourselves. For baseball needs competent umpires today almost as badly as it needs new players. Any college, still operating at a loss, would be reimbursed at the end of the season out of the general fund.

The program would be built upon a common scouting pool. These scouts, spotted all over the country and working, let me say again, for no one team would recommend the more promising high school players for scholarships. The boy would then apply to whatever college he wished. If he passed the entrance exams and satisfied whatever other conditions the college normally placed upon its students, his tuition would be paid for out of the general fund, either directly to the college or channeled through the conference.

There are about twenty conferences throughout the country. If all of them are incorporated into our program, we have—in one stroke—resurrected what was once the nursery of baseball—Classes D, C and B.

For the boys who cannot pass the entrance exams or have no desire to go to college, we would also subsidize four D leagues, two C leagues and two B leagues. Out of this fund also would come the money to pay a livable wage to the umpires, a revolutionary concept. Traditionally, the umpires in the bush leagues have been paid something from $2,500 to $4,000. Since slave labor has always been among the more unpopular professions, only the incompetent stay on.

252

After the boy was graduated from college, he would become eligible to be drafted by a major-league team, just as college football players are drafted, with the bottom teams getting the first choice. He would, however, be under absolutely no obligation to play. If he preferred to continue his education or go right into business, that would be entirely up to him.

The benefits to the colleges would reach beyond the subsidy itself, because they would be given the assurance—written into the major-league bylaws as well as into the agreements with each of the conferences—that no boy entering college under this program would be eligible to enter organized baseball until after his class had been graduated. One of the great strains between college athletic departments and organized baseball has been brought on by baseball's charming habit of plucking the best prospects right off the campus. Jim O'Toole, Carl Yastrzemski, Paul Murphy and Jackie Jensen are names that come immediately to mind.

As close as I have been able to figure, the whole program would cost baseball between $2,000,000 and $3,000,000 a year. Compare that sum to the $8,000,000 thrown to the bonus winds in 1961.

I am now about to make a statement that will confirm Ford Frick's blackest thoughts about me: There are changes that could be made in the game itself to make it more exciting and entertaining.

Baseball, like many other simple and primitive cults, practices the simple rites of ancestor worship. It sometimes seems to me as if there have been only about two rules changes affecting the game on the field in the past fifty years. One of them directs the players to bring their gloves back to the dugout between innings instead of leaving them out on the field; the other is so revolutionary that I forget it. When I had the names of the White Sox players printed across the backs of their uniforms in 1960—under the obviously misguided notion that the fans might want to know who they were—protests came in from every other team in the league. They weren't quite sure what they were protesting; all they knew was that the screwball out in Chicago was on the loose again.

Unfortunately, there is little else that hasn't changed since baseball became becalmed—or maybe the word is embalmed—back in 1902 (I understand, for instance, that the Wright Brothers have proved conclusively that man can fly), and while it is nice to feel that one is lending stability to a jittery world, I tend to take the selfish, parochial, box-office view of our business. I am willing enough to go up

253

in an airplane—if that is indeed the wave of the future—but I'm afraid that falling attendance will always make me nervous.

The game has become too slow. There would be nothing wrong with the now standard three-hour game if we were presenting two and a half hours of action. We aren't. Baseball is the best concessions sport in existence, did you know that? Why? Well, how many times have you watched a game on television, gone to the refrigerator for a snack and returned without having missed anything? Same thing at the park.

In 1957 and 1958, while I was ripening on an enforced sabbatical, I did the commentary on NBC's Game of the Week show. Having little enough to occupy me during the play-by-play, I made it a practice to time the pitchers. For twenty minutes out of every hour, I discovered, the action on the field consisted solely of the pitcher holding the ball and looking at the catcher, a tableau which I find singularly lacking in drama. I suspect that the ratio is even higher now because the pitchers seem to become increasingly timid every year. Of course, if I pitched like some of the pitchers I've had on my payrolls I'd be reluctant to let go of the ball too.

The reason, of course, is that with the lively ball and the slender whipsaw bat, any .220 hitter is capable of hitting the ball out of the park. And don't let anyone tell you the ball isn't livelier. (If you hold it gently between the thumb and middle finger, the pitchers tell me, you can catch a faint pulse.) The manufacturers' press releases point out that they are using the same amount of yarn in a baseball as they used in 1902 and could hardly be winding the yarn any tighter. They do not think it necessary to clutter our minds with statistics about the great advances made in the quality and resiliency of that yarn. Nor do they bother to tell us that while the diameter of the ball is indeed the same, the stitches are now pressed flat against the cover, giving the pitcher no raised surface to work his fingers against and providing little opportunity for wind resistance to build up against a long fly ball.

As a result, there are 40 percent more 3-2 counts than there were 30 years ago. Grover Cleveland Alexander would just throw the ball down the middle and let the batter hit it; he didn't bother to start pitching until there was a man on second base. I can remember seeing Alex pitch 13-hit shutouts. Today, anybody standing at the plate with a bat in his hand is in scoring position, and the pitchers feel it necessary to nibble around the corners of the plate.

For years I have tinkered with rules changes for speeding up the game, and last year Ed Scherick, ABC, was ready to present "The Game of Tomorrow"—an exhibition between the Los Angeles Dodgers and the White Sox—as one of the network's Sports Spectaculars. It

254

was only because of my physical condition that the game wasn't played. Better not to do it at all, I decided, than to go ahead and do a lousy job. It remains one of the things I'd most like to do when I get back into action. Among my changes were:

1. The plate would be widened by 25 percent. This alone would put the swagger back into the pitchers' stride and the sneer back on their lips. It would revolutionize the game of baseball, since it would force every hitter to accustom himself to a new strike zone and would give the pitcher the confidence to bite off good chunks of the plate.

2. Three balls would constitute a base on balls, and two strikes would be out. The four-ball, three-strike formula did not come down from Mt. Sinai. It only seems logical and right to us because we have become used to it. With the 3-2 count replaced by a 2-1 count, the balance would remain the same and a great deal of wasted time— pure fat—would be melted away.

3. A limit would be placed on the time permitted for throwing the ball around the infield after every out or, better still, the practice would be eliminated entirely. It is another one of those traditions which serve no useful purpose. If an infielder isn't warmed up by the Fourth of July, when is he going to be?

4. The pitcher would be limited to one warm-up pitch at the start of every inning, instead of seven. One is ample. A pitcher who is worried about his arm stiffening up on a nippy day is perfectly entitled to wear his jacket between innings. When I was working for the Cubs, we developed a jacket with an electric heating device built into the sleeve. (A fellow from Coyne Electric worked on it with me.) Other clubs have used it through the years.

5. The intentional pass would be made automatic instead of having the pitcher go through the tiresome ritual of throwing four pitches.

6. The ball would be "slowed up."

I would not, however, try to speed up the game by discouraging players with legitimate beefs from arguing with the umpires. On the contrary, I would encourage bigger and better arguments by limiting the umpires' powers to throw players out of the game. Oh, how I long for those dear, dead days when Frankie Frisch and George Magerkurth stood fang to jowl, eyes aflame and jugulars athrob. Part of the act? Sure. But also part of the action. I have always wandered around the stands, riling the fans up against the umpires and getting riled up myself. That's part of the fun of the day, and part of the color and excitement of baseball.

The umpires, having become sovereign entities, are arbitrary, officious and, worst of all, pompous. They should be reminded every

255

payday that they have been placed out there on the field, like the bases, only to keep the game going. If that doesn't work, vows of humility are clearly indicated.

And certainly no discussion on changes in the structure of baseball should overlook interleague play, which my father first suggested in 1919 and which was still considered visionary when I next introduced it in 1947. Today, with 14 of the 17 big-league cities represented by only one team (and one league), it is so logical that it seems impossible anyone could raise a voice in opposition.

Everybody benefits from an interleague schedule. The fans of the National League cities would be given their chance, once a year, to see Roger Maris and Mickey Mantle and Al Kaline et al.; American League fans would see the Willie Mayses and the Frank Robinsons and the Warren Spahns. The cities represented in both leagues would profit at least as much because the interest in the competition between the two Chicago, New York and Los Angeles clubs would be overwhelming. There is absolutely no argument that can be brought against it, except tradition.

But as long as Ford Frick remains Commissioner, there is, in my opinion, little hope of getting any substantial amount of progressive legislation underway. That's the whole point I've been trying to make here. It was only after expansion became inevitable that he hopped on the bandwagon and tried to make it appear as if he were leading the way. The truth of the matter is that he had discouraged expansion for years, even to the point of ordering me not to open my mouth about it when I was surveying the Los Angeles franchise in the mid-fifties.

What would be the use, for instance, of expecting any help from him on my college plan? With relations between baseball and the campus at an all-time low, Frick didn't even bother to send a representative to the last meeting of college coaches in Chicago.

At the time of the baseball meeting held in Miami in December, 1961, everybody was writing that baseball had lost its grip on the American public and was in danger of losing its standing as our national game. And nothing was discussed at all. Nothing. Frick pushed everything through so fast that he didn't even take the time to introduce the two new members. At the end, he beamed and said, "Gentlemen, I want to congratulate you. This has been our finest meeting. We finished everything in seven minutes." *

* Another record for The Little Red Book.

A Warm Spiritual Message from the Del E. Webb Corp.

18.

THE best advice I can give to any aspiring young baseball operator is that if you are going to hate another team in your league, do it right out there in public where everybody can see you. Speak out smartly. Private hating stunts the personality, brings on ulcers and does not a blessed thing for the box office.

Promotional hatred is tied very closely to both greed and geography. If I were operating in Washington, I would make it a matter of personal pride and honor to hate Baltimore loudly and publicly and often. I would hate their owners and their management and their Public Health Service and their park benches. There is a natural rivalry between Washington and Baltimore waiting impatiently to be uncorked. The fans of these two cities have been very poorly served by their owners, who have shown an alarming tendency toward mutual help and understanding.

Next to a local rivalry the best baseball feud is a rematch between David and Goliath. Given my choice, I would prefer to be David, because the little man is always the public's darling. The little man can dart in and out with the jabs and the jibes and the fancy footwork. And, oh yes, history tells us that David was a big winner. Had a good crowd, too. A real good crowd. New York City is everybody's Goliath. It is very important to other cities to beat New York. The best case in point is Milwaukee, which prided itself on being "Bushtown" the year its team was beating the Yankees in the World Series, a backdoor way of bragging that it was not Bushtown at all but a thriving metropolis with a wonderful ball team no matter what those New York city-slickers thought.

If you find yourself cast as Goliath, though, be Goliath. Be big and brutal and hateful. In my relationship with the Yankees, I have always played David to their Goliath, and if I do say so myself the role fits me rather well. The Yankees, I regret to say, have not always played their part to the hilt. There have been times when they have only been big and hateful.

The Yankees have made my job easy. Hating the Yankees isn't

257

part of my act; it is one of those exquisite times when life and art are in perfect conjunction.

George Weiss has been my unfavorite person for twenty years, and now that he has gone from the Yankees the spark may go out of the game for me. Del Webb made a good run for it for awhile, but Del hasn't George's staying power. Weiss is a hard, unpleasant man, whereas Webb is a hustler.

My distaste for George Weiss goes back to those first days in Milwaukee when I was just getting started and he was sitting, in regal Yankee splendor, as the head of their mighty and far-flung farm system.

Among the liabilities I had inherited from the old regime was a $15,000 debt to the Yankee farm system. Weiss had lent the sinking Brewers a helping hand the previous season by selling them two sore-armed pitchers, Jimmy DeShong and Frank Makosky, at $12,500 apiece. Bendinger had paid $5,000 down on each of them and the rest of it was still outstanding. Which is more than can be said for the pitchers. DeShong had retired at the end of the year and Makosky, who didn't win a game for us, gave up at the end of my first year.

George Trautman, in trying to start me off with a fighting chance, had asked Weiss, just as he had asked Louie Jacobs and one or two others, to cancel our debt. Weiss had agreed to "consider" it. As with Louie and the others, I called Weiss at his Newark office to tell him I didn't want to cancel any debts, I only wanted a little time.

"Take all the time you need," he told me.

If you remember that first team at Milwaukee, we had a couple of good pitchers, Schmitz and Koslo. Just as we were beginning to win a few games, I received a letter from Weiss, which had passed through and been approved by the minor-league office headed by Judge Branham, in which he demanded immediate payment of that $15,000. If the money was not forthcoming, the letter said, he would be perfectly willing to accept Johnny Schmitz or Dave Koslo in payment.

Now, I have nothing against opportunism. I will match opportunism with anybody in the world. If Weiss could find a lamb who would buy a couple of sore-armed pitchers from him, he had my blessings and my admiration. If Weiss had refused to cancel the debt originally and had, instead, demanded Schmitz at that moment, I'd have raised the money somehow or given up Schmitz without a murmur.

But he had given me his word. I was brought up to believe that a man's word was good, the greatest handicap I had to overcome as a baseball operator. I had to get thrown out of baseball before I could

258

get it through my head that the word of some of my colleagues was not worth the paper it wasn't written on. I can't blame George Weiss for that. Out of the goodness of his heart, George had done his level best to teach me early.

Cold with the righteous anger of youth, I reached for the telephone. "I know who you are now, Weiss," I told him. "And I know what you are. You're not going to get Schmitz or Koslo except over my dead body. But rest assured of this. You're going to pay for this $15,000. You've broken your word to me, and now I'm giving you mine. You have my word that for as long as you and I remain in baseball, I am going to get this $15,000 out of your hide over and over and over."

He didn't get Schmitz. Jim Gallagher bought Vallie Eaves from me to give me enough money to pay Weiss off.

I collected the first installment on that permanent $15,000 Weiss owes me almost at once. Within the month, the Brewers were scheduled to go into Kansas City to play a series with the Yankees' farm club. The Blues were operated by Roy Hamey, a good friend, who is now general manager of the Yankees. I rented the Kansas City park from Hamey for one day for $500, far more than he figured to realize on our last-place club. What that meant was that I, as the visiting team, had bought the gate receipts for the day. On that day, I held an Old-Timers' Game, featuring Dizzy Dean, Charlie Grimm and a collection of recently retired American Association stars, including as many former Kansas City players—meaning players once owned by the Yankees—as I could find. We drew an excellent crowd into the park, and I had some of my $15,000 back.

I never let up on George. I would have pulled that stunt of watering down the field to give myself control of the second game of that final-day doubleheader in 1942, no matter whom we had been playing. The fact that it was Kansas City was an extra bonus, and a special bow in the direction of Newark and George Weiss. When Hamey started phoning him, my heart sang.

Kansas City dominated the American Association until we came into the league. In my first full year, we pulled even with them. After that, Milwaukee dominated it.

When I came to Cleveland, Weiss was in the Yankees' office waiting for me. George didn't particularly care to deal with me, you know. About the only trade we ever made was when I got Allie Clark from him for Red Embree, a swap of no particular consequence. Lord knows I've tried to help him wherever I could, but George never seems to understand. There was a day in St. Petersburg, the Yankee training camp, when I went up to the press box during an exhibition game and observed that no refreshments had been set out for the writers. Now that isn't right. There was nothing to do but go down to the concourse, collect all the vendors in sight and lead them back up to distribute their wares. Oh yes, I was careful to tell the vendors to inform the writers that it was all coming to them "Compliments of Bill Veeck" so they would know they were not expected to pay. Weiss was terribly upset. He seemed to think I was trying to show the Yankees up as a cheap and shoddy outfit. I can't understand how a big and powerful organization like the New York Yankees could so misinterpret a humanitarian gesture toward its starving writers.

But George is touchy. He takes things the wrong way. Right after we had won the pennant in Cleveland, Weiss and I were on the dais together at a *Sport* Magazine dinner at which Lou Boudreau was the guest of honor. To take the pressure off George for the coming season, I observed that the Yankees would be doing well if they finished third. As I was speaking, I was moved to pay tribute to my two great heroes, Joe DiMaggio and Hank Greenberg, seated together just below me. And then thinking of the trouble Weiss was having in signing Joe for the new season—a story much in the news at the time—I decided to forget past enmities and suggest to George that he could solve his problem by simply paying Joe what he was worth. I even suggested a possible area of negotiation. "I'd be delighted to pay him $200,000 if I had him," I said, helpfully.

Weiss got up and stomped off the dais. It made the whole night for me. The next morning he was still so mad that he called to accuse me of meddling in the Yankees' financial affairs—which may be the only time he has ever put in a call to me. "Hey, George," I said, "why don't you call up the papers and tell them what a jerk I am? Maybe we can get something going for us."

"I wouldn't dignify you by acknowledging you," he said. To make it clear that I was among the unacknowledged he hung up.

And all I had been trying to do was help him sign his star and get himself some publicity.

George's great trouble as he makes his way through life is that he is such a serious and humorless man, as befitted a man with the fate of the Yankee empire on his shoulders, that he doesn't know when he's being kidded. And that's the greatest target in the world. In Chicago, our scoreboard has a section where we can flash any kind of message we want to pass on to the fans. When Weiss honored us with one of his infrequent visits, I had them flash: *Welcome to the*

George Weiss Fan Club. It was up there for about half the game, and George was the only person in the park who didn't see it. George takes himself so seriously that he becomes quite upset when I speak of him as a fugitive from the human race—and I speak of George often—because he seems to think there's a 50–50 chance I may not be kidding. If he had any kind of a sense of humor he'd understand that there is also a 50–50 chance that I *may* be kidding.

One of the great stunts of recent baseball history was pulled on us in Chicago by the Yankees. Message-flashing is one of the Comiskey Park's scoreboard's minor talents. Its real mission in life is to flip its lid whenever one of our players hits a home run. It shoots off fireworks, explodes bombs, plays music and puts on a gladsome display in dancing lights. When somebody from the other team hits a home run, it just stands there in austere, though never surly, silence.

Bob Fishel, whom I had better identify at this point as currently a *Yankee* public relations man, struck back by smuggling some five-cent sparklers into the New York dugout. After one of their own boys hit a home run, the Yankee players lit up the sparklers and, led by old Casey Stengel, went dancing around their dugout in wild celebration. A brilliant satire.

The Yankees were one up on us, and that wouldn't do. We played around with the idea of having them hauled into court for shooting off fireworks in a public arena without a permit. But no, that seemed a bit drastic. While the thought of Casey Stengel being mugged and fingerprinted was most appealing, we didn't want to look like sore losers. Instead, we decided to smuggle a fire bomb into the Yankee Stadium on our next visit.

The bomb was placed in with the regular team luggage. When the club got to New York, I sent our fireworks man, Tony Cartalino, east on the train. Unhappily, the Yankees figured out what we had in mind. They searched all our bags and trunks and they finally found the bomb and took it away. Ed Short called me in Chicago and I told Ed to warn the Yankees that they had better return the bomb at once or anything they brought into our park from that day on was a good bet to be missing when they left. "In addition," I said, "tell them that I'm about to swear out a warrant for theft."

Tony got the bomb back with a warning that he would be placed under arrest if he shot it off. All right, we had one more trip to New York that season, and I went to work to rent one of the empty lots behind Yankee Stadium and to get a fireworks permit. We were going to treat the Yankee customers to a massive fireworks display as they came out of the Stadium after the game, and we were going to have a big banner across the lot, reading:

COMPLIMENTS OF THE CHICAGO WHITE SOX
FOR UNDERPRIVILEGED YANKEE FANS

We got the lot all right, but the permit didn't materialize in time. Over the winter, though, we arranged everything so that we could get the permit on 24-hour notice. Unfortunately, I was too ill in 1961 to do much of anything and so, to my everlasting sorrow, I was never able to pull that one off.

For those who think I must be rotten to the core if I can't get along with such sterling characters as Weiss, Webb and their fellow predators, I must say that Bob Fishel is one of my closest friends— and the best publicity man in baseball. I brought Bob into baseball in Cleveland, and he came with me to St. Louis. When New York offered him the job, shortly after they had whisked my franchise away from me, Bob called me from a telephone booth in Baltimore to ask if it was all right with me if he went up to talk to them. "I know how you feel about them," he said. "If you'd rather I don't go up there I won't."

I told him to get up there as fast as he could. "That's the best public relations job in baseball," I said. "It's a compliment to you that they've asked you." At the same time I was fighting Weiss, Webb and Topping, I'd have done anything in the world for Fishel or Stengel. If Weiss had been willing to listen to Fishel, he'd have had one of the best publicity programs instead of one of the worst.

George is equally enthusiastic about me. In my first year in Chicago, our attendance, while good all along, came on strong toward the end. The White Sox had a history of leading through the early months and dying in the stretch, and it took awhile before the customers became convinced that we were really going to win it this time. With the crowds beginning to come I had a shot at the all-time Chicago attendance record, set by my father. I wanted it badly, and I particularly wanted it in my first year.

We had a postponed Yankee game to play off. In order to fatten up the attendance I rescheduled it as a night game on an open date at the end of their last series. That made it "getaway day"—the day they were leaving town—and, under those conditions, it is necessary to solicit the visiting team's permission to play at night. Stengel gave it. Weiss overruled him. Being fond of wasting time, I appealed to our gifted Commissioner, with the traditional result. All right, if I wasn't going to get my night game, I could at least get another installment on the $15,000 Weiss owes me. I announced that if they

262

would reconsider and play the game at night, all the money above the advance would be contributed to the Community Chest. Topping, rising very nicely to the bait, answered angrily that he would donate $10,000 to the Chest if I would. Familiar? Topping, like Saigh, had made a conditional offer to a charity, which never sounds particularly gracious and which was walking right into my (if you'll pardon the expression) web. I wired Topping: WE HAVE ALREADY SENT CHECK FOR $10,000. WILL HAVE COMMUNITY CHEST WIRE YOU TO SEE THAT YOU DON'T RENEGE AS YOU DID ON THE LAST AGREEMENT.

After Topping's matching check was received, I gave him all the credit and publicity he deserved. Charitable contributions need never be anything to be ashamed of. And while I was at it, I kept saying— to help out other worthwhile causes—"How much money do you think the Yankees will have to give to New York charities to match the $10,000 they gave to a Chicago charity?"

People I know and respect tell me that Topping is a warm-blooded guy, nothing like Webb and Weiss. I believe that he is, even though I didn't get much of a chance to see him in action in 1961 after he had shaken Weiss. Weiss and Webb are a perfect match, like two pitchers of ice water on a conference table. The trouble with the Yankee hierarchy, in my experience, is that they never give you the feeling they're enjoying themselves. They watch a ball game as if they're standing at attention in a reviewing stand watching the troops march by. I volunteered to cover the 1949 World Series for the Cleveland *Plain Dealer* to keep Gordon Cobbledick, who was ill, from jumping out of bed. Hank Greenberg, Lou Boudreau and I watched the New York games from a box between the Yankee box and the Yankee dugout, a somewhat exposed position. We rooted and yelled—not necessarily for the Yankees—just because we were in a ball park on a nice day enjoying the rich feeling of being alive. As to the occupants of the neighboring box, mine hosts, I wrote:

> I guess I'll never understand the passive approach to a ball game. Mssrs. Webb, Topping and Weiss never cheered, yelled or even smiled. They did shake hands after big John Mize got a single but that was merely to compliment each other on a very wise $100,000 expenditure.

I cannot say that Weiss is not a good operator. He is. The possibility always exists that I was never able to get along with him because I was jealous of his success. Under his direction, the Yankees always came up with a fine crop of young players.

263

Now that he is with the Mets, he has suddenly become quite promotion-minded and readily available to the press, which shows that George is able to adapt himself to changing conditions. The question is whether he will still be able to come up with all those good young players now that he has neither the Yankee prestige nor the Yankee scouting system going for him. It was interesting to note that he began by signing up scouts the way Huey Long used to sign up bodyguards. Well, each of us to our own dark fears.

With everything they have going for them, the Yankee do one of the worst promotional job in the majors, despite, let me say again, the herculean efforts of Bob Fishel. Sure, they usually outdraw everybody. Operating from a city of 11,000,000 people, how can they miss? In Cleveland, we set every conceivable major-league record in a city of 900,000. They had 12 people to every person we had, and we outdrew them. I'd be ashamed. . . . And there's even more than that involved. New York City has a transient population *every day of the year* that is greater than the entire population of Cleveland. Most of them are tourists, and a tourist, by definition, is somebody looking for something to do. With Maris and Mantle plus a close pennant race most of 1961 they drew 1,748,000.

Somehow, the Yankees don't appeal to the average guy; their appeal is to the corporation president. A good percentage of their attendance represents season boxes bought up by companies to entertain guests. Much of the time the seats aren't even occupied.

The Yankees have only one liability. Their fans are used to winning. That's just another reason, if they would only see it, why promotion and entertainment are needed to whip up enthusiasm. The accepted picture of the Yankee fan is a staid, solid, conservative citizen who latches on to a sure winner because he is used to playing everything safe. It is essentially a true picture. What the Yankees refuse to realize is that this is the kind of person who reacts best to entertainment at a ball park—the cornier, it sometimes seems, the better. Will Harridge, my favorite conservative, had the time of his life with us in Chicago after he got kicked upstairs to make room for Joe Cronin. After all the years of frowning on me from afar, Will became the best fan we had for our fireworks. The average baseball fan, my beer-drinking, shirt-sleeved guy in the bleachers, is used to enjoying himself. He expects to have a good time when he goes out. If nothing much is happening, he'll make his own good time whether it's in a ball park, in a bar or at a party. The conservative man, being more inhibited, is not used to enjoying himself. Give him a chance to get out of himself in a crowd and—I tell you I've seen it a thousand times—

264

you can't hold him down. And remembering that he has had the time of his life, he becomes your best customer.

The Yankees have many natural advantages in New York, beyond the sheer magnitude of the city. Most New Yorkers come originally from other parts of the country, which means that a very large percentage of them arrive with an inbred attachment to the big-league team of their own home area. That childhood attachment is never completely lost. To some degree it is a conditioning, and to some degree, once they have left home, it is a tie to their own youth and to their own town. What do the Yankees do to attract their huge Midwestern population when Detroit or Cleveland or Chicago come to town? I would be willing to bet that they have never even bothered to find out how many transplanted Ohioans are in the park when the Indians are playing.

I'm not going to draw them up a full promotional campaign. I don't have to. All they have to do is listen to Fishel. But I'll give them one more hint. New York City abounds in unattached females searching for a place to meet young men under respectable auspices. For a young man, there is no better entertainment buy than a baseball game. Beyond that, I am not going to go.

When the Yankees did come up with a promotion, it was invariably tasteless and embarrassing. Two of their greatest promotions were their public farewells to their two dying giants, Lou Gehrig and Babe Ruth. I'll take my midgets and my circuses. Necromancy has never been to my taste.

Their great annual promotion is an Old-Timers' Day, and while I must admit it's successful, it is, after all, another exercise in mortality. I could never understand how it either entertained the fans or benefited baseball to show the great old names as wheezing, balding, arthritic old men. To the younger generations, the fabled old stars they have read about are made to look ridiculous. To their contemporaries, there may be a temporary wave of nostalgia, but it is followed by a wave of sadness at the realization that they themselves are becoming wheezing, balding and arthritic old men. That sends them home feeling just great.

The only Old-Timers' Day I ever held was when I was getting my money back from George Weiss. Dizzy Dean had retired only that year, Grimm is a pixie at any age, and the others were mostly minor-leaguers who had never quite made it and had therefore retired at a relatively early age and were in fair shape. And still I made a vow that I would never do it again. When I had a gathering of the Old-Timers in Cleveland in 1946, I didn't let them on the field.

I can't stand such cheap and tawdry box-office gimmicks. I mean what are they trying to do, make a mockery of the game?

It would be unfair—although not undiscriminating—to leave the Yankees' Fifth Avenue offices without a short profile of Del Webb. Webb bought into the club with Topping when Larry MacPhail was putting together a syndicate to buy the Yankees from the Ruppert estate. Larry had never heard of Webb or laid eyes on him until he was pointed out to him in the lobby of a Washington hotel as a prospective backer.

(I was trying to buy the Yankees at the same time from my bedside office in the Corona Naval Hospital. The club was on the block for $2,800,000, a steal. I was a child of my times, full of brave new hopes for the brave new world and happy in my modest, idealistic belief that I was going to make a fast buck. It was one of the most frustrating times of my life. I raised a quick $2,000,000 and then I hung there. As soon as I picked up $100,000 one place, I'd lose $100,000 someplace else. James A. Farley was trying to put together a syndicate in the East and he was having the same trouble. People who would have normally been jumping out of the walls to invest with him didn't want their names associated with his because he was supposed to be *persona non grata* with Roosevelt. I suggested to Farley that we put our syndicates together but he wasn't interested. He still thought he was going to raise the money himself. Too bad, because there's no doubt New York is the best track to run on. I suspect, though, that I'd have operated the Yankees for a couple of years and then sold out. The fun is in the building, not in just holding on after everything has been done.)

During the past decade of franchise-shifting, one of Del Webb's greatest interests has been in getting the contracts to build the new ball parks. He is a businessman. He seems to be at the ear and elbow of everybody who is in the running for a franchise, promising them his support—directly or by implication—getting everybody obligated to him, as if following the principle that a man who buys a ticket on every horse in the field ends up cashing a winning ticket. An ancestor of Del Webb's undoubtedly got the contract to build the Pyramids after elbowing the Pharaoh's favorite nephew out of position.

Webb even wooed me at one point. After I lost the St. Louis franchise, Phil Wrigley gave me an option on the territorial rights to Los Angeles with the understanding that I would protect his interests by—among other things—converting Wrigley Field in Los Angeles from a minor-league park seating 20,000 to a major-league park

266

seating 50,000. Webb and I were not on the best of all possible terms at the time, possibly because he had been a prime mover in kicking me out of baseball. But if a construction job is in the offing, Del Webb is never far behind. Especially in Los Angeles, his home base. He was right there from the beginning, offering advice and assistance and intimations that if he was going to get the contract, I would be getting his vote at any American League meeting.

I never kidded myself for a moment that he'd stay with me if he dug up a better deal someplace else, although I did think I might have some claim on his loyalty since my backers in Los Angeles were Conrad Hilton, who builds nothing but hotels, and Henry Crown, who builds hotels and buys and sells things like the Empire State Building. Webb had done some work for them, and he stood willing —and, I must say, able—to do more.

The franchise that immediately was thrown up for grabs was, as we know, the Macks' franchise in Philadelphia. With Arnold Johnson in the bidding, I had little confidence that I was going to get the Yankee vote, especially since Webb and Topping were the men who brought him in to do the bidding. Arnold Johnson was their partner in several businesses, including a large vending-machine company. He was indirectly involved with them in baseball too. Johnson had bought the ball parks in both New York and Kansas City from the Yankees and then leased both parks right back to them. To make it more complicated, he had, according to published reports, borrowed $2,-900,000 from Webb and Topping in the form of a second mortgage so that he wouldn't have to put up too much of his own money.

Johnson's deal with Kansas City, as he came to the meeting, was that the city would buy the minor-league park from him (remember that Webb and Topping still held that $2,900,000 mortgage on the two parks) and then pay for a complete reconstruction job. Johnson was to award the contract to a construction company of his own choosing and, by sheer coincidence, the best possible construction company, as it later turned out, happened to be Del Webb's.

As an old wanderer, I had to admire Webb for his sheer gall. Before the meeting was held to dispose of the Philadelphia franchise, Del had been pledging his unswerving support to the old hometown, Los Angeles. Del didn't have to worry too much about me, of course. He did have to worry about offending Hilton and Crown. He also had to worry about the newspapers. In every city that has won a big-league franchise, a single newspaperman has led the campaign. In Los Angeles, it was Vincent X. Flaherty, who conducted the greatest one-man campaign over a period of years I have ever seen. Webb walked into that meeting still vowing his support to Flaherty and as soon as the door shut behind him, he got up and announced that Los Angeles wasn't ready for big-league baseball. That left me sitting with my three votes, as I knew I was going to be.

Here's where it gets funny. As soon as the franchise was voted to Kansas City, Webb dashed out of the conference room, rushed to a phone and called Flaherty in Los Angeles to assure him he had done his best to get the franchise for Los Angeles but that Clark Griffith, out of his old friendship to Connie Mack, had been hot for Kansas City. Old Uncle Clark, said Mr. Webb to Mr. Flaherty, had been too strong for him.

What made it so outrageous was that Griffith had led the battle against Kansas City. His argument had been pitched to the theme that with Johnson owing the Yankee owners all that money, there was a clear conflict of interest. His real reason for breaking with the Yankees was that he wanted to keep the franchise in Philadelphia.

This is the kind of thing that makes Webb so transparent. He cannot realize that a columnist like Flaherty has his own sources of information. Flaherty had known everything that had been going on in that presumably secret meeting, and he knew very well—and told Webb so—that it had been Del himself who had killed Los Angeles.

I have always been sure that Webb's primary interest in Kansas City, even above the sale of the park and the construction work, was in getting control of a franchise which he could eventually move to Los Angeles himself. There's no way of proving it, of course, but it's one of those things your nerve ends tell you has to be true because it is the logical explanation that would account for all of his twistings and turnings.

When I say there's no way to prove it, I'm leaning over backward. I did read later that he told Connie Hilton the Kansas City franchise was going to be moved to Los Angeles after a couple of years, but I'd hate to cite that as any kind of proof, because Del had to tell Hilton something.

It has to be true, though, because there was no other possible justification for moving a team into Kansas City. By moving to Kansas City after having already moved to Baltimore, the American League had, to all intents and purposes, taken two relatively small, constricted cities and invited the National League into the two booming western cities, Los Angeles and San Francisco—unless the Kansas City franchise jumped again in a hurry.

Even while they were voting Johnson in, everybody felt that Kansas City would have difficulty supporting a major-league operation after the original enthusiasm wore off. According to my information, the Athletics will definitely be on the wing again within two years. The other patsies in the league went along because they always go along with the Yankees and because Frick is there to throw in the weight of his office when the weight of his office is called upon.

Until Arnold Johnson died, Kansas City was not an independent major-league team at all, it was nothing more than a loosely controlled Yankee farm club. In addition to the close business ties between Johnson and the Yankee owners, the Athletics took their general manager, Parke Carroll, right out of the Yankee farm system. I have heard Carroll boast openly in baseball gatherings, "I don't have to worry. Weiss has promised to take care of me." This, needless to say, was not a thing our lively Commissioner thought worthy of his attention.

Frank Lane knew he was sending Roger Maris on a one-stop trip to the Yankees when he traded him to Kansas City. Everybody in baseball knew it; the sportswriters knew it; any well-informed fifteen-year-old boy in Des Moines knew it. I called Frank and asked him what in the world he was doing. "I know I'm handing him to the Yankees," Frank said. "But it's a trade I have to make for my own ball club."

In Del's behalf, let me say that he does have a saintlike forbearance and a forgiving heart. Every year he brightens up my dreary holiday season with a warm and sentimental Christmas greeting. In order to savor the real Del Webb that lies under that deceptively cold exterior, it helps to know that his greetings come on the letterhead of his construction company, the Del E. Webb Corp., and are typed on one of those machines that are supposed to make a form letter look personal. I have always looked forward to Del's annual Christmas message with great expectancy—especially when I haven't had a good laugh for awhile.

Unfortunately, I always have to wait until the holiday season is over. Despite the strong personal bond his message bespeaks, he always seems to send it to the wrong address. Even after the White Sox won the pennant in 1959, he was still sending it to St. Louis, a city I had left six years earlier at the end of his toe. This year he finally caught up. Now that I've moved to Maryland, he sent it to New Mexico.

What follows is Del Webb's unexpurgated Christmas greetings for the 1961 holiday season. It is typed, as I said, on the usual Del E. Webb Corp. letterhead and decorated tastefully at the bottom with bells and holly:

DEAR BILL:

Christmas comes again, as it has for hundreds of years ... a time when religion should become paramount and commercialism should take second place ... a time to rededicate ourselves to the principles of a season that stands for joy and hope, love and faith.

Peace has not yet come to the world. There will still be cruel aggression, the human suppression of freedom by violence. All this means America must be strong, with undoubted strength.

Yet we should be able to make that strength count for peace by works of humanity and friendship. If we make the rewards of peace greater than the gains of war, have we not made peace more likely?

We believe this Christmas Day deserves a moment of quiet contemplation to consider everything it symbolizes. We express gratitude for all good things. And for the priceless gift of friendship, we wish all our friends a Merry Christmas and a New Year filled with happiness and success.

Under separate cover we are sending to you one of our 1962 Del E. Webb Corporation desk calendars.

Sincerely,

Gee, that's beautiful.

Right Between the Shoulder Blades | **19.**

FOR the story of how I was kicked out of baseball, bleeding profusely, I have to go back a little before the wedding of those two great American institutions, Budweiser and baseball—a marriage most assuredly made in heaven, with only a small assist from the advertising desk, the counting room and the tax department. It begins, two months earlier, in December, 1952, with the winter meeting at Phoenix. The Phoenix meeting is worth looking into because it not only shows why the Yankees were so eager to get rid of me, above and beyond sheer personalities, but also something of how the Yankees operated under George Weiss's benevolent despotism to dominate the league.

270

During the Phoenix meeting, I officially notified the league that I might want to move out of St. Louis if Saigh should sell his club to a powerhouse. I had, in fact, been alerting my fellow owners, individually and unofficially, all during the season. A tentative meeting was set up in Tampa, in mid-March, in the event I found such a move necessary. Not a voice was raised in opposition.

I did something else in Phoenix. I introduced some measures calling for radical changes in the procurement of players and in the split of the gate receipts and the sharing of television fees. (On that last, my sights were really set on a policy for restricting the televising of home games.) All of these were issues I had raised before in one form or other. This time I introduced them all together and waited until the last moment to put them on the agenda. The Yankees were convinced I was shooting at them. I wasn't, really. I was shooting at the Yankees only insofar as they were trying to keep the league from becoming competitive.

It is fairly obvious—as these things are always obvious in retrospect —that since I knew very well that I might be asking permission to move shortly, I had not picked the best possible time to offend the Yankees. If I had been sure at that point that I was going to be moving, perhaps I would have waited another year. Beyond that, the answer to why I shook things up at that particular moment comes in four parts:

First: baseball attendance had been dwindling steadily since the big year of 1948. In the season just ended the Browns had been one of the few teams in either league to increase their attendance.

Second: I really didn't think anybody would try to stop me from moving, if only because it was to the league's best interest for me to move.

Third: I didn't think that under the conditions that would have to arise before I did move out of St. Louis, they had a legal right to stop me. I still don't.

Fourth: I have always had the vague feeling that when a man is confronted with the choice between being right and being wrong, it's just as well to be right. (This is the kind of thinking that used to get people burned at the stake, so I got off lucky.)

In order to get anything on the agenda, you need two votes. The only vote I have ever had, in all my years in the American League, has been Frank Lane's. Frank, who was then with the White Sox, gave me the other vote I needed even though he made it clear that he would have to vote against the sharing of television receipts. Like me, Frank felt that we had to come to grips with our problems.

I proposed an Unrestricted Draft rule that would have distributed players more evenly and, just as important, salvaged the minor leagues. The decline of the minors had started years earlier when Papa Branch Rickey, out of his own needs, conceived and developed the farm system, a really brilliant example of an original mind at work. My father was one of the few baseball men able to see from the beginning that in bypassing the independent minor-league operator, the farm system would, over the long haul, be a destructive—not constructive—influence. By 1952, it took far less foresight to see that television was about to deal the minors the final blow. I proposed:

1. All minor-league players would be eligible to be drafted by any team in a higher classification after their first year in professional baseball, the price to be set on a rising scale as the player moves up in classification. Regardless of classification, the player would receive 25 percent of the draft price as a reward for advancement. (Under the existing rules, they were not eligible to be drafted until they had been optioned back to the minors three times.)

2. The major-league clubs would be forbidden to sign any player who had no previous professional experience.

These two rules were, among other things, an attempt to put the minor-league operator back in business. If the minors signed all the players, they could sell their best players and then use the money to go out and find new ones. It would also strengthen the weaker major-league teams by allowing them to draft any player nobody else had been willing to pay more than $25,000 for, the price I set for the major-league draft.

3. If a major-league team televised its games beyond a 50-mile radius it would have to make a cash settlement upon any affected minor league.

In September, 1961—nine years later—the Unrestricted Draft was finally passed, a considerably watered-down version of my original proposal. Under this rule, a major-league team is permitted to option only one of its first-year men back to the minors. All others can be claimed for $8,000. Players already in baseball, however, are in no way affected. Nor is there any provision for the free movement of players within the various classifications of the minor leagues.

Since there is no attempt to strengthen even the rickety minor-league structure that remains, the Unrestricted Draft may serve to distribute players more evenly—which is all to the good—but it will hardly put an end to the bonus bidding. It could, in one way, have the opposite effect. The tendency will probably be to stop paying the $10,000 to $20,000 bonuses but to go even higher for the handful

272

of highly publicized kids everybody is after. We may very well see the $200,000 bonus before we see the 3:50 mile.

(Baseball must be the only association in the world where the first thought in the members' minds, after they pass a new rule, is how to get around it. I could give a dozen examples. But how do I—being out of baseball when this rule was passed—know it was true in this case? Because within the week I had four calls from four different clubs asking me if I had been able to figure out how it would be possible to pay a boy a bonus and not have him count on the list of first-year men.)

You could spend a few unpleasant months talking about all the things wrong with the bonus system. Everything is wrong with it. In the first place, the money goes *out* of baseball. It goes into bank accounts, it goes to buy homes, it goes into Cadillacs, it goes into stocks. If a small portion of the $60,000,000 that has gone to bonus boys in those intervening nine years had been used to strengthen the minor leagues, independent owners would be finding the kids themselves, selling the good ones to the majors and then using the money to go out and find new material.

The most ridiculous part of it is that the scouts set the bonus price, not the operator, because the scouts are scouting each other far more than they are scouting the boy. They have to. I have had big-league operators tell me, "If fifteen other clubs are bidding for a boy and we're not, then I want to know what's the matter with my scouting system." One strategically placed shill can jump the price up from $15,000 to $65,000, because once the bidding contest gets underway the operators act like a bunch of old women at a boardwalk auction. Suppose, as an example, the operator has given his scout permission to go as high as $50,000, and the scout calls later and says, "The Dodgers are willing to give him $55,000, but I'm pretty sure I can get him for $60,000." The operator has to say to himself, "If I was willing to go to $50,000, I have to go to $60,000." And all the time he is raising his bid he is hoping he isn't the lucky winner, because he knows the odds are 10–1 against any bonus boy making a major-league squad. And all the time he's hoping he doesn't get him for $60,000, he is also thinking, *But if I can get him for $70,000, I have to go the extra $10,000.* It's crazy.

In addition to everything else, it puts you in an impossible bargaining position with every player on your team who has been signed for a bus ride and a cup of coffee. For what really makes it ridiculous is that the same team that will hand over $100,000 to a kid who hasn't played a game won't give $30,000 to one of its own ballplayers who has just led the league in hitting.

And there's something even more ridiculous, something I don't think anybody has ever noticed. The only argument in favor of throwing bonus money around is that you have to sign the nine stiffs to make sure you get the one good one. All right, what about the kid who makes it big and presumably justifies all those other losses? There's this about it: If he develops quickly enough, he is *legally entitled to disaffirm*. When you sign an eighteen-year-old kid, you have to get his father's signature. By the nature of the baseball contract, the father is signing the boy's bargaining rights away in perpetuity. It happens not to be legal. A man is perfectly entitled to sign away his own rights for a consideration, but nobody is entitled to sign away anybody else's rights for him. When the boy becomes twenty-one, he is no longer bound to honor his contract.

No other club would sign a boy who disaffirmed? Yes, they would. Otherwise he would have them locked in a perfect conspiracy case, for he has already established, on his previous year's play, that he is more than worthy of playing in the major league. They'd sign him all right, or the baseball contract would face a court test under the worst set of circumstances that could possibly be found.

The Unrestricted Draft, such as it is, is now part of baseball. So is expansion to new cities, another policy I labored for without success for years. The other parts of my Phoenix program—plus interleague play—will be resisted for awhile longer, but they will be adopted eventually too:

I proposed that the visiting team be given a better break on the box-office cut. In the American League, the visiting club averages 28¢ per customer, which sounds like a carefully worked-out formula. In truth, it is just another proof that baseball has not stirred a foot in the quicksand since 1902. When baseball was first organized as a professional sport, the average price for a ticket was 50¢. The league office took a nickel off the top, and the home and visiting teams split what was left, 22½ ¢ apiece. In later years, with the league getting all its operating funds from the World Series, it returned the nickel. Since the price of tickets had risen greatly by then, with no commensurate rise in the visiting team's *per-capita* take, the nickel was passed on to the visiting team under a formula which allows 30¢ for grandstand tickets and 20¢ for bleacher seats and for kids. Other than that, there has been no change in 50 years.

With the cost of transportation and hotel accommodations having

274

risen tremendously in the postwar years, an increase in the visiting club's cut was long overdue. I proposed several formulas at different times and always they were voted down—as my proposal was voted down in Phoenix.

But what really brought the wrath of my peers down upon my head was the proposal to cut the visiting team in on the television receipts. Now, this may not sound quite so inflammatory as, say, the Communist Manifesto, but to the Yankees it was revolutionary, un-American and just about what you could expect from that fellow Veeck.

My real aim was to use the sharing of receipts as an opening wedge for coming to grips with the whole problem of television. It is self-evident that in televising home games you are competing with yourself; your customers are given a choice between watching the game in their own homes, for nothing, or watching it, live, at the ball park after a brief stop at the box office. The ideal way to handle television is to black out the home games and televise the road games. That way, you hold on to every advantage and throw back all the disadvantages. As far as the sponsor is concerned, the only drawback would be an increase in his line charges, an added expense the club could easily share with him.

Where there are two major-league teams in a city, that policy wouldn't work. You would be placed in direct competition with the other team, and the weaker of the two teams could be seriously hurt. The ideal arrangement in a two-team town is to televise all day games and Saturday games, and black out all night games and Sunday games.

Long-range plans aside, there is not the slightest doubt that the visiting team, which provides half the television show, is entitled to a share of the proceeds. Baseball itself concedes this every year by exchanging reciprocal releases. In other words, I sign some papers for each of the other teams in the league waiving my claim on their radio and TV receipts and they do the same for me.

At Phoenix, I introduced my measure, with Lane's help, and got trounced, 7–1. Now, note this vote carefully because we are going to come back to it. I had thought I had a good chance of getting this one passed. Instead, everybody voted against it. I was offering an impressive sum of money to Washington and Philadelphia, two struggling teams with lousy television contracts, and they were turning it down. In private talks at the summer meeting, where I had first intended to propose it, they had then been eager to become co-sponsors.

More was involved here than simply an exchange of money. Television in those days was just beginning to make itself felt as a source of revenue that would inevitably widen the gap between the top of the league and the bottom. I was not so worried about the imbalance that was already making itself felt, I was very much concerned about the future.

Let's stop to take a look at the importance of these television receipts, bringing the figures up to date to illustrate my point. Last year, the Yankees were paid, in all probability, $1,250,000 for their TV and radio rights. The new Washington franchise, I would guess, received $125,000.

But there is another important contributor to the cause here. The Game of the Week, on a national hookup, pays $25,000 a shot to the team it uses. The Yankees probably realized another $500,000 from this source alone, while the Senators were getting one game, as a courtesy.

In Chicago, to give a full perspective to the TV rat race, we received $300,000 from television, $292,000 from radio and $300,000 from the Game of the Week, or something close to $900,000. We are not involved with small change, obviously, when we're dealing with television.

How can the Senators, with every other conceivable disadvantage, possibly compete when the Yankees start $1,500,000 ahead of them every year on a purely subsidiary right?

The Yankees do not get that television and radio contract because of any particular brilliance on their part. They get it because they happen to be situated in the greatest commercial market in the country. (As proof that this is true, the New York Mets signed a radio-TV contract for $1,200,000 before they had ever played a game or signed a player.)

As to the Game of the Week, the Yankees get the most coverage because they are the greatest attraction. No doubt about that. There is also no doubt that since the Game of the Week originates outside each city, the contract should be negotiated by the Commissioner's office at a flat annual sum, with the money being split up evenly among all the teams. This happens to be precisely the way the National Football League handles its TV contract, and this is one of the reasons pro football has been a healthy, burgeoning sport in the same decade baseball has been on the decline.

When my proposal was voted down, I refused to sign the releases permitting the other clubs to televise their games when the Browns were in town. I did not have any television broadcasts at all in

St. Louis, which meant I was giving up my property right in their telecasts and receiving nothing in return. My legal position was unassailable and, in fact, was never questioned.

Having said that, I want to make it clear that it was not the rampant case of sour-grapeism that the Yankees tried to make it out to be. I had offered the same proposition in Cleveland where I had a good television contract, and I continued to make it in Chicago where I probably had the second-best contract in the league. Even in 1952, I told them they were perfectly free to televise their road games against us back to their home cities. "Be my guest," I told them. "No charge." But when they televised their home games, I told them, they were keeping a certain number of people out of the park and cutting down our share of the gate.

Since there was no doubt about my legal position, they had to find some other way of stopping me. Del Webb had already invited everybody to a dinner party at his home in Phoenix, an invitation I had turned down. Under the circumstances, it turned into a discussion of the ways and means of bringing me to heel. The answer was simple: if I would not permit the others to televise my road games, none of them would schedule any night games with us.

The schedule for the upcoming season, you understand, had already been drawn up, circulated and approved by every club, with the night games clearly indicated. Here was a clear case of breaking the league rules and, in the process, breaking a firm contract. Add the meeting at Webb's house and I had a cut-and-dried case of conspiracy against every team in the league. I appealed to Frick, who took the bull by the horns and ruled that it was none of his business. In any other business in the world, I would have simply taken them into court and forced specific performance. I have always hesitated to go to court. I don't know why. There's a tradition in baseball that you keep your troubles inside the locker room, no matter how bad a beating you are taking. In later years, I let it be known that I was ready to go into court at even the whisper of a conspiracy; I felt that would help me get back into baseball.

They had me. The Browns were as close to being a road-team as it is possible to be; I was absolutely dependent upon those road receipts. While we might draw some fairly decent crowds at night, we had no chance of drawing anything on week days. My choice was to sue or to throw in the towel.

I pondered it a long time before I threw in the towel.

In those days, the rules called for each team to play two night games in every other city, with a third game to be played at the option of both teams. Under normal circumstances, a night game against the Yankees is worth $30,000 more than a day game. The Yankees therefore awarded the third game to their friends and withheld it from any operator who did not take kindly to their whip.

The Yankees were also able to reward their friends with the usual patronage a winner can dispense, such as extra World Series' tickets. Most important of all, perhaps, the Yankees always had their great pool of young players, and the overflow from that pool also trickled down to their friends. When you run a tight 6 percent operation like Clark Griffith always ran in Washington, all these things were important.

And this is why my Phoenix proposals hit George Weiss right between the eyes. The Unrestricted Draft threatened both his minor-league empire and the power that empire gave him over the rest of the league. A pooling of television receipts hit him in the same place. Without minimizing the effectiveness with which the Yankees use their money, it is money that makes their operation go, far more money than is available to any other team. Take the $2,000,000 that television dumps into the Yankee coffers. Every penny of that money goes, in one way or another, to find and to sign new players. They might just as well spend it; the Government would get about half of it anyway.

Whenever I offered any plan that would give the other teams a fighting chance against them, the Yankees always cried socialism, the first refuge of scoundrels. I say it is not socialism to tighten competition; I say it is capitalism at its best. The essence of capitalism is competition, and there is no competition when you are playing with a stacked deck. Weiss made his reputation by starting off so far ahead of the field every year that he almost had to break a leg to lose. The fallacy of this kind of "competition" is that it doesn't really help the Yankees either. We are in a strange business; we are in competition and yet we are partners. Weak teams like Washington, Kansas City and Los Angeles are a drag on all of us. The best year the American League ever had was in 1948, when the Indians, Red Sox and Yankees went down to the wire together, with Philadelphia in contention all the way into the stretch. In 1961, with a little help from luck and providence, Detroit was in the pennant race into September, and in a 3-game Series at Yankee Stadium, drew a total of 171,503 customers. It was this Series—together with the home-run hitting of Maris and Mantle—that made the Yankees' season for them.

It was not wholly a coincidence, then, that the Unrestricted Draft—

278

even in its watered-down form—did not get passed until after George Weiss left the Yankees.

So remember that the Phoenix meeting was in the background, with all its heat and intrigue, when Eliot Stein called to tell me that Gussie Busch was going to buy the Cardinals. Within the hour I was talking to Russ Lynch, the sports editor of the Milwaukee *Journal,* to start the Browns rolling toward Milwaukee.

Milwaukee's attraction went even beyond my pleasant associations of the past. The county was already in the process of building a $5,000,000 stadium.

The head of the county board was Bill McGovern, an old friend. I had been in communication with Bill from the time Saigh was ordered to sell his team. I had also been in communication of sorts with Los Angeles and Baltimore.

The great complication in Milwaukee was that the Brewers no longer were owned by Oscar Salinger. Oscar had offered the club to me in 1946 right after I bought the Indians. I was in no position then to swing it, and so he had sold to Lou Perini of the Boston Braves. Before I could move to Milwaukee I had to deal with Perini for the territorial rights.

I urged McGovern to push the stadium to completion for the start of the upcoming season. "Either we'll be playing there on opening day," I said, "or someone will." My intention was to force Perini either to move to Milwaukee himself or to sell his rights to me. If he didn't move and wouldn't sell, I was going to draft the territory and move in anyway.

Perini was a problem. The whole saga of the moving of the St. Louis franchise—a two-year, two-chapter horror story—was a wonder of bad timing and, to some extent, bad luck. The whole thing had started, when you think about it, because Fred Saigh didn't make out his income tax right. There wasn't much I could have done about that. Faced with the necessity of evacuating St. Louis because of Saigh's financial *gaffe* with the Government, I now found myself butting my head against Lou Perini's attendance problems in Boston. The Braves had let their team decay. After drawing more than a million customers in 1947-48-49, their attendance had dropped, in the season just ended, to an impossible 280,000. Perini had been watching that stadium going up in Milwaukee himself.

Talk about bad timing. If the Milwaukee club had still been in-dependently operated or if I had been able to buy it from Salinger, I would have moved in with no trouble at all. If Salinger had sold to

279

anybody except the Braves, I would have been able to buy the territorial rights without any difficulty. A year earlier, and Perini would have been willing to sell. A year later, the Braves, who were rebuilding, had leaped from 7th place to 2nd and probably would have drawn well enough in Boston to make it impossible for Perini, a local man, to leave. There is a tide in the affairs of man which taken at the ebb leaves you fishing in mud flats. The tide was running low for me.

I talked to Perini perhaps a dozen times, trying to wear him down or, failing that, at least to get a definite answer. He was religiously noncommittal. He kept insisting that he wanted to stay in Boston, but he kept evading the question of his Milwaukee rights.

Talk being unavailing, I decided to try money. Perini was very closely associated in Milwaukee with Fred Miller of Miller Hi-Life beer (an old handball opponent of mine during the Milwaukee days, although I knew him only as a guy named "Fritz" until I went to his office one day to negotiate a concession contract). I met with Bobby Uihlein of Schlitz beer, in Chicago, to find out whether he would be interested in buying the radio-TV rights from me and, in the bargain, keeping Miller Hi-Life out. He was interested enough, on both counts, to offer Perini $750,000 for the territorial rights to Milwaukee. Not for the park or the players; just for the rights. I even arranged to buy the territorial rights to Toledo, which had just dropped out of the American Association, so that Perini would be able to pick up his old Milwaukee team and move right in.

I kept Russ Lynch informed of everything I was doing, so that the pressure would stay on Perini. Sell or move, Lou. Sell or move.

Perini's move was to call Frick into action to try to shut me up and shut me out. The Commissioner began to phone me regularly to tell me what a terrible thing I was doing to this nice Mr. Perini. "Yeah," I'd say, "I'm trying to give him a terrible amount of money. If he wants to move I can't stop him. If he doesn't, let him get out of the way."

"He doesn't want to leave Boston," Frick would say. "But he thinks he might want to leave next year."

"You want me to stay in St. Louis and lose money for everybody in our league," I'd say, "to protect Milwaukee for Perini in case he wants to move in some day. You're a great Commissioner, Commissioner."

Not being able to get a definite answer out of Perini, I was also talking to Baltimore, the only other city that was building a stadium. I had eliminated Los Angeles because it was already too close to the opening of the season to convert Wrigley Field into a major-league park. I only had to look at the Coliseum once to see that it was impossible to play baseball there—as Abner Doubleday and I understood the game—a fact which Walter O'Malley conclusively proved when he moved the Brooklyn Dodgers into the Coliseum six years later.

By this time, spring training had begun, and the Tampa meeting, which had been scheduled to find a new home for the Browns, was drawing near. Frick wrote me a letter—which he also released as a public statement—censuring me for "adversely affecting" the minor-league operations in Milwaukee and Baltimore with all my talk about moving a major-league franchise.

Within the space of one week he made the following statements:

a) "Attempts to transfer ball clubs at this time are nonsensical. I have no such proposal in front of me, but if I did I would not sanction it."

b) "There is nothing in the book that says they need my approval. I repeat that I believe it is nonsensical at this time but I am powerless to stop it."

c) "Move now or shut up."

Two or three days before the scheduled meeting at Tampa, the Commissioner summoned both leagues to a joint meeting in Belleair, a small Florida resort to which he retreats annually in order to rest up from those long, rigorous afternoons at Toots Shor's.

The meeting had been called, quite obviously, at Perini's urging and it was kept remarkably secret. Perini was still crying that he did not want to leave Boston. All I could do was tell him how happy that made me because, Lord only knew, I didn't want him to leave Boston either.

He was terribly upset. He got up on his feet and complained that I was forcing him to move by enlisting the aid of the Milwaukee papers to make the city dissatisfied with a minor-league club.

I said, "No, I'm not forcing you to do anything. I'm offering you three-quarters of a million dollars for something you bought for $250,000. And you're keeping your ball club and getting the rights to Toledo."

That didn't impress anybody as strongly as it seemed to impress me. The attitude of Frick and the National League was that I was perpetrating an unforgivable fraud on their nice Mr. Perini.

"Will somebody please tell me what I'm doing to him except making him a lot of money," I kept saying. "If he wants to move why doesn't he move? If he doesn't want to move, what's all the yelling about?"

Frick countered neatly with a statement that certain irresponsible operators, unnamed, were running off half-cocked and jeopardizing everybody's investments. I got a little warm myself and said I saw no reason for the Commissioner not to look ahead and try to find a way to improve the structure of baseball. "You're here yelling because you think Perini has been hurt," I told him. "I was under the impression that the Commissioner was supposed to look after baseball in general, not just one league and not just one club."

The Commissioner thereupon struck a leonine pose and delivered one of his dynamic orations. I awoke in time to hear Perini announce that due to the dirty trick I was playing on him, he had no alternative but to move to Milwaukee himself. A National League meeting was quickly scheduled in St. Petersburg, two days after the American League meeting at Tampa.

Perini loved Boston so much, though, that he could not bear to tell them. He kept insisting to the very end that he was staying on to build anew.

As a parting shot, the Commissioner ruled that Toledo was American Association territory, not International League territory. Since I now had to turn to Baltimore, which had a club in the International League, my option was no good. Frick, in a word, had turned Toledo over to Perini.

All this time, I had been buttonholing my fellow club owners and receiving their assurances that they were behind me no matter where I wanted to go. The American League rules require a ¾ majority for the moving of a franchise, which meant I needed five votes in addition to my own. I had five definite commitments, one maybe, and one probable no.

The Yankees were the only team that hedged. Del Webb's attitude was that Milwaukee was all right with him, but that he had his reservations about Baltimore. I took that to mean I wouldn't be getting his vote. Joe Cronin was noncommittal at Boston, too, but Yawkey told me he'd go along with the majority whichever way they voted.

Frank Lane, of course, was with me all the way.

Ellis Ryan at Cleveland told me, "Of course, Bill. Do anything you want."

"Either Milwaukee or Baltimore?" I asked.

"Sure," he said. "Done."

The commitments from Detroit and Philadelphia were just as firm.

Clark Griffith was very enthusiastic about Milwaukee, and while he was a bit more reserved about Baltimore, he had promised me, point-blank, that I could count on him to support me wherever I decided to go.

282

As the meeting at Belleair was breaking up, I polled them all again and found I still had my solid 6 votes.

Griffith was the man I was worried about. Baltimore is only 40 miles away from Washington, and Griffith had always enjoyed a certain amount of Baltimore patronage. That 7–1 vote against me on the sharing of television fees kept sticking in my craw. I could see where the proposal for an Unrestricted Draft might be too violent a change for old-timers like Griffith and the Mack boys in Philadelphia (although not for Connie Mack himself), but I had never been able to understand why they had voted against accepting money which they both badly needed.

The only logical tie-in I could find was the prospect of my moving to Baltimore. I could just hear Griffith telling Roy and Earle Mack, "If we let that jerk get in between us with his circuses, he's going to make us both go to work."

No, it was difficult to escape the conclusion—or at any rate, the strong possibility—that the Yankees had entered into a deal with Washington and Philadelphia. In return for the votes that would crush all further talk of sharing television fees, the Yankees could promise to prevent me from moving into Baltimore in the event that Perini stopped me from moving to Milwaukee.

For although Griffith had the votes to stop me without the Yankees, I could see where he needed the Yankees to run interference for him.

The American League—and, I would suppose, all leagues—is filled with cabals and alliances which, given the circumstances, are fairly predictable. The Mack boys were the weak link in the league. They wouldn't be sure what their self-interest was in this matter until Griffith told them. On any matter where their own self-interest wasn't involved, Boston and Detroit would always vote with Griffith too. The Boston alliance was easily explained. Joe Cronin is Griffith's son-in-law, Spike Briggs at Detroit and Griffith shared a less obvious but even closer bond than a mere blood relationship; they shared a mutual distaste for Gabe Murphy, the Senators' minority stockholder.

But for Griffith to defeat me with these four votes would be to defeat his own purpose. Griffith was in a box. He would lose most of his Baltimore patronage if he let me into Baltimore, all right, but he would lose it all if he took any part in keeping me and major-league baseball out. The Yankees' proposition, as I saw it, was that he and his friends would be able to vote for me and leave it up to the Yankees to organize the campaign against me.

The only way I could be sure I had Griffith completely tied up was to make it worth his while. I had been feeding him rosy dreams about a Baltimore-Washington feud that would more than make up for those lost night riders. Knowing that Griff was not promotional-minded, and also knowing that he liked to see the money on the table, I put what amounted to $150,000 a year in front of him.

Several sponsors had bid for the television rights to Baltimore. I had chosen Jerry Hoffberger of the National Brewing Company, who also happened to be Washington's TV sponsor, because I liked him personally. The television rights in Baltimore were far more valuable than in Washington. Jerry was paying me $300,000, twice what he was paying Griff. But when I discussed the situation with Jerry, he volunteered to sweeten the pot for Griff by offering him the same fee he was paying me *on condition that there was baseball in Baltimore.* Griff accepted with alacrity, and the contract was prepared. Now he was sewed up. No if's, but's or maybe's.

I came to the Tampa meeting with Mayor Tommy D'Alesandro and two or three Baltimore officials. We all assumed that we were merely to go through the formalities of presenting our case for the record. I was to address the meeting and make my pitch, then D'Alesandro was to make a Chamber of Commerce talk about the capacity of the new stadium and the potentialities of his city. If we could keep from being carried away by our own rhetoric, the whole meeting figured to last maybe fifteen minutes.

We were not alone in that belief. The story about the two meetings had finally broken, and every sportswriter in every American League city had been writing that the shift to Baltimore was a foregone conclusion. I know because I checked every paper in every city afterwards. As the first franchise shift in 50 years, this was a front-page story, well checked and well covered. The writers all knew the shift was going to be approved because the owners of every American League club had assured them that the meeting was just a matter of routine.

Two days before the meeting, the Griffiths had calmed the lingering fears of the Baltimore writers by assuring them that they would not oppose the move. "As far as I know," Cal Griffith said, "no club will oppose the shift."

Will Harridge was quoted as saying that the move to Baltimore had already been approved, which was something Will honestly believed. The American League owners had been telling him it was just a formality too.

The International League, having been informed that Baltimore would be moving into the American League, scheduled a meeting of

284

their own, the day after our meeting, to decide where to move their old Baltimore franchise.

And, of course, the National League, having been told at Belleair that the American League was solidly behind me, was about to hold a meeting of their own to give Perini permission to move to Milwaukee.

I walked into that meeting at the Tampa Terrace Hotel with firm commitments for a 6–2 vote, and an excellent chance for a 7–1 vote. Since the Yankees don't like to be on the losing end of that kind of score, the distinct probability was that it would be announced as a unanimous vote.

In less than five minutes, I knew that I had been had. They had let me crawl all the way out on the limb, and they were gathered there, this parliament of my peers, to cut it off.

I have been given to understand that the eastern clubs had twice caucused to line up solidly against me. I also have heard that on the day before the league meeting, there had been a third get-together in Tampa to bring Cleveland and Detroit into the ranks, undoubtedly because Griffith and the Yankees wanted it to look as if the league was solidly against me, for the good and sufficient reasons that would be laboriously worked up, rather than like an eastern cabal to keep me from competing with them.

They hit me with it while I was still delivering my opening address. Roy Mack, hardly a leader in these councils, stood up and said, "I don't see why you want to leave St. Louis. We'd never leave Philadelphia."

I broke back in to tell him that Philadelphia would most assuredly be the next franchise to take wing. "Oh, no," he said. "No. Never." He delivered a moving speech about the glorious traditions of Philadelphia baseball, interspersed with a few kind words about civic loyalty and eternal ties. When a baseball owner talks about civic loyalty *to other club owners,* you know the fix is in.

Spike Briggs of Detroit followed with an equally inspiring speech. One by one, they arose, in almost high-schoolish arrangement, each of them in turn coming up with a new objection. One expressed doubts that the schedule could be rearranged only three weeks before the opening of the season, another had misgivings that the railroad transportation could be straightened out. Still another—I forget who—had come equipped with a legal opinion that we would all be in default of our television contracts, which I found somewhat bewildering since I didn't have a television contract and I doubted whether anybody else's sponsor would be mad enough to go to court because the guys in the gray uniforms called themselves the Baltimore Orioles instead of the St. Louis Browns.

It was a good hour before Tommy D'Alesandro was called in to make his presentation. I left after another hour or so to tell him we had blown it. D'Alesandro, being a good politician, wasn't exactly shocked. "When I wasn't called in after fifteen minutes," he said, "I knew something had gone wrong."

The newspapermen camped outside in the lobby still had no idea that I was being bushwhacked, although the long delay was beginning to make them nervous. Ford Frick put them at ease, quite innocently. My colleagues had kept their secret so well that they hadn't even told him. Frick, who had wandered down into the lobby from his hotel suite long after I knew I was dead, led them to believe—as he believed —that the vote was a foregone conclusion. "It looks," he said, "like St. Louis can't support two teams."

The writers, assuming that Frick had come from the meeting rather than from his own suite, relaxed. Actually, the Commissioner never attends a league meeting. Only joint meetings. When I left the conference room to carry the news to D'Alesandro they assumed that I had been asked to leave while the vote was being taken. I hadn't. I had left because I had no appetite to watch the farce played out to the end. As the operator of the St. Louis franchise I had every right to vote. I had voted, in fact, in the preliminary ballots. During baseball meetings, they're always taking preliminary votes. A preliminary vote means: "This isn't an official vote, but if it were an official vote how would you have voted?" We play all kinds of fascinating little games in there.

The preliminary voting, like the final vote, was always 6–2, with only Frank Lane standing with me.

The assumption that St. Louis didn't vote because I was out of the room led, incidentally, to a misconception about the final vote. It was reported as 5–2 against me, with Lane and Greenberg as the two supporting votes. It was 6–2.

Greenberg, who was there with Vice-President George Medinger, was under orders to vote against me. Cleveland insisted they would have been with me if their vote had meant anything, and perhaps they would have. I know Hank would have liked to vote for me.

As a matter of fact, he almost did. The moment I left the room, George Weiss got up and said, "Veeck is a lousy operator, we all know that. He owes the league money. The American League will be better off without him."

Hank leaped up and said, "Now wait a minute. If the vote is against

286

the moving of a franchise because we think it will be harmful to the league that's one thing. But if this is going to become a personal indictment of Bill Veeck, let's review the bidding."

The money I owed the league, incidentally, was a $300,000 debt I had inherited from Bill DeWitt.

The first thing I did after I left D'Alesandro was to call Mary Frances. She had been waiting for the call, and as time kept passing and the phone remained silent she had begun to pace back and forth in the living room, her eyes on the floor. The room was done in green carpeting and draperies, and the longer she paced and the later it got, the stronger became the premonition of disaster. To her, the whole affair has a sort of greenish haze to it. Even today, she cannot see that particular shade of green without shivering.

Once the voting was announced, there was nothing left to do but to smile. I quoted Adlai Stevenson on Abraham Lincoln—which put me back with big-leaguers—about feeling like the boy who had stubbed his toe: "It hurts too much to laugh and I'm too big to cry."

"The timing is bad now," Frick said. "It's too close to the start of the season. And there are contracts involved with television and radio people and concessionaires."

The sportswriters, taking him at his word, were unanimously wrong once again on the National League meeting at St. Petersburg across the bay, a pardonable mistake in that the National League meeting took place two days closer to the start of the season.

In addition, the National League rules called not for a ¾ vote but for a unanimous vote. I knew Perini would get it. I went to the bar at the Tampa Terrace after the vote was announced to meet all comers, joke with those who wanted to joke and accept the commiserations of those who wanted to sympathize. I predicted that Perini would be allowed to move to Milwaukee, and was immediately besieged by an adoring public anxious to take my money away. "I'll do better than that," I said. "I'm not a betting man but in this case I'll bet anybody a suit of clothes that he'll not only be allowed to move but that in his first season in Milwaukee, he'll draw more people than the Yankees." The Yankee Stadium capacity is 67,000; Milwaukee Stadium at the time was 36,000.

They were jumping over tables to get at me. If I had been a betting man and I'd had any guts, I'd have owned half the state of Florida. As it was I didn't have to buy a suit of clothes for five years.

Perini, of course, got his unanimous vote. Bob Carpenter of the Phils, for one, had bitterly assailed me for embarrassing baseball.

287

"Did you ever hear of a more asinine thing than to try to put over something like this just before the start of the season?"

Carpenter voted for Perini, though.

The National League schedule was changed without any trouble at all. There were no insurmountable troubles about transportation, a tribute, no doubt, to the efficiency of the railroad industry. The radio and television contracts—and Perini *did* have a television contract—were adjusted without difficulty. So were the concession contracts.

I wired Perini:

> I AM VERY HAPPY OVER THE DECISION TO MOVE THE BRAVES
> TO MILWAUKEE. I AM SURE IT WILL STRENGTHEN THE LEAGUE,
> AND THE FANS OF MILWAUKEE ARE CERTAINLY DESERVING OF
> MAJOR-LEAGUE BASEBALL. SOME OF THE DAMAGES I HAVE AL-
> LEGEDLY CAUSED HAVE BEEN RECTIFIED BY THE ACTIONS OF THE
> NATIONAL LEAGUE. I WISH YOU AND YOUR CLUB THE BEST OF
> LUCK.

I was more than broke. Although we had finished in the black in St. Louis—just barely—I had gone into hock for almost $400,000 buying players so that we would move into Baltimore with a respectable team. I had been operating again, like in those old days in Milwaukee, by paying "five thousand down and the rest when you can catch me." I had, for instance, paid $100,000 for a shortstop, Billy Hunter. Almost all of it was still owed to the Dodgers.

After the Tampa meeting, I sat at the bar with Frank Lane drinking beer until they closed the joint down. When nobody but Frank and I were left, I said, "Frank, this club has me insured for a million dollars. The best thing I can do for it now is to jump out of a high window."

"No, you won't," Frank said. "Because if you do, you'll never be able to needle the Yankees again. If you had only been able to keep yourself from needling Weiss, you'd be in Baltimore now, do you know that? And the next time you're at a meeting with Weiss—after all this—you're going to start right in on him again. No, I'm not afraid of you going out of any windows. You've got too much to live for."

And I guess he was right. Against all self-interest and the best resolve, there is something about George Weiss I find irresistible.

Had I tried to bull my way into first Milwaukee and then Baltimore? I had. There was no other way to do it. If baseball owners ran Congress, Kansas and Nebraska would still be trying to get into the Union. Had I given them only three weeks notice as they claimed? Nonsense. I had informed them officially at Phoenix more than four months before the start of the season. That alibi died painfully when

288

the National League approved Perini's shift to Milwaukee on less than a week's notice.

If I had not tried to bull it through, I think it is quite possible that baseball would still be precisely where it was in 1952, which means it would be precisely where it was in 1902. I would have sold the Browns to some beer company or insurance men and they would still be bumbling along in St. Louis. Perini would have remained in Boston. The expansion to the west—justified, lest everybody forget, by the tremendous success of baseball in Milwaukee—would still be denounced as the propaganda of radicals, dreamers and guys who send midgets to bat. If Perini had not been riding high in Milwaukee, O'Malley would probably never have left Brooklyn for Los Angeles.

There is one other question that should not be left hanging. Since I had intended to move to Milwaukee, with or without the territorial rights, if Perini remained in Boston, why didn't I move into Baltimore, with or without league permission? We did discuss it. But here was where the strategy of gulling me along to the last minute paid off. At one time, we did have a couple of lawyers looking into the question of whether I could go to Baltimore if the league voted against me. We pulled them off after we had Clark Griffith's signature on the TV contract.

The season was about to start in three weeks. If we were going to move, we had to move almost before sundown. We weren't that sure of our legal ground.

Over the next season, though, we had half a dozen lawyers looking into every possible facet of it, and they prepared a long legal brief. Boiled down to a couple of paragraphs, the brief stated that while the American League was most assuredly a group of men bound by their own rules and regulations, no group of men has the right, under any conditions, to enter into a conspiracy to deliberately bankrupt another man. Since it was evident on the face of the situation that it was in their self-interest to have me in Baltimore and against their self-interest to have me in St. Louis—i.e., they would all make money in Baltimore and lose money in St. Louis—it was obvious that they were keeping me in St. Louis only because they did not like me personally. By that time, we had enough evidence of the meetings in Phoenix, Washington, New York and Tampa to establish a prima facie case of conspiracy according to my legal advice.

It is illegal, my lawyers said, for a group of individuals to get together to cause injury or loss to any other individual. It is not only illegal to do it, it is illegal to even discuss it. That is what the laws

289

against restraint of trade—the monopoly laws—apparently are all about.

If we were voted down again the next year, we were prepared to move to Baltimore anyway. If we were written out of the schedule, we were prepared to sue for triple damages. But that's another year, another set of circumstances and another knife in the back.

As it was, with the Tampa meeting in dust around me, Will Harridge and Ben Fiery told me that a special committee would be set up to study the qualifications of Baltimore and that I would most certainly be permitted to move the following year. I'm sure that both Will and Ben, two honorable men and two men I am extremely fond of, believed it. Would you believe it, I believed it too!

A Night at Toots Shor's | 20.

CALL me Ishmael.

I went back to St. Louis, the villain returning to the scene of the crime, and tried to stay alive through the season. I was a villain without any money, which—all things considered—is the worst kind of villain to be. I was an unrepentant villain, which didn't do me much good either.

What killed me in St. Louis in the end was that I was underfinanced. For that, I had my own greed to blame. Not circumstances, bad luck or bad timing. Good old-fashioned greed. Knowing how much work it was going to take to build up the Browns, I had easily convinced myself that I was entitled to a good percentage of the syndicate; 33⅓ percent sounded just about right. After all the stock had rolled in, our 79.9 percent cost us $1,750,000. As always, I borrowed a million from the bank in the name of the club and as always I set up the debenture-stock grouping. As always, I was short-bankrolled. Before I could pick up the percentage I had assigned myself, I had to borrow money on my own. By being that anxious to throw everything I could lay my hands on into stock, I left myself without too much of an operating cushion right from the start. Even worse, I was not in a position either to sell any of my stock or to borrow against it after the league sent us back to St. Louis. Almost all of the stock was in hock to start with. I couldn't borrow on the ball park either; it was already heavily mortgaged when we took over from DeWitt. (Due to a small fine-type

290

sentence, overlooked by everybody at the closing, we were in default of that mortgage every second we were in St. Louis. The insurance company that held the mortgage had specifically forbidden the liquidation of the original borrowing company, the Dodier Realty Co. After it was discovered, I'd go down to the bank three times a week to dance, sing and tell funny stories to discourage them from calling the loan on such a nice fellow as me.)

My principal backers in the St. Louis syndicate are important because they figure strongly in the bitter league meeting at the end of the season when the St. Louis franchise was disposed of. Art Allyn and Newt Frye, from the Chicago syndicate, came in for their usual percentages, even after I spelled out all the problems. The others contented themselves with investing small token sums. That was all right with me. I came to them offering a business deal, and if they thought it was a bad deal, they'd be crazy to invest their money. I was left, however, with the necessity of raising more than the usual 20 percent from the local representation in St. Louis. It wasn't local representation at all in the usual sense—I was looking for St. Louis backing.

My original backer in St. Louis was Sid Salomon. I had met Sidney a few times at Toots Shor's and taken to him from the first. He was well-connected politically and he knew his way around St. Louis. He also knew his way around baseball. Salomon had been the partner of Steve Hannegan, Truman's Postmaster General, in an insurance company. Sid had set up the deal by which Hannegan had bought control of the Cardinals in 1947, and he had come out with a 10 percent interest in the Cards.

My main backer, the man who had the largest block of stock next to myself, was Mark Steinberg, another of the remarkable men I have found myself associated with in baseball. Mark had gone bankrupt during the Depression and, after great difficulties, had battled his way back up to where he owned his own brokerage house. He was a great baseball fan. I had seen him at just about every World Series, a short, spare, quiet man; one of those men you know by sight but not by name. Sidney Weil, who had owned the Cincinnati Reds in the early thirties, had put me in touch with Mark as soon as he heard I was trying to put together a St. Louis syndicate. Weil had taken a liking to me when I was a kid traveling around with my father and, like so many of my father's friends, he had always been very kind to me.

Weil set up an appointment at the Coronado Hotel in San Diego where Steinberg vacationed annually to get the sun and play the horses. I didn't say bet the horses, I said play. That's what it was for Mark— play. He bet small amounts, and he kept meticulous records of his

291

handicapping and his bets and his current balance. It was the winning that was important to Mark, not the winning of money. I can understand that. Despite all my talk about greed and finance, it is the winning that has always been important to me. If I can set up the deal I want and put all the elements together just as I planned, that's winning. If, through dozens of trades, I can piece together the kind of team I've set out to build, that's winning too. The money is secondary. Money I can always make. Hank Greenberg has told me often that if I'd put what promotional abilities I have to work in fields where there is real money to be made, I'd be a millionaire. I have no objection against being a millionaire that can't be easily overcome, but, all things being equal, I'd rather be in baseball.

What I'm trying to say is that Mark and I hit it off right away. He was eager to back me. He felt, as I did, that we could take Fred Saigh. He was eager to give me names of friends in St. Louis who would want to come into the syndicate. He was eager to throw himself into the task of collecting the 75 percent we needed to complete the purchase. He was an enormous help in untangling the Browns' finances, which wove back through DeWitt to the two previous owners.

Perhaps he did too much. Mark died in our first year in St. Louis. If Mark Steinberg had been alive in 1953, I do not think I would have lost the franchise.

All cities have a major luncheon or dinner the day before the season opens. In St. Louis, it was the Chamber of Commerce press luncheon honoring both the Browns and the Cards.

To everybody's surprise, the villain showed up and took his place at the head table. When I was introduced, a volley of silence rang out through the room. I didn't try to kid them or con them or woo them. I told them our prospects were not bright and that I would probably have to do something I had never thought I'd be doing as a big-league operator—sell players to keep a club going. In closing, I told them a lot of moves would be made to try to build up the club in the face of whatever difficulties we encountered. "But," I said, laying it on the line, "not all the moves we would have liked to make."

I sat down to the biggest hand I had ever been given in St. Louis.

But what can you do in a city that knows you are there against your will and have every intention of getting out as soon as possible? In the first week or so, I made some appearances. The first question, always, was whether I intended to remain in St. Louis. As soon as I said I was going to make every effort to move at the end of the year, a certain warmth went out of the room. So, in fact, did much of the audience. I couldn't blame them. I gave up trying to promote and just settled back in my cell and dug in to last out the season.

Don't let anyone tell you that a team is not affected by the attitude of the crowd. The apathy in the stands brought on a lethargy in the field. We had a good team, a team that had figured to make a run for the first division. We finished dead last. I couldn't blame the players, either. The little Brownies who lived through both the Hornsby regime and the cold war of 1953 are entitled to wear a couple of campaign ribbons on their uniforms.

The apathy hanging heavily over the ball park was broken only by the happy folk ritual of hanging Bill Veeck in effigy. If we could have charged admission for effigies and let the fans in free, our books might have come closer to balancing. I suppose there is something funny in watching some deserving wretch hung in effigy—until you find yourself being cast for the title role. And when they started burning those effigies, my sense of humor left me. What is it they say about coming events casting their shadow before?

At the beginning, I was a little worried about Mary Frances. Anybody who has a television show becomes readily recognizable in the street, and the cabdrivers and truck drivers had become accustomed to yelling greetings as she passed. Fortunately, Mary Frances can take care of herself. Whenever a cabdriver challenged her about moving the club, she would tell him, frankly and simply, that while baseball was a sport it was also a business. The Veecks, she would point out, had no brewery or construction company going for them. "Bill has only one means of supporting our family," she would tell them. "The ball club. If you were in his position, what would you do?" Put in those terms, the cabbie was willing to agree that he'd catch the next freight train out of town. The working man understands that economics begin at the grocery store.

The press wasn't as willing to see our side as the cabdrivers were. I expected a bad press. I expected to be stuck up on the spit and roasted through the year. I also expected that in our personal relationship the writers and I would remain friends. What happened was exactly the opposite. In their columns, they urged the customers to come out to the park to prove to the world that St. Louis could support the Browns. In our personal relationship, they cut us dead. It hurt. These were men who had spent hour after hour with us in the ball park apartment. They were so close to us that Mary Frances could have lectured on the state of their respective digestive tracts. Sure, I had done something they disapproved of. But as a person I was the same guy they had laughed with. They didn't act as if I had run off with their daughter, they acted as if I had run off with their wife.

I have a philosophy about the press. The only time I have ever taken exception to anything written about me was the garbling of the facts in the Hornsby cup presentation. The most cutting and caustic writer in Cleveland was Whitey Lewis. Whitey could take me apart in the afternoon paper, and in the evening we would meet at Gruber's, two guys who enjoyed each other's company. If I mentioned the column at all it would be to congratulate him on the felicity of a phrase or the fine cutting edge of his prose.

Well, I had other things to worry about. Like survival. I don't believe in going back to my stockholders for money. Even if I could, I had led them into this mess and it was my problem to get them out. The problem can be expressed in fairly basic economic terms: we were deeply in debt, we had no money and we had no credit. Bills were going to fall due all during the season on the players I had bought on the prospect that we would be in Baltimore. Payrolls were going to have to be met. To balance those bleak prospects, season tickets were being canceled by the hundreds.

I had two sources of immediate revenue: my ranch in Arizona and Sportsman's Park. Before the season began, I was negotiating to sell them both.

A deal had already been set up for Gussie Busch to buy the park if I had gone to Baltimore. The first time Busch visited the park, I had invited him to the apartment, confided that I was about to be run out of town and suggested that the least he could do was buy the park. The terms were $800,000 when we got permission to move and another $300,000 when we did move. As a public relations gesture, Busch had to deplore our imminent departure when the news broke out of Tampa and express his confidence in the city's ability to support two teams. I would have done much the same thing myself. Practically speaking, he was the first outsider to know we were leaving. Financially speaking, he was putting up $300,000 to speed us on our way.

I was a disappointment to him; I came back. I was willing to make amends by selling him the park anyway. After that first meeting we dealt entirely through emissaries, but Busch could hardly have been unaware that I needed that money desperately. He was perfectly willing to pay me the $800,000. He did not see why he should pay me the $300,000 for leaving when any fool could see that I was still there.

There was an even more pressing reason why I had to sell it to him before the season opened. Sportsman's Park was old and run-

294

down to begin with, and I had not had the money to keep it in repair, something that violated my basic precept of operation and broke my heart. The park was so badly run-down that upon my return to St. Louis the city handed me four full pages of repairs, all of them vital and urgent and all of them costing money. Unless the more flagrant violations were rectified by opening day, the park was going to be condemned. For awhile, it looked as if I was going to find myself in a position where the league wouldn't let me move and the city wouldn't let me play.

Let me tell you something. When you own a park which is in default of its mortgage and about to be condemned, you are not in the best position to drive a hard bargain. Still, there was no doubt in my mind that I was going to get the full price.

In that old, ramshackle park of mine we had one little oasis of class, the private box with the connecting bar where, if you remember, the Falstaff people had sat to watch Eddie Gaedel come to bat. It was a fine little box with a fine little bar, and Gussie Busch's eyes lit up at the sight of it when I first showed him through the park.

I informed his people that as long as I owned the park, the box was off-limits to him, just as it had been off-limits to Fred Saigh. Busch had invited his best friends and customers to the park for his first opening day and, as his emissary made clear, he lusted after that box so that he could entertain them in style. Not a chance, I said.

A week before the season opened, he agreed to pay the full $1,100,-000—which now broke down to $800,000 for the park and $300,000 for the box.

I mentioned, rather casually, that before he signed the contract he would do well to check the list of repairs ordered by the city, so that he would understand what he was getting into. "Never mind that," he said.

"It's important," I told him, "because I'm going to attach the list to the contract as part of the deal."

"Fine," he said, "fine."

The repairs cost him over a million—maybe more than he paid for the park itself. But minor items like repairs didn't bother him.

The mortgage on the park took almost one-half of the sales price; the rest of the money went to pay off the debts already due. The sale of the ranch gave me operating funds to start the season.

After the ranch money went, we lived from day to day. To show how tight things were, Rudie came in one morning and told me, "Well, we'll meet another payroll. I just mortgaged my house." That's the kind of guy Rudie is.

We did have some treasury stock; that is, stock which had been voted in the original incorporation but had never been issued. Colonel Shoenberg, a close friend of Mark Steinberg's and a small stockholder himself, kept us going by buying a block of this stock for himself and his sons, a great kindness since I don't think I have to point out that the St. Louis Browns, at that moment, hardly rated as a blue-chip investment.

When things are going wrong, all you have to do is keep a smile on your face and a song on your lips and you can be sure they will get worse. Everything that could conceivably go wrong, went wrong.

It was bad enough that we had no income from television. I had fixed it so that we had no income from radio either. I had been so sure we'd have the Browns in contention within three years that I had proposed a rising-scale contract to Falstaff's for both 1952 and 1953. If we didn't finish above 7th place, they were to pay us only $1 for the rights. If we got up to sixth, it was $5,000, fifth was $20,000 and if we reached the first division we would get $50,000. If we won the pennant, Falstaff would have paid us $250,000 and I would have been able to ride an open car in another victory parade and toss pennies to the children in the streets. With a team like the Browns, which has little chance of doing the sponsor any good unless it is winning, that's the only fair way to do it. But while we were scrambling for pennies thrown by kind and charitable children we were getting nothing from radio.

And finally, there was visited upon us in our time of travail the final affliction of Bobo Holloman's no-hitter. Now really. I know Job had a hard time of it, in spots, but Bobo's no-hitter would have broken his spirit.

I had bought Bobo Holloman from Syracuse on a trial basis, for $10,000 down plus another $25,000 if I kept him after the June 15 cutdown date. Bobo turned out to be a character. He called himself "Big Bobo," and he had charm and he had humor and he had un-limited—if sadly misplaced—confidence in himself. Big Bobo was born to be a hinterlands drummer. He could outtalk me, outpester and outcon me. Unfortunately, he could not outpitch me. In spring training, he was hit harder trying to get the batters out than our batting practice pitchers who were trying to let them hit. That sounds as if I'm trying to make a point through exaggeration. I'm not. It is literally true. I knew he had to be better than that, once he rounded into form. I had a $10,000 investment that told me he had to be better than that.

He did little to encourage me in that simple, capitalistic faith. In his

296

few relief appearances after the season started, Big Bobo was bombed. He was a lot of fun and I loved him dearly when he was away from the pitcher's mound, but the only thing left for me to do was to write off the $10,000 and hustle him back to Syracuse in time to get out from under that $25,000. So Bobo reached into his drummer's bag and went to work on us. "You haven't given Big Bobo any chance," he'd tell Marty Marion. "Big Bobo isn't a relief pitcher, he's a starter. Big Bobo can pitch better than half the guys you've got starting."

When he felt he had Marty softened up, he turned his con on me. What a salesman Bobo was. At last Marty asked me whether I wanted to give Big Bobo the start he was pleading for, a standard courtesy when a manager knows the operator is about to send a player away. "All right," I said. "Let's give Big Bobo his big chance or he'll be on our ears all the way to the train station."

Big Bobo went out and pitched against the Athletics, the softest competition we could find, and everything he threw up was belted. And everywhere the ball went, there was a Brownie there to catch it. It was such a hot and humid and heavy night that long fly balls which seemed to be heading out of the park would die and be caught against the fence. Just when Bobo looked as if he was tiring, a shower would sweep across the field, delaying the game long enough for him to get a rest. Allie Clark hit one into the left-field stands that curved foul at the last second. A bunt just rolled foul on the last spin. Our fielding was superb. The game went into the final innings and nobody had got a base hit off Big Bobo. On the final out of the eighth inning, Billy Hunter made an impossible diving stop on a ground ball behind second base and an even more impossible throw. With two out in the ninth, a ground ball was rifled down the first-base line—right at our first baseman, Vic Wertz. Big Bobo had pitched the quaintest no-hitter in the history of the game.

Big Bobo Holloman was one with the immortals. Even among immortals, Big Bobo was immortal; he was the only pitcher in the twentieth century to pitch a no-hit game on his first major-league start. I'm not any more superstitious than the next man, but I don't think it's really wise to send a man back to the minor leagues right after he's become immortal. I mean it looks as if you're punishing him for throwing a no-hitter. I bought him a TV set as a reward for his splendid work and resigned myself to digging up $25,000 for Syracuse. There was always the chance that Big Bobo was rounding, in his leisurely fashion, into form. There was even an outside chance that a few people might pay their way into the park to see Big Bobo the next time he pitched. If they did, they didn't see much of him. Big Bobo didn't last two innings.

Bobo Holloman, piling laurel upon laurel before he departed, became the only pitcher to ever pitch a no-hitter in the only complete big-league game he ever pitched. Before the year ended, I managed to sell him, slightly frayed but a certified immortal, to Toronto for $7,500. Big Bobo's dandy little no-hitter had cost me $17,500 and a TV set.

That isn't the end of what Bobo's day in the sun (with intermittent showers) cost me. Shortly after I sent the $25,000 to Syracuse, I lost Ernie Banks for want of $31,500. Bill Norman, whom you may remember from Milwaukee, was scouting the Kansas City team in the American Association, and while he was there stayed over to watch the Negro team, the Kansas City Monarchs. Bill called, in great excitement, to tell me that the Monarchs' shortstop, Banks, was tremendous. I knew Tom Baird, the Monarchs' owner, fairly well, and I asked him what he wanted for Banks.

"Thirty-five," he said.

I said, "Gee, I don't have thirty-five thousand. I'll give you thirty-five hundred down and the thirty-one-five when you catch me."

He began to laugh. "That's the way I'm doing business myself, Bill," he said. "I have to get thirty-five thousand for Banks to pay off my own debts."

"Listen," I said, "just please don't sell him in our league. Norman tells me he's tremendous."

"All right," Baird said. "Where do you want him?"

I phoned Jim Gallagher at Chicago and told him to grab Banks quick. Jim was already scouting him. Banks, of course, has been the entire Chicago franchise for ten years.

Add Banks to the players we would have brought to Baltimore if we had been allowed to move at Tampa, and we'd have had a contending team. We had three good young pitchers coming up, Turley, Larsen and Duren (who between them won all 4 games for the Yankees in the 1958 World Series). We had Satch Paige and Virgil Trucks. We had Roy Sievers, Vic Wertz, Clint Courtney, Johnny Groth, and Billy Hunter.

I had to sell Trucks to Frank Lane for $95,000 to keep going. I know the record books say I sold Trucks and Bob Elliot for $65,000; that's what Mrs. Comiskey thought too. I had asked Lane for $100,000. Frank, who needed another starter, was willing, but Mrs. Comiskey refused to approve more than $50,000. Lane knew Trucks would help him, so we worked out a gimmick. I put Bob Elliot, whom

298

I was about to release, into the deal, and Frank added $15,000 there. As the season went on and we kept making our cat-and-dog deals, Frank would add another $10,000 here and there to make up the price on Trucks. In the end it came to $95,000 and a pitcher. Lane made himself a good buy. Trucks kept the White Sox in contention for two straight years.

We made it through the season so narrowly that when our last game went into extra innings, we ran out of new baseballs. The era of the Browns came to an end in St. Louis with nicked and dirty baseballs flying around Sportsman's Park. In the background, an effigy of Bill Veeck hung from the upper deck of the right-field stands. Well, you know those *avant-garde* writers and their obvious symbolisms.

I was sustained to the end by the knowledge that beyond the parched and effigy-bearing desert of St. Louis lay the fertile fields of Baltimore.

I did have some clues that my fertile fields were a mirage. Connie Mack made a special trip from Philadelphia to tell Mary Frances and me that he wanted us to know that if the Athletics voted against us, it was his sons' doing, not his. As if we didn't know that. Elliot Stein and Sid Schiff were both advised during the year that if I sold out to the Baltimore interests there would be no problem about getting a quick and unanimous approval. The implication that if I did not, there *would* be, was not wholly lost on me. There already was a Baltimore syndicate set up. We had set it up ourselves, before the Tampa meeting, to take the 20 percent we always give to local representation. Baltimore attorney Clarence Miles, the head of that syndicate, informed us that he had been told the same thing.

At the All-Star break in July, Will Harridge assured me that a committee would be appointed to meet in Chicago in early September to hear evidence that we were meeting all the requirements that had been laid down to insure a big-league operation. Representatives from New York, Boston, Chicago and Detroit were duly commissioned to sit on the committee. It was purely a face-saving device to make the original vote in Tampa look legitimate, but I appeared with James Anderson of the Baltimore park board to testify to what they already knew about such things as the parking facilities, the television and radio contracts, and to show them that the size and capacity of the Baltimore Municipal ball park were up to the standards that had been set. In future transfers, these standards suddenly became advisory only. We were the only ones who ever met every requirement, and we were the only ones who were ever turned down.

The committee released a statement announcing that it would recommend the transfer of the Browns "to a city to be determined later."

My mind was set at ease. New York and Boston had been represented on that committee, and that was the power. Clark Griffith had already lost his Baltimore clientele because of his opposition at Tampa, and the Baltimore press had not let up on him all year. Griff seemed eager to be given a chance to redeem himself—and also to get that extra television money from his contract with Jerry Hoffberger.

The league meeting was set for late Sunday morning at the Commodore Hotel in New York, just prior to the Yankee-Dodger World Series. Earlier in the morning, the advisory committee met again and recommended the move to Baltimore.

I couldn't see anything less than a unanimous vote.

The first notice that it was going to be Tampa revisited came when Del Webb asked for a 30-day delay to study alternative cities. I objected vigorously. In 30 days, as everybody in the conference room knew, I would be bankrupt. If ten of my creditors had gotten together, they could have thrown me into bankruptcy in 48 hours. If it hadn't been for my legal briefs, my escape hatch, the meeting might have become a little violent.

Sidney Schiff, speaking as our attorney, outlined the steps we had taken to meet their requirements and warned them that if we weren't allowed to leave St. Louis this time we were prepared to take them into court on a conspiracy charge. "I don't want to threaten you," he said, "but consider it a threat if you will."

Ben Fiery arose quietly to tell the owners that he felt it necessary to advise them, as league counsel, that I did indeed seem to have a prima facie case of conspiracy against them. "You are putting yourself in a very dangerous position," Ben told them. "You have set the standards for Baltimore and he has met them. You have appointed a committee to pass judgment and the committee has recommended the transfer. That has all the force of a commitment. If he sues, he could well win."

That put a new face on matters. Having looked upon the corpse and found it still capable of striking back, they withdrew to discuss strategy. The meeting was adjourned until that evening.

I put in a quick call to Elliot Stein in St. Louis to tell him that things were collapsing all around us again. I asked him to find Sidney Salomon and rush to New York as quickly as possible. Salomon
300

knew Webb. More to the point, Sidney was the Democratic National Treasurer, which made him no man for Webb to tangle with.

When the night meeting was convened, there was no more talk about a delay. Following the preliminaries we got right down to voting. I would have been far more encouraged, though, if the ballot had not turned out to be secret. In all my years in baseball, I have never been able to find out when a ballot is supposed to be secret and when it is not. It seems to depend entirely upon whether someone has slipped the chair the word that he wants to hide his vote. All I did know was that a secret vote had never done me any good. I left the Commodore with my record still intact.

The vote was 4–4. I was two votes short.

Now, at least, it was out in the open. Now no alibis about the shortness of time or the inadequacy of the ball park or all that gobbledegook about transportation and television and concessions.

In voting down Baltimore, they had voted down the only park in the country that met their own specifications. As far as I was concerned, they could grope their way out of that one without any help from me. I didn't call for another vote. I was prepared to sue. Nobody else asked for another vote either. If there was now no place for the Browns to go, there was no place for the meeting to go either.

The night meeting was not held in the regular conference room of the hotel, it was held in what seemed to be a medium-sized ballroom. Since nobody seemed to know quite what to do, they went wandering aimlessly around the room, scratching their heads, admiring the Louis XIV chairs that lined all the wall, or collecting in small and shifting groups.

While the meeting was in this stage of suspended animation—or, more accurately, animated suspension—Sidney Salomon and Elliot Stein came bursting into the room, not quite so dramatically as Bob Goldstein arriving at the Cleveland bank with his bagful of money but still dramatically enough to influence the course of the proceedings. The meeting was temporarily adjourned to allow Sidney to hold a conference with Webb.

We retired to the waiters' room, a little antechamber connecting to the ballroom. While Sidney and Webb were talking at the far end of the room, Topping remained near the door with Elliot and me. Topping was nothing if not frank. When Elliot asked him what they were trying to do to us, Topping told him, "We're going to keep you in St. Louis and bankrupt you. Then we'll decide where the franchise is going to go."

"Daniel," I said, "you should live so long."

Meanwhile, Webb—only a few feet away—was assuring Sidney Salomon that he wasn't trying to louse us up, he was in reality trying to help us. He was against putting a team in Baltimore, he told Sidney, and so he was going to find us a much better city.

As soon as Webb had begun to talk about alternative cities in the morning meeting, I had smelled Los Angeles. But with Webb, all is confusion. For Sidney Schiff had come to us, during the meeting, with another fascinating piece of information. Clarence Miles had been told, once again, that if he could get us to sell out to him, the transfer to Baltimore would be approved. Miles was prepared to offer $2,475,000 for our stock, an excellent price. Taking everything into consideration, our stockholders would be realizing a 48 percent profit on their investment. (For me, the profit would be less. I had diluted my stock from 33⅓ percent to 27.5 percent. Some of the money I had put into the club to keep it going was a total loss. Some of it had gone to buy treasury stock with the understanding that the new stock would not appreciate in value.)

The reason for the secret vote was now reasonably clear. By their actions at the meeting, it could be assumed that New York, Boston, Philadelphia and Cleveland had voted against me. Boston was apparently the vote that wanted to be hidden. It wouldn't do Griffith much good to vote for Baltimore if it were known that his relatives up in Boston had voted against it. Griffith had apparently decided that if he couldn't stop Baltimore he could at least stop me. His contract with Jerry Hoffberger didn't say that Bill Veeck had to be in Baltimore, it only said there had to be an American League team in Baltimore.

With Sidney Salomon and Elliot Stein now in town, most of our major stockholders were present. We caucused in the suite Mary Frances and I had at the Biltmore Hotel, right around the corner from the Commodore, and I passed on the information about Miles' offer. I also told them the league could not prevent us from moving to Baltimore and that it was my firm belief that we could all make far more than a 48 percent profit. "Even if they succeed in bankrupting us," I said, "we might do all right on the triple damages."

In order that they would have all the pertinent information, I also had to pass on the news that a guy in St. Louis, who had 8 shares of stock for which he had paid $24, had been awarded a temporary injunction against our moving. While the St. Louis suit didn't sound as if it was really anything to worry about, it did mean that we could end up fighting one suit in front of us and another suit in back.

302

And then I said, "I got you into this thing, so I'm not going to vote my shares. You decide among yourselves what you want to do."

Right here is where Mark Steinberg's death—in addition to the loss of his personal support—killed me. Mark had about 20 percent of the syndicate, and with me not voting, his shares were the big block. In calling for the vote, I knew those shares had to go against me. I also knew that I was putting Elliot Stein, the executor of Mark's estate, in a terrible position. Elliot had been Mark's protégé. It was only after Mark's death that Elliot had taken an active interest in the club. Remember what I said back in the beginning that wherever I have been, I have always had the good fortune to stumble across exactly the man who would be the most help to me? In St. Louis, that man was Elliot Stein. He had saved the club for us countless times, and he was the best friend I had in the city.

Elliot voted his own shares for holding on, but he was ethically bound not to gamble with the estate's money. If he hadn't exercised reasonable prudence, he could have been severely censured by the court. With some of the other stockholders voting to sell, the estate's shares were just enough to tip the balance. I think it is interesting, though, that those who had been closest to the situation—Elliot, Sid Schiff and Sidney Salomon, together with Art Allyn—voted to fight it through the courts if necessary. At the same time, I could hardly blame the others for being happy to take the handsome profits instead of the troubles.

Miles went hurrying back to Baltimore that same Sunday night. It seemed advisable that he be back, with his loan and his syndicate all in order, before Webb had the team headed for Alaska.

In the morning, word was sent to us that another meeting had been called for that evening. As I had been expecting all along, Webb arrived on the scene talking Los Angeles. Webb's big pitch was that "as a Westerner," he could guarantee that Los Angeles was ripe for big-league baseball. (A year earlier when I was sounding him out, he had assured me that as a Westerner he could guarantee that Los Angeles was not ready. A year later, while I was trying to buy the Philadelphia franchise for Los Angeles, he assured everybody, as we know, that Los Angeles was still not ready.) By sheer coincidence, the price Webb's Los Angeles syndicate was ready to pay was $2,500,-000, one notch above the Baltimore offer.

I was sure he was playing both ends against the middle. He had first used Miles' Baltimore group to get me to agree to sell the franchise and also to establish a price. Now, it seemed to me, his plan could be to bypass Miles, pass the loose franchise to his

Los Angeles friends and eventually sell his Yankee stock and take over the Los Angeles team himself. I still don't discount that theory entirely.

At any rate, Webb asked for a vote to move the franchise to Los Angeles and he got it, unanimously. I voted for it myself, for many reasons. It was still my franchise he was throwing up for grabs. I would have been delighted to permit Webb to go all the way out on the limb with his Los Angeles friends and then flatly refuse to sell. I even played momentarily with the heady dream of taking the team there myself; I could just as easily start suit on one coast as the other. But only for a moment. We had Clarence Miles running all over Baltimore, and it was too late in life to start breaking my word. The main reason I voted for it was because I wanted the unanimous vote on the record. Don't you see what they had done? After all the talk about meeting big-league standards, the owners—at a mere request from Webb—had voted unanimously and without debate to move to a city that had nothing resembling a big-league park. After all the crying about transportation difficulties, they had voted to travel to the West Coast to play only one team. After all the attacks on me for having assaulted poor Mr. Perini with a $750,000 offer for his territorial rights, they had voted to go into Phil Wrigley's Los Angeles territory without even bothering to pay him a courtesy phone call.

That was the way the meeting ended. For almost 24 hours, the American League was committed to go to Los Angeles.

Clarence Miles returned late the same night, his syndicate set. We met with him again in the suite and assured him that the Los Angeles vote was nonsense. We had given him our word to sell the club to him and we promised that we would battle the rest of the league to live up to it.

The next meeting—the fourth and last—had been scheduled for late Tuesday morning. As our sad group came into the conference room before the meeting had convened, Webb was waving a million-dollar check from Howard Hughes and chanting the glories of Los Angeles. I never saw the face of the check, but I'm sure it was legitimate.

The meeting was cut-and-dried. I got up and made one of the unhappiest little talks I have ever had to make. I told them about the vote of our stockholders and our agreement to sell to Miles. "I am selling against my own desire," I said. "Obviously, though, you want to get rid of me. All right, you have succeeded. I have my partners to consider. It has been my understanding that Baltimore is acceptable without me, and that these people are acceptable to you.

304

We dealt with Miles in good faith. I am sure the league dealt with him in good faith too. If not, he should be able to find recourse in the courts. You have kept Baltimore hung up from the beginning of this season to the end. I suggest that you vote them in without any more delay."

The vote for the Miles group was routine. Webb's talk and check-waving dwindled away, and the vote was unanimous.

I was unhappy to be out of baseball. I was unhappy for another reason. It is clear by now that I had no regard for most of the baseball operators of the American League. I knew they had no regard for me. With all that, it had been a shock to me that Sunday evening to learn that they were out to break me, not just to teach me a lesson. I hadn't thought they hated me that much.

I except Tom Yawkey and, it goes without saying, Hank Greenberg. The Boston vote was Joe Cronin's vote for his father-in-law. At Toots Shor's that night, Yawkey told me, "We voted against you, Bill, but I never thought it would come to this." And when I returned to baseball, Yawkey alone among those owners sent me a message to welcome me back.

One other little chore remained to be run, it developed, before I was out of the St. Louis mess. The temporary injunction was still in force and we were unable to get it vacated. No judge in the city of St. Louis, it seemed, was going to put himself on record as the man who had let the Browns get away. The legal grounds for either an injunction or a suit were questionable, but if we had let the case go to trial they could have charged me with mismanagement and demanded to examine every check I had written and every bill we had received. That would have kept us in court for a year. In order to deliver the club to Baltimore, it cost us—hold your breath—$50,000.

Before Webb would agree to accept the Baltimore syndicate, he squared himself with his Los Angeles friends by insisting upon a constitutional amendment to allow enlargement of the league to ten clubs "if it should become desirable to bring major-league baseball to the Pacific Coast." I had been talking expansion to the Coast for years, and had been pushed aside as a crackpot. Webb had only to open his mouth and he had a unanimous vote.

At the same time, he told the writers that his hopes for Los Angeles had collapsed because the Los Angeles syndicate had not come up with the necessary money. And, finally, he brought on waves of laughter from the galleries by confiding that he had gone along with the unanimous vote for Baltimore because he "did not want any dissension."

I had sent a message back to the hotel for Mary Frances to meet me at the Commodore. She was waiting there at the door of the conference room as I came out. "Come on," I said, "let's go over to Toots Shor's. They can chase us out of baseball but they can't chase us out of a friend's restaurant."

Toots is a friend. Back in the days when I was hustling around Milwaukee, I would always hang out at Shor's when I was in New York. Toots knew I had no money, so he would always tell his waiter to have me sign the check. I'd pay later when I could afford to.

We arrived at Shor's early, no later than 6 o'clock. We walked in there with our heads up and sat at the front booth, ready to greet all comers. At various times, different friends came to sit with us. The DeWitts sat with us for awhile. Even though Bill was protected by a contract, which still had two years to run, they were as unhappy as we were. Margaret DeWitt, in fact, was crying.

And then one of those unbelievable things happened. Del Webb came over to our table, sat down, and began to exchange small talk. I mean meaningless small talk on the order of how's-the-world-treating-you-these-days-Bill-old-boy. I like to think I can react to a situation, but this was too much for me. I wasn't going to give him the satisfaction of rising up in anger and ordering him away; I wasn't going to pass the time of day with him, either. I could feel Mary Frances seething beside me.

Del casually summoned the waiter. He was going to have dinner with us, wasn't that nice? The waiter seemed even more stunned than I was. He looked over at me questioningly. I didn't know what to do. I just shrugged, and the waiter came and took his order. Jimmy and Mary Dykes were in the booth right next to us, and Mary Dykes reached for Mary Frances's hand and said, loud enough I'm sure for Del to have heard her, "You don't think anyone will think *he* invited us here, do you?"

But Del just kept chattering away. We paid no attention to him. We didn't look at him, we didn't speak to him, we didn't acknowledge he was there. It was one of those moments of unreality that come back to you as soon as you wake up the next morning and leave you wondering whether it actually had happened or whether it was something you dreamed during the night. I leaned toward the opinion that I had dreamed it.

The waiter apparently went over to tell Toots about it before he put in the order. Because before Del's dinner arrived, Toots came to the booth and told him, "Get lost. They don't want you here."

Del got up pleasantly and, I trust, got lost. Toots took his place.

He sat with us through most of the evening, like a bulldog warning enemies away.

For some reason of his own, Webb wanted to make it appear as if he and I were friends. In the next issue of the *Sporting News,* there was a fair-sized box letting the baseball world know that our mild difference of opinion about whether I was fit to be in baseball had left no hard feelings between us. The final sentence read: *Webb was the guest of the Veecks for dinner at Toots Shor's after the final meeting.* You figure it out.

He could have been trying to convince Sid Salomon that he had not been against us. It's possible that he had been telling his Los Angeles friends that he had me in the bag. In both cases, a pleasant dinner after the meeting would prove that he had been telling the truth. At the time, I didn't care what his motives were. He wanted me out of baseball, and I was out. For the long year scrounging along in St. Louis, I had only the mental anguish and the undoubted strengthening of my character.

I had been kicked out all right. It took me six years to get back. In the intervening years I tried unsuccessfully to buy other franchises. I lost out in Detroit, even though I bid $500,000 more than anybody else. I finally managed to get back, though. I got an option to buy the Chicago White Sox before anybody knew I was negotiating for it and I sent around word that three seconds after I heard even a rumor that anyone was trying to stop me, I would have him in court.

I returned to Chicago, my hometown; Chicago, where my father had operated and still held the all-time attendance record; Chicago, where I would be in competition with my old boss, Phil Wrigley. Given the world to choose from, Chicago was the place, all right, to show them that William Veeck's screwball son wasn't through.

But most of all I wanted to come back to show Mary Frances that she hadn't married a loser. In the nine years of our marriage, it had been nothing but the second-division clubs, the disasters of St. Louis, the humiliations of the league meetings and the year-and-a-half runaround in Los Angeles. And I'd think, *If only she could have seen me in Cleveland when it was going good and I was riding high and no matter where I turned I was a big winner.*

And, of course, I was lucky. I was adequately financed in Chicago and I took over a good ball club. So good a ball club that first crack out of the doghouse we won ourselves a pennant.

Dynasties Are For the Dinosaurs | 21.

NEVER once did my father ever suggest that I follow him into baseball. All he ever did was provide me with summer employment. I have followed the same policy with my own sons. I am neither for nor against any of them making a career in baseball; they have their own lives to lead. I do think, however, that the greatest favor a father can do for his children is to stand back and let them carve out their own careers in their own ways and in their own good time. If I owned a baseball club today, I am quite sure there would be a paragraph high up in my will directing that the club be sold immediately upon my death. I am against dynasty-building in baseball because I have seen too many cases where it has only led to bitterness and unhappiness. I am against dynasties anyway because I have seen little evidence either in baseball or in history that intelligence or leadership is an inherited trait.

Baseball dynasties have usually ended in failure and, worse, in public squabbling. Baseball is too much in the public spotlight not to magnify every difference. The Griffith family has been constantly embroiled in lawsuits with its minority interests. Connie Mack's sons "inherited" the club before Mr. Mack died and ended up in discord. In Detroit, Spike Briggs and his sisters stopped speaking to each other after an argument over the disposition of the team. In Chicago, Chuck Comiskey battled with his mother and kept his sister in a revolving door to the courthouse.

It was these family arguments that put Philadelphia and Detroit on the block during the six years in which the forces for good within baseball were holding me at bay, and it was the family argument between the Comiskeys that finally opened the door for me in Chicago.

After I failed to buy the Philadelphia franchise in the winter of 1954 and the Detroit franchise in the summer of 1956, I spent three or four months in 1957 trying unsuccessfully to buy the circus from the Ringlings, who were also entertaining the public with an intramural battle.

John Ringling North owned 51 percent of the Ringling Brothers-Barnum & Bailey Circus. The rest of the Ringling family owned 49 percent. There had been constant discord, lawsuits and threats of lawsuits.

In addition, the circus was in trouble. The economic problem the circus had never been able to lick was the enormous expense of carrying around a huge crew just to throw up the tent upon arrival and tear it down again upon departure. With the Teamsters organizing the roustabouts, the cost of labor seemed about to become prohibitive. North had therefore announced that the circus would no longer be playing under canvas. A proud and colorful—and to a circus buff like me, glorious—era in American entertainment was coming to a close.

If I had been able to close my deal, the circus would still be playing the small towns today and—using the term loosely—playing under canvas. Working with a Cleveland engineering firm, I developed an inflatable, dome-shaped nylon tent which would be easily transportable and which would require, as a maintenance crew, only four engineers. The nylon was double-walled for strength. When blown up, there would be an inside wall and an outside wall, with a pocket of air sandwiched in between. The tent was fully blueprinted and the engineers had no doubt that it would work. Well, there is no doubt at all that it would have worked because these nylon domes are in fairly widespread use today, although they are not called tents but "air houses."

Before I could buy the circus, I had to negotiate both with John North and with the lawyer who represented the 49-ers—which is what the rest of the family was always called. I met with them perhaps a dozen times and we worked out an overall purchase price of $2.7 million.

Although I was broke again by that time, financing was no problem. My old baseball syndicate was, as always, prepared to back me. In addition, I was working on a most attractive deal with Chrysler Motors. Instead of carrying the usual sideshow around the country, I was going to carry the Chrysler Motorama, for which *they* were going to pay *me* a million dollars a year. With everything developing so nicely, I had discussed with the State Department the possibility of importing the Russian Imperial Circus, which had never before been seen in this country.

My own credentials were, of course, unimpeachable. Throughout my entire baseball career, kindly sportswriters and solicitous colleagues had been telling me, "Veeck, you ought to be running a circus!"

The deal collapsed because, although both sides had agreed upon

309

the price, a slight difference of opinion developed about the distribution. When it came down to the closing, both John North and the 49-ers advised me that the only fair way to split the loot was for themselves to get the $2 million and the other side to get the $700,000. Each side, you will be pleased to know, had great confidence in my ability to make this kind of distribution not only palatable but apparently appetizing to the other. After a few fast gallops around that 2-ring circus, I could only come up with one solution. "We'll all gather together in a little room," I told them. "I'll bring the money in cash and I'll throw it on the middle of the table. Then you can all jump in and fight for it."

I dabbled in many other things during those six in-between years. The first year and a half were spent in Los Angeles, surveying every conceivable angle of bringing major-league baseball to Los Angeles and San Francisco. I would like to make one thing clear here. Despite the reports that came out at the time, I was not working for Mr. Phil Wrigley. I was working for me. Immediately after the New York meeting in which the St. Louis franchise had momentarily been voted into Los Angeles, he called me in and presented me with an option to the territorial rights so that his own interests would be protected. Wrigley's asking price was $1,000,000 for the territorial rights and $2,000,000 for the ball park. He paid me $1,000 a month in expenses for one year. I spent $70,000 of my own money before I left Los Angeles, whipped, after the Philadelphia franchise was voted to Arnold Johnson.

Following the subsequent failure to buy the Detroit Tigers, I formed a public relations firm in Cleveland with Marsh Samuel and Jim Gallagher. One of our clients was the Plymouth Dealers Assn. of Cleveland. This being during the time of the severe 1956 Repression which brought on the worst automobile sales in memory, we were put immediately on our mettle. President Eisenhower had suggested that the nation go out and do a little more spending, so we coined the slogan U-AUTO-BUY-NOW, which not only proved to be helpful to our little group of local clients but got completely out of hand and swept the country.

Another of our clients was Jerry Hoffberger and National Brewing Co. With the Game of the Week about to be launched on the NBC network, Jerry picked up the telecasts for the southeastern part of the country, his main distribution area. Jerry wanted his own broadcasting crew so that it would not seem as if he were just buying local spots, and he picked me, of all people, to do the commentary. Well,

310

as we advertising men say, anything for a client. I teamed up with Chuck Thompson, who was a good and patient teacher. Along with Buddy Blattner, Chuck is, in my opinion, the best play-by-play announcer in the country. I have been very fortunate in my announcers. In Chicago, we had the dean of them all, Bob Elson. Broadcasting was really a lot of fun. In addition, it brought me into all the ball parks and kept me abreast of the latest developments in what I, if I alone, still considered my natural habitat—the major leagues.

I did a few other things which lowered my status, in the opinion of many, without even making any money. Mary Frances and I had bought a ranch in New Mexico after we left Los Angeles, and I became a sectional scout for the Cleveland Indians. A few of my friends asked me in the most discreet possible way how I could bring myself to become a scout for a team I had once owned and operated. It was easy. I like to watch baseball games. I like to find players. By becoming a scout, I was only doing officially what I would have been doing unofficially anyway. Nothing annoys me more than to be told I am not supposed to do something I enjoy because it is lacking in dignity. That has nothing to do with dignity. That's insecurity masking itself as a dignity.

I lowered myself further in 1956 by running a minor-league team for Sid Salomon and Elliot Stein, who had inadvertently bought a ball club. On this one, I suppose, I preserved some shred of dignity by serving without pay.

How can two intelligent, level-headed and worldly men like Elliot and Sidney inadvertently buy a ball club? Well, that's one of the nuttier stories I've been involved in. Elliot and Sid were in Columbus, Ohio, to close a deal for a St. Louis restaurant that Salomon was selling to Louie Jacobs. Louie was in Columbus for the minor-league meetings. In the previous day's meeting, the American Association had voted down a motion to move the Toledo club to Miami, and while they were having lunch Sidney, who had a home in Miami, was remarking that he thought the Association had made a terrible mistake. What he really meant was that, being a great baseball fan himself, he was disappointed that they hadn't given him a Triple-A team to watch. "If I could buy a club," he said, overcome by local pride and Caesar salad, "I wouldn't hesitate to move it to Miami."

A fellow sitting at the next table tapped him on the shoulder and said, "OK, you've just bought yourself a club."

The fingers that had tapped Sidney so lovingly were, it turned out, connected to the arm of the owner of the Syracuse club in the International League. Well, Sidney did want to be able to see baseball in

311

Miami, even if he had to present it himself. So he and Elliot bought the club on the spot. With friends like that, who needs circuses?

Sidney then called me at the ranch to pass on this marvelous news. "What do I do now, Bill?" he asked. "I've got a ball club but I haven't any park and I haven't any working agreement so that I can get some ballplayers."

"I am about to give you some very good advice," I told him. "Go back to the restaurant, tap the shoulder of the guy at the table on the other side of you and ask him if he wants to buy a ball club. If that doesn't work, go out into the street and try to spot some lamb walking by. If you don't have a buyer by nightfall, see if you can't give it to somebody. Believe me, it will be cheaper."

He said, "Will you come down and help me get started?"

I said, "Sure."

It was kind of fun operating on a small minor-league scale again. The ball club finished third and we were second in attendance. I'm sure we set a record of sorts, though, when Satchel Paige pitched a charity game against Columbus in the Orange Bowl and drew 51,713.

I negotiated the deal with the city fathers for the park and made a good working agreement with Roy Hamey of the Phillies, but after the season got underway I'd come down only when the club was in some kind of trouble or the attendance seemed in dire need of a shot in the arm. Toward the end of the year, I told Elliot and Sidney that my days as a commuting operator were over. I sold the club for them and they got out, against all logic, with a handsome profit.

The bid for the Detroit Tigers came during that same season. On this one, I was a lamb among riverboat gamblers. I was not only the high bidder, I had two bids higher than the group that won out.

Walter O. Briggs Sr., of Briggs Manufacturing, had left the club in trust to his son Walter O. "Spike" Briggs Jr. and his three daughters. But the bank, which was executor of the estate, had gone into court and obtained a ruling that a baseball club was "not a prudent investment" for the unborn grandchildren. That meant the Tigers had to be sold. Spike, who had been running the team himself, offered his sisters $2,500,000 for their interests and, when they turned him down, raised his bid to $3,500,000. They rejected that offer as wholly inadequate too—which it was—and brother and sisters stopped speaking.

Spike, as a man of great weath, influence and a considerable baseball background, could have gone to the bank for a loan and, if necessary, put together a syndicate to meet their price without any trouble at all. But Spike had that rich man's confidence that he could

312

just as easily sell the club to the highest bidder and still stay on to run it. He was, after all, a Briggs, and like all men who come into possession of a big-league franchise—be they heirs or insurance hustlers—he seemed to be under the impression that he ran the Detroit Tigers by divine decree.

Eight syndicates entered the bidding. The ground rules, we were informed, called for us to submit one bid, sealed, against a deadline. The assumption of any reasonable man was that the high bidder would win.

At the time I first learned from Spike that the club was going to be put up for sale, I had been wandering around town for Jerry Hoffberger, who had just purchased a brewery in Detroit. Jerry was understandably eager to get the TV rights for National Brewery, which meant I had a backer before I started. My other major backers were John Hilson of New York, who had been one of the small St. Louis investors, Elliot Stein and, of course, various members of the old Chicago and St. Louis groups.

The circumstances being what they were, I felt that it would be important to have, in the local representation, the flossiest possible collection of well-connected young men in the city. We had, among others, Bill Breech, son of the chairman of the Board of Ford Motors; Edward Wilson, son of Defense Secretary Charley Wilson, the former chairman of the board of General Motors; Ernest Kern of the Kern Department Stores; and Palmer Watling, head of one of Detroit's largest brokerage firms—all put together by Dick Van Duzen.

With it all, it became fairly evident from the first that I was not going to get the club no matter who was behind me or how much I bid. The Briggs sisters, I had good reason to believe, had been warned that if they sold the club to me, the American League would not approve the deal.

Considering the circumstances under which I'd departed, the don't-sell-to-that-guy-Veeck rumors were probably inevitable. Ordinarily, I would have discounted them. And yet, there were a few small things in the Detroit bidding that convinced me they were true. The Negro community of Detroit, for instance, was solidly and vocally behind me, especially after I came under personal attack. One of the reasons was that under the Briggs family, Detroit had never had a Negro player. One of the Briggs sisters was married to Philip Hart, the lieutenant-governor of Michigan. With the Negro vote such a powerful political factor in the state, every rule of politics dictated that Hart should have, at the very least, issued a statement that my bid would be accepted without prejudice and considered on its merits. Instead, he maintained a complete silence.

Another indication came, paradoxically, from Chick Fisher, who was also married to one of the Briggs sisters and who I knew was rooting for me. Chick, you may remember, was the Detroit banker who had offered to lend me the money to buy the Cleveland Indians. When I sold the Indians, I had recommended that the new owners give Chick half the loan, and I had myself given him half the loan when I bought the Browns.

Chick authorized a million-dollar loan both for my syndicate and for the syndicate led by Fred Knorr, John Fetzer and Kenyan Brown, three radio-TV men whose main interest lay in gaining control of the broadcasting rights. Shortly afterwards, however, Chick authorized one of his officers to inform me that the National City Bank was prepared to lend me half a million more than anybody else, "if you get the club."

"Great," I said. "I'll come right down to make the arrangements."

"Well," he said, "let's wait to see whether you're going to get it."

Now, Chick Fisher was treasurer of the Tigers and a member of their board of directors. If he was that dubious about my chances of buying the club even with an extra half-million, I knew my chances were practically nil.

Acting under the assumption that I was probably going to be blackballed, I made a second approach, along the flanks, by bringing in Bob Goldstein, the hero of that last-minute purchase at Cleveland, to enter a bid on behalf of his own "Hollywood syndicate." To decoy the opposition, Bob talked up a bid of $5 million. I kept my mouth shut—the upset of the year—and with the extra half-a-million credit from the bank I submitted a bid of $5½ million.

In order to justify that extra half-million, I decided it would be wise to sell the ball park and lease it back. With Detroit management and capital figuring so prominently in my syndicate, I wanted to bring labor into the picture too. The ideal union to be connected with in Detroit was, to my way of thinking, Walter Reuther's Auto Workers. My second choice was Jimmy Hoffa and the Teamsters.

I had an entree to Hoffa. His chief lieutenant, Harold Gibbons, had been the Teamster leader in St. Louis during the time I was operating the Browns. The Teamsters had rented the park from us a few times, I had made a few speeches for them, and Harold and I had become pretty good friends. As a matter of fact, if Mr. Busch had not broken down and bought Sportsman's Park when he did, it

314

quite probably would have been sold to Gibbons and the St. Louis Teamsters.

Harold set up a meeting in California, and Hoffa and I discussed the terms under which he would buy Briggs Stadium if we were successful in buying the club. I had made it clear that I still reserved the right to try to sell the park to Reuther, and Hoffa, a practical man, understood perfectly.

About a year later—to digress for a moment—Gibbons asked me to come to Washington to advise Hoffa on whether it would be wise to make a million-dollar loan to a Washington figure who was involved in a deal to buy the Redskins from George P. Marshall. From my point of view, the most interesting part of my investigation was the chance to look over the drawings for the new Washington stadium that was about to go under construction.

As to the question at hand, I advised Hoffa that with the seating capacity in the new stadium, the loan would not only be a good one for the Teamsters but that if he could buy the Redskins himself, he'd probably be able to triple the union's investment in a few years. There was only one drawback that I could see, and it had nothing to do with finance. As part of the deal, Marshall was to stay on and run the team, on a lifetime basis, at his regular salary. I had to point out to Hoffa, who is not a sports fan, that it would be foolish for him, as a union leader, to involve himself with Marshall, even on anything as indirect as the prospective loan, unless he had a clear understanding that Marshall's color line would have to go. I must say also that in my two contacts with Jim Hoffa, I found him to be most prudent about investigating every angle and seeking expert advice before he invested his union's money. I also found—and this surprised me— that he is able to digest a complex financial statement as fast as anybody I have ever run across in my life.

I never did see Reuther. A few days before the bids were to be submitted, I had a conversation with Spike Briggs at the Statler Hotel bar that convinced me, beyond all doubt, that I had no chance. Fred Knorr, he told me, had offered to keep him on to run the club. I told Spike, "Look, you can be chairman of our board if you want to, for as long as you want to, and you won't have to put in a penny. But I'm not going to tell you I'll let you operate the club. I've always been president of any club I've been involved with and I intend to operate it myself."

That wasn't good enough for him. "All right," I told him. "But watch out. These guys are going to get the club and then throw you out."

Now, Spike is not naïve. He is an experienced, intelligent man. Here, though, was another case of the rich boy who had always found that people were willing—and sometimes anxious—to do anything he wanted, as people always seem willing to do things for rich people they wouldn't dream of doing for poor people. Besides, he owned 7½ percent of the Knorr Broadcasting Co. Unfortunately for Spike, Knorr owned only one-third of the purchasing syndicate.

I was so certain I was out of the running that I went back to the ranch in New Mexico before the bids were opened. And then Harry Salsinger, the sports editor of the Detroit *News,* delivered a front-page broadside against me that brought the people of Detroit and columnists throughout the country leaping to my defense and almost brought me back to life.

He wrote:

> Veeck has been described as a "man with the heart of a carnival barker and the soul of a medicine show pitchman"... the various promotional stunts that Veeck used to swell attendance in Milwaukee, Cleveland and St. Louis and in Miami this spring, were often marked by vulgarity rather than ingenuity. He at times humiliated his manager and embarrassed the American rival club owners and baseball in general.

As everybody promptly pointed out, Spike Briggs had only recently blasted his own manager and coaches so badly that Joe Gordon, one of the coaches, had handed in his resignation.

Salsinger could be described as the J. Roy Stockton of Detroit. He had been extremely close to Walter Briggs Sr., though, and I don't doubt for a moment that he was completely sincere in viewing me as a threat to the dignity of Detroit baseball and an insult to Briggs' memory. Unfortunately, he went on to misrepresent the presentation of the Hornsby Cup—his most damning evidence against me—and he did it not by means of the usual flat misstatement, which would have indicated that he was merely misinformed, but by carefully hedged innuendo:

> Veeck was "presented" with a loving cup, presumably from the players, and the engraving on the cup expressed their appreciation for emancipating them. There were enough letters on the cup to have kept an expert engraver busy for a couple of days completing the inscription, and the cup was supposed to have been bought by the players after they were informed of Hornsby's release. If some of them suspected that Veeck had

bought the cup several days earlier, or that one of his employees bought it and ordered the inscription, they could not very well be blamed.

Elliot Stein phoned down to New Mexico to let me know about the column. I had better explain that the ranch was so far back in the hills that the phone company had not run any lines in. My phone was therefore in a little box on top of a fence post on the main road, five and a half miles away. I'd have to drive down every second day or so, ask the operator for any messages and stand there for a couple of hours returning calls, with the wind whipping the sand up all around me. You would be surprised how many phone calls suddenly become unimportant when you're standing on a road with sand blowing down your tonsils. When I returned Elliot's call we could barely hear each other. "We have a terrible connection," he shouted. "It sounds like a windstorm."

I yelled back, "It is!" The wind and sand were blowing so hard that I was sitting on the road with my legs wrapped around the post to keep me from blowing away.

I went back to Detroit on the next plane to defend myself against this most shocking and most welcome attack. Not that it did any good. On the original bidding, I was high with my $5,500,000. Jack Cooke of Toronto was second. (Salsinger disposed of him nicely in the postmortems by calling him "the Bill Veeck of Canada," which is a heck of a thing to say about a guest from our good neighbor to the north.) Bob Goldstein, who had tacked $50,000 onto the $5 million he had been advertising, was third. Knorr, with a bid of $5,000,000, had, according to all reports, run fourth.

Despite the one-bid stipulation, though, the Knorr group, having learned of my bid, had raised its own figure to $5,500,000 too. I learned about their new bid upon my return to Detroit and so I raised my bid to $6 million. Knorr got the club anyway. I had been in there as a shill to raise the price for the Briggs family.

Salsinger let the cat out of the bag the next day when he wrote:

> It was perhaps just as well that Bill Veeck's bid for the Detroit baseball club was turned down. Had it been accepted, Veeck would have needed the approval of at least six American League club owners before taking possession and there was the rub.

Fred Knorr, obviously a master salesman, was able to prevail upon Spike Briggs to accept the job as general manager. "Spike," Knorr said, as thousands cheered, "you are going to be with us a long time. We value you as a great executive and a wonderful baseball man."

Spike announced, "It was a condition of Knorr's offer that I remain with the club. I have agreed to do that for a reasonable length of time."

Before another year was over, Spike "resigned." (And Knorr quit as president of the club in protest.) Spike phoned me in Cleveland and said, "Well, Bill, you were right."

I had made the largest bid ever made for a big-league club and I had been shut out. At that moment it did not seem to me that, barring a miracle, I would ever get back into baseball.

Chuck Comiskey and the National Debt | **22.**

IN buying the White Sox, I found myself involved, in a far more intimate way, with another heir, Charles A. Comiskey II. The White Sox had been founded by Chuck's grandfather, the original Charles A. Comiskey, known for reasons of state as the Old Roman. After the death of Chuck's father, Lou Comiskey, in 1939, his mother, Mrs. Grace Comiskey, fought the attempt of the trustees to sell the club and assumed the title of president. There were two surviving children, Dorothy and Charles. Dorothy married a White Sox pitcher, John Rigney, and in the course of time, Chuck and John became vice-presidents.

Chuck had grown up firmly convinced that the divine order of the universe called for the earth to spin on its axis, the sun to rise in the east and Charles Comiskey II to preside over the fortunes of the White Sox. As a boy in his early twenties, he stalked out of a board meeting and resigned because his mother refused to appoint him president and turn the club over to him at once. He was back in a few months.

When Mrs. Comiskey died, in December, 1956, Chuck was thirty years old, no longer a boy. Still, Mrs. Comiskey made a specific bequest of 500 shares of her stock to her daughter, Dorothy, before splitting the remaining 2,082 shares between Dorothy and Chuck. Dorothy was also named executor of the estate, which gave her control of the bulk of the shares issued by the White Sox corporation.

With the stock already inherited from their father, Dorothy owned 54 percent of the club and Chuck, 46 percent. To state it bluntly, Mrs. Comiskey, for reasons sufficient unto herself, had thought it better to leave the club under the control of her daughter rather than her son. Dorothy did her best to treat her brother as a partner. Chuck and Rigney were vice-presidents with equal rank. But Charles, completely unable to reconcile himself to a situation in which the team had fallen out of his hands, instituted a series of lawsuits against his sister which kept the tabloid readers entertained and won the owners of the White Sox the sportive title, "The Battling Comiskeys."

Charles was a litigant of fire and spirit and determination. We may never see his like again. But he had one very bad weakness. After we got started, he kept losing. In all his suits against his sister, and later against us, he won only one major victory. This was a victory so brilliantly conceived and executed that it lost him the ball club.

Dorothy Rigney, as majority stockholder, was entitled, after their mother's estate was distributed, to 3 of the 5 board members; Charles, with his 46 percent, would be entitled to two members—himself and, after the stock was distributed, also his father-in-law. Through a series of events and legal maneuvers, Charles ended up with him and his sister having equal representation on the board, thereby throwing the affairs of the club into a deadlock. Unable to run the company she had a majority ownership of, except by committee or compromise, Dorothy was left with no logical alternative except to sell out.

In June, 1958, word came to me that Dorothy, having wearied of life in the public laundromat, was ready to sell her stock and retire to private life. Naturally, I hurried to Chicago to investigate. Not that I ever saw Dorothy during any stage of the conversations. All negotiations were carried on between myself—flanked by my lawyers—and her lawyers.

Contrary to what has been said or may be said in the future, Dorothy was not only fully prepared to sell to her brother, she preferred to sell to her brother. Her lawyer's opening words at our first meeting were that Mrs. Rigney wanted me to understand that she was going to use my offer to establish a price for Charles. If I did not want to negotiate under those conditions, her lawyer said, there would be no hard feelings on her part. But if I did make an offer and found the club being sold to Chuck at the same price, she did not want there to be any hard feelings on my part. Nothing could be more frank and honorable than that.

Negotiating under those conditions, our final offer was $2,700,000. As optimistic as I always am when I have a ball club in my sights, it should be perfectly apparent that I had no great hope that Charles, with the club his for the taking, would let it slip away from him.

I was traveling from city to city with Game of the Week, and so the deal hung there, half forgotten, through the rest of the season. Charles had from June to November—six solid months—to meet my figure.

Toward the end of the season my television duties took me to Boston, where the Red Sox were playing the White Sox. After the game, I went out with Ed Short, the White Sox publicity man (and now general manager) for some steamed clams. Ed had no further information on Dorothy's plans but he agreed to query John Rigney for me when the team returned to Chicago. A couple of weeks later, I phoned Ed and he said, "I think I'd talk to John if I were you."

So I called John Rigney and he said, "Well, I'd just as soon keep out of it. Why don't you check with the attorneys?"

That was all I needed to send me rushing back to Chicago to instruct my attorneys to resume negotiations. Chuck had blown it. Given the opportunity to buy complete control of the White Sox, he had offered his sister a full million dollars less than I had. And this, despite the fact—as we shall see in a moment—that her stock was worth at least a million dollars more to him than it was to us or to anybody else. Either he could not bring himself to believe that Dorothy would really sell to anybody except him, the last of the Comiskeys, or he could not believe we would really pay that much for her 54 percent.

Negotiations were resumed in earnest. And this time there was no proviso from Dorothy that Charles was going to be given another chance to match my offer. Chuck had filed another lawsuit, asking that Dorothy be removed as executrix, and her patience had run out.

Although I did 99 percent of the negotiating myself, making frequent trips between Cleveland and Chicago, there was not—surprisingly—the hint of a leak. Even if it had become common knowledge that Dorothy was ready to sell, though, Charles's lawsuits would probably have frightened all competition away. One of the conditions laid down by her attorneys was that we would have to buy the deadlocked board along with the club. In other words, if we found no way to break the deadlock, we would have no claim against Dorothy.

The best legal opinion of our attorneys was that we had better than an even chance of winning all the cases. They made it clear, however, that the legal points were not so clearly defined that anybody was handing out any guarantees that we would win. It was a gamble. What made it even more of a gamble was that they could anticipate additional lawsuits, the results of which were, of course, undeterminable at this time.

Even with our 54 percent, we would not have control unless we could win a reversal of the ruling setting up the 4-man Board. Otherwise, the club would remain paralyzed at the top, an impossible situation.

And yet, it was inconceivable to me that any court could rule that Mrs. Comiskey had not had the right to distribute control of her property between her children as she saw fit. Nor could I believe that the court would hold to a ruling that the majority interest, in any business, did not have a self-evident right to control the board of directors and set policy.

My attorney in these final negotiations, for the first time, was not Sidney Schiff. Sidney was beginning to limit his activities. We were represented by two other attorneys from the same firm, Milton Cohen, one of the finest men I know, who had done most of the work in St. Louis for us, and John Yonko, who has been associated with me in every purchase and sale in which I have been involved.

I should also mention that Dorothy soon had a new trial attorney representing her, Don Reuben, one of the brightest men I have ever met. Don and I worked together closely while Chuck's suits were being disposed of and we became close friends. After Don took over, Dorothy lost no new legal battles.

Once Dorothy had expressed that completely unhedged willingness to sell, I called Hank Greenberg to ask him if he wanted to come in with me.

"Sure," Henry said, "if you can get it, count me in. But I don't think her stock can be bought."

"I think it can be," I told him. "Let's begin to casually put together some partners."

Hank immediately suggested Charles and Andrew Baxter, who had been associated with him in Cleveland (and who, as you will remember, dropped out later in order to take Hank's Cleveland debentures off his hands). My first visit, needless to say, was to Art Allyn Sr. As always, Art was not only willing but enthusiastic.

Mr. Allyn did something else. He set up an appointment for me at the Continental Illinois Bank so that I could make my pitch for my usual million-dollar loan. Despite the suits, the bank did not hesitate. They were not overly impressed by the logic of Chuck's case either. And, of course, the stock had a basic value even if I wasn't able to assume control.

With the backers all present and the money accounted for, the time had come to put all talk behind us, present a definite, clear-cut offer and, if it was acceptable, get Dorothy's signature on a piece of paper. Our offer had two "if comings," deductible from the $2,700,000. Putting it backwards, she would lose $175,000 if we were unable to get 80 percent of the stock and $200,000 if we were unable to win control of the board of directors. We never did get the 80 percent and so the actual purchase price was $2,525,000.

If, on the other hand, we had been able to buy Charles's stock, Dorothy would not only have received the $175,000, she would have been recompensed for any difference between the price we paid for a share of his stock and the price we paid for hers.

On December 20, a Saturday, an appointment was set up for Milton Cohen to meet with Dorothy at her attorneys' office in the Prudential Building and, we hoped, buy our option. Milton believed, from our conversations with her attorneys, that she would sign. The commitment was not absolute, however, and we could not be sure that all the terms were acceptable to her.

Still holding to the policy that it is just as well if the buyer and the seller do not meet until the day of the closing, I left Milton at the Prudential Building and walked over to the Wrigley Building restaurant to have a few beers. He was going to phone me the moment he came out of the meeting. The Wrigley restaurant was closed. I went on to the Boul Mich bar, a couple of doors away, and left word at the attorneys' office that Milton could reach me there.

There followed another of those seemingly interminable waits. But when Milton's call finally came through, it was to tell me that everything had gone smoothly. We had the option. At that moment, standing in the phone booth of a bar, I was back in baseball.

The option cost only $100, but the sum itself is meaningless. The $100 was just a convenient figure to bind the deal—it could just as easily have been $1 or $100,000—because her attorneys knew that we had the money and that there was no question of our overwhelming desire to exercise the option.

Immediately, from the same booth, I phoned Chuck Comiskey at his home and asked if I could come out to see him the following evening. Charles lived in Hinsdale, about four blocks from my mother's house. I was staying with my sister, Mrs. John Krehbiel, in nearby Downers Grove. In every negotiation in which I have ever been involved, I have worked out of my sister's home at one time or another, not too surprising when you consider that my financial backing has always come from Chicago. Peg is a couple of years older than I, but we have always been extremely close, even as

322

children. John Krehbiel is a man of uncommon common sense and his advice—since I never seem to be able to buy a club without a few crises thrown in along the way—has been invaluable. Instead of running home to mother, I always ran home to Peg and John.

It was perfectly apparent upon entering Charles's house that he did not know why I was there. "Charles," I said, "I'd rather you hear this directly from me than read it in the paper or hear about it secondhand." And then I broke the news that I had the option for the majority interest. I could see that he was startled, and yet he seemed quite resigned to accepting an accomplished fact as an accomplished fact. Good. "Charles," I said, "I'd like to buy your shares too."

He answered that under the circumstances he might very well want to sell them to me.

Everything went so pleasantly that I called Hank afterwards to tell him that I felt we had an excellent chance of getting the full 100 percent. I'll let you in on a secret, it being this late in the game. Hank is the practical member of our partnership. I have wandered through life on the philosophy that if you wish for something to happen and do everything possible to make it happen and convince yourself that it's going to happen—who knows?—it may happen. It is a philosophy that leads to many a rude awakening, but it can occasionally buy you a ball club in Chicago.

"Chuck won't sell," Hank said, in a tone of finality. "Not a chance in the world."

"That," I reminded him, "was what you said about our chances of getting Dorothy's stock."

This time, though, Henry was right.

Soon afterwards Chuck filed a new suit—across his other suits—to halt the sale. He was basing his action, as near as I could see, upon that ancient doctrine of divine right. Charles claimed—and I'm sure this was his honest conviction—that the White Sox belonged to him because his name was Comiskey; that is, that his mother had never intended that the club should leave the family. Dorothy's defense was that Mrs. Comiskey, by leaving the majority interest to her instead of to the only male member of the family, had knowingly and deliberately let it pass out of Comiskey control. The decision went against Charles, but his appeal was still in the courts when we bought the club on March 10.

Our backers, who had been fully informed on the risks from the beginning, held firm. For the only time in my career as a baseball operator I was not the single largest stockholder, for when the Baxter brothers bought Hank's Cleveland debentures, Hank had to buy their

323

Chicago stock. Between us, Henry and I had 80 percent of the new company; I had something like 34 percent and he 46 percent. Art Allyn took most of what was left, with the stockholders who had voted for me in the St. Louis showdown all coming in for small shares too.

And speaking of stockholders, large and small, let us not forget Charles O. Finley, the current owner of the Kansas City Athletics. Finley, a Chicago insurance broker, called to ask if he could have a piece of the local representation. I knew Finley. He had first appeared on the baseball scene during the bidding for the Philadelphia franchise, waving a check for something like $250,000 and offering to permit innocent bystanders—like me—into his syndicate. He had popped up again in the Detroit regatta and submitted the fifth highest bid.

I had Charles O. penciled in for a piece until it suddenly developed that he was calling Jerry Holtzman of the *Sun-Times*, who didn't know him from Adam, to tip him off that I was never going to be able to exercise my option because my backers were going to run out on me unless I could deliver Chuck's stock along with Dorothy's.

Shortly thereafter, it was revealed that Finley had gone to Dorothy's attorneys and signed a purchase agreement, exercisable in the event I let my option lapse. Finley was putting up $500,000, which made me and my $100 look pretty sick.

Being rather narrow-minded about having people in my own syndicate working the other side of the street, I informed Finley that he had disqualified himself. One thing you have to say for Finley, he's not a man to nurse a grudge; he promptly offered to buy my $100 option for $250,000.

Finley apparently felt that he would be able to handle Chuck without too much difficulty, and work out some sort of an arrangement on the 80 percent. That would have been interesting. When you consider that Finley gave Frank Lane a fabulous eight-year contract at Kansas City and then bought it up about eight minutes later, I sometimes feel I deprived the world of one of its great acts in not permitting the Comiskey-Finley relationship to get off the ground.

A great deal has been written, unfortunately, about why we needed 80 percent of the stock in the Chicago White Sox. I say unfortunately because nobody would have been the least bit interested if we had been able to work out a way of buying it. Since the sports page doesn't specialize in finance, and the *Wall Street Journal* has other fish to fry, I don't think I have ever seen it adequately or accurately explained. I'm not sure that it's possible to explain it adequately without writing a minor treatise. I'll volunteer to take on the job, but only with the understanding that what follows is condensed and oversimplified.

When you buy a ball club, you buy three things. You buy a place to play, either through ownership or by lease; you buy a franchise, which is the right to play; and you buy the players' contracts.

(You buy a host of intangibles, too. That's why there is such a difference of opinion about what the park, the franchise and the players are worth. I have always felt, for instance, that the longer a city has been without a pennant, the more valuable the franchise becomes. The White Sox hadn't won a pennant in 40 years.)

The park, if you own it, is the only part of the package that makes the lawyers happy. It is mortar and brick; it can be seen and touched and it lights up in the dark—except, of course, when it falls under the baleful influence of Chicago's North Side. Because it is mortar and brick, the park can be depreciated, as real property, according to an established government scale.

The players are not mortar and brick, except in rare cases. I knew a third baseman once . . . well, that's another story. The Government has never quite got around to figuring out a schedule for depreciating flesh and sinew although there was a time when it did allow a 14.2 percent composite rate of depreciation on all ball club assets, ballplayers included. In 1933, a test case involving the Chicago Cubs overthrew that schedule and a new system for carrying player contracts was put into force.

I like to poke around the financial statements, in the early morning hours at the park, looking for opportunities for fun and profit, in much the same way I like to poke through the rule book looking for ways to keep the adrenalin flowing in the Commissioner's office. In Cleveland, I found something.

I had always been struck by a basic inconsistency in the way we carried our players on the books. When you buy a ball club, you list your whole roster of players as a cash item, which means you cannot depreciate them. And yet, if you buy a player any time thereafter, you carry him as an expense item, which means that you can write him off immediately just as you would write off paper clips, stationery or any other business expense.

The difference, technically, is this: When you buy a ball club, you are buying stock, not assets, because the seller—for his own tax reasons—will seldom negotiate on any other basis. Although possession of the stock gives you control of the assets of the company, the position of the Government has always been that there has been no real change in the company itself. Management can come and go but the books—and the established accounting procedures—go on forever. The logic there is sound. Since the previous stockholders had already enjoyed the benefits of writing off the players' contracts at the time of original purchase, the Government could not see why the same contracts should be written off a second time.

When, on the other hand, you are buying an individual player you are buying him, purely and simply, as an asset. He is income to the team that has sold him; he is a business expense to you.

To be able to write off all the player contracts at the time of purchase, then, I had only to find some way of converting them, in strict accord with legal definition, into assets.

An interesting idea to play around with, obviously, because the money involved here is tremendous. To show how much is involved, let's bring it up to date by using the Chicago White Sox as an example, instead of Cleveland.

Projecting the price I paid for Dorothy's stock to the club as a whole, we can establish a total sales price—for our purposes here— of $5,000,000.

Let us allocate $250,000 of that sum to the cost of the franchise. (This is low, but for tax purposes, a starting place.)

Let us say that Comiskey Park, including all real property and equipment, is worth $1,750,000. (This is somewhat higher than book value.)

By simple subtraction, that means the player contracts, major and minor league both, have cost us $3,000,000.

All right, let's play around with that $3,000,000. You can do something else, according to the tax laws. After you buy a company, you are entitled, under certain conditions, to liquidate it, tax-free, and reorganize: that is, establish a new corporation with a completely new stock setup. In normal business practice, liquidation and reorganization have many advantages, one of them being the right to call in all the outstanding stock of the liquidated company at a fair market price. Unless there is a tax-loss carrying over from the old company—as I had in Milwaukee—the new owners of a baseball team always did reorganize. I had to reorganize in Cleveland, for instance, if only to set up the debenture-common stock grouping.

But, of course, in setting up the new company in Cleveland, I had, in accordance with the established procedure, picked up the old company's books and carried on. But why? I hadn't bought stock in the new company; I had created it out of thin air. There had been no previous stockholders enjoying any benefits because there had been no previous stockholders.

326

Why, in short, couldn't the new company *buy* the contracts from the liquidating company? I'm not talking about buying them as a bookkeeping gimmick, a mere paper transaction, I am talking about literally buying the players' contracts individually by writing out checks to the account of the liquidating company. Isn't this what liquidating really means, turning the assets of the company into cash? When you come right down to it, the old system, in which the assets were simply assigned from one company to another on paper, was the bookkeeping gimmick.

And if the old company, in liquidating, was selling the players' contracts, the new company was obviously buying assets and entitled to write them off as a business expense.

There are—wouldn't you know?—limitations. In the first place, the law does not permit management to liquidate if it controls only a bare majority of the stock. If it did, there would be no problem at all. The theory is that while a small minority should not be allowed to frustrate the will of a large majority, neither should a mere majority be able to override the wishes of a sizable minority. In most states, management is required to have 80 percent of the stock behind it (although in Missouri it was only 75 percent).

There is a second limitation. In order to take advantage of this tax-free liquidation, you have to liquidate within a year of the purchase date (to be exact, within 360 days). After that, the ship has sailed.

Let me clear up one point that seems to be confusing in the public mind. The Government is not giving you any automatic tax rebate. All you are getting is a tax deduction.

My original plan had been to write off the entire sum—the entire $3,000,000, if we hold to the White Sox illustration—over a short period of time. Since losses can be carried forward for five years, this would have meant that the first $3,000,000 we earned over a five-year period would be tax-free. The tax on corporate earnings being 52 percent, the savings would amount to $1,600,000.

The Government, while accepting the concept as perfectly valid and legal, proposed, instead, a three-to-five-year depreciation, depending on the individual club and the players involved—with the value of the players' contracts to be determined by independent appraisal. The potential deductions, in other words, were spread out over a longer period of time. But all this, you will notice, assumes a profit. If the profits are not there, the tax savings are not there either.

Now comes the tragic chapter of this personal chronicle of high finance. I—with my night-school course in accounting—uncovered

327

this tax formula and I alone among the men who have bought ball clubs in the past decade have never been able to take advantage of it. Even though I lead both leagues in buying ball clubs.

I was not able to use it in Cleveland because I had been in operation for more than a year before it was worked out. Nate Dolin, of the purchasing syndicate, developed the idea further, and it was his use of this formula when the new Cleveland owners liquidated my old company that brought on the government ruling discussed above.

In St. Louis, I left myself so badly underfinanced that I never did have the money to liquidate and buy up the outstanding stock. In any case, there were no visible profits from which to deduct even the paper clips and stationery. But I wonder whether something else hasn't sprung to your mind? Remember the stockholder who sued me with his 8 shares of stock? If I had been able to liquidate, I would have bought those shares for $56, the established price, and saved the $50,000 it later cost me to free myself from the injunction.

And, finally, I wasn't able to liquidate in Chicago because we were never able to tear Chuck Comiskey loose from even one share of his stock. It does seem only fair that I should return to baseball, if only to enjoy some slight taste, one might say, of my own cake—or, at least, to find out whether I can find some new way of blowing it.

Chuck never really could accommodate himself to the fact that the White Sox had slipped out of his hands. Even after the court ruled that Dorothy was perfectly entitled to sell the club to me, Chuck announced that it would be impossible to pay the players unless he signed the checks. Since the ruling came down on March 6, a week after spring training had begun, this did worlds of good for player morale.

He did have to sign the checks. The club was still frozen in that evenly divided 4-man Board, and while I was, to all intents and purposes, running the team, I was not an officer of the company. Technically, I was just a guy with a big mouth, hanging around the ball park.

I was not without sympathy for Charles, or, to put it more mildly and more accurately, I had some understanding that he would have to make a difficult and painful adjustment. It is never easy for the crown prince to find, upon reaching the age of accession, that François Villon and his beggars have taken over the palace.

From a public relations aspect—an aspect to which I have always been sensitive—we had been placed in the position of outlanders who had seized his birthright from him, a role I did not relish. In all my years of striking up conversations with the fans in the stands, I can

328

think of only a handful of times when anybody was rude or angry. Early in the first season at Chicago, I sat beside a guy in the left-field grandstand who let me know in no uncertain terms that he felt we had behaved very badly toward Chuck when we bought Dorothy's stock. "Well," I said, "I'm sorry you feel that way, but the stock was for sale. Chuck had a chance to buy it. If he didn't want to, he had to anticipate that somebody else would." It turned out that this particular fan identified so closely with Chuck because he had gone to school with him. But I'm sure there were many other people in Chicago who felt the same way.

The day we bought the team, Henry and I asked Charles to meet with us at Comiskey Park the following morning so that we could begin to iron out out difficulties and get on with the business of running the ball club. Chuck answered, through the press, that he probably would be too busy to show up at the suggested time.

Actually, he was at the park when we arrived. He wasn't there to meet us, though, or even greet us. He dashed out of another exit, jumped into his Cadillac and—ignoring the pleas of the photographers—drove off. Instead of a posed picture of Chuck, Hank and me looking at each other, the photographers got a picture of the departing potentate driving stiffly past while Hank and I waved forlornly from the sidewalk.

If we had set out to rig a picture, we could not have conceived of a more dramatic way to bring home our message that far from being usurpers, we were just a couple of well-meaning, hard-working guys being pushed around by a rich minority stockholder.

Chuck had hired a public relations man who, we can imagine, put his head between his knees and wept. And so the next day, Charles returned to Comiskey Park to make a comeback. He wasn't quite up to giving us another of those classic action shots, but he did present us with a semiclassic family portrait. Dorothy was still a member of the Board of Directors and she was scheduled to meet us at Comiskey Park to discuss club affairs. As we were posing for the cameramen, Chuck came bursting into the room, just as determined to have his picture taken with us this time as he had been *not* to have it taken the day before. Poor Dorothy, I thought she was going to die. He had accused her, among other things, of trying to deny him of his just inheritance, and taking things out of their mother's home that rightly belonged to him, and the last thing in the world she wanted to do was to pose with him. Being a gracious lady, though, she couldn't very well refuse, and being an outsider, I couldn't very well refuse on her behalf. What resulted was a picture of the three of us seated

329

around a low table drinking tea, all of us trying desperately to look pleasant and all of us looking as if we were suffering from a severe case of gastric disturbance. It was hardly a picture to inspire the National Tea Council to break out 4-color ads in the national magazines.

We increased the board to five after winning a case to fill a vacancy on the Board of Directors. Thus by April 30, two weeks after the season started, I finally became a director. On May 8, I was elected president of the White Sox while I was off somewhere making a speech. By that time, I had already made close to a hundred speeches and we had a record advance sale.

Chuck Comiskey became a minority stockholder, with the same rights as a minority stockholder in U. S. Steel. He had the right to name his two members to the Board, to attend the Board meetings and enter his objections to our policies. We had the right to duly note his objections and move on to the next order of business. He and his father-in-law were the two minority Board members. They had no suggestions for improving our operation, they were simply against any improvements we wanted to make. For the most part, they were watchdogs over the purse strings. We had, for instance, instituted a new method for feeding our park personnel and guests and they objected strenuously that we were spending too much money on food.

I did want to have a good relationship with Charles at first. I was always civil to him personally and I have never said an unkind word about him publicly. We raised his salary from $28,000 to $35,000 and gave him a liberal expense allowance. We promoted him from vice-president to the more imposing position of executive vice-president so that he would be able to hold up his head at class reunions. I left him his old office and secretary and worked out of a desk, just off the reception hall, that had always been used by one of the secretaries.

He wanted a written contract, so we gave him one. He objected to the routine clause in the contract calling for a 15-day notice of dismissal, so we crossed it out. When we went to Los Angeles to play in the World Series at the end of the year, I gave him the tickets to the White Sox box. Mary Frances and I watched the games from out in left field.

As executive vice-president, he could have made a real place for himself in the organization. I have never told officials of any of my clubs what to do although, of course, I'll suggest things at times. Charles never showed any inclination to do much of anything. He came and went as he pleased. Mostly, he stayed away. In all fairness, though, it wasn't that he didn't want to work; he didn't want to work with us.

And he couldn't seem to break that habit of litigating with us, even with his sister gone. I mean he treated me just like one of the family. His litigations were pretty hopeless, and I stopped paying any particular attention to them. I stopped paying any attention, in fact, to Charles. I had a club to run, starting from scratch, and I couldn't be bothered. I spoke to him about the 80 percent only once, and then turned him over to Hank and put him completely out of my mind.

Hank couldn't understand my attitude. "You spend all your time hustling bellboys and charming elevator boys," he'd say, "and here's a guy who means so much to all of us and you won't even try." Even today, Hank believes that if I had turned my boyish charm on Chuck, full force, I could have come to some kind of an understanding with him on the 80 percent. But, I tell you, I have no patience with people who think everything is coming to them. If a man wants to work, I'll work right alongside him. And if he extends his hand to me in friendship, I'll extend my own. But don't let him tell me that I owe him anything because his grandfather struggled to build a ball club sixty years ago.

I don't think he'd have sold one share of stock to me no matter what I did or how charming I became. Hank had him on the edge at least three times, but in the end he would always find a reason to back off. There was another way we could have worked out the liquidation, although it would not have been as clean-cut or saved us quite as much money. Chuck could have sold the stock, and then bought back his original 46 percent in the new corporation, in the names of various members of his family. He was willing to do it, he said, if we would let him buy back 50 percent, which would have been fine if we were interested in fighting the Civil War instead of winning the pennant.

The inability to liquidate cost us about $1,300,000 in extra taxes, and what made it so senseless was that 46 percent of it was really Chuck's money. "Well," he told Hank, "I'm patriotic. I don't want to beat the Government out of any taxes." There wasn't much Hank could do after that except lower his head and leave quietly—with Charles humming the Star-Spangled Banner softly in the background. I had to keep a firm grip on myself for two weeks to prevent myself from firing all the accountants in a fit of patriotic fervor.

Early in our second season, Charles surprised me by sending in a letter of resignation.

When I had to retire from baseball myself because of illness, Art

Allyn bought the club from Hank and me. As a new owner, Art had another 360 days in which to convince Charles that it was to their mutual advantage to work out some way to liquidate. Chuck did sell out before the year was up, but he sold to outside interests. It was not until May, 1962, that Art was able to buy full control and look forward to a few happy years of tax benefits. It is to be hoped that the nation will survive.

The South Side Shall Rise Again | 23.

IT may be rough on the nervous system to buy a ball club the way I, because of forces beyond my influence, control and bankroll, always seem to, but there is one thing to say for it. I'm always riding a big publicity buildup to the day I take command. From the time it became known that I had an option from Dorothy to the time I was elected president, we had more than two months' worth of controversy, conflict and conjecture. Being a well-known supporter of the Constitution, and most particularly of the First Amendment, which guarantees freedom of the press, I have never felt I had the right to discourage newspaper coverage. I mean, I, in my quiet unassuming way, am just as patriotic as Charles Comiskey.

In Cleveland, there was rumor followed by confirmation followed by anticipation. In St. Louis, we had the day-by-day countdown on the stock trickling into the bank, as we presented a thrilling cliff-hanger to the background music (with apologies to Louis Jordan) of "Will he will or will he won't collect his 75 percent?"

In St. Louis, Helen Traubel held about 10 shares of the old stock. Being a good sport, she helped us get some free space by selling it to us publicly and urging her fellow stockholders to send their certificates in. After the first story broke in Cleveland, Bob Hope's lawyer, Colonel J. J. Klein, phoned to inform us that he thought Bob, a Cleveland boy, would like to be cut in for a piece of the local representation. We were delighted. The addition of Hope not only kept the story moving, his name—like Miss Traubel's—lent a touch of tone and glamour to our arrival.

Because that's what you're selling. Anticipation. Excitement. Excitement is contagious. It jumps from the fan to the non-fan and, to a degree that is astonishing, it spills over onto the field and infects

332

the players themselves. The first order of business when you take over a franchise that has been in the doldrums is to create the atmosphere that the new order has arrived, that we are living in historic times, that great things are in the air and ultimate triumph inevitable.

Chuck Comiskey, who felt—and not without justification—that he deserved the credit for putting the team together, was particularly unhappy when he found himself practically blotted out of the publicity that accompanied our drive to the pennant. I would submit, on my own behalf, that without the excitement generated by the new management the White Sox would not, out of the blue, have won their first pennant in forty years.

Viewed purely as an engineering problem in building attendance, we won the pennant too soon. In Cleveland, where we whipped up excitement for half a year with a sixth-place team, jumped to the first division the next year and won the pennant the next, it was handled much more efficiently. Ideally, you should build to a pennant over four years, jumping from sixth to fourth to second to first. The Milwaukee Braves gave us something close to a textbook example of keeping a city panting for five full years. In their first year the Braves, considered a second-division team, caught the imagination of the city by finishing second. They then dropped back to third, came up to second, had the pennant apparently sewed up the crucial fourth year and blew it (an ingenious plot twist) and then, with the town just about to run out of aspirin and patience, bounced back to win the pennant and, to send everybody home happy, beat the Yankees in the World Series.

The man who walked into Chicago in 1959 was not the same carefree, confident young man who had walked into Milwaukee 18 years earlier. I was more nervous about operating the White Sox than I had ever been about any project in my life, because I knew that this might very well be the last roll of the dice. I was like a chronic gambler going back into action with one last stake. I didn't have Rudie Schaffer there to backstop me, either. Rudie was stuck in Toronto and he wasn't able to join me until the end of the regular season. Hank stepped in wherever he could. So did Mary Frances. The bulk of the work we simply threw onto the shoulders of the old White Sox staff, and they did their jobs superbly.

And, again, my luck held; I went into a new operation and found exactly the man I most needed. He was Aaron Cushman, about the brightest young P. R. man I have ever come into contact with, and my luck in bumping into him was the first sign that the dice were going to fall for me in Chicago.

I'm sure that everybody who has been to more than half-a-dozen ball games has experienced the feeling that a rally is about to start. It is impossible to explain, it is just there; the sudden realization that everything that has taken place to that point has been building to a big inning. The same feeling, greatly intensified, takes over a city that feels a pennant coming on. It's a physical and invigorating thing, like a freshening wind. The press is an almost foolproof barometer. Once we got rolling, the Chicago writers began to arrive at the park earlier and leave later, a very good sign. Pretty soon, the writers from the little dailies and weeklies of the area began to drop in on us, an even better sign. Generally, the out-of-town guys are made to feel rather like outsiders, indulged rather than welcomed. We greeted them all with open arms, made them part of the family and gave them the same courtesies and information that we gave the Chicago writers.

And finally the columnists, John Carmichael and Dave Condon, began to join Warren Brown and the others who regularly covered the games, an even surer sign. The columnist has his choice of sports and subjects. When he begins to appear regularly at your ball park, you know that his antennae are picking up signals that the big story— the pennant—is developing.

The last person in Chicago to see the light, I suspect, was me— although I am normally a devout optimist. I never enjoyed a season so much or suffered so intensely. Or was so astonished. Since my early days in Milwaukee, I have been an advocate of power and pitching. In modern baseball the winning equation is Power + Pitching = Pennant. Teams like the White Sox which depend upon speed and defense delight the hearts of all old-timers and generally finish in the second division. As the 1959 season began, we were, it seemed to me, far better equipped to battle McGraw's Giants than Stengel's Yankees.

I spent the first two-thirds of the season predicting that we didn't have enough power to beat the Yankees, which seemed to me to be self-evident. I spent the rest of the season sticking happily to my prediction, not because I believed it any more but because the White Sox fans were getting such a kick out of badgering me about it.

I should have listened to Al Lopez. Al told me from the beginning that we were going to win it. "This," he kept telling me, "is my kind of team." I have always respected Al's ability and judgment. I had, after all, been the first operator to look upon him as a major-league manager. But as far as I was concerned, it was his kind of team and he could have it. Al got his chance to prove his point mostly because I wasn't able to make a deal for any of the power hitters I was after. Particularly Roy Sievers. I offered Cal Griffith as much as $250,000 for him, plus players. As much as Cal wanted the money he was afraid of the reaction of his Washington fans.

If Al Lopez has a weakness as a manager—and I said *if*—it is that he is too decent. Unlike me, he will not have a roistering or even troublesome player around, a prejudice which, as you may imagine, severely limited my range of action. I wanted to sign Satchel Paige. I felt Satch would help us. I knew he'd help us at the gate. But Al wants only the players who catch every plane and meet every roll call, and Satch wasn't a particularly good bet to catch the next streetcar.

Al and I had no real personality conflict, though, even though I sometimes had the feeling that he would have been more comfortable had I worn a tie. We lived in adjoining hotels and we breakfasted together almost every morning. Our early-season conversations generally went like this:

ME: Are they really going to count that one we won last night?
AL: It was a little close at that.
ME: I talked to Calvin again about Roy.
AL: What'd he say this time?
ME: (*Shrug*) I don't know who's hurting more, Cal or me.
AL: Why waste all that money, Bill? Those phone calls are expensive. We'll be all right. Just relax.

Al was completely relaxed. In that cool, calm way of his he squeezed every possible drop of talent out of his team. When I think of that season, I think of a squibbling hit and everybody running. Our battle song (with apologies to the composers of the musical *Kismet*) was "Bobbles, Bingles and Bunts." A typical White Sox rally consisted of two bloopers, an error, a passed ball, a couple of bases on balls and, as a final crusher, a hit batsman. Never did a team make less use of the lively ball. We won 35 of our games by one run, and it seemed as if we won most of them in the ninth inning or extra innings. At the end of the season I offered my services to the Heart Fund. Having brought them so much unsolicited business, I felt as if I owed them a year.

When you have that kind of a team, the fans can be enormously helpful. It is possible, I suppose, that the last group of fans always seems to have been the best. I never thought I'd find fans to equal Milwaukee's, and within a year I had found them in Cleveland. There was no doubt in my mind that Cleveland was the ultimate until I found myself among the White Sox fans of Chicago, better known to experts in this field as "the long-suffering White Sox fans."

The White Sox hadn't won a pennant since 1919 and they had yanked that one away from their rooters by throwing the World

Series. During one slack period they finished in the second division 16 years in a row. When their fortunes improved, with the arrival of Frank Lane, they were a team which would break fast, lead the league for half the season—or three-quarters of the season, or seven-eighths of the season—build up the hopes of their fans and then, as any real White Sox fan knew in his heart all along, fold in the stretch.

The Cub and the White Sox rooters break along social and economic and geographic lines. The Cub fan comes from the suburbs and from out of town. He will come to a Sunday game, preferably after an early-morning round of golf, to relax. To the White Sox rooter there is nothing casual or relaxing about baseball. Wake him up in the middle of the night, ask him who he is and he will say, "I am a carpenter and a White Sox fan." He may or may not have inherited his trade from his father, but the chances are very good that he inherited his rooting interest in the Sox. This kind of family solidarity can only come out of adversity and trial by fire. The White Sox had long ago tested the loyalty of their rooters; the weak and the faint of heart had fallen by the wayside and only the strong, the dedicated and the masochistic remained.

If there is any justice in this world, to be a White Sox fan freed a man from any other form of penance.

They had adopted a surface cynicism about their team—nothing but scar tissue. They pretended that they never expected another pennant to fly over Comiskey Park—protective coloration only. They were loyal to the bitter end and they faced each new season with renewed hope. And when they came to the park, they came, by golly, to root! We had some very good base runners, particularly Luis Aparicio, an incredible shortstop from Venezuela who turned the impossible play into an everyday occurrence. Luis brought the stolen base back into baseball, and whenever he would get on base the chant would arise, spontaneously, from every corner of the park: "GO ... GO ... GO ..."

When they became convinced, in 1959, that after 40 years their time had finally come, they got behind the team and almost pushed us to the pennant. We'd come into the ninth inning, three runs behind, and they'd fill the park with a sort of electric excitement that told us they *knew* that one way or another we were going to pull it out. So there'd be a base on balls and an error and a squibbling hit and a wild pitch and a sacrifice fly and we'd win.

They were so enthusiastic that I couldn't complete my rounds in the usual six innings, in order to spend the last three innings in the press box. Everybody wanted to talk, and most of them wanted auto-

336

graphs. I signed hats and shirts and jackets and tennis shoes and whatever other exotic haberdashery came to hand.

The problem of attracting other Chicagoans to the games, particularly women, was complicated by the noisome reputation of Comiskey Park, a problem made even more difficult by the competition from "Beautiful Wrigley Field," on the other side of town. Comiskey Park is in the grimy industrial back-of-the-yards section of the South Side, and although it was a basically sound and solid structure, the maintenance had been neglected so completely over the years that it had all the appearance of an outdoor slum. The neighborhood's reputation was about the same as Central Park in New York. You did not walk your dog at night unless you wanted both yourself and the dog mugged.

Our greatest asset, we discovered, was Lieutenant John L. Sullivan, the best handler of crowds—as a copper—I have ever seen. John L. and Andy Frain had achieved a remarkable record over the years in the face of all the difficulties; that is, nobody had been murdered on the premises and the park had not been burned to the ground. Given a little help from management, he cut the rowdyism rate 50 percent in our first year despite the tremendous increase in attendance.

John L. was somewhat Irish. He was tall and square of build, and he had crisp black hair, a red face and a perpetual smile. Most important of all, he had an ample tummy which he had learned to use to good effect. He could jostle a prospective troublemaker along in a gentle and jovial way which left no doubt that the offender would be very wise to keep moving.

We kept the rate of rowdyism going down the next year by putting a coat of white paint on everything that didn't move or talk, and over-ushering by 25 percent.

We were warned, of course, that it was a waste of time and money to paint anything white in *that* neighborhood, so we painted everything a shining, glistening white, and it is still a shining, glistening white. The bill for painting the outside of the park alone came to $148,000. As a man who had suffered the agonies of watching the St. Louis park crumble all around me, it was a pleasure to sign every check.

We had started cleaning up the park the day after we took over by bringing in a crew of about 300 guys to wash down the stands and the seats with soap and water. I was right in there scrubbing with them, and I tell you we uncovered layers of dirt that had been piling up from the day the Old Roman had first his flag unfurled. By 1961, we had a steam-cleaning unit to keep the stands spotless.

To dispel any fear about the neighborhood, which was not nearly as bad as its reputation, we set out to turn the whole area into an "Isle of Light." When a night game was being played at Comiskey Park, there was as much light outside the park as inside. Until the day I was no longer able to operate, there was never a moment in which we were not involved in some kind of a program for park improvement. In all, we spent well over a million dollars.

The most satisfying part of it was that once we had brightened up the park, everybody around us began to renovate. The whole neighborhood bloomed. Instead of hanging the usual bunting around the inside of the park at World Series time, we had baskets of flowers decorating the four blocks around the park. To hold to that motif, we presented roses to the first 20,000 women to come into the park.

As always we aimed to please. On one of my first trips to the center-field bleachers, a fan asked me why we didn't tear down the loudspeaker parapet which had been blocking everybody's view for years. Why not, indeed? There were architectural difficulties involved but, with a little effort, we were able to overcome most of them.

On the last game of our first brief home series, a woman in the bleachers stopped me to tell me how terrible it was that we had no ladies' toilet anywhere out there. I had been a vendor out in the bleachers when I was a kid and I had never known that there was not a single Ladies' Room there. "Next time you come," I said, "there'll be one."

"I come every day," she said.

"Fine," I said. "The day we come off the road, I guarantee you there'll be one."

The exclusive grandstand clubs and the executive boxes were left to the Yankees and their fellow aristocrats. For our part, we built a picnic grounds in the open space between the left-field fence and the permanent stands to enable the common folk to drink their beer, grab a bite and still watch the game in comfort.

Because the weather in Chicago tends to be a bit brisk in April, we arranged to have 20,000 pairs of gloves on hand for opening day to pass out to the customers. Little things like that are important, I think. There is, for instance, a radar screen set up around Chicago as a warning system against surprise attack. The radar also picks up approaching rainfall, always a hostile force to a ball club. Since we pay taxes, too, we established a working agreement with the weather bureau. As soon as we received a flash that a rainstorm was on its way, we'd pass out thin plastic rain capes to the customers in the open areas. The expense was negligible. At the quantity in which we bought the capes, they cost us a big 4½¢ apiece. The fans didn't care how much it cost us; they were impressed by the mere fact that we cared enough about their comfort to have the thought and make the effort.

They were impressed in another way, too. As the rain came whipping across the field, right on schedule, you could hear them gasp and turn to each other to ask what kind of black art we were brewing back in the clubhouse. (The truth, which I shall now reveal, was that we had a witch doctor, a lineal descendant of Phil Wrigley's whammy man, who could read entrails with the best of them. The Yankees didn't have to hire any witch doctor, of course; in those days they had Casey Stengel.)

The Fun & Games Dept. was thrown open for business about five minutes before the first game started. I had suggested to Chuck Comiskey that we bury the hatchet on the field of play (if you're waiting for me to say "but not in each other" forget it) by forming a stockholders' battery, with me pitching and him catching. After due thought, Chuck agreed. Unfortunately, my first pitch hit in front of the plate and bounced past him.

I hadn't done it on purpose. If anybody looked bad, it was yours truly. I got the ball over on the second attempt, though, which almost made me eligible for a $50,000 bonus.

Nothing went right that first day except the only thing that counted —we won the ball game. I had planned to celebrate my return with a fireworks display. The crew was set up behind the scoreboard where there would be no danger of any of the bombs drifting into the park. The pyrotechnical engineer, however, turned out to be an independent thinker. He moved his equipment to a playground behind left field and deliberately lobbed the bombs toward the playing field on the theory that a little excitement would be created if it appeared as if the players were being bombed. It sure was. The bombs would explode over the field, the debris would come showering down on the out-field, and Billy Pierce, our normally imperturbable pitcher, would back off the mound, shuddering visibly.

If you really want to find out how sensitive I can be, all you have to do is tell me that my stunts interfere with the play of the game. The powers-that-be had been belaboring me with that charge, quite un-fairly, throughout my career. And here, in my first appearance in Chicago, after all the court fights, it appeared as if I intended to amuse the customers by sending the players scrambling for cover.

I went running to the top of a ramp opening on the second deck of

339

the left-field bleachers. (I use the word "running" loosely, which is pretty much the way I run.) "Go back where you're supposed to be!" I yelled down.

He looked up and said, "Get lost, you joker. I know what I'm doing, and I'm shooting these things."

"Not any more you're not."

That gave him pause. "Who are you?" he asked.

"My name is Veeck, and I'm running the park and I guarantee you won't get another dime no matter how many you shoot off."

That ended the fireworks display for our grand opening.

The next day, I plucked the phone number of another fireworks company out of the Red Book. A short, chunky guy named Tony Cartalano showed up. I let him know right away I was no novice around fireworks.

"Oh," he said, "what do you like?"

I told him I liked Japanese stuff.

He looked at me with real admiration. "Boy," he said. "You really got taste."

Well, I could see I had found a man of discernment. I asked what he wanted to put on a good show.

"Three hundred and fifty," he said.

"I'll pay you four hundred. Will you make it good?"

"Listen," Tony said, "I've been knocking around this business all my life, and nobody ever paid me more than I quoted before. You want to knock your joint down, I'll knock it down for you."

The fireworks crew became a real part of our organization. They rooted for us and they suffered through our coronary finishes with us, although when Tony came back after a game and asked, "How'd it go tonight?" I knew he was talking about the fireworks, not the game. For Tony took his business no less seriously than I take mine or Auturo Toscanini took his. When we installed the exploding scoreboard the next year, Tony was placed in charge of loading it. I used to hustle him all over the countryside—Detroit, Cincinnati, Kansas City —because I could recommend him as the best I had ever seen.

On July 4, 1961, a month after I had sold my interest in the White Sox, Mary Frances gave birth to our fifth child, Juliana. The others are Mike, Marya, Gregory and Lisa. I had gone to the hospital to be with Mary Frances. The White Sox were out of town, but I called the park and asked Ed Holstein if it would be too much bother to send out a small blast on the scoreboard as a welcome to my new daughter and, I suppose, a Last Hurrah for myself.

The fellows at the park took over from there. The Fourth of July

340

is the day a fireworks man like Tony lives for, but he managed to get down there between jobs and they had him load the board as it had never been loaded before. The resulting blast rocked the city of Chicago. The South Side may have risen again, but Tony darn near knocked it down.

We went in big for the door prizes that we'd had so much fun with in Milwaukee. The name of our game was Lucky Seats. One fortunate woman won 10,000 cupcakes, which were delivered to her home. Do you have any idea how much room 10,000 cupcakes take up? We told the supplier, "Just keep on moving them in." He filled the kitchen and the hall and moved out to the back porch and he was still unloading cupcakes.

We gave a thousand cans of beer to one winner. To give one can of beer to a thousand people is not nearly as much fun as to give 1,000 cans of beer to one guy. You give a thousand people a can of beer and each of them will drink it, smack his lips and go back to watching the game. You give a thousand cans to one guy, and there is always an outside possibility that 50,000 people will talk about it.

We latched onto the baseball-card craze by putting a picture of one of our players on the back of every ticket. Anybody who assembled a complete set won a trip to the park. After awhile, people stopped ordering their tickets by seat or section. Customers would call and ask for "a Nellie Fox ticket," without ever bothering to ask where they were going to sit.

On Mother's Day, we opened the gates to any woman who could show a picture of a child, preferably her own. Almost 4,000 mothers passed through the turnstiles.

We didn't neglect the kids either. One of the most colorful—and certainly most ear-splitting—days we ever had was "Little League Day." We had 20,000 kids parading around the field in uniform before they went upstairs to yell.

Gags we had aplenty. Between the games of one Sunday doubleheader, we presented the whole Cristiani Bros. Circus, complete with the parade of elephants and a high-wire act. There were rumors that I presented the circus as much for my own benefit as for the fans. This is a most serious charge and upon careful examination of all the available data, I can definitely state that it is true.

Some of the gags backfired badly, an occupational risk. To commemorate the end of National Dairy Week—an occasion which most of us, in our selfish pursuit of fame and fortune, allow to pass unmarked and unhonored—we gave away all kinds of dairy products. As a topper, I conceived the truly brilliant idea of holding a milking

341

contest between the White Sox and the visitors. All the cows submitted in good spirit except for the one drawn by Nellie Fox, who was on his way to winning the award as the league's Most Valuable Player, and whom we needed no more than your baby needs milk.

I always thought Nellie had a good pair of hands myself; the cow, a far more exacting critic, seemed to think otherwise. The cow kept kicking, and Nellie kept trying, and I started writing mental headlines again. This one read: FOX IN HOSPITAL IN CRITICAL CONDITION AS RESULT OF VEECK GAG. Nellie's cow lost no milk that day, and I lost no more than three buckets of blood.

As always, I found that some of the best ideas were stimulated by some extraneous incident or offhand remark. I was speaking before a University of Illinois advertising class after the 1960 season, and in the question period that followed, one of the students asked why a vendor always seemed to be blocking his view during the key play of every game. Well, this did not come as a revelation. I can assure you that many a Roman left the Colosseum moaning that he had missed that magic moment when the lion first sank his teeth into martyred flesh because some big slob selling roasted chestnuts had cut off his view.

But all of a sudden I thought, Why not have midget vendors for one game next year so that for once everybody will be happy?

On opening day in 1961, midget vendors were patrolling the grandstand. We dressed them in little uniforms and had them carry little trays. They distributed the little shorty beers and the little cocktail weiners and other midget-sized edibles. Eddie Gaedel was one of the vendors, the last job he ever did for me. A couple of months later, little Eddie died.

The best promotional gimmick I have ever come up with, and certainly the least ignorable, has been the exploding scoreboard at Comiskey Park. Like many of my inspirations it came, alas, not in a flash of native genius but by applying an old idea to a current need. Years ago, I was very much impressed by a scene in William Saroyan's *Time of Your Life*. Through the entire show a guy had been battling a pinball machine in the background and finally, just before the curtain, he hit the jackpot and the machine erupted into an exploding, light-flashing, flag-waving finale. To me, it was an exciting scene, and I made a note to adapt it one day to my own uses.

And that brings us back to baseball. It had seemed to me for a long time that the home run, which had once been the single most spectacular and exciting event in a ball game, had become so commonplace that it was being greeted not with cheers but with yawns.

342

I could not see why it should not be possible to put the kick back into the home run by having it trigger something else. The memory of the pinball scene came naturally to mind because isn't that what a home run is, after all—the jackpot? And why the scoreboard? Well, why should a scoreboard just stand there doing nothing when it can contribute to the day's enjoyment?

This idea was developed, unfortunately, during my six years of penance, when I was in no position to pick up the phone and order an exploding scoreboard. One of our first clients when I joined Samuels and Gallagher in the public relations firm had been, briefly, the Cleveland Indians. I urged the exploding scoreboard upon them, and they weren't the least bit interested. So much the better, it developed, for me.

We built a scoreboard at Comiskey Park with 10 mortars bristling from the top for firing Roman candles. Behind the scoreboard, the fireworks crew shot off bombs, rockets and anything else they happened to think of. Nor was shooting rockets and bombs all our talented scoreboard could do. Far from it. In flipping its top, the scoreboard never flipped the same way twice. Unpredictability was part of its charm. The spectator could first look forward to the home run as a trigger to the scoreboard, and then he could look to the board itself to find out what in the world it was going to do *next*.

In the front of the board, there were colored "strobe" lights that flashed on and off crazily. The lights were controlled by a tape, which meant there was an infinite number of patterns they could be made to follow.

Built into the scoreboard also was a speaker system so powerful that if we had ever turned it all the way up, we could have blown 50,000 people out of the park. With a speaker system, we could obviously play any kind of sound track, or combination of sound tracks, that suited our mood and purpose.

My own favorite performance, I think, was the rendition of the chorus of Handel's *Messiah,* a glorious and exalting passage under any circumstances but, as you can imagine, a thing of sheer exultation when combined with the bursting bombs and the rockets' red glare in celebration of a White Sox home run.

Try to picture it. The ball has disappeared over the fence, the batter is rounding first base and the lights have already begun to chase themselves madly up and down and around the board. From the speaker come the strains of the *Messiah* chorus, but just as it has built to its marvelous climax, there is a moment of silence (as the amplifying system is pushed up) and then, in a beautiful and booming

343

choral arrangement: HALLELUJAH! HALLELUJAH! HALLE-
LUJAH!

Now comes another classical passage, a passage known to us
opera lovers as The Lone Ranger Galloping Theme:

Da-dada da-dada da-dada da da. Awaaaaaaaaayyyyy!

And away we go, again, to the full-voiced *Messiah* chorus and
HALLELUJAH! HALLELUJAH! HALLELUJAH!

And as the last HALLELUJAH! fades away, there is a BOOM!
And a BOOM! And a BOOM! BOOM! BOOM! BOOM! BOOM! as
the bombs explode and the rockets splash across the sky.

The scoreboard became such an attraction that it was the leading
subject for questions as I wandered around the city making speeches.
People who had seen it in action on television made special trips to
the park to see what it looked like live.

I have always tried to have a symbol for my ball clubs—in Cleveland it was the Laughing Indian. In Chicago, the people themselves
made the scoreboard the symbol for the team or, at least, for me.
As I'd walk into a hall to address a group, I'd be greeted by a volley
of bursting bombs, a marvelous way to start off the day. One group
rigged up a replica of the scoreboard itself that was so beautifully
done that it now sits in the Cooperstown Hall of Fame, preserved for
the ages.

I had a thousand variations figured out for the scoreboard had I
been able to remain in Chicago, because in any kind of entertainment
there should always be a topper. You get them to say *aaaah* and you
get them to say *ohhhhh,* but the real success comes when you can
then get them to gasp and bulge out their eyes and say, "Ho-ly
smoke!"

Which reminds me. For the 1961 season, I added smoke to the
scoreboard. When the bombs went off, smoke came pouring out from
all portholes, making it appear as if the whole board was going up
in flames.

One of the toppers, which, to my great regret, I was not able to
present before I left, was reserved for the New York Yankees. I had
arranged to rent about a hundred homing pigeons from the Bronx,
which for some strange reason seems to be a veritable hotbed of
pigeon breeding. After the bombs and the rockets and the rest of the
display, a section in the right-hand side of the board was going to
swing open and the pigeons were going to come streaming out, circle
around and head due east—carrying the news of the home run back
to New York. But you only do it once, understand. And, of course,
unadvertised.

344

Some of these things are expensive. I believe you have to spend money to make money, even if you don't think you can afford it. One of the secrets of being a promoter is never to doubt for a moment that if you spend your money right, the fans are somehow going to come. I have always run the most expensive operation in baseball. But sometimes the best promotions come the cheapest. The scoreboard cost $350,000. Now I could tell you that it cost *us* $350,000. It didn't. I didn't put up one dime. The fellow who built the scoreboard for us and helped to design it, Charlie Gibbes of Spencer Advertising Co., advanced the money and is being paid back from the receipts of the billboard advertising. My contribution was to conceive the idea and help to sell some of the ads. By 1964, the scoreboard will be completely paid for and it will then become a source of considerable income for the White Sox.

It has been a great thing for Gibbes. Out of the publicity from our scoreboard he has sold six or eight others around the country at a minimum price of $200,000.

While we were having fun with the scoreboard in Chicago, we had a bit of good, clean, malicious fun with the umpires too. The umpires, as a class, have never really impressed me. Not as greatly, at any rate, as they have impressed themselves. In the words of Lord Acton, power tends to make them lazy and absolute power tends to put them to sleep. I don't mind an umpire blowing a decision now and then, that's going to happen to the best of them. But there's no excuse for an umpire to be out of position just because the day is hot and he doesn't feel like hustling.

The umpires have it made because nobody checks up on them or grades them as they do ballplayers. Besides, they always stick together. As an operator, I have no idea what the umpires say in their reports to league headquarters after a controversy, which means there is no way I can dispute their endorsement of their own infallibility.

After we had some trouble with umpires being out of position, back in the old Milwaukee days, I announced that I had arranged to borrow two Eye-in-the-Sky cameras from the race track in Chicago, one to be trained on home plate and the other positioned to take pictures at both first and third base.

Actually, I didn't have the money to dismantle the cameras and have them shipped from Chicago. I doubt whether the track would have been happy to cooperate anyway. To save them the necessity of making a decision, I didn't bother to ask them. The umpires didn't know that, though. Rudie picked up three empty wooden boxes and we painted them a metallic gray, built rims into the front and painted wheels on the sides. The whole deal cost maybe $20. We installed them on top of the roof in left and right field, and from the distance they looked very authentic.

The umpires, always quick to take offense, refused to go ahead with the game, and George Trautman, the league president, came up to investigate. I told George what my cameras really were made of, and he, being a singularly unstuffy official, was not against shaking his umpires up a little. The game went on, and you never saw a team of umpires show so much hustle. We had excellently officiated games, I must say, for the rest of the year.

In Chicago, in 1960, with my finances and the world of science both having made great advances, I reverted to the plan of my youth. After a couple of bad decisions had cost us a couple of ball games, I installed a real Eye-in-the-Sky behind first base and had the operator accredited as a one-man newspaper agency so that he could legally service the papers. If I had been able to work through 1961, I was prepared to have the pictures hung up in the park 30 seconds after a disputed play, so that the paying customers could gaze upon every miscall in sadness and disbelief.

If I am not a fan of the umpires, I am, of course, a great fan of ballplayers. Along with the Chicago franchise came Early Wynn, who had been my ransom price from Clark Griffith ten years earlier. Early was one of my favorite players and a great personal friend. During the years I was out of baseball I would always run out to his home for barbecued steaks when I was passing through Cleveland. Wynn is a pitcher who, it is rumored, can be provoked into knocking a batter down should the batter show any foolish notions of digging in at the plate. I would shake my head sadly and tell him, "You'd hit your poor old mother," and Early would say, "Only if she was digging in."

Actually, he insists that he has never even pitched to his mother let alone knocked her down. He has, however, pitched to his son. "I was pitching batting practice to the kid," he says with paternal pride. "and he hit my outside curve against the left-field wall." Needless to say, Early knocked his son down on the next pitch. "What else could I do?" he says. "He had just hit my best curve ball against the fence."

In a tight pennant race, that kind of combativeness and competitive drive can communicate itself to a whole team.

Wynn had come to Chicago from Cleveland a year earlier, along with Al Smith, in a deal involving Minnie Minoso. Smitty was one of the boys we had signed in Cleveland—actually Hank had signed him

346

—and he was the closest thing to a power hitter we had. Theoretically, at any rate. Actually, Smitty wasn't doing anything except getting booed roundly whenever he showed his head. The fans in left field had loved Minoso, one of the last of the flamboyant players, and as will sometimes happen they took out their resentment at Minnie's departure on Smith. If Smitty had come into Chicago and hit a couple of home runs his first day, he'd have been adopted at once and all memories of Minnie would have faded away by the end of the week. But Smitty had a poor year, and they never let up on him.

By the time we arrived, in 1959, they weren't only booing him out on the field, they were booing him every time he came to the plate. It had reached the point where he wouldn't permit his wife or his son or daughter to come to the park.

I liked Al. We needed Al. I sat myself down, at last, to try to find some way of overcoming this feeling against him and maybe even swinging the fans behind him. The hook that seemed most promising was his name itself. If all the Smiths in Chicago would get behind Al, he would be off to a running start. The obvious thing to do was to hold a night for Al, with all Smiths, Schmidts, Smythes and any variants thereof admitted into the park as our guests—which meant, really, as the guests of their namesake. The idea was to pack them into the left and left-center field bleachers, right behind him, and hope they would form a personal cheering section.

Assuming Smith had a good night, the gag would make a great story; and since everybody likes to go along with a good story, we could expect the other fans to pick it up. If we were really lucky, the booing fad—because that's what these things are, fads—would be transformed through my alchemy into a cheering fad.

To buoy Smitty up even further, I sat beside him on the bench before the game and I said, "I've just been looking at the register and I see that you were cut $2,500 this year. I think you've been hitting real well even though the records don't show it. It seems to me that you've just been hitting in bad luck. So I'm going to give you a $2,500 bonus to make up for the cut."

Now that I had him primed for the big effort, he went out and had one of the great nights of his career, right? Well, no. He went out and had one of the worst nights he or any other big-league ballplayer has ever suffered through. He struck out and he hit into a couple of double plays and to make his night in front of all the Smiths and Smythes and Schmidts a boyhood dream come true, he dropped a fly ball to let in the winning run. The Smiths, the Smythes and the Schmidts booed and hooted and catcalled according to their predilections and national origins and read him out of the tribe. It was brutal. Instead of solving all his problems, I could see where I had probably ruined him forever.

The next day, I was down on the bench alongside him again. Smitty was trying to take it all in his stride, like a pro, but he'd have had to be abnormal not to be a little dejected. After some introductory small talk, I said, "Oh by the way, I meant to tell you. I hope you understand that the $2,500 bonus was just up to now. If you can go out and have a good season from here on in, I think I can work out another bonus."

There was no sense kidding myself that he wasn't very well aware what I was doing. At the same time, I was also showing him that he had at least one firm rooter in the city, who was with him all the way. I believe, as you know, in handing out the rewards when a player is down, not when he is on top of the world. Still, there always has to be a reason or you make him feel like a charity case and that only makes matters worse. If Smitty hadn't done well over the final six weeks, I wouldn't have been able to give him the bonus no matter how much I might have wanted to.

Over the last six weeks of the season, he led our team in home runs and runs batted in, and won game after game with the clutch hit in the ninth inning or in extra innings.

I gave him the bonus, of course. I also put him to work selling tickets over the winter, because I wanted him to call on people personally so he could discover that they really didn't have anything against him.

The next season the booing stopped, and Smitty finished with the second highest batting average in the league.

Everything in Chicago pales alongside the winning of the pennant. The night we clinched it by winning at Cleveland, I was in Bloomington making a speech for State Farm Mutual, the insurance company which sponsored Mary Frances and me on TV. Since the team was returning to Chicago that same night, I drove to the Midway airport with Dizzy Trout and Hal Smith, an advertising man from the insurance company's agency. Diz left me at a bar near the airport and went on into the city to pick up Mary Frances.

Before we drove on to the airport to greet the players, Mary Frances and I toasted our comeback with a bottle of champagne.

It was one o'clock in the morning when we headed for the airport, and yet at least 300,000 people had turned out to welcome their champions home. There were people standing on cars and trucks and

348

buses, and there were others on top of telephone poles. There were people who had jumped out of bed and into their cars without bothering to change from their pajamas. We were driving in a car which had the word WHITE SOX splattered all over it, and that helped to clear a path through the early going. Then we hit a solid mass of people and had to leave the car behind and try to battle our way through. We lost Hal Smith somewhere in the mob and never recovered him. Mary Frances lost one of her shoes, and was hopping along on one foot until a policeman fought his way through to return it to her, clearly above the call of duty.

We were going nowhere at all until word of our troubles reached Mayor Richard J. Daley, who was also having his troubles despite a police escort. Like Mayor Burke in Cleveland, Mayor Daley was not just an election year fan or an opening day fan or a World Series fan. He had grown up on the South Side only five blocks from Comiskey Park, had attended our games regularly for years, and was a visceral White Sox fan. The mayor sent a squad to pick us up and bring us over to his car and we managed to get through. The crowd was so huge that it spilled all over the runway. When the plane arrived two hours late, it had to land in the International Terminal.

Mayor Daley and his wife, and Mary Frances and I climbed to the top of the ramp, preparatory to being wheeled up to the plane to greet the players as the door opened. There were so many people hanging onto the ramp that it became impossible to move it into position. We all had to return to the runway until a portable staircase could be hustled into service. As we climbed up, the fireman's band was playing "My Bill" for me. In honor of Mary Frances, they played "It's a Grand Old Name," a grand old song which she looked upon with the same affection with which firemen look upon arson.

The victory parade through the streets of the city was scheduled for the following day. Mary Frances and I and Hank—who had been on the plane—held our own victory celebation that night. Too keyed up to sleep, we roamed the clubs of Chicago through the rest of the morning, ending up at the Singapore on Rush Street and arriving home with the dawn.

While I had been at Bloomington delivering a speech, and the team had been in Cleveland being interviewed in the locker room, we had performed a real public service for Chicago. The city council, in recognition of our victory and of the coming election, had passed a resolution decreeing that "there should be hilarity in the streets and shouting and celebration." While they were about it, Fire Commissioner Bob Quinn authorized the sounding of the sirens throughout the city to alert the citizenry to the victory. I'm not sure that last was really necessary. The game had been on television and the audience had been the largest to ever watch a baseball game in the city's history. It was a reasonable assumption that anybody who really cared already knew.

The sirens' wail made the night memorable, since there was no way for the people of Chicago to know whether the sirens were announcing the White Sox victory or the imminent arrival of the Russians. I mean, if you were a White Sox fan, you had to figure that it was just your luck for The Bomb to be dropped right after the White Sox won the pennant. What else could follow 1919? The newspapers and radio and television stations were inundated with calls from people curious to know whether the attack was coming from Russia or from Mars. The night clubs emptied as their patrons rushed out to look to the skies. The phone company reported that its switchboards hadn't been so busy since the death of President Roosevelt. The siren blew on for five minutes.

The only people in Chicago who kept their heads through it all were the air-raid wardens, who showed little disposition to rush to their posts, possibly because they were too busy lending their aid to the first spontaneous—and purely unofficial and unauthorized—hilarity in the streets. Chicago has never quite recovered from the lawless days of Capone.

By winning the pennant, we had filled the streets with a nicely balanced mixture of hilarity and panic, and uncovered a basic weakness in our national defense. The Director of Civil Defense, whom nobody had thought to consult or inform, let it be known that he was about to lodge a vigorous protest to national headquarters.

As in Cleveland, the fans got all the Series tickets above and beyond our normal commitments. Before we clinched the pennant, Birdie Tebbetts, the executive vice-president of the Milwaukee Braves, phoned to suggest a ticket exchange. Tebbetts proposed that we reserve 2,000 tickets for my old friend Lou Perini, in the event we won and, in return, Milwaukee would reserve 2,000 tickets for me in the event they won. Making the choice between handing 2,000 tickets to Perini's friends and customers or putting them into the hands of 2,000 Chicago fans was not one of the most soul-searching decisions I've been forced to make in my career.

Let me give you an idea how valuable World Series tickets are. When we were getting ready to take orders in Cleveland in 1948, a friend I hadn't seen in years came into the office early in the morning

350

while I was alone. I had known him as a kid and we had run around together in the early Chicago days when I was with the Cubs and he was working as a ticket broker. Naturally, I was happy to see him. He said he wanted some tickets. "Fine," I said, "I can give you a set."

He placed a little black bag in front of me on the desk. "I'll tell you what," he said. "You take out your season's reservations and what you need for the other clubs and the press, and I'll take the rest at face value. I'll also walk out without this little bag."

"I think you'd better leave," I told him. "Now and with the bag. I'd throw you out myself except I've known you all my life and I know this is how you make your living."

He picked up the bag and started out. "By the way," I said. "How much is in there?" Look, I'm as curious as the next man and I didn't want to spend the rest of my life wondering whether I had been a little noble or a lot noble.

He turned back hopefully. "A quarter of a million dollars," he said, rounding his consonants nicely.

"It's guys like you who make life so hard for guys like me," I said. "So get out now while I still have my resistance up." He started out again. "Come on back," I said. "I'm going to let you buy two strips of tickets for old times' sake." It seemed the least I could do for a man so concerned about my financial welfare. (This was the first of the safe-deposit offers I turned away—with, let us say, some regret. The political offer didn't come until almost two years later.)

The fans got all the tickets. We had conducted surveys during the year to find out where our customers were coming from, which meant we were able to weigh our ticket distribution quite accurately. Sixty-five percent of the tickets went to the South-Siders. After that, as might be expected, the percentages diminished as the distance from Chicago increased. We didn't assign them only by radius, though; to be as accurate as possible we allotted them by the town.

To make certain everybody knew we were trying to be as fair as humanly possible, we rented an office downtown, in the same building where Will Harridge had his headquarters, and conducted a public drawing. Some of the city's outstanding citizens were among those picking the applications out of bushel baskets, including my first backer Phil Clarke; Truman Gibson, Sr.; Richard A. Aishton, retired president of the Continental Illinois Bank and Trust Co.; and William V. Kahler, president of the Illinois Bell Telephone Company. A couple of the regular bleacherites—one of them was a retired streetcar conductor—were among the dignitaries too.

But not even the most careful geographical lottery could insure that the regulars, the guys who had been coming every day for years, would end up with tickets. And I was determined that this was one time when the old, loyal rooters were going to be at the Series. In traveling around the park, I had come to recognize most of the regulars. A full month before the end of the season, I began to take their names and addresses without telling them why. Since the regulars all knew each other by sight, I'd ask each of them to point out the others, and also to let me know about anybody who might not be there that day. "There's this baldheaded guy," one of them would say. "He usually sits right over there. Never has too much to say, but he's been coming since, oh, right about the year Luke Appling hit .388."

"OK," I'd say, "the next time you see him, tell him I want to talk to him, will you?"

I collected something like 3,000 names before I was through, all of them hard-core fans who had been supporting the team through the good years and the bad.

"These are our vvvvips," I announced. "Our very, very, very, very important persons."

I trust that Lou Perini's customers were able to see the games in Los Angeles.

As for me, I finally brought a team into Los Angeles, even if it wasn't quite the way I had originally planned. There are some cities where you aren't meant to prosper; I still haven't walked out of Los Angeles with anything. For that matter, we didn't do any better in Chicago; we lost two out of three in each city.

Things began to go badly for us from the singing of "The Star-Spangled Banner" before the opening game of the Series at Comiskey Park, and you have to start working pretty early in the morning to beat that. Nat Cole, an old friend from the Cleveland days, was our opening-day singer. Nat forgot the words and had to make up his own National Anthem as he went along. He showed a real flair for it, too. If Fort McHenry is ever bombed again, Nat's prospects will be unlimited. On the second day, Miss Vivian Della Chiesa sang the National Anthem. Miss Della Chiesa's memory was faultless and her voice, of course, superb. The sight of the flag rising to the top of the pole behind her gorgeous voice would have been a moment to remember, if only the flag hadn't got stuck halfway up.

We hastily called around for a steeplejack and learned that the steeplejack had apparently disappeared from the American scene. You turn your head away for ten or twenty years and all of a sudden, no more steeplejacks. In the entire city of Chicago, we discovered, there was only one specialist in disentangling flags from flagpoles—a female flagpole sitter.

Naturally, we wanted her to rush down and strut her stuff during the game. These are my people. I didn't visualize anything quite so dramatic as the raising of the flag at Iwo Jima, but still there is a certain drama in the picture of 50,000 people watching breathlessly as one lone brave woman shinnies up a pole and sets the flag free to wave in the breeze. (I'm sure I would have been accused of planning the whole thing and making a travesty of flag-raising.) Our intrepid flagpole expert couldn't come to the park until the game was over, though, and we had to play out the game with the flag flying, prophetically, at half-mast.

In case anybody from *Variety* is listening, Nat Cole, given a chance to redeem himself, sang the National Anthem for the White Sox on opening day in 1962, and this time he gave Francis Scott Key a much better shake.

How We Brought the Minor Leagues Back to Los Angeles | **24.**

THE great expansion move in baseball was finally voted in the winter of 1960, a season wisely chosen to coincide with an even greater expansion in my head. It is sometimes amazing how completely you can be carried away by your own fond estimate of your own strength. Or, to get it right down to the language of the dugout, I had delusions of grandeur with marked tendencies toward euphoria.

My modest little plan was to slip my own friends into the two new franchises, Washington and Los Angeles, and there being little to gain by halfway measures, also to put a friend into the Kansas City franchise. Arnold Johnson had died that spring, and his widow, who was independent of the Yankees, was seeking to sell.

At the very worst, I would have a bloc of four votes (counting my own), and nobody would be able to pass anything detrimental to us. At best, I was going to isolate the Yankees and try to jam through a progressive program that would lift baseball, kicking and screaming, into the twentieth century.

Like all great concepts for universal good, my inspiration came to me in a flash of sheer egotism during my first year in Chicago. It came out of—and was dependent upon—Cal Griffith's desire to move his team from Washington to Minneapolis.

My feelings were that it would be basically wrong and even worse, stupid, for the American League to leave Washington. I had not the slightest doubt that the moment we moved out, the National League in its own expansion program would quickly move into Washington and back to New York and have itself all the great cities from coast to coast plus the prestige of the nation's capital. If Presidents are going to toss out baseballs on opening days, better in an American League park than a National League one. Washington also happens to be an untapped gold mine. If I couldn't make a club go there I would turn in my shield. (That's the shield on which I have been carried off of so many battlefields, including the one we are now talking about.)

At the same time, I was in no position after my own experience in St. Louis to tell anybody he had no right to move. My attitude when Cal sounded me out was that I'd be for him only if there was another team ready to move into Washington to take his place. Yes, Cal said, that's what everybody had been telling him. And, right there, I became Cal's ally. You see the possibilities, don't you? If Cal left Washington, it would mean we would have to have an expansion to ten teams.

But there was far more to it than that. The lineup of the other teams in the league left me in the strangest position of my career in baseball. The Eastern clubs were solidly behind Cal, and with Johnson still alive in 1959 the Kansas City vote went with the Yankees. The only thing that could hold Cal to Washington was the solid opposition of the other three Midwestern cities, Cleveland, Detroit and Chicago.

The background music went like this: Minneapolis had built a municipal stadium because it had expected to get the New York Giants as soon as Horace Stoneham achieved complete disaster in New York. Stoneham was just about ready to jump to Minneapolis and its out-stretched stadium when Walter O'Malley picked him up and carried him piggyback out to the Coast.

The Minneapolis stadium had been built at the urging of sports-writers Charlie Johnson and Sid Hartman, who have never been given the credit they deserve. After he lost the Giants, Hartman went after the Cleveland Indians, whose attendance had been slipping badly. Being a man of taste, Hartman did not want Washington nearly as badly as the Senators wanted Minneapolis. Still, they were a big-league team, duly entitled to use baseballs signed by Joe Cronin. Hartman might gag a little but he'd take them.

Here was the situation that opened up for me: While the Indians weren't ready to depart from Cleveland, it comforted them to wake up in the morning and know that Minneapolis was there in case of dire emergency. This meant that Cleveland was against Cal moving in. In the old days, Cal could always count on Spike Briggs and the Detroit vote. But Spike was gone. Fetzer had become the majority stockholder in Detroit, and Fetzer was showing himself to be a man of independence. In general, he and Nate Dolin—who had become the strong man at Cleveland—had formed a loose alliance. In this case, Detroit was following the official Cleveland line, which was, "What do we want Griffith going up there for?"

That left Chicago as the only uncommitted franchise. For the first time in my life I found myself not only aligned and allied with the majority, I found myself sitting with the *control vote* in my hands.

I made an agreement with Cal. In return for my vote to permit him to move to Minneapolis, he was to vote for my candidate to replace him in Washington. Cal agreed, gratefully and absolutely. My candidate for the franchise was Jerry Hoffberger of National Brewery. Jerry owned a good hunk of stock in the Baltimore Orioles, which was a complication, but I felt he would be great for both the city of Washington and the American League.

Hank Greenberg was going to get the new team in Los Angeles. Hank was already a member of the committee that had been set up to study the possibilities of expansion. The committee appointed him to go out to investigate Los Angeles, with the understanding that he had what amounted to an option on the franchise.

Our man in Kansas City was Elliot Stein. Elliot obtained an option on the 52 percent majority interest owned by Arnold Johnson's widow without any difficulty and went on to try to buy out enough of the minority stockholders to give him the 80 percent he needed to liquidate. (Johnson's death had not changed the voting lineup on Minneapolis because as much as his widow disliked the old board of directors, it still had another year to sit before she could replace them.)

By the time the league met to vote on expansion, it had become more important than ever for Hank to be awarded the new Los Angeles franchise. In June, 1960, I had undergone the final amputation on my leg, this time above the knee. And for the first time in my life I hadn't bounced right back. It was becoming increasingly evident that it wasn't the leg but something else.

By the end of the season, I knew I was going to have to sell my interest in Chicago and take a long rest. Charles O. Finley, with that instinct of his for an available franchise, jumped out of the weeds again with an offer of $4.2 million for the club, a good enough price. Finley's reasoning was that if Hank was going to Los Angeles, I was going with him. The funny thing was that Finley was right, even though he was right for all the wrong reasons. I *didn't* want to sell the White Sox so that I could go to Los Angeles; I just wanted to put my affairs in order, a grisly expression but an accurate one. Before we sold to Finley, though, I wanted to see Hank settled down with another club, mostly for his own sake but also, I must admit, for my own. With Hank in Los Angeles, I knew I could always come back as a full partner—assuming an improvement in my health—just as Hank knows he could always come into any operation with me.

If I was able to come back, Finley would still give us a friendly vote in Chicago and my master plan would hold.

All of these plans began with Cal Griffith's move to Minneapolis. Cal, of course, could not negotiate himself, because once it became public knowledge that he wanted to leave Washington he would find himself in the same situation I had found myself in St. Louis. I carried the ball for him. At the end of 1959, I went to Minneapolis, ostensibly to appear on a television show for Sid Hartman between halves of a Minneapolis basketball game but actually to sell him on Washington. I had breakfast with some of the leading citizens and explained why I thought the shift would be good for them and for baseball and, more to the point, to let them know that Cal was willing.

By the time the 1960 season opened, Cal was beginning to vacillate. "If it could be arranged and I don't get embarrassed . . ." he was saying.

"That's right, Cal," I'd say. "If anything goes wrong, you have to be in a position to say you never asked."

I attended routine league business meetings I otherwise wouldn't have been caught dead at, just to keep after him. While I was there, I'd poll the owners again on the basis of "he's not asking, understand, and I'm not asking for him but let's just see what would happen if he did ask." And always the vote was the same.

Over the last part of the season I kept telling him, "Either you leave the minute this season's over, or somebody's going to beat you to it. You see what's happening to Cleveland's attendance?"

Cal had to play it close to the vest to the very end. He was being sued by his minority stockholder over an entirely peripheral issue, the sale of the real estate on his Chattanooga farm club, and if it had been known he was moving his own club, his whole case might have been prejudiced. The American League had to push its meeting back a week so that the verdict would be in before we voted.

By this time, my master plan had already sprung a couple of leaks. The first crack in the façade came when Elliot Stein found he was going to have trouble buying enough of the minority stock in Kansas City to get his 80 percent. The minority stockholders were not particularly disposed to cooperate with Johnson's widow—or, for that matter, with me. For by this stage of the game, there were a few of my fellow operators who had put two and two together and come up with the glimmering of an idea that they added up to four franchises.

Elliot's feeling was that if he bought the majority interest, he could —with a lot of effort and at great expense—work something out. I didn't think that I, in good conscience, could recommend that he lock himself in without being sure of that 80 percent. It was bad enough that we were in that position in Chicago. To be stuck in a marginal operation like Kansas City without tax benefits would be murder. I had to advise him to drop the option.

I was in trouble in Washington, too. In my own defense, I must point out that I came to the meeting in poor health. I had been doing a bad job running the ball club and I had been meeting my speaking commitments with difficulty. Between one thing and another, I had badly neglected my plot to take over the world.

Jerry Hoffberger had never given me a firm commitment on Washington. Jerry's dilemma was that he owned 27½ percent of the Baltimore Orioles and it appeared, at that particular moment, as if he had some chance of buying control. That left him with a choice between the two cities, because if he headed up the Washington syndicate he'd have to get rid of his Baltimore stock. On the eve of the meeting, Jerry informed me that he really preferred to remain in his home town.

That was really no difficulty, though. Edward Bennett Williams, who is perhaps the best of the modern criminal lawyers, had been in the syndicate with Jerry; Ed—who is one of my favorite people— stepped in quickly and the financing was completed overnight. To all of you who are aware that Ed Williams is the counsel for Jimmy Hoffa and the Teamsters and who therefore jump to the conclusion that Williams was being backed by Teamster money, forget it. Hoffa wasn't involved at all.

All chances for an easy victory in Washington had gone by then anyway, because both the Yankees and the Red Sox had a candidate in the field. The Yankees were backing Admiral Bergen of Graham-Paige, the organization that owns Madison Square Garden. Admiral Bergen was no great problem. He seemed like a nice enough guy and he was probably relatively independent of the Yankees, but it wasn't too difficult to weaken his position by asking the other clubs whether they wanted to give the Yankees another farm club to replace the one they had just lost in Kansas City.

The bad break I got, discounting for the moment my own sloppy job of organization, was that Tom Yawkey had decided it would be nice if his old friend General Elwood Quesada, who was about to leave his job as head of the FAA, got the franchise Quesada was in and out and up and down and around and about for awhile, but two weeks before the meeting I was reliably informed that he was going to be a candidate. I had been hoping that Cal Griffith would bring Boston along as part of the package and that between Cal, Boston and Hoff-berger, the Baltimore vote would fall to us too. As it was, I entered the meeting with only myself, Cal and Cleveland. That was all right. I had three votes, an absolute veto. I was sure that Bergen could be eliminated quickly. Quesada had little beyond Yawkey's blessing and whatever good Joe Cronin could do him as league president. In the end, it seemed to me, they'd have to come around to Ed Williams.

Right to the end, I rode shotgun for Cal Griffith. There had been a Minneapolis "club" in the Continental League, a third major league that I looked upon as wholly a figment of Branch Rickey's imagination. Rickey, still a man to reckon with as he approached the age of eighty, had been using his phantom league as a wedge to get a New York franchise in the National League. A controversy somehow developed as to whether Griffith would be bound to take this local Minneapolis group in as partners. "This is the most ridiculous thing I've ever heard of," I said, still battling for my man. "Just because some guys get together and say they've got a club and a league, and we've been willing to listen to them talk, does that mean we've given them an interest in our own clubs?" After a little debate, the Continental League was buried. At least, it would have been buried if anybody could have found a body.

We proceeded, at last, to the business of expansion.

I delivered the control vote, as per agreement, and Cal was given permission to move to Minneapolis. The meeting itself moved on to the next order of business, the new franchise in Washington.

A secret ballot was called the first time around and, needless to say, I started screaming. I was confident that Cal had told the Red Sox that he had a prior commitment, but I would just as soon have heard Cal honor that commitment, loud and clear.

First, they voted on Bergen. He received two votes. That would be New York and Kansas City; he was well contained. Then they voted on Ed Williams. We got three votes: Chicago, Cleveland and good old Cal. Quesada got three votes too, Boston plus Baltimore and Detroit, two votes that Cronin had probably hustled up. Those last two votes would be easily detachable in a deadlock. My three votes, thank goodness, were firm.

Two or three more secret ballots were taken, always with the same result. Since Yawkey hadn't come to the meeting, Boston was represented by Dick O'Connell, who had just become the Red Sox business manager. O'Connell seemed a bit bewildered. He called for an open vote, not by candidate now but by a poll of the individual teams. It was perfectly clear that he had expected another vote on his line and was anxious to know who the defector was. I knew who it was. Cal hadn't been able to bring himself to tell Boston that he wouldn't be able to go along this time. All right, now they'd find out. Right in the open.

The vote was called in the order in which the teams happened to be seated around the table. That put Cal second in line. He sat there unhappily, his hands folded beneath his chin, and said, "Minneapolis votes for Quesada."

A chip off the old block. Uncle Clark had reneged on the Baltimore vote and Cal was in the old tradition. He remained hunched over the table, half turned away, and never looked at me. After the voting was completed, he sent over his traveling secretary, Howard Fox, to explain to me that in an open vote he had to go with the family. Fox is a very decent guy and he was terribly embarrassed. "Don't talk to me," I said, before he could get it out. "I did what I agreed to do and I expected him to do what he agreed to do. As far as I'm concerned, he ran out on me."

So Cal took a powder and Fox is embarrassed, and my plans are all loused up. The Yankees moved over to Boston, and General Quesada was quickly voted the franchise.

Nothing remained except to vote in Los Angeles as the tenth team in the league. A meeting was scheduled at the Plaza Hotel in New York the following month to assign the franchise. On this one we seemed fairly safe. Hank Greenberg was the only candidate.

Hank had done an enormous amount of work in Los Angeles. His prospective partner was an old friend, C. Arnholt Smith, a Los Angeles banker who owned the San Diego Padres in the Pacific

Coast League. Hank and I both believed he had a good chance to get his own park built before O'Malley completed the Dodgers' long delayed, suit-ridden project at Chavez Ravine. They already had some land picked out just off the Freeway, the only location that means anything in Los Angeles. The park was going to be built by the Del E. Webb Corp. For the year coming up, Hank had no difficulty arranging for his dates at the Los Angeles Coliseum.

Ford Frick had opened the way for the American League to go to Los Angeles and the National League to return to New York by proclaiming them both "open cities." Not once. Not twice. The words "Open City" came to Frick's lips every time a sportswriter called up to ask for an interpretation of the rules. After opposing expansion for years, Frick was not only scrambling to get on the bandwagon, he was trying to make it appear as if he were the driving force.

His Open City proclamations were necessary because of Rule 1(c) which states:

> ... the circuit of either Major League shall not be changed to include any city in the circuit of the other Major League except by the unanimous consent of the clubs constituting both Major Leagues.

This is so central to the story of the Los Angeles franchise that we had better dwell upon it a moment longer. Commissioner Frick, in invoking his power to do anything that was "for the good of baseball," was overriding any right the Yankees or the Dodgers might have to bar the other league through the use of Rule 1(c). This was what the words "Open City" meant, this was what everybody understood the words to mean, otherwise they had no meaning at all. The National League, operating under the Open City principle, had already voted to expand to New York and there had not been a murmur of protest from the Yankees.

As we met to vote for the Los Angeles franchise, we discovered that Walter O'Malley was loaded down with objections about anybody coming into his private grazing grounds in Los Angeles. We discovered it when Ford Frick, that erstwhile apostle of the Open City, sent word from his office that some kind of fair and equitable settlement had to be made with O'Malley. Los Angeles wasn't an Open City any more; it was an Open City only to the degree Walter O'Malley wanted it to be. New York was still an Open City but Los Angeles was not.

Emissaries began to race back and forth in both directions. There were hints that O'Malley wanted indemnifications and the right to dictate his opposition's television policy. His main message to the American League, as passed on to us through the Commissioner, was that he—Walter O'Malley in person—would not permit an American League team to play in the Coliseum. O'Malley did not want two teams in the Coliseum, we were told in all seriousness, because if baseball monopolized all the dates during the summer, other worthy causes would be shut out.

There was the suggestion that O'Malley, being a reasonable man, would have no objection to an American League team playing in the Rose Bowl in Pasadena, where presumably a few stray citizens who had lost their way on the Freeway might stumble upon them while searching for a gas station. (Some connoisseurs of O'Malley were unkind enough to opine that in addition to trying to protect the people of Los Angeles from the temptation of squandering their money on American League baseball he was also taking a sideswipe at the Coliseum Commission, which he felt had been overcharging him unconscionably.)

Hank went to see Frick and was told that it was not up to the Commissioner to meddle in these private matters. It was up to Hank, he said, to negotiate with O'Malley himself. "Oh no," Hank told him, "I don't have to negotiate with O'Malley. I don't have to be anything but friendly with him and that's only because I like him."

The American League merely had to tell O'Malley to go jump, vote the franchise to Hank or to anybody else and move into the Coliseum. There was not a thing O'Malley could have done about it, and there was certainly nothing Frick, after strumming that Open City theme for so long, could have done except spit his foot out of his mouth.

Instead, the American League told Hank: "It's your problem. You have to solve it."

Frick told him: "It's the American League's problem, not mine."

Free translation: "Go see O'Malley, preferably on your hands and knees."

Hank had no intention of seeing O'Malley. It all became academic anyway when we saw the plan by which the new teams were going to be stocked.

Hank had gone to Los Angeles on the understanding that the new teams would be allowed to buy some decent players. The plan we intended to suggest called for the eight established teams to submit their regular starting lineup, with four of these regulars listed as untouchables. Each of the new clubs would then be entitled to buy one of the remaining starters for $150,000. Under this system, Los

Angeles and Washington would be starting out in life with four good established players who would be attractions in their own right and who would also form the nucleus for a sound ball club.

Instead, the established teams were being permitted to reserve all their top players, leaving nothing for the new teams except the culls and the hangers-on. As soon as we saw the generosity with which players were going to be dealt out Hank decided that even the undoubted pleasure of an intimate association with O'Malley would have to be foregone. I agreed with him. "This is your own bankroll you're putting in," I told him. "You have to lose from $400,000 to $500,000 a year for the foreseeable future, and that means you have to have a business you can write it off against."

Del Webb's capacity for confounding confusion has already been amply commented upon. With confusion in the air, Del swung into action. His solution predictably was to fly out to Los Angeles himself and deal with O'Malley on behalf of the entire league.

It is entirely possible that someone, somewhere, could have found a worse way to handle the situation. By offering to pay O'Malley off, Webb was recognizing, on behalf of the entire league, that he had a valid claim despite Frick's constant Open City talk.

Again, one is always bewildered by Webb's motives. Del was going to build Hank's park and therefore had been on our side until Hank withdrew. The relationship between Webb and O'Malley is hard to figure. At one time, they had been so close that I suspected they were working on a plan to go to Los Angeles together. By the time of the expansion meeting, this was no longer true. Webb had been confident that he was going to build O'Malley's park at Chavez Ravine. He had been so confident, O'Malley let it be known, that his bid had been about $6,000,000 higher than the winning bidder's.

The sportswriters jumped to the conclusion that Del was running out to Los Angeles to help O'Malley establish his position. Because the Yankees had been claiming, with perfect logic, that whatever was true for O'Malley against an American League team was also true for the Yankees against a National League team.

The sportswriters are often baffled by Webb because they keep thinking that his only interest is the Yankees. We know better than that. Webb had just lost the chance to build Hank's ball park. That was a loss, yes, but it was also an opportunity. The franchise was now wide open. You could be sure that Webb had a roomful of candidates waiting to fill the gap.

Now, there may have been a certain amount of politicking at the Democratic National Convention of the same year, but believe me, it
362

was nothing to the politicking that went into the assigning of the Los Angeles franchise. When Hank decided he did not choose to run, the dark horses came galloping from afar. The first to arrive to present his credentials and bank balance was our old friend Charles O. Finley. Del Webb, always the friend of all candidates, was there to lend him aid, comfort and encouragement before he himself went galloping off to Los Angeles to huddle with O'Malley. Finley somehow adopted me as his unofficial consultant and adviser, a role I found fascinating in that it kept me abreast of the latest gossip and gave me an unparalleled opportunity to follow the Odyssey of a man who takes Del Webb as his guide. Odyssey, students, is a Greek work meaning "wild-goose chase."

With Hank out of the Los Angeles picture, Finley suspected that I wouldn't be selling the White Sox. He was wrong, of course—a mistake that cost him his golden opportunity to end up with a contending team. Charles O. was hot for the franchise that was available at the moment, though, and for that I couldn't blame him. I had to warn him, however, that on the unlikely chance he did get the Los Angeles franchise, he could only get hurt. "Charles," I said, "you can go to Kansas City right now and buy the majority interest in the club from Arnold Johnson's widow. And from what Elliot Stein tells me, you'll be able to pick up the minority interests if you're willing to put in a little work."

But no. Finley was confident that the Los Angeles franchise was practically in his pocket. Webb, he said, had complimented him on the fine presentation he had made and advised him to firm up his syndicate with some local Los Angeles representation. The man Webb particularly advised him to see was Kenyon Brown. Brown was one of the radio-TV men who had been in the Detroit syndicate.

"Now we know who Webb's man in Los Angeles is," I told him. "Take my advice, Charles. Forget Los Angeles and go to Kansas City."

Finley called me from Los Angeles the next day. Brown, he said, had not been alerted by Webb, which seemed rather strange since Webb had left Brown's office only an hour or two before Finley arrived. "But," he said, "Brown is thinking over my invitation for him to join my syndicate. He's going to let me know tomorrow."

In short order, Finley was back in New York. No, Brown hadn't joined his syndicate. Brown, in fact, had never called back. Finley had therefore hopped to San Francisco to find Casey Stengel and offer him the job of manager of the Los Angeles team—which didn't yet exist and which Finley, in any case, didn't own. It had been

363

Finley's feeling that if he could stroll back into the Plaza with Casey on his arm, he'd stampede the meeting. I could have saved him that trip. I had already offered Casey any job he wanted in the Chicago front office at his own figure. Casey had informed me that he wasn't interested in a front-office job and had already turned down a couple of good offers to manage.

With nothing much developing, the question of the Los Angeles franchise was put off until the regular baseball winter meetings, which were scheduled for St. Louis in about two weeks. In those two weeks, I received daily calls from Finley from every conceivable section of the country. The most memorable call, I would say, came from Arizona. By that time, it had become evident that the Kenyon Brown syndicate had the inside track, and the most newsworthy name in Brown's stable was Gene Autry. Charles O. had decided that if cowboys were what was wanted, he would counter Autry with Roy Rogers. Good solid thinking. Rogers wasn't interested. Also good solid thinking.

Just before the St. Louis meeting, Finley called me in great excitement. He was right there in Chicago, he said, and he was going to fly to the St. Louis meeting with Walter O'Malley himself. No true servant of the Empire ever intoned the name of Queen Elizabeth with greater awe. "O'Malley," he said, triumphantly, "is for me."

I don't think I groaned outwardly. How could I expect Finley to know my compatriots as I knew my compatriots? He would learn the hard way, as I had learned. Meanwhile, he had broadened himself through travel and an intimate association with movie cowboys.

During the period between the New York and St. Louis meetings, Hank and I had reversed our fields completely. We didn't want Los Angeles in the league any more. Not just yet, anyway. If Los Angeles could be held off for one year, we could make an all-out push for interleague competition.

With Washington already voted in, we had a nine-team league. You cannot schedule nine teams. The two new National League teams, Houston and New York, were not supposed to start playing until 1962. Our plan was to bring New York in immediately, so that both leagues would have nine teams. The setup couldn't have been more perfect. There was only one city at the time with two teams, Chicago. If New York came in, that would make two. An interleague schedule would therefore give fourteen one-league cities a chance to see the great stars of the other league. It would particularly help the new teams, who needed all the help they could get. By giving Washington fans a chance to see the National League teams for the first time,

364

we would be salvaging the season for them. By giving the New York Mets seven games against the Yankees, their season would be salvaged too.

For awhile it seemed to have a pretty good chance, despite its logic. The American League was for it. O'Malley was supposed to be for it too, as we had anticipated, because it would automatically keep the American League out of Los Angeles for another year.

As the first business of the St. Louis meeting, the National League voted it down. Either O'Malley had lost a round, making him no longer undefeated, untied and unscored upon, or else O'Malley had the new American League syndicate so nicely under his control that he was better off with them in than out. (As for me, my record was spotless. I hadn't won a minor skirmish from the time Cal Griffith changed his vote.)

Despite Finley's confidence that he had received the blessings of O'Malley, it was obvious from the beginning that the Brown-Autry group was in the saddle. (Finley finally flew to Kansas City and bought the Athletics.) The Kenyon Brown group had undergone a fast shuffling, with Brown himself shuffled to the bottom of the deck. Gene Autry was now the head of the group, along with Rob Reynolds, the old Stanford All-American tackle who ran Autry's string of radio stations for him. Brown, it was generally understood, had stepped down because he wasn't acceptable to Walter O'Malley.

Before he would grant permission for an American League team to come into the Open City of Los Angeles, O'Malley insisted on naming who the owners would be, where they would play and how much television they could use. Oh yes, he also wanted indemnities to the amount of $350,000.

On television, he was willing to allow them a grand total of eleven games in Wrigley Field.

His demands about the park were, I thought, most outrageous. The new team, said O'Malley, had to play its first season in Wrigley Field—no place else—and also had to sign a contract to come into his own park at Chavez Ravine, as his tenants, as soon it was ready.

The Coliseum, where O'Malley was to play until his park was built, has a capacity of just under 100,000 people. Wrigley Field seats only 20,500, and with Chavez Ravine scheduled to be ready for the 1962 season, it would be ridiculous for the new club to rebuild the park along the lines I had proposed when I was surveying Los Angeles. If the Coliseum was a joke as a big-league baseball field—and it was—then Wrigley Field was a farce. The playing field was so small that any well-hit fly ball was a home run. Now, it is possible that a midget or a collection of Grandstand Managers can have some minor effect on a ball game. They cannot begin to compare with the influence of the playing field, which can be as important a factor in the game as the players themselves. In the one year the Los Angeles Angels played in Wrigley Field, all records for home runs hit in a ball park in a single season were broken.

The only thing more incredible than the conditions O'Malley laid down was his attitude that he was entitled to special consideration because he had somehow been forced to take his club from the golden borough of Brooklyn, where he had been making a lot of money, to the golden land of the West where he was making a lot more.

Even more incredible, though, was the willingness of the American League to accept his terms. I tried to point out, first of all, that for O'Malley to even attempt to dictate such terms to us, a fully sovereign league, was an insult. For us to negotiate on those kind of terms was to shame ourselves; to accept them was to degrade ourselves. I then pointed out, knowing my colleagues could always be appealed to on a high moral level, that since we would all be traveling to the Coast to play only one team, it would be impossible to show a profit *even if we sold out the park for every game.*

My plot for world conquest had ended in total disaster. I had lost out in Kansas City, I had been outmaneuvered in Washington, and now I had created a Frankenstein in Los Angeles. And instead of putting friends in the two new cities as I had planned, I had opposed the new owners and thereby added a couple of potential enemies to the rolls. So much for my delusions of grandeur.

Everybody was running around the Park Plaza Hotel holding informal meetings. Nobody more than Del Webb. Webb was running between O'Malley and Frick making deals, and then running back to the American League clubs to press for unconditional surrender to O'Malley. When we finally met to discuss the terms, his argument was that it was none of our business what kind of a deal the new club made with O'Malley as long as the club itself was willing to make it. I was screaming that the new owners, being unfamiliar with operations, couldn't possibly have any idea what they were getting into. And I'm screaming that it most certainly is our business because we will all be losing money. And I'm screaming that by placing what amounts to a minor-league club in a minor-league ball park we would be branding ourselves a minor-league operation and a bunch of patsies.

But, of course, Webb was right. The great difficulty, all along, was that everybody liked the Autry group, myself included, and the Autry group was so anxious to get the club that they were willing to do whatever they thought they had to. Sometimes in moments of acute depression I find myself wondering whether Autry really outdrew all those guys with the black mustaches.

The big mistake we made was in not paying Autry and Reynolds more court ourselves, instead of leaving them to the tender counsels of O'Malley, Webb and Frick. Autry and Reynolds had their own suite in the hotel and I never once went up to talk to them. At one point, I ran across Reynolds in the lobby and told him, "Rob, you can't go for this. You don't have to accept any terms you don't want."

Rob seemed to think otherwise.

In a final attempt to put some marrow into our colleagues' bones, Hank and I launched a noisy campaign to force Frick into the open. The slogan of our campaign was "Make him vote!" Hank and I ran from club to club, doing everything except grabbing the owners by the scruff of the neck to try to convince them that all the American League had to do was refuse to accept O'Malley's terms, and Frick would be placed in the position of having to vote, for once in his life, to break the deadlock between the leagues.

"He can't duck it," we'd tell them. "He can't put off letting Los Angeles in the league because then he's sticking us with a nine-team league and they've already voted down an interleague schedule. If he backs away from all those Open City statements, he's publicly labeled himself a National League tool, and he's made himself ridiculous. Make him vote!"

The last thing in the world Frick wanted to do was to vote. Frick was so anxious not to vote that he looked ill. Frick has a slogan of his own, a slogan that has served him throughout the years. It goes: "You boys settle it among yourselves." For that he gets paid $65,000 a year, not bad as things go these days.

And right at this point, a very interesting thing happened, the most interesting thing, I think, that has happened in an American League meeting in years. Dan Topping got up in the course of the meeting and said, "Look, if it will help solve this thing in our favor, I'll waive any rights I may theoretically have in New York, provided the same rights are waived in Los Angeles."

Topping had taken over from Weiss, you have to remember, only a couple of months earlier. He was getting a first-hand, close-up look at the inner workings of a meeting for the first time and he didn't like it. There would have been nothing extraordinary about making a gesture to give up something he had never claimed—until O'Malley claimed it—if it hadn't been for one thing: his partner Webb was the

367

guy who had been working the hardest to give O'Malley whatever he wanted. Dan Topping showed me something that day. Class.

So I jumped right in behind Topping. "Let's just stay firm," I said. "We're going to vote to go to Los Angeles and we're going to play in the Coliseum and that's the end of it. Why should O'Malley have special treatment in Los Angeles that the Yankees aren't afforded in New York?"

The meeting broke up with an agreement that we were going to force Frick to vote. Hank and I remained in our seats, talking. Webb and Topping were standing against the wall not far from us, and there were perhaps two or three other stragglers still in the conference room. All at once, Topping's voice began to rise angrily and it could be seen that Webb was trying to pacify him. "You're meddling into everybody's business and lousing everything up," Topping said clearly. "Well, we're going to expand and we're going to play where we want, regardless of who approves and who doesn't. Go tell that to your friends."

Webb said something we couldn't hear, and then Topping said, "Oh no? I'll buy *you* out!" And Topping broke away from him, went stalking to the door and yelled back, "I'm going home!"

He didn't go home. He came back the next day to face the inevitable fact that the American League was prepared to go along with O'Malley. Whatever had happened overnight, Frick wasn't going to be put to the vote.

Our battle ended on December 7 (a date which Roosevelt, in a flash of prescience, once characterized nicely), in a joint meeting of the two leagues presided over by Ford Frick and his commanding officer, Walter O'Malley. O'Malley, like MacArthur, affects a cigarette holder.

I made another attempt to rally them, but the spirit that had flared up briefly the previous day had been spent. O'Malley made a speech about how he was the first man to have built a new park since the beginning of time, poor-mouthing it all the way. He neglected somehow to bring along his books to show how much he was losing, possibly because they would have shown he was making a fortune. Commissioner Frick, the master of these revels, offered the opinion that O'Malley was being more than reasonable.

In a last attempt to save some shred of dignity, I called a quick caucus to try to get our league to at least protect Autry from being stuck in Wrigley Field in the event O'Malley didn't have his park finished on schedule. I couldn't even get that.

The vote was 6–2, with only Cleveland and Chicago voting against accepting O'Malley's terms.

Every time the White Sox played a series in Los Angeles in 1961, it cost us—taking everything into consideration, including the profit we would have normally made if we had been playing elsewhere—$20,000. Projecting that sum throughout the American League, it cost the individual teams $500,000 to move into the most promising city in the country. What makes it even more galling is that the first year is the year any city will normally support a new team, even as bad a team as we foisted off on Los Angeles.

You build up your attendance on the big weekend and holiday crowds, but there was no place in Wrigley Field to put a big crowd. A small park kills your attendance in many ways. The Yankees, for instance, might very well have sold out a 50,000-capacity park on their first appearance in Los Angeles. They didn't attract a sellout crowd to Wrigley Field, because too many people were sure they wouldn't be able to get in. The Angels didn't have a 20,000 crowd all year. They averaged less than 7,300 a game finishing tenth in attendance in a ten-team league.

As far as I know, the contract the Autry group signed with O'Malley for Chavez Ravine has never been made public. But I am not far off, I can guarantee you, in saying they will be paying him something around $1,000,000 in rental fees over the four years. In addition, O'Malley is their concessionaire, another source of profits. There is no doubt, pardners, who's the top gun in Los Angeles.

It was the most brutal thing I have ever seen in my life. And yet, I have to make one reservation. Autry went into it with his eyes open. He knew what was happening to him and he was willing to let it happen.

The Angels are going to be a financial drag on their league for, possibly, the next three or four years. We built ourselves a problem, just as we built ourselves a problem—again with Del Webb's invaluable assistance—in Kansas City.

And worst of all, we humiliated ourselves and downgraded our league.

Del Webb was awarded the contract to refurbish Wrigley Field for the one season's play. I am willing to bet anybody in the house a suit of clothes that when the Angels start building their own park, the Del E. Webb Corp. will be very much in evidence. No takers? Oh well. . . .

After the American League had collapsed at the final joint meeting,

O'Malley and Frick took turns congratulating each other on their statesmanship.

"I want you all to know," said the Commissioner to the press, "that without the complete cooperation of Mr. O'Malley, baseball would have been in one of the damndest messes ever seen."

It was nice to know that Frick was suitably grateful to O'Malley for being willing to accept everything that O'Malley had asked for.

Said the cooperative Mr. O'Malley, "The Commissioner steered a straight course. If he had lost his sense of direction, we would have wound up in an awful mess."

I don't know about that. If the Commissioner had lost his sense of direction, I have every confidence that Walter would have propped him up again and pointed the way.

They both took a final potshot at their fallen foes, Hank and me. Said that peerless navigator of our fates, Ford Frick: "That first group that applied for a franchise didn't sound very stable. They sounded like some fly-by-night operation that might drain the territory in one year and then move off to San Diego or some place else."

Only a man with Frick's highly developed sense of direction could conceive of anybody leaving Los Angeles to go to "San Diego or someplace else." I have to give the Commissioner credit for being so alert, though. He and O'Malley made certain that Autry didn't fill his saddlebags full of money and ride off into the sunset.

O'Malley's contribution was: "With one particular group I would have been at least half a million dollars harder to deal with. But I was willing to make concessions to these people. These are people I can live with."

What concessions he made remain a state secret, for good and sufficient reasons I'm sure. I can only assume that Walter, like an earlier American conqueror, one U. S. Grant, allowed Autry's men to keep their horses and side arms so they would be able to plow their fields when they got home.

O'Malley wasn't going to be half a million dollars harder on Hank. He wasn't going to get ten dollars from Hank and he knew it. You can't blame the man for not wanting a noncontributing opposition in town.

The last thing in the world I'd do would be to disparage Walter O'Malley. He won every round in Los Angeles, just as he has won every round since he came into baseball. There are a lot of people in baseball ready to say he's been lucky. They say he walked into Brooklyn with a string of pennant winners, inherited from Branch Rickey; they say he was lucky to beat the field to the bonanza in

370

Los Angeles; they say he antagonized everybody in Los Angeles unnecessarily with his moneygrubbing and he still was lucky enough to be in a position where he couldn't help but make a fortune.

Lucky, my eye. O'Malley is smart. He's smart mostly for O'Malley, but if everybody you could say that about was put behind walls, you'd be able to gather all the unwalled people into Budweiser . . . oops, Busch Stadium, and have J. Roy Stockton lead them in group singing.

He's also smart enough to hire good people. In Buzzy Bavasi he has one of the finest general managers in baseball. One of the few pleasant passages I can recall out of the meeting at the Park Plaza was the night Hank and I spent with Bavasi and Fresco Thompson, the head of the Dodgers' farm system. I kept telling them they deserved a stock deal from O'Malley. Buzz and Fresco, not quite able to appreciate that my concern for their future was the paramount issue, kept defending O'Malley and changing the subject. No matter what they talked about, though, I kept being amazed, indignant and outraged at the thought that two such brilliant operators had been left without a stock deal. I trust they both have a little stock by now. Hey, Buzz, you deserve it. . . .

It's easy enough to say that anyone could have made a fortune in Los Angeles. The only thing that counts is that O'Malley was the man who did it. I had the first option on Los Angeles and I couldn't do it. It's like putting a legislative program through Congress. It's not enough for the President to have a fine, progressive program; the program means nothing unless he can get it passed.

For O'Malley to move to Los Angeles, he had to work his way out of Brooklyn and he had to bring Horace Stoneham to the West Coast with him. Do you think that happened overnight? I know better. My first plan when I went out to the Coast with Phil Wrigley's option was to buy an established club, preferably the Dodgers, since they and Los Angeles seemed made for each other. I sounded O'Malley out, and he wasn't interested in selling. If you think back on the chronology, you will remember I went to Los Angeles the year after I had pushed Perini into Milwaukee. O'Malley couldn't stand to sit back and watch Perini rake in all that money. When I left his office, it was with the distinct impression that O'Malley wasn't going to sell the club to me because he had already mapped out Los Angeles for himself. And that was four years before he moved.

To get out of Brooklyn, O'Malley had to make demands upon the city that the New York politicians couldn't meet. (They couldn't have met his demands, of course, because if they had given him what he wanted he'd probably have kept changing them.) What fascinated me as I watched him wriggle his way loose was the ease with which a man of O'Malley's political power was unable to get the politicians of New York and Brooklyn to bend to his rather modest demands.

But that's all part of it. O'Malley is a good politician and I'm a bad one. I made the first passes at Milwaukee and Los Angeles, the two bonanzas of recent years, and lost out because my timing was bad and my finances were weak. Well, timing and finances are part of the package.

Personality is part of the package too. Sure, an O'Malley is going to get all the cooperation from the other owners and the Commissioner (and the lack of cooperation from New York politicians) while I'm always going to be wrestling single-handed. I'm a maverick. I'm a maverick the way O'Malley is a politician, by nature and by inclination. You cannot set yourself against the *status quo* and expect that the *status quo* isn't going to fight you back. Look up the two words in the dictionary; they snarl at each other. The trouble with the country today is that it is full of rebels who get all upset because the *status quo* resists being overthrown and even tries to stamp them out. A price-tag rebel is no rebel at all. The *status quo,* by definition, wins almost every battle; otherwise it ain't the *status quo* any more. So you pick yourself up, dig the dirt out of your ears and try again.

I have my own satisfactions. I know I have been proven right. About Milwaukee. About Los Angeles and San Francisco. About expansion. About the unrestricted draft. I have a track record I can play back to myself when I come up with another idea that seems outlandish by the accepted standards—like the scoreboard in Chicago —and knowing I have been right before, I can go ahead without having to second-guess myself.

And who knows, the *status quo* of baseball might just look at the track record the next time I push for something like interleague play and say, "All right, let's humor the jerk for once." And you know something? That's when it's time to start worrying. When they listen to your ravings with indulgence and, heaven help me, affection, you know you've joined the herd.

IN THE play *Finian's Rainbow,* there is a scene of ultimate justice in which a bigoted Southern senator turns black. Until I lost my leg, I—with my own occupational bigotry—always felt uncomfortable in the presence of a cripple. I had grown up in a world where men made their living and earned their reputation and, when you come right down to it, were judged almost solely on their physical abilities. There was something about any kind of physical incapacity that was distasteful to me. Fear something enough, as many far more brilliant men than I have observed, and you will bring it on.

When I was first injured, I refused to have my leg amputated despite all medical advice. I continued to hold out for more than two years. Nobody wants to be dismembered, of course, but it seems to me, looking back, that I felt there was something shameful about it—as if the loss of a leg would make me less of a man. I am not saying, understand, that my background in baseball made such a loss a greater blow to me than to anyone else; all I am saying is that it was more central to my way of life. One of the oldest axioms in baseball says, "The first thing that goes is the legs." It's true. Even with a pitcher, the legs go before the arm. And when the legs go, a ballplayer is through.

My Marine career was short and undistinguished. I was an albatross around Uncle Sam's neck. I injured my right leg at Bougainville, and eighteen of my twenty-two months in the service were spent in hospitals.

The injury was complicated through the years by an infection which ate away every bone graft.

By the time I had finished bouncing around the country to buy the Indians, sores had erupted all over the leg, like boils. It was a mess. The infection was bad, and I was running a high fever. Dr. J. A. Dickson of the Cleveland Clinic advised me to take it off right there and then, but I insisted upon waiting until the season was over. For the rest of 1946, I was in and out of the Cleveland Clinic, running the club more from the hospital bed than from my office.

At the end of October, with the World Series over and the leg rotting away again, I was back in the hospital. Dr. Dickson made it clear that the time had come.

"When?" I asked.

"Tomorrow," he said.

I still wasn't rushing into anything. "Let's make it the day after."

The leg was cut off nine inches below the knee on November 1, 1946, the same day, by coincidence, as the baseball draft. The draft must have been very much on my mind because the first thing I did when I came out of the anesthetic was to reach for the phone and call Frank Gibbons of the *Press,* who had become one of my closest friends.

I have to rely on Gibby's recollection here because the anesthetic had left me not only groggy but, quite literally, drunk. He, of course, was flabbergasted to hear me mumbling over the phone. "Bill," he said, "take it easy. I'll be up to see you tomorrow with the whole list."

You know how drunks are. Nothing would do but that he read the list then and there. I'm sure I listened with great interest if no comprehension. "Thanks," I mumbled. "I'll see you at the dance."

The dance was the coming-out party I was secretly planning for my peg leg.

My period of recuperation was really one long three-week party. Flowers arrived by the truckload, most of them from Cleveland fans. A couple of days after the operation, I had Larry Atkins send me up a good steak, a bottle of wine and such other creature comforts as make up the good life. If there was a hospital rule we didn't break, it was only because we hadn't heard of it.

Shondor Birns sent in all my meals from the Alhambra Tavern. At least, he started by sending in meals. He ended up as a caterer. I had enough visitors every night for a complete dinner party.

Ten weeks after the amputation, the leg arrived. It was delivered to me at 4 o'clock in the afternoon and we had about 1,000 people in the Hollenden ballroom that same night. I had never so much as tried an artificial leg on before, but by the end of the evening I was quite attached to it. I couldn't have parted with it even if I had wanted to. The stump was still so tender that it had been rubbed raw, and the blood, in drying, had glued it solidly to the wooden leg. When the party was over, the stump was so sensitive that I had to crawl out of the elevator and down the hall into my apartment and then sit in a hot tub for an hour or so to soak the darn thing off.

I am absolutely convinced of one thing. A cripple cannot coddle himself. Once you coddle yourself, you're admitting you can't do what anybody else can do and then you're through. Coddling yourself is a way of apologizing for yourself, and I am darned if I will apologize for anything beyond my control. I'd like to be handsome, too, but I'm not going to stay home and lock myself in a closet because I'm not.

Now, all this may seem quite obvious on the face of it. Let me assure you that it is not. In addition to the natural feeling that you may be embarrassing other people, there is tremendous pressure from the outside world pushing you to apologize for yourself. You will notice that I always use the word "cripple." It isn't a word you normally hear, is it? It has become customary, in our euphemistic world, to describe us cripples as "handicapped"—a word that has become a sponge. No. Webster defines a cripple as "a lame or partly disabled person." I'm not handicapped; I'm crippled.

It would be far more accurate to reverse the emphasis. Webster defines handicapped as: "to place at a disadvantage." I don't believe I am. I believe I can do anything anybody else can do that doesn't involve quick sprints, high jumps and a fast buck-and-wing. And so, far more important, although I am crippled, I am *not* handicapped.

Most important of all, by making no apologies to anybody else, you are debarred from making them to yourself. By saying, "All right, I am a cripple," and accepting it, you can go on and say, "But I will function as before." You are giving yourself no out, no excuses. The opposite is true. It can act as a spur.

Mary Frances and I were once attending a hockey game at the Cleveland Arena, along with Larry Atkins, and we arrived rather late. The parking lot was almost filled up, and I was waved to the far end. Not wanting to miss the start of the game, I indicated the crutches and said, "I'm sorry, I can't walk that far. I don't get around very well."

As soon as I'd said it, I was ashamed of myself for stooping to that kind of thing and ashamed *for* myself because I had admitted that I couldn't do what anybody else could do. I tried to reverse myself and drive on, but it was too late. Everybody had become extremely sympathetic and they insisted on helping me park as near as possible to the Arena. Mary Frances was disgusted with me, and the whole night was ruined. When you act small and helpless, you feel small and helpless.

Not that I would hesitate for a moment to use a little legmanship when the moon is low and the cause is just. In operating the Miami ball club, I negotiated a routine contract with the city fathers for the use of their park. I had negotiated similar contracts at Cleveland and Baltimore, and had gone through the preliminaries at Los Angeles and Milwaukee, so I had a good working knowledge of the standard contract. The contract I offered them was as fair as humanly possible.

Well, everything was fine until one of the council members convinced the others that I was a city slicker trying to take the country boys. After they had accepted the contract, they reneged and asked to reopen the negotiations.

All right. I came into the meeting, listened to their demands and saw at once that they had not the slightest idea what they were talking about. I howled in pain, threw my leg on the table and cried out, "Why don't you take this, too?"

After they had exchanged pleased and covert smiles, we entered into an all-night negotiation, during which, step by step, I reluctantly surrendered my pennies in return for their dollars. They agreed, for instance, to pay the cost of the lights in return for an extra 2½ percent of the parking receipts, a brilliant maneuver by which they cost the city $3 or $4 for every dollar it could possibly get back. When I departed in the morning, broken and bent, they had pulled a contract out of me that was about half as good as the one I had given them voluntarily. They were very happy about it until the bills began to come in.

There was another time when I had Gene Mako come to Tucson to build me a cement tennis court designed solely for the purpose of allowing me to defeat Hank Greenberg. You might not think it to look at Hank, but he is very quick on a tennis court, a retriever. I have to make up for lack of maneuverability with power, and although I had to switch from left-hand to right-hand because of my inability to pivot, I can really put the ball away. The court would have done credit to Emil Bossard; it was so hard that the ball didn't bounce when you put it away, it skidded. I caught Hank at the airport after he had been flying all night and insisted that he change for a quick game of tennis and then, after all that plotting and intrigue, I unaccountably turned gentleman and gave him his choice of courts. He naturally took the wind at his back and beat me in five sets. Hank won the three sets where he had the wind, and I won the two where I had it. There I was with the best tennis court in the state of Arizona on my hands and no place to go.

Tennis is a wonderful game because it not only allows me to keep in shape, but it is great for working off frustrations. During my stay in Los Angeles, I would play at the Beverly Wilshire every day with Frank Feltrop the pro. I used to team up with Pancho Segura, who is

376

a lot of fun, against Pancho Gonzales and whomever he picked up. Don't misunderstand me; I didn't belong in their league even with two legs. But I could play well enough so that I wouldn't louse up their game. Obviously, if they ran me, I'd be done. Gonzales, though, was very good about setting up my forehand.

I'd be the last person in the world to suggest that the human race would be better off with one leg. Still, a wooden leg does become a sort of cachet once it ceases to embarrass you. You know, a man with a wooden leg is automatically colorful. Long John Silver would hardly have become an immortal character in fiction if he had been nothing more than a handsome bloke who killed people. The peg legs—the leg below the knee—are hollowed out to keep them as light as possible. I always cut a hole in my leg (you go through a couple a year) and used it as an ashtray. All I had to do was drop the butts and the ashes into the hole and empty out the leg when I took it off at night.

The full leg, the leg with a knee, has to be heavier. I sometimes feel that my F.O.B. price has been greatly diminished now that I no longer come equipped with optional ashtray.

The peg leg gave me a natural gambit when I was visiting friends with children. I'd pull that old one about sticking a knife clean through my pants leg, in one side and out the other, and while the kids were gasping in amazement, I'd say, "Aw, that's really not so hard. Your daddy can do it too. Ask him to show you after I go home tonight." I've loused up more father-son relationships that way.

Our radio sponsor in Chicago, General Finance, was a sitting duck. When I'd appear at some company function with Al Wonderlic, the president, I'd say, "You notice I'm on crutches tonight. I spent a very pleasant afternoon with Al. As you can see I left a little collateral with him. [Loud and appreciative laughter] Oh, I'm not worried. He has it planted out in the windowsill with all the others."

And then, patting the other leg, I'd say, "Of course, it was only a small loan."

What made the final operation—the operation that took the knee— such a blow was that it came after the infection had completely disappeared. The last operation was brought on by a failure of the tissue.

Nor was the illness that forced me to sell the White Sox in 1961 was not brought on by either the leg or by that final operation—although we thought at first that it was. I had always found that a stay in the hospital sent me back to work with by batteries charged. This time, I came out with a permanent headache which I am just starting to lose. I came out dragging.

In addition to the headache, I began to have coughing spells which would last until I blacked out. I'd be sitting in a room talking to friends, and all of a sudden I'd lose control of the right side of my body and, on occasion, black out. The last thing in the world I wanted to do was return to the hospital. I was loaded down with commitments and besides, the expansion meeting was coming up and we all know about the grandiose schemes I had cooked up for that.

I was afraid to drive a car, though, because I was quite aware that I would be a menace on the road. Dizzy Trout did all the driving. I'd fall asleep in the car, something that had never happened before. To tell the truth, the speeches—which I had always enjoyed so much—had become a chore. I lived in fear that I might pass out in the middle of a talk or, even worse, in the middle of our TV program. To protect myself against the coughing spells, I'd fill myself up with throat lozenges before any appearance.

I tried to kid myself that if I could hold on until the 1961 season started, I'd be able to slide the rest of the way on momentum. On opening day, I just ran out of gas.

At the Mayo Brothers Clinic, they were almost sure that I had a case of lung cancer which had spread up to the brain. I had suspected that myself, since I knew I had every one of the classic symptoms. I had suspected it so strongly that I had drawn up a will and put my affairs in order before I left Chicago. When I walked into the Clinic, I literally did not expect to walk out again.

The tests showed that it wasn't lung cancer. Subsequent tests showed that it wasn't a brain tumor or a stroke either. I found out as time went on that I didn't have a lot of things. It was a long time, though, before they could find what it was.

I was allowed to return to Chicago under orders to stay away from anything that might precipitate the attacks. That meant that I was not to leave the apartment. I did not step outside the door for months.

I had become what I had always hated and inveighed against, an absentee owner. I knew I was doing a terrible job of operating, and I knew in my heart that I was collecting money under false pretenses. Well, you don't say things just to say them, you say them because you believe them. I took myself out of the picture and turned the clubs over to Hank. Art Allyn Jr., son of my old benefactor, solved my problem finally by buying Hank and me out.

The doctors at Mayo wanted me to return to the hospital. Well, I've served my time in hospitals. We worked out a compromise. I was to settle somewhere out of the mainstream—I eventually bought a home in Easton, Maryland—with the understanding that I would not leave the grounds except to come back to the Clinic for periodic tests.

378

By the process of elimination, they discovered I had what amounted to a chronic concussion. The blood vessels had been stretched in my head, and when I went into a coughing spell, the blood pounding through expanded them just enough so that exerted pressure on the brain. They had only one prescription: rest.

Just after I sold the club and left for Easton, a Chicago columnist criticized the players for not visiting me while I was confined to my apartment. The column brought a letter from my old friend, Early Wynn. Early also asked the *Sun-Times* to give him equal space. His letter was printed on their back page. It went, in part:

DEAR BILL:

I'm a better pitcher than I am a letter writer—at least I hope I am—but I'm writing now, not just for myself but for all the other fellows who have played and worked for you on the White Sox. None of us want you to leave town without some sort of a good-bye, or at the least a so-long, because we know you'll be up and kicking, bad leg and all, and that you'll be back with us soon.

Firstly, I want to clear up some accusations that I saw in print here recently. . . . Everybody wanted to come up and say hello but a lot of the players didn't do so in respect to the doctor's orders. He said you had to have rest and quiet and that's why we weren't all knocking the door down.

I've never written a letter like this before, especially to my boss—and I've had quite a few of them. Probably the others were a little stiff-necked but whatever the reason, I know I speak for all of us when I say that you've been a helluva lot more than just a boss. You've been a wonderful friend. All of us will always cherish your friendship.

I know people might say that for the kind of salaries you've been paying us we should all be grateful. But this isn't just a matter of money. Heck, a ballplayer can make good money a lot of places so it can't be just that. It goes a lot deeper and I'm sure you know this just as well as we do.

There are a lot of other people who should be grateful to you, especially the other club owners. You've helped all of them at the gate and even though they don't always seem to approve of some of the entertainment you've offered I haven't seen an owner yet who didn't like a packed house. To me and the other players, you'll always be the No. 1 club executive of all time. . . .

The most important thing, though, is that you enjoyed it. It's the same thing about all the prizes you gave away at the ball park. You enjoyed seeing someone stand at home plate and discover that he had just won two dozen live lobsters or a barrel of chocolate-covered butterflies. You weren't the only one who laughed. We all did.

My answer has, I think, been bound between these covers from beginning to end:

Sometime, somewhere, there will be a club no one really wants. And then Ole Will will come wandering along to laugh some more. *Look for me under the arc-lights, boys. I'll be back.*

AFTERWORD

The lights went on again at 7:40 P.M., on December 10, 1975, when Veeck came out of the elevator of the Diplomat Hotel in Hollywood, Florida, surrounded by a cordon of League lawyers and, in the sheer exuberance of the moment, kicked his prosthetic leg high in the air. At the end of the long corridor the photographers were waiting, and as they proceeded toward the conference room where his fellow owners were gathered to welcome him, unenthusiastically, back into the most exclusive men's club in America, he was suddenly moving . . . perhaps not under the arc lights but certainly in a pool of light.

Bill Veeck had never been able to buy a club the easy way, and his second time around with the White Sox (1975–1980) was no exception. Once again, he had slipped in through the side door by getting an option to buy the White Sox, a bankrupt club, before anybody knew what had happened. Only this time, he wasn't merely outflanking Baseball's blacklist, he was upsetting some of baseball's most carefully laid plans.

Unable to meet his final payroll, Art Allyn Jr., the outgoing owner of the White Sox, had sent word to Bill that the American League was ready to take the club off his hands so that they could move it to Seattle. For baseball, that would have solved a couple of problems that had been festering out on the west coast. Like, for instance, the $32.5 million lawsuit the city of Seattle had filed against baseball for granting it an expansion team in 1969 and removing it the following year after an impoverished ownership had dropped the franchise back into its lap. The city fathers had agreed to hold the suit in abeyance and proceed apace with the construction of a shining new domed stadium on the promise that Seattle would be awarded a new team by 1976 when the stadium was completed.

And then there was the Oakland-San Francisco factor, otherwise known as the inability of the Bay Area to support two teams. Once the White Sox had been shipped to Seattle, the maneuvering could commence to pry Charlie Finley out of Oakland and move his club into Chicago, which was the base of operations for his insurance business.

The lords of baseball did not take the shattering of such a lovely plan lying down. One week before the annual winter meeting in Florida, they held an emergency meeting in Kansas City, told Veeck that his finances were unsatisfactory, and voted him down. When he threatened to sue, they gave him a week—five business days—to raise another $1.2 million in capital and, while he was about it, change his whole financial structure around so that his stockholders would no longer be enjoying the capital-gains leverage of Bill's traditional debenture—common stock grouping.

Clearly an impossibility. In addition to scouting up the new investors, he was going to have to inform the 40 stockholders he already had that their equity in the ball club was being undermined to the extent that they now owned 25 percent less of the club that they thought they had bought.

There was only one way it could have been done, and Veeck found it. He was taking a 15 percent override (as a finder's fee) for his work in putting the deal together and running the club for the corporation. If he gave up his override, just threw it back into the pot, he would be able to tell the stockholders that their equity was actually going to be increased. As for Bill himself, all he was doing was giving up everything that had made the deal worthwhile for him. Before coming to any final decision, he flew home to Maryland to discuss and consider what to do.

"What you are telling me," Mary Frances said, "is that it isn't an investment any more, it's a vendetta. So what else is new?"

So he came to the winter meeting in Florida, with everything in place, and they voted him down again anyway.

He needed nine positive votes to be accepted. The vote was 8-3, with one abstention. It was John Fetzer of Detroit, never a friend of Bill's, who turned it around. Because Fetzer, who was a powerful voice in those counsels whenever he chose to be, was incensed. He berated his fellow owners for the slipshod way they had been handling their affairs during his 20 years of the game. He accused them of being more interested in running out to the bar for a drink than in doing the right thing. "We have left these people over a barrel," he said. "We told them to go do it and they did it. Now we can't cry over spilt milk. We've got to be men about this. Look, I don't like it any more than you do that we're allowing this guy in here. But, gentlemen, we're just going to have to take another vote."

Veeck needed nine votes. He got ten.

Having been officially approved and accepted, Veeck went into the ballroom, where amidst a mob of sportswriters and a forest of television cameras, he held a triumphant press conference. It was difficult to tell who was enjoying himself more, Veeck or the writers.

382

"I hope it's as much fun as I expect it to be," he told them. "It's not often a one-legged, 61-year-old man gets started again in a new go-around doing something he loves."

Why did he think there had been so much opposition to his return? "I have not always led an exemplary life. I am not Galahad riding in on a shining white charger . . . *[big, flashing smile]* . . . I think of myself more as Merlin."

"Our first priority," said the ancient prestidigitator, "is to make the White Sox better. To win, to bring some small degree of honor to our city and some small degree of profit to ourselves."

The fun began the following day when he set up a trading post in the hotel lobby. The lobby of the Diplomat could perhaps best be described as Miami Garish, a splendid setting for trade and commerce if you happen to have a passion for monster chandeliers adrip with gold. Off in the corner, however, there was a little sunken alcove, featuring high-backed chairs and low coffee tables. Within that alcove Veeck set up his sign, hand-painted and topped off with a perky little American flag:

Open for Business

By Appointment Only

Bill and his general manager, Roland Hemond, sat there for 14 straight hours, "operating in the open like honest men," with only a small break at lunchtime to munch hot dogs and sip milkshakes with the press. During that period, they made four trades, the last one beating the midnight trading deadline—as the crowd cheered—by a matter of seconds.

And if most of the baseball operators were either willing accomplices or amused spectators themselves, there remained, as always, those who were going to be outraged.

"This is a meat market," grumped Bud Selig, the Milwaukee owner.

"Why can't he do this in his own room?" asked Houston official John Muller, "This is a disgrace."

"So now I'm making a travesty of trading," said Veeck, perfectly delighted. "Who says you can't go home again?"

Two weeks later, he was trimming the Christmas tree in his own home when word came to him that the Messersmith decision had come down against the owners, something the League's lawyers had told him couldn't happen. And he knew at that moment that it was going to take a miracle for him to survive.

A flagrant case of life being unfair. For 25 years, Bill had been telling his fellow owners that they were doing something illicit with the Constitution and urging them to moderate the Reserve Clause while they were still able to exercise some modicum of control. In testifying for Curt Flood in 1972 (an act which confirmed the Baseball Establishment's darkest thoughts about him), he had recommended that baseball adopt some version of the old Hollywood 7-year contract, with its built-in structure of automatic raises. The Players Association, which was financing Flood's suit, was perfectly willing to go along with that solution. The owners weren't. Instead, they agreed to allow the players to submit their grievances to binding arbitration, and four years later it was an independent arbitrator who was doing what neither the courts nor Congress had ever been willing to do; overrule the Supreme Court decision that had been written by Oliver Wendell Holmes.

All Peter Seitz, the arbitrator, had actually done was to rule that since Messersmith had played out the season without signing his contract, the option clause under which the Los Angeles Dodgers had reserved his services for the following year was no longer in force. And if nobody yet realized how vast and far-reaching the repercussions from the ruling were going to be, the first impact was felt when the owners announced that there would be no spring training until a new labor contract had been negotiated with the players. The announcement also said that the vote had been unanimous. Wrong by one.

"It used to be 15-1 against me," Bill Veeck said. "And now it's 23-1."

To Veeck's way of thinking, spring training had very little to do with conditioning the athletes, and everything to do with conditioning the fans. He had taken over a club which had a pre-season ticket sale of exactly zero, and he had been counting upon the publicity coming out of the training camp to give new impetus to the wave of ticket buying that had erupted at the news of his return.

Ever the master of the loophole, Veeck once again found a way. Since the ban had referred specifically to the players on the roster, he announced that he was going to open with non-roster players and free agents. "I am complying exactly with the rules," he informed League president Lee MacPhail.

"I don't care what you do," MacPhail told him. "I just don't want to know about it ahead of time."

For two weeks, Veeck garnered all the publicity coming out of the South, as half the sportswriters in the country descended upon his camp in Sarasota. Except for Veeck, they didn't have much to write about. The winter roster consisted of 40 players, the 25 players on the major-league roster plus the 15 most promising players in the minor-league system. Not only had the White Sox finished in last place, but so had every one of their farm teams. The non-roster players were so con-
384

spicuously lacking in talent, or the promise thereof, that the best player in camp was Cleon Jones, the former New York Mets star who had been out of baseball with a bad back.

His two main objectives, however, had been to sell tickets and to make everybody aware that there was going to be fun at the old ballyard again. And in those two objectives he succeeded.

The Opening Day crowd was 40,318, the third largest opening day attendance in White Sox history. He had promised that he was going to give the fans something special, and he came through with a promotion that hit the front pages and 6 o'clock news shows all over the country. For as the Opening Day ceremonies were coming to a close, the voice coming over the public address system said, "We direct your attention toward second base, where three White Sox veterans are coming back home to Chicago to honor America's Bicentennial with an exact re-enaction of 'The Spirit of '76'."

And there, marching down from second base to home plate in a perfect re-creation of the Three Minutemen in "The Spirit of '76" were Bill Veeck, Rudie Schaffer and Paul Richards. Veeck was the pegged-legged fife player, complete with the blood-soaked bandage around his wig. Rudie Schaffer was the drummer boy, down to the buckled shoes. And Paul Richards, marching between them, was carrying the Revolutionary flag with the 13 stars.

"If you've got the guy with the wooden leg," Veeck has said when the Bicentennial connection hit him, "you've got the casting beat."

It was the participation of Paul Richards that came as the real surprise. In agreeing to return to the dugout, Richards had made it clear that he could not appreciate having any of Bill's promotions intrude upon himself or the ballgame. But everybody has their own pet projects and obsessions. For as long as anybody could remember, Paul Richards had been lamenting the fact that nobody ever sang anything except the first stanza of "The Star-Spangled Banner," which asked, rather plaintively whether the flag was still waving. While nobody even knew about the fourth stanza, which sent forth the stirring message that "Yes, the Star-Spangled Banner still waves o'er the land of the free and the home of the brave." And, yes, Paul Richards had leaped upon the suggestion that he might want to take advantage of the opportunity to march up to home plate, flagpole in hand, and recite the entire 4th stanza for the edification of the spectators, the press and the generations yet unborn.

To make the day perfect, Wilbur Wood, the knuckleball pitcher, threw a 5-0 shutout, with the whole crowd coming to its feet in the ninth inning, and applauding steadily through the final two outs.

After that, it was all downhill. What more do you have to know about the 1976 season after you have been told that the high point was reached on Opening Day?

Well, how about this: In 1977, he almost pulled it off.

The 1977 season opened with the White Sox consigned to last place, and Veeck so broke that he had to trade his shortstop, Bucky Dent, to the Yankees in order to meet his first payroll. Dick Dozier of the *Chicago News* picked them to finish in the American Association. Another columnist wrote, "Bill Veeck is deceiving the fans with the players he is putting on the field." And when it was over, the White Sox had come very close to pulling off the Upset of the Century. They had led the league for 61 days, set a new attendance record, and Veeck had been voted Executive of the Year.

He did it by going against the wisdom of Comiskey Park. Because the park had always been looked upon as a slugger's graveyard the White Sox had always been built on pitching, speed and defense. Given the state of his finances and the unattractiveness of his team, Bill made the calculated decision to trade pitching and defense for power.

To put the season in context, 1977 was the first year of the Re-Entry Draft: i.e., the season which ended with Reggie Jackson's World Series heroics.

Unable to bid on the big games, he drafted a couple of cripples off the list, pitcher Steve Stone and third-baseman Eric Soderholm. Stone had a torn rotator cuff, an injury no pitcher had ever come back from, and Soderholm had missed the entire previous season due to torn knee ligaments and broken ribs. Bill coaxed them back by making them an offer that was hard to refuse. Give it a try, he urged them, and if they couldn't make it they would still be paid for the full year.

He inaugurated his Rent-a-Player system by trading for two power hitters, Richie Zisk and Oscar Gamble, knowing that he would be losing them at the end of the year. Gamble, who had become available when the Yankees signed Reggie Jackson, came along with the money in the Bucky Dent deal. Zisk came for Chicago's two best short relief pitchers, Goose Gossage and Terry Forster. "A trade of questionable worth," was the kindest thing the Chicago writers had to say about it. But Veeck knew exactly what he was doing. The best relief pitcher in the world has little value on a team that rarely has a late-inning lead for him to protect; the attempts to turn Gossage and Forster into starting pitchers had failed miserably—and, in the era of the Free Agent, he was going to lose both of them at the end of the year, anyway.

And, of course, there was that other consideration. Relief pitchers do not bring fans into the park. Home-run hitters do.

386

The infield was atrocious. Eric Soderholm had gone through spring training with his leg so swathed in bandages that he looked as if he were wearing a light cast. The shortstop, Alan Bannister, had been a part-time left-fielder and fill-in third baseman. As a final gamble, Veeck put Jorge Orta, whose fielding had made him a natural designated hitter, back on second base in order to insert another big bat into the lineup at the designated hitter slot.

They had no pitching and less defense. As a rule of thumb, the White Sox threw away one run every game with their fielding, and gave away another on their base running. And after 100 games, they were 6½ games ahead in their own division and had a better record than the New York Yankees, whose gaudy collection of high-priced stars had won them the title of The Best Team Money Could Buy. Nobody could believe it, least of all the players. Richie Zisk seemed to have the most reasonable explanation: "I think Bill Veeck has sold his soul to the Devil."

They were doing it on sheer power. Oscar Gamble's 31 home runs set an all-time White Sox record for lefthanded hitters. Richie Zisk, who was everybody's choice for the Most Valuable Player Award over the first half of the season, finished with 30. Soderholm, whose knee still couldn't stand up on artificial turf, hit 25 home runs and was voted the Comeback Player of the Year. Jim Spencer and Lamar Johnson, who alternated at first base, each had 18. Chet Lemon, the fleet center-fielder, had 19. Catcher Jim Essian, who had never hit a home run in the big leagues before, had 10.

All in all, they hit 192 home runs, shattering the old record of 138. Only the Red Sox, who were hitting them in that home-run paradise, Fenway Park, had more.

Never did any fans have more fun at the ballpark. From the beginning, Veeck had attracted a very young crowd and, in the manner of the day, they provided their own entertainment. It was the White Sox fans who introduced the Standing 'O,' and the prolonged cheering to bring the hero of the moment out of the dugout for a curtain call. They created their own battle song to inform the opposing pitcher that the end was drawing near, the *nah-nah, nah-nah* from an all but forgotten record called "Kiss Her Goodbye."

As a final touch, Veeck talked his gravel-voiced announcer, Harry Caray, into leading the fans in the singing of "Take Me Out to the Ballgame" during the 7th inning stretch. "But I can't sing," Harry had protested when Veeck first put the idea to him. "That's the whole idea," Veeck told him. "If you could sing, I wouldn't want you to."

There were two games which will remain forever verdant in the

387

memory of all White Sox fans. Through the early months of the season, the White Sox had been battling the Minnesota Twins, the other poor man's team for the lead. On July 1, with 35,709 fans in the park, the White Sox took over first place (and started a 9-game winning streak) by defeating the Twins, 5-2, on Richie Zisk's two-run home runs. The first drive had gone to deep left field, and when he came up for a second time with a man on base, everybody in the park knew—just knew—that he was going to hit it out again. In deepest right-center at Comiskey Park, there is a kind of notch cut out of the wall above the elephant gate, and it was through that notch—as through a knothole—that Zisk hit it.

In his other two times at bat, Zisk struck out, and it was hard to tell whether he received a greater ovation for striking out than for hitting the home runs. After the game, nobody wanted to leave the park. And when they did, they wandered around the neighborhood for hours, in a mardi gras mood, chanting their *nah-nah, nah-nahs* at each other.

Up in the Bard's Room in Comiskey Park, the celebration went on through the night. From the opening of the season, the Dozier column predicting that the team would finish in the minor leagues had been taped to the mirror behind the bar, and Veeck entertained the celebrants by holding forth on his bewilderment that sportswriters could get away without knowing what they were looking at, while practitioners of any other profession who were so consistently myopic and intellectually impoverished would have been given the bounce.

On July 31, the White Sox played a Sunday doubleheader against Kansas City, before a record crowd of 50,412 (capacity is 44,492). In the top of the tenth, the Royals broke a 2-2 tie by scoring 2 runs. In the bottom of the inning, Chet Lemon tied it with a 2-run home run, his second of the day, sending everybody into such a paroxysm of joy that a few stray spectators in the overflow crowd were all but blown off the roof. When they went on to win the game, after sanity had been restored, their lead was up to 6½ games.

That was the high-water mark of the season. They lost the second game and twelve days later they were out of first place. The thinness of their squad had finally caught up with them. Zisk had injured his knee and he stopped hitting. Alan Bannister, who had been leading the league in runs scored at the All-Star break and had been second to Rod Carew in base hits, hurt his shoulder, which had been sore all year anyway, and could no longer make even his scatter-arm throws to first. To make the loss of Bannister even more disastrous, Kevin Bell, a good-looking young prospect who had been counted upon to fill in at all the

388

infield positions when the dog days of autumn came, had already torn up his knee on a play at home plate.

Not that the White Sox suffered a complete collapse. Even after they had fallen out of first place for the final time, they won more games than they lost. The trouble was that neither Kansas City nor Texas could lose. Kansas City won 35 out of 39 games. Texas won 14 of their final 16. The White Sox won 90 games and finished in third place.

The pursuit of a new attendance record went down to the final day and—if such a thing is possible—ended in a draw. Veeck's primary goal wasn't merely to break the White Sox record, which had been set by his 1960 team. He was out for the all-time Chicago record, which had been set by the Chicago Cubs in 1969.

As they came to the final weekend against Seattle, an expansion team in last place, he still needed 14,060 to break the White Sox record and 44,590 to break the all-time Chicago record.

Chicago is a Friday night town, and Bill always enlivened Friday night at Comiskey Park with a post-game fireworks display. On top of that, it was Polish night, and Chicago has the largest Polish population of any city in the world.

The Friday night game was rained out.

Saturday turned up cold and wet. There were only 5,778 of the staunchest shivering through the game.

For the final game on Sunday, the crowd was 20,953. A new White Sox record, but almost 18,000 short of the ultimate goal.

Still and all, they had won 90 games, set an attendance record, and turned a profit. And if the other owners had not gone into another feeding frenzy at the appearance of a new batch of Free Agents he would have been in good shape. No such luck. The era of constantly escalating salaries had begun, wherein the "ridiculous," "outrageous" and "insane" contracts of one year became the starting place for the bidding next time around.

The one player Bill had hoped to keep was Oscar Gamble. Oscar was always loose and witty, a great man to have in the clubhouse as well as on the field. Veeck loved him. And so when Oscar was unable to attract an offer that was any better than the $325,000 which Veeck had offered him, Bill flew to Oscar's home in Louisiana and sweetened it to $350,000 a year for three years. In the interim, unfortunately, Gamble's agent had been contacted by Ray Kroc of San Diego, and a few days later, the agent called to apologize for breaking his promise to give Bill a chance to match any offer San Diego might make. Ray Kroc, he explained, had offered Gamble $3,000,750 over six years—almost as much as Goose Gossage, who had been the jewel of that year's Re-

Entry Draft, was getting from the Yankees. "But," Kroc had said, "you've got to take it or leave it right now. I'm not going to let you guys get me into a bidding war."

"Of course you had to take it," Bill laughed. "You'd have been crazy not to." What else do you do when someone offers you twice as much as anybody else is willing to give you, on a take-it-or-leave-it basis?

"That was the frustrating part," remembers Rudie Schaffer. "The mere fact that we were able to survive in 1976 and bring it to the pinnacle in 1977 was great up to a point because it proved that you could do things by other means than money. But it didn't last long enough for us. If we'd had the money at that point, then we would have been able to keep some of the fellows who disappeared because of Free Agency, and 1977 would have just been a forerunner of 1978 and 1979." But it wasn't that simple either. "The whole situation kept changing. It wasn't only the Free Agency thing. The arbitration thing became the real killer."

What arbitration did was to turn the pay scale over to the members of the Arbitration Association, a group of men whose knowledge of baseball seemed to be limited pretty much to statistics. The arbitrator had to select either the figure offered by the club or the figure demanded by the player. There were no compromises, and the ability of the club to pay could not be taken into consideration. The decision was based on what some other player was being paid in that position. If the agent cites a player who was paid $500,000 for hitting .301, and his client had hit .303 then obviously his client deserved more than $500,000.

Every time a record-breaking award was handed down, it became the high-tide upon which all salaries rose. By the same token, every time the ball club established a new high in signing a free agent or resigning one of its own players, the tide was up again for everybody.

Veeck knew that the bell had tolled for him in 1979, when John J. McMullen of Houston signed Nolan Ryan to the first of the million-a-year contracts. "It doesn't matter how well you may have operated," Veeck would later explain. "When a Nolan Ryan is paid a million dollars, everybody's pay structure is shattered."

The final crusher came the following year when Ted Turner went gaga over Claudell Washington. Washington had come to the White Sox in 1978, in a trade with Texas. Washington could hit a little, but the casual attitude he took toward ground balls was immortalized by a sign that sprouted behind him in the right-field bleachers: "Washington Slept Here."

All told, he did so little for the Sox that Veeck practically gave him to the Mets in the early part of 1979, just to get rid of his salary. At the end of that year, Washington went free agent, and Turner signed him to something like $750,000 a year for five years (there were incentive clauses which left the actual figure hazy), plus a $250,000 bonus for being good enough to take it.

Every outfielder in baseball slept well that night. Every club operator went to bed with a cold compress over his forehead.

Still and all, Veeck had put together the best young pitching staff in baseball by the time he sold the club at the end of the 1980 season. And he had put it together the old-fashioned way. By a sharp eye for talent, some shrewd trading and a lot of luck.

The five young pitchers were LaMarr Hoyt, Dick Dotson, Britt Burns, Steve Trout and Ross Baumgarten. Steve Trout became Veeck's first #1 draft choice, over the objections of his farm department, solely because he was the son of Dizzy Trout, who had, of course, been Veeck's chauffeur and constant companion during Bill's previous incarnation in Chicago. Bill was betting on the bloodline. "And I was afraid Dizzy would put a curse on me if I didn't take care of his kid."

Britt Burns was recommended by Bob Cromie, the book critic for the *Chicago Tribune*. Cromie, who had once been a sportswriter, sent Bill a newspaper article about Burns from a Birmingham newspaper, along with the notation that he was sure the White Sox knew all about the kid. The White Sox had nothing at all on him, and neither did the scouting combine. (Bill didn't actually subscribe to the scouting combine, but he had a spy in their office, and the office had a copying machine.) Britt Burns was getting all kinds of high school pitching records around Birmingham, and yet somehow in this age of total computerization, had fallen through the cracks. When Veeck went down to Birmingham to sign him, he was told by Britt's father that nobody had even bothered to come by.

If Burns was recommended by a book critic, Ross Baumgarten was recommended by a furniture salesman. Ross is an heir to the Baumgarten furniture stores, and there is a branch of Baumgarten's in the Merchandise Mart in Chicago. The manager of that store, Marv Samuel, was a former minor leaguer. He was also the head of Chicago Charities which includes the Sherm-Lollar-Nellie Fox Cancer Society. Samuel kept telling Roland Hemond that Ross had grown several inches since his high school days and was pitching for a junior college in Florida with great success. The Sox got kind of a lukewarm report on him, but they made him their twentieth and final draft choice as a favor to Marv Samuel.

A year later, Ross Baumgarten was pitching in the big leagues. He wasn't particularly fast, but he had a good left-handed curve ball and he knew how to pitch. In the opinion of many, Baumgarten would have been the most successful of the young pitchers Veeck left behind if a shoulder injury hadn't brought his career to an end.

Dick Dotson and LaMarr Hoyt came as throw-in trades. Dotson was a legitimate prospect. He had been a #1 draft choice for California, but Veeck had been able to talk the Angels into putting him in a trade he was making for Bobby Bonds, a Rent-a-Player who didn't work out. LaMarr Hoyt was a throw-in in the deal for Bucky Dent. Originally, the Yankees were supposed to give Bill $705,000 as well as Oscar Gamble for Dent. When Commissioner Kuhn ruled that no more than $400,000 could change hands in a player deal, Gabe Paul agreed that Veeck would be given a relief pitcher in lieu of the lost money.

At various times through the spring, Veeck almost had Spark Lyle or Ron Guidry. He didn't get Lyle only because Guidry, who was supposed to replace Lyle in the Yankee bullpen, couldn't get anybody out. He didn't get Guidry only because Gabe Paul said, "Over my dead body."

When the deal was finally closed on the last day of spring training, Gabe told him he could have Bob Polinsky (a sore-armed lefthander who never pitched another game), and a righthander named LaMarr Hoyt, who Gabe assured him would be able to do the job for him out of the bullpen.

Hoyt went to the minors where he was so ineffective that he was included on the year-end list of farmhands who were going to be released. "When LaMarr Hoyt goes out the door," Veeck told his youthful farm director, Charlie Evranian, "you can go with him." And so, he said, could the minor-league manager who had put Hoyt on the list. And then he told Evranian the facts of baseball life. The $400,000 he had received for Dent was gone. Gamble was going to declare free agency. Veeck was not about to admit to the Chicago fans that he had been stuck with two useless pitchers. Not yet, anyway.

He talked Hoyt into going down to Class A, the lowest minor league classification, in the hope that he could be able to hang on long enough so that his release would pass unnoticed. Hoyt dominated the league in Class A, pitched moderately well in a higher classification the following season, and a year later was pitching for the White Sox. And then, all of a sudden, the guy who had such trouble winning in the high minors couldn't lose. He won 15 straight over the 1980–81 seasons mostly in relief, and in 1983, won 24 games, pitched the White Sox to the Division championship, and won the Cy Young Award.

And if he had come to the White Sox in any other way, he'd have been cut loose, gone home and been known for the rest of his life, in all probability, as a guy who was not quite good enough for Double-A ball.

And always, of course, there were the promotions. Veeck was either the Toscanini of the Ball Yard or Baseball's Barnum, depending on the weather conditions and the background music. He viewed the baseball park as the theater in which he operated and he was bursting with the ideas that had been accumulating for 15 years.

The fireworks were resumed, and the exploding scoreboard reactivated. There were belly dancers and circus acts. Teen Nights, Family Nights, Senior Citizens Nights. Shakespeare Night, featuring a couple of scenes from a local "Friends of Shakespeare" troupe. In honor of the best-selling novel *Ragtime,* he gave away 10,000 paperback books and turned the park into a tableau of the Gay Nineties, complete with Keystone Cops and Gaslight girls.

He put a portable shower in the bleachers to allow the kids out there to cool themselves off. He had a woman barber out there too, before the union lodged a protest.

There was a continuous series of Ethnic Nights to honor the multitudinous nationalities to be found in Chicago. In what other ballpark, at what other time, could you have found yourself celebrating Croatian Night?

It was during the never-to-be-forgotten Mexico Fiesta Night that Minnie Minoso, in full matador regalia, took on a bull. No, not a real bull. A guy in bull's costume. Neither Veeck nor Minoso was *that* crazy.

He even invented his own sporting event, if that's what it was. Beer-case stacking. The inspiration came to him full blown, as he observed a trio of hefty workmen tossing the beer cases off a truck. If the national sport of Scotland could be something called kaber tossing, Veeck saw no reason why the national sport of the Polish-Americans and Irish-Americans and German-Americans and anybody else who wanted to get in on it shouldn't be beer-case stacking. He divided the city into sections, and held elimination contests at the park. The way it worked, each team consisted of three guys working in harmony. The idea was to stack the cases as high as possible, as fast as possible, and pray that a vagrant breeze didn't come along and knock them over before the laws of balance and gravity took their natural course.

And then there were the various Music Nights and Band Nights and Dance Nights. The first music night came out of the need to publicize a makeup game that had been thrown into an open Thursday night. The way it worked out, anybody who came to the park with an instrument was admitted at half price. Those who didn't have and instrument were

393

handed a kazoo at the gate. The rules were that anybody could play their instrument as the muse struck them, just so long as they understood that they were on their honor to join the festivities during the seven-inning stretch.

A couple of young girls pulled up to the gate with an old player piano in the back of a pickup truck. The ground crew hauled it in, and set it up on the concourse behind the box seats. Among the novelties provided for the pre-game ceremonies were an organ grinder and his monkey, the world's largest guitar, a calliope, a band of bagpipe players, a 25-foot trumpet, and stuff like that.

When the moment of truth arrived, Henry Mazer, the associate conductor of the Chicago Symphony Orchestra, came strutting out of the dugout in his white tie and tails, walked the track line to home plate and mounted a 4-stair podium that was placed at his feet. The Maestro raised his baton, gave them the down beat and led the world's largest orchestra into the playing of "Take Me Out to the Ballgame."

The Disco Demolition can be looked upon as either his greatest promotion or his greatest disaster. "Looking at it as objectively as possible," Veeck decided. "It was both." It was a great promotion because it drew 50,000 paid, plus another 5,000 or so illegals and undocumented who rushed the gate, plus another 15,000 hopefuls outside the park clamoring to get in, plus perhaps 20,000 unfortunates trapped in a traffic jam which extended the full length of the Dan Ryan Expressway from Chicago to Comiskey Park. It was a disaster because it was a disaster.

The premise of the evening was that a young Chicago disc jockey who had been making a name for himself as a implacable foe of disco music was going to blow up a gigantic wooden boxfull of the despised records out in center field, before the game. His fellow discophobes supplied the fodder by dropping the records off, along with 98¢, as they entered the park.

The disc jockey hit the detonator, the records went flying and as the smoke began to clear, it could be seen that the youthful music lovers were pouring onto the field from every corner of the park.

There were two broken ankles. One kid fell off the mezzanine ramp as he was racing toward the field. The other had been throwing firecrackers out in the bleachers until his neighbors heaved him over the center-field fence as an expression of their displeasure.

The batting cage was dragged out onto the field and destroyed. There was a small fire in the center-field bleachers, and a banner that had been tied to the left-field foul pole was ablaze.

The mounted police arrived soon enough, along with the tactical police force in their blue helmets and face visors. Also the fire department. Also Mayor Jane Byrne, who had picked up the police call on her car radio. When Mayor Byrne was asked to state her position on the great disco controversy, she answered, "Oh no, you don't," and showed what a splendid politician she was by getting the hell out of there.

The police couldn't enter the park without permission, and permission was something which Veeck was going to withhold. Bill had stationed himself at home plate with a mike, and was calling out, over and over again, "Please get off the field . . . Please get off the field . . ." The kids, filled with defiance and marijuana, were running around the field and sliding into the bases, but since there was no real meanness in them that he could detect, he had decided to let them run themselves out. Which, soon enough, they did. By the time he brought the police in, the intruders had become so weary that they were only too willing to be directed back to their seats.

With Veeck, promotion was such an integral part of his operation that there was an area—about the size of East St. Louis—where his promotional juices and his feuding instincts intersected. The best promotion, as he always said, was David vs. Goliath—as in "If it's big, hit it"—so perhaps it was only natural that his favorite targets would be the Commissioner, the umpires and—oh, blessed day—the New York Yankees.

But with a difference. Commissioners were boobs, and he gave the back of his hand to them. He viewed Bowie Kuhn, the Commissioner of his last go-around, as little more than Ford Frick with a law degree. A creature of the National League, courtesy of Walter O'Malley. Mean-spirited and vindictive.

Yankee-bashing was part of his act, and also one of his pleasures. As if to prove that there was a God, and that God was good, he returned to baseball to find George Steinbrenner waiting for him in New York. (Since the Lord giveth and the Lord taketh away, the White Sox had such a horrendous record against the Yankees that Bill could show you—if you promised not to tell anybody—how the White Sox were the best thing the Yankees had going for them in those tumultuous pennant races of 1977 and 1978.)

Bill disliked the Yankees, and everything they stood for. He did not really hate them. True hatred is a grim and humorless thing, and Veeck had too much fun with the Yankees over the years not to understand that if the New York Yankees did not exist he would have had to invent them.

Umpires he hated. Not the way the fan hates them, as part of the fun of the day, but with a deep-seated sense of loathing and contempt.

He did not subscribe to the belief that umpires were the last bastions of honesty in a sinful world. He believed they were arrogant bully boys who committed acts of institutionalized dishonesty daily.

The very act of wanting to become an umpire rendered them suspect in his eyes. "Who would want to be an umpire? They know they are going to be despised, they know they are going to be spending most of their time alone. And still they go to umpire school to train for the job." What did that make them? "Masochists, with a sadistic bent."

They would throw a player out of the game for cursing at them. "Do you think they don't curse out players and managers themselves? They do it all the time." And then lied to the league office in their reports, knowing full well that the league had no choice but to take their word for it.

Their primary concern, in his view, was not to call an honest game, but to make things as easy as possible for themselves. They punished players who argued with them, especially if they were rookies, and most especially if they were black or Caribbean rookies. They made up the rules as they went along. The only difficult call they had to make was on the pivot at second base, and so they had passed the word around that they were not going to require the pivot man to have his foot on the base.

In their most recent excursion into the delights of petty dictatorship, they had granted themselves the right to prevent the home team from replaying a bad call on the scoreboard screen. "He has the right to eradicate his mistakes as far as the people who have paid their way into the park are concerned. Pure censorship."

The umpire strike of 1979 confirmed everything he had always believed about them. On the first day of the strike, the networks did such a brutal job on the amateur umpires who had been brought in that Lee MacPhail came to Veeck and asked him to say something nice about them. "Help me out on this thing," MacPhail said, "and I'll see that you're not hurt."

MacPhail knew his man, all right. Veeck came out, fervently, for the amateurs. He praised them at the skies. He announced daily that the amateurs were not only the equals of the striking umpires, but were superior. Not only superior, but perfect. And when the strike ended, he showed how much he appreciated their fine work by throwing a party for them and their wives at the ballpark; which may well have been the smartest thing anybody has done since Napoleon mounted his horse and said, "What winter? We'll be in Moscow before the leaves begin to turn."

For the rest of the year, Veeck would say the White Sox never got a close decision when it counted. When Bill called upon MacPhail to make good his promise, MacPhail replied, "Oh, come on, Bill. You know they wouldn't do that."

When he approached an umpire to berate him for a particularly outrageous call, he was told, "You're the guy who thought the scabs were so good, aren't you?"

Every time there was a bad call, he would send the film to MacPhail. "It's trivial," MacPhail would say. "Just trivial."

It got so bad that Bill was ready to bug the umpires' dressing room in order to catch them gloating over what they were doing, until he learned that Illinois had a very stringent law against that kind of thing.

What made his attitude toward umpires such an anomaly was that umpires aside, Bill Veeck was the most nonjudgmental man who ever lived. He delighted in the foibles of mankind. He reveled in the human comedy. He loved to sit and drink and talk and laugh.

The most remarkable thing about Bill Veeck, when you come right down to it, was that he was able to look at the world with such high hopes and unfailing humor in the light of the infirmities that beset him.

The stump on his amputated leg, sliced away at annually, was down to "about a pound and a half of prime thigh," he would say. What he didn't say was that after the infection had taken what was left of the stump it would continue to move up, inexorably, toward his vital innards.

His one knee was a cross-patch of scars. Having endured the poundings of a thousand hard airport floors and ten thousand stadium steps, all the cartilage had been removed and replaced by plastic.

He was legally blind, he would say. He was deaf in one ear, and he had an electronic hearing aid in the other. "I have an ear that whistles," was the way he put it. "The good news is that with a little deft fingerwork on the adjustment, I can play a fair approximation of Yankee Doodle Dandy. The bad news is that I can no longer creep up on mine enemies, unawares."

He had been a four-pack-a-day smoker for 50 years, a contributory factor, certainly, to his chronic case of emphysema. Every year, he would go into the Illinois Masonic Hospital for some new operation, and every year the doctors would insist on cleaning his lungs out by forcing oxygen into them for a couple of days before they'd risk the operation.

Toward the end of the 1980 season, with the White Sox about to pass from his hands, he suddenly found himself in his apartment, unable to breathe. He was rushed to the hospital with his head hanging out the window to force the air into his lungs.

On the following day, the club was holding its annual party for the ground crew in what had been scheduled as Bill's farewell to the troops. Guess who arrived on a stretcher, with an oxygen mask clamped over his face. Bill had called a couple of guys at the park, and told them to come and get him. He had then told the nurses that he was ready to negotiate with them. If they would sign him out and place an ambulance at his disposal, his friends would have him back in a couple of hours. Otherwise, he was going to walk out and take his chances.

In 1984, shortly after the Cubs had blown the league playoff to San Diego, a malignancy was discovered in one of his lungs. But he seemed to have that one licked too. His first public appearance after he was released from the hospital was at Lino's, where the movers and shakers of Chicago were gathering to greet Ed DeBartolo, the man to whom Bill had wanted to sell the White Sox. DeBartolo was the owner of the San Francisco 49ers, the 49ers were about to play in the Superbowl, and DeBartolo was coming to Chicago with a batch of Superbowl tickets for his friends.

Veeck arrived late, and with everybody worrying about the state of his health, he strode to the seat that had been held for him at the head of the table, looked around and said, "Holy smoke, every hustler, con man and swindler within 50 miles of Chicago is here. The citizenry is safe for 24 hours."

"And from there on," says Nick Kladis, who was one of Bill's partners in the White Sox, "he completely dominated the proceedings for two straight hours."

It was the lung that got him exactly one year later. More accurately, an embolism in the pulmonary artery leading out from the lung.

And when he was gone, everybody realized what a void had been left.

At what Bill Veeck did, he wasn't only the first, and he wasn't only the best. He was the only.